REINCARNATION IN PHILO OF ALEXANDRIA

Society of Biblical Literature

Studia Philonica Monographs

General Editor
Thomas H. Tobin, S. J.

Number 7

REINCARNATION IN PHILO OF

ALEXANDRIA

by
Sami Yli-Karjanmaa

SBL Press
Atlanta

Copyright © 2015 by SBL Press

All rights reserved. No part of this work may be reproduced or transmitted in any form or by any means, electronic or mechanical, including photocopying and recording, or by means of any information storage or retrieval system, except as may be expressly permitted by the 1976 Copyright Act or in writing from the publisher. Requests for permission should be addressed in writing to the Rights and Permissions Office, SBL Press, 825 Houston Mill Road, Atlanta, GA 30329 USA.

Library of Congress Control Number: 2015954535

Printed on acid-free paper.

STUDIA PHILONICA MONOGRAPHS

Studies in Hellenistic Judaism

Editor
Thomas H. Tobin, S.J.

Advisory Board
Ellen Birnbaum, Cambridge, Mass.
Jacques Cazeaux, CNRS, University of Lyon
Lester Grabbe, University of Hull
Annewies van den Hoek, Harvard Divinity School
Pieter W. van der Horst, Zeist, The Netherlands
Alan Mendelson, McMaster University
Robert Radice, Sacred Heart University, Milan
Jean Riaud, Catholic University, Angers
James R. Royse, Claremont, Calif.
David T. Runia, Queen's College, University of Melbourne
Gregory E. Sterling, Yale Divinity School
David Winston, Berkeley

The Studia Philonica Monographs series accepts monographs in the area of Hellenistic Judaism, with special emphasis on Philo and his Umwelt. Proposals for books in this series should be sent to the Editor: Prof. Thomas H. Tobin, S.J., Theology Department, Loyola University Chicago, 1032 W. Sheridan Road, Chicago IL 60660-1537, U.S.A; Email: ttobin@luc.edu.

TABLE OF CONTENTS

Preface x
List of Figures and Tables xiii
List of Abbreviations xiv

CHAPTER ONE:
INTRODUCTION

1.1	The Issue	1
1.2	The Terms of Reference of the Study	4
	1.2.1 Definitions...	4
	1.2.2 The Research Task and the Structure of the Work	6
1.3	Methods...	7
1.4	Earlier Research..	9
	1.4.1 From de' Rossi to Wolfson	9
	1.4.2 David Winston and the Endless Series of Reincarnations	19
	1.4.3 The Work of David T. Runia on Philo and the *Timaeus*.....	20
	1.4.4 The Most Recent Research on Philo and Reincarnation...	25

CHAPTER TWO:
THE INDIRECT EVIDENCE

2.1.	Anthropology	30
	2.1.1 Dualism...	30
	2.1.2 Pre- and Post-existence of the Soul.................................	31
	2.1.3 The Structure of the Soul and the Location of Corruption within the Human Being	36
	2.1.4 Why Does the Mind Incarnate?	44
2.2.	Afterlife and Salvation	81
	2.2.1 The Fate of the Imperfect	81
	2.2.2 The Role of Monadization in Salvation............................	85
	2.2.3 The Driving Forces of Reincarnation and the Prerequisites of Salvation in Plato: A Comparison with Philo	90

2.3	Does Philo Rule Out Reincarnation?	101
	2.3.1 Pre-existence of the Soul Questioned?	101
	2.3.2 Freedom at Death?	106
	2.3.3 Predestination of the Wicked?	109
	2.3.4 Agnosticism Regarding the Hereafter?	110
2.4	Platonic Reincarnational Terminology and Imagery in Philo	111
	2.4.1 Being Bound to a Mortal Body	113
	2.4.2 The River Metaphor	114
	2.4.3 Paying Back the Elements at Fixed Periods	117
	2.4.4 The Body as a Grave and a Prison	119
	2.4.5 Changing to Animal Form	120
	2.4.6 Practising Death	122
	2.4.7 Being Weighed Down	124
2.5	Conclusions on the Indirect Evidence	127

CHAPTER THREE:
THE DIRECT EVIDENCE

3.1.	*Somn.* 1.137–139	129
	3.1.1 Introduction	129
	3.1.2 Text, Translation and Commentary	130
	3.1.3 Review of Scholarly Opinions	143
	3.1.4 Conclusions	149
3.2	*Cher.* 114	150
	3.2.1 Introduction	150
	3.2.2 Context, Text and Translation	152
	3.2.3 Regeneration—Merging into the Divine?	154
	3.2.4 The Incorporeals	159
	3.2.5 "The Soul Rules Us"—What Is Wrong Then?	160
	3.2.6 Philo's Use of παλιγγενεσία Elsewhere	163
	3.2.7 Conclusions	166
3.3	*QE* 2.40	167
	3.3.1 Introduction	167
	3.3.2 Texts, Translations and Preliminary Remarks	169
	3.3.3 Final Salvation without Death?	173
	3.3.4 The Contingency of the Return	176
	3.3.5 The Plunge into Tartarus	180
	3.3.6 Conclusions	185

3.4	Fragment 7.3 Harris	186
	3.4.1 Introduction	186
	3.4.2 Text, Translation and Preliminary Observations	187
	3.4.3 Is It Philo?	189
	3.4.4 Later Writers	195
	3.4.5 Some Tradition History	202
	3.4.6 Congruity with Philo's Thought	205
	3.4.7 Conclusions	211
3.5	Conclusions on the Direct Evidence	212

CHAPTER FOUR:

SYNTHESIS

4.1	The Journey of the Soul According to Philo	214
	4.1.1 A Synthesis of the Reincarnational Passages	215
	4.1.2 Towards a Reincarnational Understanding of Philo's Individual Eschatology	216
	4.1.3 The Prerequisites of Salvation	242
4.2	Concluding Remarks	243
	4.2.1 Some Reflections on the Results of this Study	243
	4.2.2 Philo's Reticence about Reincarnation	244
	4.2.3 Further Work	247
Appendices:		
	Appendix 1. Philo's Use of παλινδρομέω	251
	Appendix 2. The Text-critical Issues of *Cher.* 114	255
	Appendix 3. Two Text-critical Issues in *QE* 2.40	260
Bibliography		265
Indices		283

PREFACE

This book is a revised and shortened version of my doctoral thesis which I defended at the Faculty of Theology of Åbo Akademi University (ÅAU) in Turku, Finland, in July 2013. I am grateful to several people for their contributions. My supervisor, Professor Antti Laato, unfailingly encouraged me throughout the lonely years of work far away from the Akademi, provided many useful suggestions and helped shape the structure of the work. Whenever I visited the research seminars at the ÅAU to present parts of the dissertation, I usually had the privilege of enjoying the knowledgeable and witty opposition by Professor Emeritus Karl-Gustav Sandelin. And it was Adjunct Professor Erkki Koskenniemi without whom this book would be on some other subject, for he fortunately persuaded me not to change the topic after I had written my Master's thesis on Philo and reincarnation at the Faculty of Theology of the University of Helsinki. His basic argument was that a monograph on the subject was still lacking. Here it finally is. I thank Adjunct Professor Pauli Annala for his comments as one of the two external examiners of my thesis and for our many fascinating discussions. Thanks are also due to two Professors Emeriti for their kind help with certain points in the Armenian Philo: Abraham Terian and Jouko Martikainen. My skills in this language remain very limited, and all lack of expertise in this regard is entirely my own. Nevertheless, studying some of my key texts only as translations of translations was no option.

There are also institutions to thank. This study was made possible by the financial support of the ÅAU, its Foundation and Rector Jorma Mattinen. I received grants also from the Emil Aaltonen Foundation and the Waldemar von Frenckell Foundation, and a 12-month scholarship from the Finnish Graduate School of Theology. A debt of another kind but no less important I owe to the Thesaurus Linguae Graecae at the University of California at Irvine. Earlier generations of scholars of antiquity could not have even dreamed of being able to access and search almost all relevant Greek texts while sitting at their own desk.

I also want to thank my dear wife Minna and our beloved daughter Siri. They provided me with the much needed balance of *vita activa*. It is to Siri, who at the time, from the age of two, was also working on her own "dissertation," that I dedicate this book.

Last but certainly not least I want to express my gratitude to Professor David T. Runia (Melbourne, Australia). During the time I have read on

Philo, he has for me become a model of Philonic scholarship of the highest order. I was deeply honored and overjoyed to have him first as an external examiner and then my opponent at the public defense of my thesis. Our two-hour discussion, in which we agreed on some points and disagreed on others, was a real debate and an extremely pleasant and rewarding experience as such. This preface gives me the opportunity to follow a recommendation of his to state some of my *assumptions* regarding Philo and his project at the outset, and I will use the rest of this Preface for a short discussion of my approach to the Alexandrian exegete.

The process of reworking the manuscript has given me the opportunity to rethink everything once more. The text has significantly benefited from this, although in essence the work has remained the same. Just like in the original thesis, I here also build a cumulative case. It is important to note that the case is not, to begin with, one for or against Philo's acceptance of the doctrine of reincarnation. Rather, as I have in some instances half-seriously stated, in some respects it is like a "courtroom trial" which aims to settle how the matter stands: all evidence is taken into account as completely as possible regardless of the outcome it favors. As the case proceeds, I also make observations and draw more general conclusions regarding Philo as an author. It is some of these conclusions, and especially the assumptions they involve, that Professor Runia suggested I should explicitly share with my readers earlier on. Although we may not entirely agree on their character (I would emphasize that they are the result of my study of Philo's writings), I am happy to follow his advice and briefly discuss two issues.

First, it is my view that Philo does not always say everything he thinks but leaves some connecting of dots to his reader. His way of using allusions is a good example. Whether he is paraphrasing parts of the biblical text under interpretation, or using Platonic language in his allegories, or giving almost the same exegesis for different scriptural verses, there are very often unacknowledged intertextual elements present. For example, with regard to the last case, it is clear that Philo did not write each of the three closely parallel accounts of the souls of the air in *Gig.*, *Plant.* and *Somn.* (see section 3.1.2) unaware of the other ones, nor could he reasonably expect his audience not to recognize their connections. It is my conviction that reading such close parallels together will lead to a fuller picture of Philo's message, even though he himself makes no statement to this effect. Would this not also hold for passages which feature allusions to Plato's dialogues? Surely the passages that he refers to need to be closely examined and their relation to Philo's thought world assessed. In the context of this study this issue becomes particularly acute when the allusions are to the Athenian philosopher's descriptions of reincarnation. Here again, no explicit comment by Philo is to be found, and yet the allusions serve some purpose with regard to what he is aiming to say. It is my view that this purpose may, in the absence of evidence to the contrary, be taken to be one of expressing approval—the extent and limits of which must be analyzed case by case.

The second point too is related to parallels. When Philo gives a very similar interpretation to entirely different biblical verses, I think we need to ask questions about the relationship between the *explanandum* and the *explanatio*. There is no question about the unparalleled standing of the "holy word" of Moses or about Philo's staunch loyalty to Judaism. At the same time his midrashic, allegorical method gives him a very large freedom of maneuver as far as the contents of his interpretations are concerned. And it is through the door thus opened that Greek philosophy, first and foremost the ideas of Plato, enters. Here I have found myself to be in considerable agreement with the way of reading Philo represented by David Winston.—Given these two points (and perhaps some others as well), it is my hope that this work will generate debate not only about Philo's individual eschatology but, in addition, about the way his works, especially his allegories, are read. Both issues have implications that also extend beyond Philonic studies.

I humbly thank Professor Thomas Tobin, S.J., for accepting the work to be published in the Studia Philonica Monographs series. I also thank Leigh Andersen and Nicole Tilford of SBL Press for smooth cooperation and Gonni Runia for professional typesetting of the manuscript.

LIST OF FIGURES AND TABLES

Figure 1. Aggregated Factors Leading the Soul to Reach Salvation or to Reincarnate in Plato 95
Figure 2. The Mean, Minimum and Maximum Frequencies in *Corpus Philonicum* of Words that Occur in Nine Random Passages Plus Fragment 7.3 Harris 194
Figure 3. The Comparison between Sleep and Death by Socrates in the *Phaedo* 204
Figure 4. Comparison between Salvific Second Birth and Sleep 210

Table I. The Causes of the Soul's Incarnation in Three Thinkers According to Winston 45
Table II. Summary of Nine Potential Causes of Incarnation in Philo 81
Table III. Passages in Plato and Philo Illustrating the Salvific Relationships in Figure 1 and the Resulting States in Philo 99
Table IV. Passages in Plato and Philo Illustrating the Anti-Salvific Relationships in Figure 1 and the Resulting States in Philo 100
Table V. The Greek Expressions Used for Some of the Items That Occur in the Accounts of the Souls of the Air in *Gig.*, *Plant.*, *Conf.* and *Somn.* 145
Table VI. Descriptions of Return in *QG* 1.85, 4.45 and *QE* 1.7, 2.40 178

LIST OF ABBREVIATIONS

ALGHJ	Arbeiten zur Literatur und Geschichte des hellenistischen Judentums
Arm.	Armenian; (a reading attested in) the ancient Armenian translation of Philo's works
BJS	Brown Judaic Studies
BZNW	Beihefte zur Zeitschrift für die neutestamentliche Wissenschaft
CBQ	*Catholic Biblical Quarterly*
CQ	*Classical Quarterly*
CRINT	Compendia rerum iudaicarum ad Novum Testamentum
DK	*Die Fragmente der Vorsokratiker*. Edited by Hermann Diels and Walther Kranz. Sixth edition. 3 vols. Berlin: Weidmann, 1951–1952.
ex.	exegesis of [a biblical text]
fr.	fragment
HO	Handbuch der Orientalistik
HTR	*Harvard Theological Review*
HUCA	*Hebrew Union College Annual*
HWS	Smyth, Herbert Weir. *A Greek Grammar for Colleges*. New York: American Book, 1920.
JAOS	*Journal of the American Oriental Society*
JBL	*Journal of Biblical Literature*
JPS	Jewish Publication Society, or *JPS Hebrew-English Tanakh: The Traditional Hebrew Text and the New JPS Translation*. Second edition. Philadelphia: JPS, 2003.
JSJ	*Journal for the Study of Judaism in the Persian, Hellenistic, and Roman Periods*
JSJSup	Supplements to the Journal for the Study of Judaism
JSPSup	Journal for the Study of the Pseudepigrapha Supplement Series
LCL	Loeb Classical Library
LSJ	Liddell, Henry George and Robert Scott. *A Greek-English Lexicon: Revised and augmented throughout by Sir Henry Stuart Jones with the assistance of Roderick McKenzie*. Oxford: Clarendon 1940.
LXX	The Septuagint
MAAR	Memoirs of the American Academy in Rome

MI	Marcus, Ralph. "An Armenian-Greek Index to Philo's *Quaestiones* and *De Vita Contemplativa.*" *JAOS* 53, no. 3 (1933): 251–82.
MPG	Patrologia graeca [= Patrologiae cursus completus: Series graeca]. Edited by Jacques-Paul Migne. 162 vols. Paris, 1857–1886.
NBHL	Awatik'ean G., Siwrmēlean X., Awgerean M. *Nor Baṙgirk' Haykazean Lezui. [New Dictionary of the Armenian Language].* Venice: Mechitarist Press 1836–1837.
NETS	*A New English Translation of the Septuagint.* Edited by Albert Pietersma and Benjamin G. Wright. New York: Oxford University Press, 2007.
NHMS	Nag Hammadi and Manichean Studies
NovTSup	Novum Testamentum Supplements
NTAbh	Neutestamentliche Abhandlungen
OL	The Old Latin translation of *QG* 4.154–245 and the eleven *quaestiones* between 4.195 and 196 not present in the Armenian version. Critical text: Petit, Françoise. *L'ancienne version latine des* Questions sur la Genèse *de Philon d'Alexandrie.* 2 vols. TUGAL 113–4. Berlin: Akademie, 1973.
PACS	Philo of Alexandria Commentary Series
PAPM	*Les oeuvres de Philon d'Alexandrie.* Edited by Roger Arnaldez, Jean Pouilloux, Claude Mondésert. 37 vols. Paris: Cerf, 1961–1992.
PCH	*Die Werke Philos von Alexandria in deutscher Übersetzung.* Translated by Leopold Cohn, Isaac Heinemann et al. 7 vols. Berlin: de Gruyter, 1909–1964.
PCW	*Philonis Alexandrini opera quae supersunt.* Edited by Leopold Cohn, Paul Wendland and Siegfried Reiter. 7 vols. Berlin: Reimer, 1896–1915.
PhI	Borgen, Peder, Kåre Fuglseth, and Roald Skarsten. *The Philo Index: A Complete Greek Word Index to the Writings of Philo of Alexandria.* Grand Rapids: Eerdmans, 2000.
PLCL	*Philo.* Translated by F. H. Colson et al. 12 vols. LCL. Cambridge, MA: Harvard University Press, 1929–1962.
PRSt	*Perspectives in Religious Studies*
ps.-	pseudo-
QGE	Philo's *Quaestiones in Genesim* and *Quaestiones in Exodum* collectively

QGUM	The German translation of Philo's *Quaestiones in Genesim* ongoing at the Institutum Judaicum Delitzschianum of the University of Münster. Texts are available online at http://www.uni-muenster.de/EvTheol/ijd/forschen/philon.html.
ResQ	*Restoration Quarterly*
SBLDS	Society of Biblical Literature Dissertation Series
SFSHJ	South Florida Studies in the History of Judaism
SPhA	*Studia Philonica Annual*
SPhA	Studies in Philo of Alexandria
TLG	Thesaurus Linguae Graecae (http://stephanus.tlg.uci.edu)
TUGAL	Texte und Untersuchungen zur Geschichte der altchristlichen Literatur
VC	*Vigiliae Christianae*
VCSup	Vigiliae Christianae, Supplements
WUNT	Wissenschaftliche Untersuchungen zum Neuen Testament

CHAPTER ONE

INTRODUCTION

1.1 *The Issue*

The original impetus for my research on Philo's position on the idea of reincarnation, first in the form of a Master's thesis, then as my doctoral dissertation and now as its revised version, came from a single sentence and the related footnote in an article by Samuel Vollenweider.[1] As an undergraduate student of theology, I had been wholly unaware that this doctrine might have had supporters within Second Temple Judaism, and was thus surprised to find Vollenweider writing, "Darüber hinaus zeichnet sich nur gerade einmal bei Philon von Alexandrien das Seelenwanderungsmotiv am fernen Horizont ab."[2] The passage referred to states the following about the incorporeal souls which, according to Philo, inhabit the air:

> Of these souls some, those that are closest to the earth and lovers of the body, are descending to be fast bound in mortal bodies, while others are ascending, having again been separated (from the body) according to the numbers and periods determined by nature. Of these last some, longing for the familiar and accustomed ways of mortal life, hurry back again, while others, pronouncing that life great folly, call the body a prison and a tomb but escaping from it as though from a dungeon or a grave are lifted up on light wings to the ether and range the heights for ever. (*De somniis* 1.138–139)[3]

---

[1] Samuel Vollenweider, "Reinkarnation—ein abendländisches Erbstück," in *Horizonte neutestamentlicher Christologie: Studien zu Paulus und zur frühchristlichen Theologie*, WUNT 144 (Tübingen: Mohr Siebeck, 2002), 327–46, p. 332; repr. from *Der Evangelische Erzieher* 47.2 (1995): 141–58. My doctoral thesis is "Reincarnation in Philo of Alexandria" (Th.D. diss., Åbo Akademi University, 2013).

[2] Vollenweider "Reinkarnation," 332. In a note he refers to *Gig.* 6 ff. and *Plant.* 14 with regard to the idea of the pre-existence of the soul and concludes by stating that "erst in der *Kabbala* wird die Seelenwanderung bedeutsamer."

[3] All English translations of Philo's texts are from the PLCL with the following exceptions: For *Opif.* I use David T. Runia, *On the Creation of the Cosmos According to Moses: Introduction, Translation, and Commentary*; PACS 1 (Atlanta: Society of Biblical Literature, 2001); for *Gig.*, David Winston, *Philo of Alexandria: The Contemplative Life, The Giants, and Selections: Translation and Introduction* (London: SPCK, 1981); for *Agr.*, Albert C. Geljon and David T. Runia, *Philo of Alexandria: On Cultivation: Introduction, Translation and Commentary*; PACS 4 (Leiden: Brill, 2013); for *Virt.*, Walter Wilson, *Philo of Alexandria: On Virtues: Introduction, Translation and Commentary*; PACS 3 (Leiden: Brill, 2010); and for

Two questions arose: (1) Is reincarnation merely "discernible in the faraway horizon" in the above passage? (2) Is this the one and only place where Philo refers to the doctrine? My *prima facie* answer to the first question was "no," and further reading of Philo not only confirmed this but also elicited the same response to the second. Granted, all the other possible mentions of reincarnation are less explicit and seem to form a continuum from probable to ambiguous. Nowhere in his surviving writings does Philo openly name or discuss the doctrine itself.

This state of affairs makes it imperative for the researcher to try and understand Philo's views about the soul in their entirety. This means delving, first of all, into Philo's anthropology and soteriology in order to see whether or not they are in harmony with the tenet of *metempsychosis*. As Philo is so vague about the matter and his references to the fate of the imperfect souls in the hereafter are few and undetailed, understanding his statements will require that the researcher be well acquainted with his writings and ways of argumentation in order to recognize relevant parallels that complement each other.

Another part of the task of establishing Philo's position on reincarnation is to assess his debt to authors who espoused the doctrine. While there may be several such thinkers, one of them can without hesitation be given the prime position. Plato may have adopted the doctrine from Socrates whom he presents as its proponent, but it was also part of the Pythagorean thought world to which he stood near.[4] The expressions Philo uses of the soul in general, and the passage quoted above to a high degree, exhibit Plato's influence, and when a Platonist speaks of the soul, rebirth is in the air. Hence also the title of this book. For it is self-evident Philo knew the idea; he also knew it had a bearing on what he said about the soul's need to orientate away from bodily things, and he also knew he was leaving out

---

Legat., Mary E. Smallwood, *Philonis Alexandrini* Legatio ad Gaium: *Introduction, Translation and Commentary* (Leiden: Brill, 1961). Where I have deemed it warranted, I have modified the translations (as in several places above). Only significant changes are mentioned. In this passage I have chosen to translate διακριθεῖσαι πάλιν as "having again been separated (from the body)" rather than "selected for return" (PLCL) for reasons to be returned to (p. 136). For the Septuagint, I use *A New Translation of the Septuagint* (NETS). Proper names are in the form they appear in PLCL to avoid the use of different versions of a single name. For all other primary texts, the translations used are those indicated in the bibliography.

[4] In the dialogues *Phaedo*, *Phaedrus* and *Republic* it is Socrates who explains the tenet; the passages in question will be dealt with below (pp. 91–95). In the *Meno* Socrates refers to "wise men and women" (81b) who hold it. In the *Timaeus* it is brought forward by the title character (a leading Pythagorean according to later tradition), in the *Laws*, by the Athenian, and in the *Statesman* it is mentioned in passing (272e) by the Stranger.

explicit discussion of the doctrine even where it would have been most natural. He neither rejects or adopts the doctrine itself in so many words, but he cannot—so I maintain—have considered it so insignificant a part of Plato's views as to simply ignore or forget it. From these premises it follows, *a priori*, that the tenet has to be somewhere in Philo, *regardless* of what he thought of it. The task is to comb his *oeuvre* to see what his words reveal of his thoughts.

Familiarizing myself with previous research on Philo and reincarnation revealed a surprising state of affairs. The subject has not enjoyed popularity, even though transmigration was among those Platonisms that led to the important development of Philo's losing his position as "honorary Church Father."[5] Other typical features of the scholarly treatment of this question include taking a position on what Philo thought without having actually studied the matter, and a virtually complete lack of interaction and debate between researchers. Hence it is no wonder that the views adopted vary widely. Compare, for instance, the following two quotations:

> But natural death brings [the entire liberation from the body] only to those who, while they lived on earth, kept themselves free from attachment to the things of sense; all others must at death pass into another body; transmigration of souls is in fact the necessary consequence of Philo's premises, though he seldom speaks of it expressly.[6]

> Although both Philo and Plato emphasize the connection between the soul's conduct and its fate, Philo posits no successive incarnations of the soul according to fate in which the wicked soul will ultimately be purified and freed from the body ... Philo's rejection of successive incarnations for the soul and his emphasis upon God's providence lead him to different conclusions from Plato about the soul's fate.[7]

After this preliminary sketch of the landscape in which we are moving in our exploration to determine Philo's views concerning the afterlife of those souls which do not meet the preconditions for salvation it is time to define more precisely the scope of our inquiry.

---

[5] The quoted epithet is by David T. Runia, *Philo in Early Christian Literature: A Survey*; CRINT 3.3 (Minneapolis: Fortress, 1993), 31 who does not mention reincarnation in this context.

[6] Emil Schürer and Charles Bigg, "Philo," in *The Encyclopaedia Britannica*, 11th edition, 21:409–13, p. 411. (As will become obvious in subsection 1.4.1, this view, in all likelihood by Schürer, comes almost directly from Eduard Zeller.)

[7] Fred W. Burnett, "Philo on Immortality: A Thematic Study of Philo's Concept of παλιγγενεσία," *CBQ* 46 (1984): 447–70, p. 466 n. 83.

1.2 *The Terms of Reference of the Study*

1.2.1 *Definitions*

In this study the following key terminology will be used in the sense defined below.[8]

Acceptance: The following two main senses for the verb *to accept* are applicable:[9] (1) 'take or receive with consenting mind,' 'receive with favour or approval'; (2) 'receive as adequate or valid,' 'admit,' 'believe,' 'tolerate,' 'submit to.' Of these, the last one can be omitted, and if the outcome of this study shows that Philo "tolerated" reincarnation, it will then need to be discussed separately as to whether this qualifies as acceptance. The words *believe* and *belief* will, accordingly, be used interchangeably with *accept* and *acceptance* and do not refer to an explicit creed. All other corresponding expressions (adopt, approve, endorse, espouse, etc.) are used in the sense defined above.

Doctrine, tenet: In this study the expressions "the doctrine of reincarnation" or "the tenet" thereof are used undogmatically: they do not refer to an explicit creed or dogma. They are used synonymously with such phrases as "the idea of reincarnation," "the notion," et cetera.

Imperfect soul: This expression is used for referring to souls that do not meet the prerequisites of salvation. Those who do will in any case not be liable for reincarnation, and so it is the fate of the "imperfect" ones in Philo's thought that is vital for his stance on reincarnation. It is not implied that perfection is a precondition for salvation.

Individual eschatology: Views held by a person, or forming part of a belief system, that concern the events which an individual soul undergoes after being separated from the physical body at death.

Pre- and post-existence of the soul (or mind etc.): Its existence, respectively, before entering the human body and after separation from it at physical death.

Protological/universal allegory: A protological allegorical interpretation maintains the protological orientation of the text being interpreted (and thus is chiefly applicable to the exegesis of Gen 1–3), whereas a universal interpretation ignores the context of a protological text and extracts from

---

[8] Certain specific concepts will be defined later, after the necessary preliminaries have been discussed: *double dichotomy* on p. 39, *monadization* on p. 40 and *the corporealization of the mind* on p. 70. These are tentative concepts that I have found practical.

[9] Taken from the *New Shorter Oxford English Dictionary*.

the biblical narrative concerning "how things happened in the beginning" a general truth on "how things are."[10]

Reincarnation: In this study the terms reincarnation, rebirth, transmigration (of souls) and *metempsychosis* are used synonymously to mean a repeated process in which a fundamental, incorporeal part of the individual is thought to pass from one body to another through physical death and birth. In practice, if Philo is found to accept the doctrine, this part will be the soul (ἡ ψυχή) or its highest part for which Philo's three most important terms are the mind (ὁ νοῦς), the intellect (ὁ λογισμός), and the understanding (ἡ διάνοια).[11] For convenience, the term *soul* may be loosely used to refer to the incarnating entity, whatever it is. The purpose of reincarnation is the liberation, purification and restoration of the soul to its original, heavenly state.

Reincarnational: This adjective is used in two ways: (1) Of belief systems that include the doctrine. (2) Of texts, terminology or images etc., to denote the presence of the idea of reincarnation: the tenet is either explicitly mentioned or implied, e.g., mentioned before or after a passage in such a way that the terms or images in question have a connection to the idea. This definition as such entails no position on what the use of reincarnational texts means. They can be quoted or alluded to for the purpose of either espousing or refuting them.

Salvation: Philo's words in *Gig.* 14 serve as a succinct definition of salvation: "incorporeal and immortal life in the presence of the Uncreated

---

[10] This distinction is related to the tension noted by Runia, *On the Creation*, 333–34 "between a presentation as *history*, i.e. an account of the life of early mankind, and a presentation in terms of *actualization* and *idealization*, i.e. seeing Adam and Eve as types of human beings" (emphases original), although he, in the context of the *Exposition of the Law*, restricts the former to "the origins of human culture and civilization." His characterization of the latter very well suits what I see as the purpose of Philo's universal allegory: biblical themes are "applied to the human situation as it is for the contemporary reader." Cf. also Folker Siegert's reference to "mankind as it is in the present" in connection with Philo's exegesis of Gen 2:7 in *Leg.* 1.31–38 ("Philo and the New Testament," in *The Cambridge Companion to Philo*, ed. Adam Kamesar [Cambridge: Cambridge University Press, 2009], 175–209, p. 184).

[11] I have chosen "mind" as the general term when speaking of the highest part of the soul. It is my aim to adhere to the translations above throughout this study—also in quotations from published translations, in which I do not mention the possible change of words unless the terminology itself is of consequence. The consistency sought admittedly comes at the cost of reduced idiomaticity in English, when, e.g., "understandings," as entities, are spoken of. For the structure of the soul in Philo, see below, pp. 36–44.

and Immortal."[12] This is understood to mean never-ending immaterial existence with God.[13]

1.2.2 *The Research Task and the Structure of the Work*

The central problem of this study is this: *does Philo accept the idea of reincarnation?* Ultimately, therefore, the result of this study will be condensable to a single word. It is, however, to be expected that solving this issue will lead to enhanced understanding of also other aspects of Philo's individual eschatology, soteriology, anthropology and ethics.

As previously mentioned, the number of passages where Philo explicitly discusses the post-mortem fate of imperfect souls is low, and the matter cannot be judged by them alone. A broader approach that takes into account all available indirect evidence is mandatory. Chapter 2 is devoted to this evidence: It is necessary to examine Philo's views of the origin, composition, incarnation, afterlife and salvation of the human being to see whether they are reconcilable with what reincarnation presupposes. Ch. 2 also includes the assessment of the occurrence in Philo of the essential characteristics of reincarnational belief systems, the pre- and post-existence of the soul and the existence of potential driving forces of reincarnation.[14] A belief system where the soul does not exist both before birth and after death or where it does not need to develop in some predetermined way in order to be saved, is unlikely to accommodate the idea of reincarnation.[15]

Another set of indirect evidence is related to the fact that while Philo nowhere explicitly denounces the doctrine, his works do contain passages

---

[12] ἡ ἀσώματος καὶ ἄφθαρτος παρὰ τῷ ἀγενήτῳ καὶ ἀφθάρτῳ ζωή.
[13] A brief remark on the resurrection of the body is perhaps in order at this point. In this study no attention is paid to this doctrine, as it is entirely alien to Philo and incompatible with his anthropology and soteriology. There is a consensus about this in modern Philonic scholarship. See, e.g., Harry Austryn Wolfson, *Philo: Foundations of Religious Philosophy in Judaism, Christianity, and Islam I–II* (Cambridge, MA: Harvard University Press, 1948), 1.404; Runia, *Philo in Early Christian Literature*, 72; Siegert, "Philo and the New Testament," pp. 190–91; Cristina Termini, "Philo's Thought within the Context of Middle Judaism," in *The Cambridge Companion to Philo*, ed. Adam Kamesar (Cambridge: Cambridge University Press, 2009), 95–123, p. 108.
[14] These characteristics have been adopted from Carl-A. Keller, "La réincarnation: vue d'ensemble des problèmes," in *La réincarnation: Théories, raisonnements et appréciations*, ed. Carl-A. Keller (Bern: Lang, 1986), 1–35, pp. 11–35.
[15] It must be emphasized that these features are to be understood as *necessary but not sufficient* conditions for the acceptance of reincarnation: A belief in the pre- and post-existence of the soul does not mean endorsing rebirth, and positing requirements for the soul's development in order for it to achieve salvation does not entail that these requirements function as driving forces for reincarnation.

where an anti-reincarnational interpretation seems possible. These texts must be analyzed in order to establish whether they amount to precluding Philo's approval of the tenet. Examples include references to children being brought from non-existence to existence and the soul's return to God at death.

Thirdly, Philo's active use of terminology and images that occur in reincarnational contexts in Greek philosophy (mainly in Plato but also in both earlier and later traditions) also has to be studied. It is usually assumed that Philo's audiences knew Plato well enough to recognize the allusions to the latter's dialogues. Thus the question is raised: what did Philo *aim at* by alluding to reincarnational texts? This question itself may not be answerable before the central problem of this study is solved, but this solving is aided by analysis of the use to which Philo puts Plato's rebirth language.

Chapter 3 deals with the available direct evidence, in which category I place *Somn.* 1.137–139, *Cher.* 114, *QE* 2.40 and fragment 7.3 Harris. The question to be answered with each is: is Philo speaking of reincarnation, or can or should his words be interpreted in some other way? The passages are examined in their different contexts: the Philonic treatise in question, the biblical lemma together with the possible proof texts or parallels from the Septuagint and, as is the case with each, the references or allusions to Plato. In addition, in all cases there are also important parallels in Philo's own writings, which, when read together with the main passage, help us understand it.

Chapter 4 builds on the results of chapters 2 and 3 and aims at a synthesis that captures Philo's essential view of the journey of the soul. The understanding reached in the earlier chapters is applied as an interpretative key to a significantly larger number of Philonic texts. In addition, the reasons for Philo's reticence about reincarnation are addressed. The chapter closes with some reflections on the results attained and areas of further work.

This chapter now continues with a discussion of the methods used in this study and an overview of the history of research on Philo's position on reincarnation.

1.3 *Methods*

The general approach followed in Chs. 2 and 3 is that of two-sided argumentation. In other words, all relevant evidence is taken into account regardless of which answer to the main problem it tends to support; no solution is sought to be shown to be the correct one. The situation changes in the last chapter, because it applies the results of the earlier chapters to Philo's thought generally with the aim of demonstrating their feasibility. However, there as well I try to remain as open as possible to any contradictions and anomalies. The more specific methods applied in this study include the following.

A *database of thematically encoded passages* is utilized. In the context of close reading of the Philonic corpus I created a database of relevant text passages and assigned each passage one or several numerical codes (out of some 200) which denote pertinent ideas, themes, expressions and images that I consider to appear in the text. At the end of the research the database contains approximately 2200 Philonic passages with ca. 5700 codes. Interrogating the database provides a fast way of finding the occurrences of a particular notion or combination of notions in Philo's surviving *oeuvre*.

In addition, the search functions and other resources of the *Thesaurus Linguae Graecae* have been absolutely indispensable in finding almost any ancient text written in Greek as well as in searching for the occurrences of words and expressions and exploring the meanings of various key terms in Philo and others. The TLG presently enables one to look for a maximum of three words or expressions occurring within a specified distance from each other. I have developed a software tool for accumulating any number of TLG search results on Philo and post-processing them into *a graphical concordance*, so that the occurrence in his extant Greek works of selected words and expressions, combined with any number of the thematic codes, can be seen in a few glances and clusters identified for further analysis.

The texts themselves are examined through *tradition-historical, semantic* and *philological analyses* as required. By tradition-historical examination I mean mapping out the history of ideas or concepts in Greek and/or Jewish literature (i.e., in written texts) as far as possible. The purpose is to enhance the understanding of the background of the text being considered, and the identification of the possible sources Philo has used or the influences he has been subject to, as well as the eventual modifications made by him.

A very important way of working with Philo's works is the *reading together* of parallel passages: It seems clear that when an author speaks of the same or very similar things in different places using the same or very similar terms, concepts and/or images, a researcher is entitled to assume that the passages complement each other so that any one of them can be assumed to fill in what is not explicated in the others. This approach also enables one to make observations of specific senses Philo attaches to specific words.

INTRODUCTION 9

The method cannot be used blindly, however. It is not an exercise of harmonizing passages whose mutual consistency is in question; genuine contradictions do exist. The degree to which passages in different works may be treated as one whole will also depend on the overall mutual harmony of the treatises regarding the subject matter being discussed. In Philo, particular caution is called for when different genres of writings are concerned.[16]

1.4 Earlier Research

1.4.1 From de' Rossi to Wolfson

It is perplexing to find that there has, in practice, been no scholarly debate over the issue of Philo's position on reincarnation. As will be seen, many a scholar has expressed his or her view about the matter, but cases where reference is made to someone *else's* opinion, not to mention *arguing* for or against them, are exceptions. The lack of debate is all the more difficult to understand as many of the statements made fall into mutually exclusive categories as exemplified by the quotes above.[17]

The earliest explicit reference to Philo's having taken a position on the idea of reincarnation that I am aware of is included in the long assessment of Philo which the well-known Italian Jewish scholar Azariah de' Rossi gives in his *The Light of the Eyes*, first published in 1573–1575.[18] De' Rossi writes,

> He also believed that the soul once separated from carnal existence eventually returns to it. This is shown in a lengthy passage from his book entitled *On Dreams* which I will quote in translation in a successive chapter if God so wills.[19]

---

[16] On Philo's different genres, see, e.g., James Royse, "The Works of Philo," in *The Cambridge Companion to Philo*, ed. Adam Kamesar (Cambridge: Cambridge University Press, 2009), 32–64. The most important ones are the three Pentateuchal commentary series, the *Quaestiones*, the *Allegorical Commentary* and the *Exposition of the Law*.
[17] See p. 3.
[18] I am thankful to Professor David T. Runia for alerting me to de' Rossi's relevance to my study.
[19] Section 1, chapter 4; page 113 in Azariah ben Moses de' Rossi, *The Light of the Eyes: Azariah de' Rossi: Translated from the Hebrew with an introduction and annotations by Joanna Weinberg*, Yale Judaica series 31 (New Haven: Yale University Press, 2001). De' Rossi's statement is mentioned without comment in Ralph Marcus, "A 16th Century Hebrew Critique of Philo (Azariah dei Rossi's *Meor Eynayim*, Pt. I, cc. 3–6)," *HUCA* 21 (1948): 29–71, p. 38.

The quotation (*Somn.* 1.138–146) follows two chapters later.[20] It is interesting to note that de' Rossi does not seem to have anything against Philo's belief in reincarnation. He does not criticize Philo's views of the soul, but instead calls them "apposite."[21] After the quotation from *Somn.* de' Rossi does present a critique, but not regarding reincarnation. What he cannot accept is Philo's "belief that the souls and angels belong to one order of existence;" this is "alien to rabbinic opinion."[22] Overall, de' Rossi sees Philo as one of the Essenes, whose views he takes from Josephus and from Philo's *Prob.* and also *Contempl.*[23]

On the Christian side the first reference to Philo's stance on transmigration comes in the 1640s, in the *Dogmata theologica* by the French Jesuit theologian Denis Pétau (Dionysius Petavius).[24] Part III of the massive work begins with angelology, and Philo's views are discussed. After quoting *Conf.* 176–177 Pétau turns to the *De somniis*, notes Philo's use of Plato's philosophy and says that he "expounds a belief which is minimally suited to a pupil of the Holy Scriptures and Moses and the prophets, that the species of the soul is fourfold."[25] This is a reference to *Somn.* 1.138–139 which Pétau paraphrases by listing different kinds of soul as follows: (1) those who, "seized by the enticements of the earth and bodies,"[26] descend into bodies to be held by fetters, (2) those that are released in times determined by nature "and no longer return to bodies,"[27] (3) "others who again return to them,"[28] and (4) the angels, on whom Pétau quotes *Somn.* 1.140–141. In making explicit the notion of re-embodiment and in labelling the

---

[20] De' Rossi, *The Light of the Eyes*, 156.
[21] De' Rossi writes in the earlier passage (p. 113): "If you examine the entry for 'soul' in the index to his works you can acquaint yourself with his apposite remarks on any aspect of the subject which interests you."
[22] This is also Marcus's ("A Hebrew Critique", 56) understanding of de' Rossi's point here. The quotations from *The Light of the Eyes* are from p. 157. On the following page de' Rossi states, "his statements about *souls and angels* as described above do not demonstrate convictions which are consistent with those of our sages." (Emphasis added.)
[23] De' Rossi, *The Light of the Eyes*, pp. 154–58. De' Rossi conflates the various accounts. He includes among the Essene beliefs also reincarnation (p. 106).
[24] Most of the literature older than approximately a century that I cite can be found on the Internet as scans of the original documents, which has made this overview possible. The works can be found using search engines fairly easily.
[25] My tr. for "Scripturarum Sacrarum, ac Mosis, & Prophetarum alumno minime congruentem opinionem explicat de quadruplici animarum specie" in Denis Pétau, *Opus de Theologicis Dogmatibus, in Hac Novissima Editione Auctius* (Venice: Andreae Poleti, 1745), 3:2. Parts 1–3 of the *Dogmata theologica* were originally published in 1643.
[26] My tr. for "terrae, corporumque captas illecebris."
[27] My tr. for "nec ad corpora amplius reverti."
[28] My tr. for "alias iterum in illa relabi."

whole as a Platonically oriented scheme which is not faithful to the Scriptures, Pétau is here presenting the first printed criticism against Philo's accepting the tenet of reincarnation. Yet it is fairly mild, and Pétau does not include Philo among the "heretics" whom he moves on to discuss.

Half a century later came an "important turning point" in the development that led to Philo's "los[ing] his status as honorary Church Father:" the twelve-page dissertation by Johann Albertus Fabricius.[29] As the title *Exercitatio de Platonismo Philonis Judaei* reveals, the emphasis is on showing Philo's debt to Plato. Reincarnation figures in sections X and XI. At the end of section IX, Fabricius quotes Photius's (d. ca. 893) statement on Philo: "He goes wrong in many things, adopting ideas and some other things of (*or*, foreign to) Judaic philosophy and having them written down."[30] In section X Fabricius then cites Pétau's account just discussed. He begins section XI by extolling the work of Giovanni Battista Crispo on Plato's psychology. A century earlier Crispo had published an almost six hundred-page corrective to Plato where he had enumerated twenty-four propositions concerning the soul—including reincarnation in part III, book I—and debunked them with the help of the Bible, Church Fathers, Councils etc.[31] Fabricius writes:

---

[29] The quoted characterizations are from Runia, *Philo in Early Christian Literature*, 31.
[30] Johann Albertus Fabricius, 'Exercitatio de Platonismo Philonis Judaei' (diss., Leipzig, 1693) (no page numbers), my translation. The text in Fabricius differs slightly from what Henry's edition gives for Photius. The latter runs (cod. 105), Ἁμαρτάνει δὲ ἐν πολλοῖς, ἰδέας τε ὑποτιθέμενος, καὶ ἄλλα ἄττα τῆς Ἰουδαϊκῆς φιλοσοφίας ἀλλότρια συγγραφόμενος. Apart from changing the words referring to Philo into accusative, the word ἀλλότρια ("foreign [things]") is missing from Fabricius's quote. The similarity between Photius's and Pétau's judgements (which Fabricius proceeds to quote) and the general tendency of Fabricius's work makes me surmise this is just a mistake and that the latter's text should be amended. —It is interesting to note that Photius does not charge Philo with believing in transmigration *in distinction* to, e.g., Clement of Alexandria (cod. 109) and Origen (cod. 8).
[31] Giovanni Battista Crispo, *De Ethnicis Philosophis Caute Legendis Disputationum ex Propriis Cuiusque Principiis* (Rome: Aloysij Zannetti, 1594). Jill Kraye, "Ficino in the Firing Line: A Reneissance Neoplatonist and His Critics," in *Marsilio Ficino: His Theology, His Philosophy, His Legacy*, ed. Michael J. B. Allen, Valery Rees and Martin Davies (Leiden: Brill, 2002), 377–97 sees Crispo's work in the context of a more general turning of the tide in Rome against Plato, whose philosophy was regarded by Crispo as the source of most heresies, "including Protestantism" (p. 394). Against this background it is worth noting that Pétau was a Jesuit, Fabricius, apparently, a Lutheran (he published a Lutheran bibliography, *Centifolium Lutheranum*, in 1728). In any case the rise of anti-Platonism thus seems to lurk behind Philo's depreciation as well at least on the Catholic side. However, examining this link and the reception of Philo by the different parties of the reformation disputes goes beyond the scope of this study.

> Of these 24 Platonic propositions on the soul I dare affirm that among them might be one or two which Philo did not similarly defend in his writings. Of the transition of souls to other bodies we have already heard.[32]

Philo is not among those accused by Crispo of believing in reincarnation. His name is invoked very seldom, and when it is, it is in defence of *orthodoxy*, whereas Origen is named under almost all propositions among the heretics.

The impact of Fabricius's work can be seen in the preface of Thomas Mangey's great edition of Philo's works (1742). After writing that Philo took from Plato the ideal of assimilation to God and the notion of the creation of the world in accordance with the invisible ideas, Mangey continues:

> In fact, when he adds the pre-existence of souls and reincarnation, the tripartition of the human soul and the four cardinal virtues, and further asserts that the stars are living beings together with the world itself, he does not show himself to be so much an interpreter of Moses but a pupil of gentile philosophy, principally a devotee of Plato's. If someone really desires to learn more about Philo's Platonism, I will not pursue a closed case, but let him examine the short and eminent pamphlet that presents the judgement of Ioh. Alb. Fabricius, with Iohannes Ionsius as the opponent.[33]

But not all saw the relationship of the two thinkers in the same way. E.g., Peter (Pierre) Allix (d. 1717) maintained, rather inconsistently, that while Philo was "very conversant" with Plato and other Greek authors, he was, nevertheless "little acquainted with Plato's works," and that in any case "if Plato had any distinct notions in religion, he most certainly had them from the Jews."[34] Allix's comments reveal the superficiality of his knowledge of

---

[32] My tr. for "Ex quibus 24. Platonicis de anima propositionibus ausim affirmare vix unam vel duas esse, quas non in scriptis suis Philo similiter asseruerit. De transitu animarum in alia corpora jam audivimus." Fabricius then moves on to the pre-existence of the soul and other matters. In his renowned *Bibliotheca Graeca* 12 vols.; (Hamburg: Christianum Liebezeit, 1705–1728)—the chapter on Philo of which (4.104–22) Runia, *Philo in Early Christian Literature*, 31 calls "the first scholarly account of [Philo's] life and writings"—reincarnation is not discussed.

[33] Thomas Mangey, *Philonis Judaei opera quae Reperiri potuerunt Omnia* (London: Typis Gulielmi Bowyer, 1742), viii; my tr. for "Denique cum praeexistentiam animarum et metempsychosim adstruat, animam humanam esse τριμερή, quatuor etiam virtutes cardinales, stellas porro animatas cum mundo ipso esse contendit, non se tam Mosis interpretem, quam Gentilis philosophiae alumnum, et plane Platoni praecipue addictum ostendit. Si quis vero plura de Philonis Platonismo cupiat ediscere, ne ipse actum agam, perlegat brevem et egregium libellum Ioh. Alb. Fabricii sententiae Iohannis Ionsii oppositum."

[34] Peter Allix, *The Judgement of the Ancient Jewish Church against the Unitarians in the Controversy upon the Holy Trinity and the Divinity of Our Blessed Saviour,* 2nd ed., corr. by the author (Oxford: Clarendon, 1821), esp. 283–93; the quotations are from pp. 284, 287. The work originally appeared in 1689.

INTRODUCTION   13

both authors. The debate seems to have centered on other aspects of
Philo's Platonism than reincarnation and on what he was seen to say about
the Trinity.[35] Reincarnation received little attention, even when the *Somn.*
passage was commented on and notions related to reincarnation discussed.[36] When the tenet was mentioned, scholars saw no need to refer to

---

[35] See, e.g. Jean Le Clerc, *Joanni Clerici epistolae criticae et ecclesticae* (Amsterdami: Typographiae huguetanorum, 1700), 256–99; J. L. von Mosheim's 14-page footnote in Ralph Cudworth, *The True Intellectual System of the Universe: To Which Are Added the Notes and Dissertations of Dr. J. L. Mosheim*; translated by John Harrison (London: Thomas Tegg, 1845), 320–33 (Cudworth's work was originally published in 1678, and Mosheim's notes first appeared in his 1773 Latin translation); Joseph Priestley, "Of the Platonism of Philo," *The Theological Repository* 4 (1784): 408–20, and Moritz Wolff, *Die philonische Philosophie in ihrem Hauptmomenten dargestellt* (Gothenburg: Bonnier, 1858). Additionally, there is no reference to reincarnation in James Drummond, *Philo Judaeus, or the Jewish-Alexandrian Philosophy* (London: Williams and Norgate, 1888), although Drumond does discuss the idea of pre-existence (see below, section 2.1). Harry A. A. Kennedy, *Philo's Contribution to Religion* (London: Hodder & Stoughton, 1919), 80–81, referring "esp." to *Gig.* 6–15, regards "one of [Philo's] most discordant hypotheses, that of the pre-existence of souls in the air" as a "side issue" and does not mention transmigration. I can also find no reference to reincarnation in Joseph Gross, "Philons von Alexandreia Anschauungen über die Natur des Menschen" (diss., Tübingen, 1930), a study on Philonic anthropology, and the situation is the same with Joseph Pascher, *Η ΒΑΣΙΛΙΚΗ ΟΔΟΣ: Der Königsweg zu Wiedergeburt und Vergottung bei Philon von Alexandria*; Studien zur Geschichte und Kultur des Altertums, Bd. 17.3–4 (Paderborn: Ferdinand Schöningh, 1931).

[36] See, e.g., D. Grossman, *Quaestiones Philoneae* (Leipzig: Friedricus Fleischer, 1829), 27, 31; August Gfrörer, *Philo und die alexandrinische Theosophie*, 2 vols. (Stuttgart: Schweizerbart, 1831), 2.357–60; August Ferdinand Dähne, *Geschichtliche Darstellung der jüdisch-alexandrinischen Religions-Philosophie* (Halle: Buchhandlung des Waisenhauses, 1834), 1.162, 260, 310–11; Heinrich Ritter, *The History of Ancient Philosophy*; translated from the German by Alexander J. W. Morrison (London: Bohn, 1838–1846), 4.438; Karl Herzog, *Spekulativ-psychologische Entwicklung der Grundlagen und Grundlinien des philonischen Systems* (Nuremberg: Rottner & Keller, 1911), 96; Franz Cumont, *After Life in Roman Paganism* (New Haven: Yale University Press, 1923), 154. Worth a special mention is Thomas Billings's work *The Platonism of Philo Judaeus* (Chicago: University of Chicago Press, 1919), which remarkably fails to mention reincarnation at all. For instance, on p. 41, when discussing Philo's views on daemons and souls of the air, Billings says "there are two main passages" that are relevant, *Gig.* 6–18 and *Somn.* 1.134–143. He chooses the former for analysis and says of the latter no more than that "[t]he ideas are repeated" there. The reincarnation aspect would have informed Billing's discussion, e.g., of the fact that "some souls are swept away and overwhelmed by sense" in *Gig.* 15 (p. 58). In dealing with the reincarnational images of Plato that Philo utilizes Billings does not note their original context in this respect (pp. 88–92, 101). Billing's work, however, led me to the earliest works discussed in this section and is useful also in other respects. An *index locorum* thereto has been drawn up (Albert C. Geljon and David T. Runia, "An Index Locorum to Billings, *The Platonism of Philo Judaeus*," SPhA 7 (1995): 169–85. A much more recent example of a scholarly discussion of themes close to reincarnation lacking an explicit discussion of Philo's position is Dieter Zeller, "The Life and Death of the Soul in Philo of Alexandria: The Use and Origin of a Metaphor," in SPhA 7 (1995): 19–55 (esp. pp. 44–45).

their predecessors; e.g., Eduard Zeller writes that those who have been freed from attachment to the body may after death enjoy their higher life, whereas "den übrigen stellt Philo, so selten er auch davon redet, die Seelenwanderung in Aussicht, welche seine Voraussetzungen forderten."[37] The only reference is a quotation of *Somn.* 1.139. Similarly, Édouard Herriot states—again in connection with Philo's views on angels—that those souls who had descended "dans des corps d'hommes non vertueux" will after death be "précipitées dans le corps d'autres hommes" of the same kind.[38]

Zeller for his part is the only scholarly reference of Emil Schürer who gives more than usual attention to delineating the *Stellenwert* of reincarnation in Philo's thought. He writes,

> For those who have not freed themselves from sense, Philo has to accept, after the occurrence of the natural death, a transition to another body, that is a *transmigration of souls*.[39]

This is preceded by the quotation of *Leg.* 1.108 and not the usual *Somn.* 1 passage, although Schürer does refer to the souls, angels and daemons of the air of *Somn.* in discussing Philo's "chiefly" Platonic anthropology four pages earlier.[40] He further notes Philo's views of the body as a prison or a grave and his ethics whose most important principle is "the *utmost possible renunciation of sensuousness*, the extirpation of the passions."[41] This Schürer sees as a Stoic ideal, but notes that the Platonic "imitation of the Deity" is also very important for Philo;[42] after all,

> the origin of man being transcendental, the object of his development is likewise transcendental. As it was by falling away from God that he was entangled in this life of sense, so must he struggle up from it to the direct *vision of God*. This object is attainable even in this earthly life.... Beyond it

---

[37] Eduard Zeller, *Die nacharistotelische Philosophie*, vol. 3.2 of *Die Philosophie der Griechen in ihrer geschichtlichen Entwicklung*, sixth edition (Hildesheim: Olms, 1963), 446. (Zeller's great work originally appeared during 1844–1852.) It seems evident that this formulation is behind Schürer's (above, p. 3).

[38] Édouard Herriot, *Philon le Juif: Essai sur l'ecole juive d'Alexandrie* (Paris: Librairie Hachette, 1898), 248. He actually refers to *Gig.* 6–18 and gives the *Somn.* passage as a comparable text only. Cf. p. 329: "la theorie ... sur la transmigration des âmes a dû faire sur [Philon] une vive impression." Previous scholarship is not mentioned.

[39] Emil Schürer, *A History of the Jewish People in the Time of Jesus Christ*, tr. Sophia Taylor and Peter Christie; 2 divs., 5 vols. (New York: Scribner's, 1885–1891), 2.3:380 n. 185. Emphasis original. (The English translation was published in practice simultaneously with the German original.)

[40] Idem, 2.3:377. For *Leg.* 1.105–108 see below, esp. pp. 57–64.

[41] Idem, 2.3:378. Emphasis original.

[42] Idem, 2.3:378–79.

lies only complete deliverance from this body, that return of the soul to its original incorporeal condition, which is bestowed on those who have kept themselves free from attachment to this sensuous body.[43]

When one compares the entire section on Philo's anthropology in the article in the *Encyclopaedia Britannica* by Schürer and Charles Bigg (from which the quotation on p. 3 was extracted) with the above summary, their likeness is so close that it is clear the text in the former is Schürer's and that these are the premises of Philo's of which reincarnation is "the necessary consequence."[44] Schürer's is clearly the most thorough description so far of the basis on which Philo could be seen to hold the doctrine. But can he be deemed to have settled the issue? Quite apart from the fact that the virtual consensus of the seventeenth to nineteenth centuries has since dispersed into a spectrum of views that in the extremes are mutually exclusive, my answer is no. He certainly succeeds in making it seem plausible that Philo believed in transmigration, but his account is nevertheless so brief that no more should even be expected of it.

It is interesting that up to the nineteenth century it is difficult to find anyone expressing an opinion to the effect that Philo *denied* reincarnation, or that even if he wrote approvingly about it, he did not really mean it. The later scholarly view that Philo rejected rebirth could be thought to have stemmed from the rise of critical research, but as the matter stands, this is not the case.

In the twentieth century, scholars continued to make their statements usually in passing. For example, Norman Bentwich has one sentence:

> The unrighteous souls, Philo sometimes suggests, in accordance with current Pythagorean ideas, are reincarnated according to a system of transmigration within the human species (παλιγγενεσία).[45]

---

[43] Idem, 2.3:380. Emphasis original.

[44] Bigg apparently did not write anything on Philo's position on reincarnation. The tenet is in Charles Bigg, *The Christian Platonists of Alexandria: Being the Bampton Lectures of the year 1886* (Oxford: Clarendon Press, 1913) briefly mentioned as having been rejected by both Clement of Alexandria (p. 318) and Origen (p. 241) but it is not referred to in connection with Philo.

[45] Norman Bentwich, *Philo-Judaeus of Alexandria* (Philadelphia: JPS, 1910), 180. Other examples of very brief mentions of Philo's acceptance of reincarnation are Walter Stettner, *Die Seelenwanderung bei Griechen und Römern*; Tübingen beiträge zur Altertumswissenschaft 22 (Stuttgart: Kohlhammer, 1934), 53, 61 (based on *Somn.*); Irmgard Christiansen *Die Technik der allegorischen Auslegungswissenschaft bei Philon von Alexandrien;* Beiträge zur Geschichte der biblischen Hermeneutik 7 (Tübingen: J. C. B. Mohr, 1969), 59 (*Somn.*); Carl R. Holladay, *Theios Aner in Hellenistic-Judaism: A Critique of the Use of This Category in New Testament Christology*; SBL Dissertation Series 40 (Missoula: Scholars Press, 1977), 139 (no reference to any Philonic text).

This time the text explicitly referred to is *Cher.* 114. There a "regeneration" after death is mentioned without spelling out its meaning.[46] The word "sometimes" implies that Bentwich saw the idea also elsewhere but he does not tell us where, nor does he refer to previous research.

Another feature characterizing the way in which scholars have treated the issue is the use of elusive language. For example, Émile Bréhier, after giving his own translation for *Somn.* 1.134–143 speaks of Philo's classification of souls in three groups.[47] If we use Pétau's classification as a reference,[48] we note that Bréhier takes the first and third groups together as "les âmes du corps."[49] He says of the second one (with regard to the body) that they "l'ont quitté définitivement" and goes on to identify the time periods mentioned at *Somn.* 1.138 with those that Plato mentions in the *Phaedrus* in the context of reincarnation. He can hardly mean anything else than that Philo too means that souls transmigrate, but he does not make this explicit.[50]

Isaak Heinemann is very brief on Philo and reincarnation: after having stated that Pythagoreanism did not have such an authoritative position for Philo as Platonism and Stoicism, he continues,

> mit dem Glauben an die Seelenwanderung setzt [Philon] sich nie auseinander, auch wo er der Bibel zuliebe tierfreundliche Lehren entwickelt oder im Widerspruch zu ihr das unblutige Opfer rühmt.[51]

Heinemann is right that in those contexts Philo does not "enter into debate" with reincarnation, but otherwise his remark is quite perfunctory.

---

[46] This passage is the object of examination below, section 3.2.
[47] Émile Bréhier, *Les idées philosophiques et religieuses de Philon d'Alexandrie* (Paris: Alphonse Picard, 1908), 127–28.
[48] See above, p. 10.
[49] In effect the same is done by the French translator of *Somn.* in the PAPM series, Pierre Savinel. See below, n. 475 on p. 148.
[50] Also Colson in PLCL 5.600 (1934) and Michael J. Reddoch, "Dream Narratives and Their Philosophical Orientation in Philo of Alexandria" (Ph.D. diss., University of Cincinnati, 2010), 203 substitute a reference to the reincarnational time periods of the *Phaedrus* for an explicit mention of the doctrine of reincarnation when commenting on the *Somn.* passage. Another type of elusiveness is found in Jaap Mansfeld, "Heraclitus, Empedocles, and Others in a Middle Platonist Cento in Philo of Alexandria," *VC* 39 (1985): 131–56: e.g., on pp. 135, 145–46 he mentions transmigration when discussing the traditions behind certain Philonic passages (*QG* 1.70–71 and *Leg.* 1.108, respectively) but does not make explicit what he thinks Philo's stance on the tenet was. See below, n. 206 on p. 61.
[51] Isaak Heinemann, *Philons griechische und jü dische Bildung: Kulturvergleichende Untersuchungen zu Philons Darstellung der jü dischen Gesetze* (Breslau: M. & H. Marcus, 1932), 550.

Henrik Elmgren considers *Somn.* 1.139 an unambiguous reference to reincarnation: "This passage about rebirth cannot be misunderstood."[52] He says it is not an isolated case, but the other passages he refers to, *Mos.* 2.263 and *Opif.* 78 (dealing with the memory of past catastrophes and that of the music of the spheres) are quite open to other interpretations. More relevant is his mention of the recurrence of the theme of migration in Philo. He concludes that "[a]ll these statements do not of course have to be put in relation with a developed doctrine of transmigration in Philo."[53] Elmgren in fact seems to be the first to express doubts about the *seriousness* of Philo's references to reincarnation. In a somewhat patronizing manner he says, "[i]t is hardly credible that Philo in the first place drew the conclusions from a doctrine of transmigration of souls." The implication is surely that in Elmgren's mind such a tenet would not be in harmony with Philo's other views. He continues that "[i]t does not have to be particularly emphasized, either, that one can easily set forth expressions of his that are in direct contradiction" with reincarnation. Alas, such expressions, which would have been most interesting to analyze in this study, are not presented for the reader by Elmgren. His meager overall conclusion is that we must be content with noting that this doctrine was not unknown to Philo.[54]

Erwin R. Goodenough does not discuss reincarnation in his famous 1935 monograph.[55] However, in a later article he finds Philo opposing the tenet. He lists this opposition among three items of "Philo's deviations from the Platonic tradition" and writes that "Philo seems completely to have rejected the Platonic doctrine of metempsychosis."[56] What are the grounds for this view? "In each of these rejections it is his Jewish foundation which has been the censor." No Philonic texts are referred to; other scholars are not mentioned.

---

[52] Henrik Elmgren, *Philon av Alexandria med särskild hänsyn till hans eskatologiska föreställningar* [*Philo of Alexandria and his eschatological views*]; diss., Lund (Stockholm: Svenska Kyrkans Diakonistyrelse, 1939), 171. All the quotations from his work are my translations from Swedish.
[53] Idem, 172. The quotations that follow are from the same page.
[54] Like so many others, Elmgren leaves the impression that no scholar has addressed Philo's position on reincarnation before him; none are cited.
[55] Erwin R. Goodenough, *By Light, Light: The Mystic Gospel of Hellenistic Judaism* (New Haven: Yale University Press, 1935). He does touch on two of the passages examined below in Ch. 3 as direct evidence, i.e., Philo's interpretation in *Somn.* 1 of Jacob's ladder dream in Gen 28 (p. 169) and the one in *QE* 2 of Moses's ascent to the mountain in Ex 24:12 (p. 214) but does not seem to see any reason for raising the possibility that Philo is speaking of transmigration of souls.
[56] Goodenough, "Philo on Immortality," *HTR* 39.2 (1946): 86–108, pp. 106–7.

18   CHAPTER ONE

In his massive two-volume work Harry Austryn Wolfson discusses Philo's position on reincarnation on a single page. He takes as his starting point in this question a rather dubious reading of Plato: "the Platonic view with regard to the reincarnation of the souls of the wicked" does not imply "a belief in individual providence and individual reward and punishment. According to Plato, reincarnation follows wickedness by the necessity of a predetermined law of fate."[57] The reference Wolfson gives is *Timaeus* 41e–42d, but what we find there is the determination of reincarnation based on precisely individual behavior;[58] and there is no contradiction between a law and individual responsibility. It is true that the punishment of reincarnation is in *Tim.* not *individually declared* on souls by some tribunal, but even that is present in other dialogues, albeit in mythical form.[59] When Wolfson then goes on to state that in Judaism "both resurrection and immortality are considered as acts of individual providence, coming to each individual as a reward or a punishment for his actions," one wonders where the difference he sees from Plato's views is to be found.[60] Moreover, since this difference is his only argument supporting the implication of what he says—that Philo could not have accepted reincarnation—his view must be judged to be without foundation. Wolfson too mentions no other scholars in this context.[61]

---

[57] Wolfson, *Philo*, 1.408.
[58] For a quotation, see below, p. 91.
[59] In the *Phaedrus* an individual judgement is mentioned (249a; similarly *Republic* 614c), but it is concerned with the souls' inter-incarnational location only and not with whether they reincarnate or not. This latter is determined by the predefined time period (10,000 or 3,000 years). In the *Phaedo*, no formal judgement is involved in, e.g. 81c in the description of impure souls being dragged back to the visible world, but later (113d) it is mentioned. In the account of the post-mortem judgment in the *Gorgias* (523b–524a), reincarnation does not figure at all—explicitly, that is, but cf. n. 203 on p. 60 below. On the use of myth by Plato, see the brief discussion below, pp. 24–25.
[60] Wolfson, *Philo*, 1.408.
[61] Wolfson himself is the only reference that Burnett, "Philo on Immortality," 466 n. 83 gives for his already cited statement of "Philo's rejection of successive incarnations" (above, p. 3). It is illustrative of the marginal position of reincarnation in Philonic studies that in the three annotated bibliographies of research covering the period 1937–2006 (Roberto Radice and David T. Runia, *Philo of Alexandria: An Annotated Bibliography 1937–1986*; VCSup8 [Leiden: Brill, 1988]; David T. Runia, *Philo of Alexandria: An Annotated Bibliography for 1987–1996 with Addenda for 1937–1986*; VCSup 57 [Leiden: Brill, 2000]; David T. Runia, *Philo of Alexandria: an Annotated Bibliography 1997-2006 with addenda for 1987–1996*; VCSup 109 [Leiden: Brill, 2012]) only the first one mentions *s.v. reincarnation* a single item, Burnett's article—which does not merit the mention in terms of having made some scholarly contribution on this topic.

Anita Méasson has thoroughly examined Philo's use of Platonic myths. Her work will be referred to in numerous places below; with regard to reincarnation it can be stated that she sees Philo referring to the doctrine at *Somn.* 1.139.[62] There are also other researchers whose statements on Philo and reincarnation are mentioned when the Philonic texts which their remarks pertain to are analyzed in Ch. 30. In the following two subsections of this chapter we will discuss the comments on Philo's position on reincarnation by two leading Philonic scholars who have written more than is usual on the subject: David Winston and David T. Runia.

1.4.2 *David Winston and the Endless Series of Reincarnations*

David Winston is one of those researchers who see Philo as accepting the idea of reincarnation. But he is quite unique in positing reincarnation as *an eternal punishment* in Philo.[63] His starting point is that the attainment of "joyful immortality" is, according to Philo, "conditional on the soul's assimilation to divine wisdom and its pursuit of the life of perfect virtue." Winston subsequently paraphrases various texts by Philo to the effect that "it is virtue that gives immortality and vice that brings on destruction," and that the wicked are dead already and can expect nothing but eternal death. He writes,

> Since Philo further indicates that the earth is the beginning and end of the evil and vile man (*QG* 1.51), we may conclude that in his view the destruction of the wicked very likely consists in an endless series of reincarnations. This would fit precisely his definition of folly as "a deathless evil, never experiencing the end that consists in having died, but subject to all eternity to that which consists in ever dying" (*Det.* 178).

He then specifies that this would be the fate of only those who are incurably wicked. With regard to the curable souls that fall short of perfect wisdom, Winston surmises that "it is quite likely Philo thought they needed to undergo further transmigrations to purge them before they could escape the wheel of rebirth."[64] In another context he mentions one of the

---

[62] Anita Méasson, *Du char ailé de Zeus à l'Arche d'Alliance: Images et mythes platoniciens chez Philon d'Alexandrie* (Paris: Études Augustiniennes, 1986), 286.
[63] David Winston, *Logos and Mystical Theology in Philo of Alexandria* (Cincinnati: Hebrew Union College Press, 1985), 38–42. The quotations that immediately follow are from pp. 38–39.
[64] Idem, 42.

passages which I discuss in Ch. 3 when he states that Philo "certainly ... envisages reincarnation" in, "e.g., *Somn.* 1.139."[65]

I think the Philonic passages Winston appeals to are not (with the exception of *Somn.* 1.139) *specific* enough to prove his views, nor is his analysis sufficiently detailed for that purpose. Philo's comments in the passage mentioned thrice by Winston, *QG* 1.51, on Adam's having to return to the earth (Gen 3:19) are very intriguing. The idea seems to be that the transgression in Paradise rendered the originally divine part of the human being earthly, and *this* made the curse of returning to the earth apply to it too and not just the body. We will be in a better position to evaluate Winston's views further after examining *QG* 1.51 and its parallel at *Leg.* 3.251–253 in detail below.[66]

1.4.3 *The Work of David T. Runia on Philo and the* Timaeus[67]

The *Timaeus* has been described as the most important of Plato's dialogues for Philo.[68] The *magnum opus* on the subject is David T. Runia's immensely

---

[65] David Winston and John Dillon, *Two Treatises of Philo of Alexandria: A Commentary on* De Gigantibus *and* Quod Deus Sit Immutabilis; BJS 25 (Chico, CA: Scholars Press, 1983), 237. I take this as Winston's text, because Dillon has expressed contrary views: In "The Descent of the Soul in Middle Platonic and Gnostic Theory" in *The golden chain: Studies in the Development of Platonism and Christianity* (Aldershot: Variorum, 1990), 357–64 (section XII) he on p. 362 writes that "Philo has certain difficulties with the concept of reincarnation, which is an essential part of Platonic doctrine, but this does not prevent him from having quite developed notions about the soul's descent to the body." The difficulties are not described. In "Philo of Alexandria and Platonist Psychology," in *The Afterlife of the Platonic Soul: Reflections of Platonic Psychology in the Monotheistic Religions,* ed. Maha Elkaisy-Friemuth and John M. Dillon (Leiden: Brill, 2009), 17–24, he says (p. 23): "There is no need, however, to postulate a preincarnate existence for individual souls, and so no problem about re-incarnation, which is not a doctrine of which Philo would approve." The reasons for this supposed disapproval are not presented. In neither case does Dillon mention any previous scholars' views.

[66] See pp. 70–79.

[67] This section is a reworked version of pp. 221–26 in my "The *Timaeus*, Philo Judaeus and Reincarnation" pp. 217–43 in Gunnar af Hällström ed., *Människan i universum: Platons* Timaios *och dess tolkningshistoria: Texter från Platonsällskapets symposium i Åbo 2007* [*The Human Being in the Universe: Plato's* Timaeus *and Its History of Interpretation: Papers from the Symposium of the Nordic Plato Society in Turku*], Finland, 2007 [Åbo: Åbo Akademi University]). Runia's other views will be returned to in the following chapters. His sceptical view about Philo's accepting the idea of the pre-existence of the soul is examined when we discuss Philo's anthropology (section 2.1), and his statements regarding *Somn.* 1.138–139 are reviewed in section 3.1.3.

[68] Runia, *Philo and the* Timaeus, 4; Bentwich, *Philo-Judaeus,* 74. John Dillon, *The Middle Platonists: A Study of Platonism 80 B.C. to A.D. 220* rev. ed. with new afterword (London: Duckworth, 1996), 140 says Philo particularly favored the *Timaeus* and the *Phaedrus.* If the references to Plato's works in Geljon and Runia's "Index locorum to Billings" are

thorough 1986 work *Philo of Alexandria and the* Timaeus *of Plato.*[69] Runia concludes that "Philo had direct access to the actual text of the dialogue and was intimately acquainted with its contents."[70] He finds twenty direct references to the *Timaeus* in the *Corpus Philonicum* in addition to which he lists several dozen Pentateuchal passages in the exegesis of which Philo "calls on ideas and texts from Plato's dialogue."[71] Runia notes that Philo may also have used secondary material such as commentaries on the *Timaeus*, and that some parts of the dialogue were more important for him than others.[72]

The aim of this section is to examine Runia's statements about Philo's relation to reincarnation. In the *Timaeus* souls are punished for their wickedness in that they are made to be reborn, not only as humans but also in animal bodies (*Timaeus* 42a–c, 91d–92c). In Runia's view "[i]t is highly problematic whether Philo accepts the doctrine of metempsychosis in *any* form."[73] As he points out, there is no evidence that Philo accepted the idea that human souls enter animal bodies.[74] This is not surprising, for Philo subscribed to the view that animals lack the highest part of the soul (νοῦς; *Opif.* 73; *Deus* 45, 47; *Anim.* 85).[75]

In *Timaeus* 91e Plato mentions that the heads of those souls who are born as land animals are dragged downwards because of their kinship with the earth, and Philo uses the same image when discussing the wicked in *Gig.* 31 and *QG* 4.111. Referring to these two passages, Runia writes:

---

counted, the *Republic* emerges as the clear winner. The relative importance of the various dialogues will depend on the subject matter at hand. The present study contains more references to the *Phaedo* than to any other dialogue.

[69] Philosophia Antiqua 44 (Leiden: Brill, 1986).
[70] Runia, *Philo and the* Timaeus, 371.
[71] Idem, 367, 353–62.
[72] Idem, 371–78.
[73] Idem, 347 (my emphasis).
[74] Idem, 348.
[75] According to Helmut Koester, *History, Culture, and Religion of the Hellenistic Age*, vol. 1 of *Introduction to the New Testament* (New York: de Gruyter, 1995), 270, this lack represents a Stoic doctrine. Plato does imply that animals have greater or lesser amounts of νοῦς depending on the changes they undergo in the process of reincarnation (*Timaeus* 92c). However, this is not necessary for rebirth as animals, because νοῦς in Plato is not an essential part of the human being: "of Reason (νοῦ) [partake] only the gods and but a small class of humans" (*Tim.* 51e). Philo's view of νοῦς appears to be much closer to Aristotle's; cf. *De anima* 413b25–28, 429a22–26, 430a22–23. Thomas H. Tobin, *The Creation of Man: Philo and the History of Interpretation* (Washington, DC: Catholic Biblical Association of America, 1983), 149 states that the notion of mind being the highest part of the soul appears in *Tim.* 30b. This is true, but there Plato is talking about the soul of the *universe*.

> Plato's description of the earth-bound animals is transferred metaphorically to men who exercise no restraint over their irrational passions and appetites. Platonic metempsychosis is converted to Philonic allegory.[76]

The first of these two sentences is no doubt correct in the sense that in both passages Philo utilizes Platonic imagery from the *Timaeus*. In this sense it can be said that the Timaean image is transferred from animals to humans. But what kind of associations did Philo expect these references to reincarnational passages from Plato to arouse? Did he make them in spite, because, or irrespective of the metempsychosic overtones? If because, did he want to reject the doctrine, or allude to the possibility that the unvirtuous may be reborn as animalistic people?

Regarding Runia's second sentence in the quotation above, "Platonic metempsychosis is converted to Philonic allegory," I take it to mean that since Philo is utilizing parts of Plato's explicit descriptions of metempsychosis in a context that does not necessitate the idea rebirth, he is "converting" and thus perhaps even *rejecting* the idea of reincarnation as animals.[77] But is this Philo's point? He nowhere explicitly rejects rebirth as animals, most probably because there was no need for him to state the obvious. It would be more accurate to say, "Becoming animals is not present, becoming in some respects *like* animals is." Philo is, after all, not explaining the *Timaeus* but Genesis—and for some reason he is doing so with an allusion to Plato's description of reincarnation in the dialogue.

According to Runia, *QG* 2.56 is "a particularly apposite example" of "Philo's use of *Timaeus* 91d–92c."[78] Here Philo gives an allegorical explanation of the four categories of animals mentioned in Gen 9:1–2 which are the same as in Plato. However, in my view the contents of Philo's exegesis have practically nothing in common with what Plato says about the wickedness of the men being born as different kinds of animals.[79] Philo may have been inspired by the Timaean scheme in some general way, but if we did not know that he knew the dialogue, this passage would give us no special reason to think that he did. It is thus questionable whether it can be

---

[76] Runia, *Philo and the* Timaeus, 347.
[77] Indeed, on pp. 512–13 in his list of "instances of independence of mind and doctrinal divergence in relation to both Platonic text and Platonist interpretation" Runia includes "the rejection of the theory of metempsychosis and its replacement with allegorical explanation." But whether in the examples discussed Philo is *rejecting* reincarnation is questionable, and, moreover, if he does, the justification for generalizing this beyond rebirth as animals is not clear.
[78] Runia, *Philo and the* Timaeus, 348.
[79] Cf. "Philo appears not to have used the thematic material which the dialogue offers" (*ibid.*).

classified as an example of Philo's use of the *Timaeus*; the similarity is between the Bible and Plato.

Runia further considers *Decal.* 80 as "another interesting example of Philo's use of the idea of metempsychosis."[80] Philo pities the Egyptians who worship animals and says that they have their "souls transformed (μετα-βεβληκότας) into the nature of those creatures they honor, so that they ... seem beasts in human shape." Philo again uses the image of animals to depict the wicked, and Runia seems to imply that this amounts to a similar conversion and rejection of transmigration as was discussed above. But what makes this passage "use" of metempsychosis? Runia refers to the verb μεταβάλλω, which is "the *terminus technicus* for the transformations that take place in the process of metempsychosis." It is true that Plato employs the verb in this sense in the *Timaeus* (42c, 92c), but Philo, however, uses it (and its cognates) dozens of times and mostly in contexts where it cannot refer to reincarnation (e.g., *Opif.* 113, *Somn.* 2.259, *Mos.* 1.204). On the other hand, if we look only at such passages where Philo uses the verb about the soul, in many of them the idea of rebirth would *prima facie* make sense.[81] However, the mere appearance of the verb is insufficient to prove a reference to the doctrine even where rebirth might be meant.

Runia's main point about Philo's position on reincarnation in the light of his use of the *Timaeus* is that the Platonic metempsychosis and the Philonic allegory achieve more or less the same "result" or "effect:"

> On the day that the man eats of the tree of knowledge of good and evil, he will "die the death" (Gen 2:17). The death must be interpreted symbolically as the death of the soul, for the protagonists evidently keep on living (*Leg.* 1.105). Plato achieves the same result with his doctrine of metempsychosis.[82]

> But Philo is able, as we have indicated, to achieve a similar effect through his method of allegorical exegesis. All references to beasts, birds and fish in the Biblical texts can be interpreted to represent the degrees of human wickedness and degradation which Plato punishes with transmigration into animals.... [W]hen one considers that folly and ignorance automatically result in the loss of control over the irrational parts of the soul and the

---

[80] Idem, 348–49.
[81] E.g., *Post.* 73: "soul-death, which is the *change* of soul under the impetus of irrational passion;" *Migr.* 225: "the soul ... *becomes* again a virgin;" *Mut.* 124: "a *change* to proved excellence of the whole and entire soul;" or, *Virt.* 205: the fallen soul is "*changed* to a life of pain and misfortune."
[82] Runia, *Philo and the* Timaeus, 264.

24   CHAPTER ONE

> body, it is clear that the Platonic transmigration schema and the Philonic allegory, for all their differences, come close to achieving the same result. [83]

> Certainly [Philo] has no use for the more overt mythical features [of the *Timaeus*], which are found especially in the account of the soul's descent and man's successive reincarnations. Moses, by encouraging the use of allegory, achieves the same result in a more wholesome way.[84]

These three cases are not identical. I understand the first one to mean that just as reincarnation is a punishment for wickedness in Plato, the same can be said of the death of the soul in Philo. This is fine as far as it goes, but it does not tell us much of Philo's stance on reincarnation until we examine his important notion of the death of the soul, linked with the punitive union of body and soul in *Leg.* 1.106–107.[85]

In the second case Runia apparently means that the wickedness of the bad leads to their changing into human brutes and that this also constitutes their punishment.[86] This case is thus close to the first one, and its validity is similarly dependent on whether this is the way Philo uses the image of becoming *like* animals.[87]

In the third case Runia, as far as I can see, argues that Philo's general distaste for myth implies a dislike for reincarnation as well. This is problematic. Let us briefly discuss the reincarnational myths of the *Phaedrus*, the *Republic* and the *Timaeus*. If we define myths as "[n]arrations through which ... religious affirmations and beliefs are expressed,"[88] I would say that the narrative, mythical elements in these three dialogues include, respectively, the heavenly chariot race and the notions of the soul's heaviness and its losing and regaining its wings; Er's journey to the hereafter with its various details including judgement, the underground and heavenly journeys, geographical features, the drawing of lots etc.; and, in

---

[83] Idem, 348. In no other dialogue of Plato's is reincarnation as *animals* given such prominence as in the *Timaeus*, and even there it is not the primary form of metempsychosis, but secondary (42c). According to Simo Knuuttila, Notes on the *Timaeus*, in Plato, *Teokset* 5 (Helsinki: Otava, 1982), 363–81, p. 376 Plato is "undoubtedly playing with the Pythagorean doctrine of transmigration of souls," for taking him literally would imply that even animals have vices and virtues; it is also unclear by what means the animal soul could ascend back to a birth into a human body, except somehow through "gain of reason (νοῦ ... κτήσει)" (92c).
[84] Runia, *Philo and the* Timaeus, 415–16.
[85] This examination will be done below, pp. 57–64.
[86] Runia speaks of "remedial punishment" in the context of reincarnation in *Tim.* 91a–c (p. 324).
[87] This will be discussed below, subsection 2.4.5 on pp. 120–22.
[88] *Oxford Concise Dictionary of World Religions*, ed. John Bowker (Oxford: Oxford University Press, 2000), s.v. "Myth."

the *Timaeus*, the souls' native stars and perhaps also their being born in a female or animal body in case of prolonged wickedness.[89] A religious belief these elements serve to express is reincarnation. So when Runia says that

> [i]f pressed, Philo would argue, I think, that ... [a]ll Plato's talk about reincarnation and metempsychosis, not to speak of souls being sown in the organs of time (42d), distracts the reader from the central and all-important conflict in man's soul[90]

he is juxtaposing a mytheme (the sowing) with a belief (reincarnation), and what I miss here is a distinction between them and an analysis of the significance of that distinction.[91] The idea that if Philo rejected one he *must* have rejected the other as well is not convincing. Furthermore, I do not think it is warranted to call the idea of transmigration *per se* mythical or to sever its close tie with the soul's ethical battle.[92]

We will return to Runia's views of Philo's position on reincarnation below, especially when dealing with Philo's use of the Platonic image of changing into animal form and in the discussion of *Somn.* 1.137–139 as the most important piece of direct evidence on our subject.[93]

1.4.4 *The Most Recent Research on Philo and Reincarnation*

In the Philonic research carried out in the twenty-first century, Philo's position on reincarnation has received hardly any scholarly attention, even

---

[89] That the narrative details vary belongs to the nature of myth; myths may even be "strictly incompatible with each other" (*ibid.*); there need be no effort to reconcile them, because it is not so much the narrative that matters as the beliefs it conveys.
[90] Runia, *Philo and the* Timaeus, 389 n. 122.
[91] For an enlightening discussion of the role of myth in Plato, see Harold Tarrant, "Myth as a Tool of Persuasion in Plato," in *From the Old Academy to Later Neo-Platonism: Studies in the History of Platonic Thought*, Variorum collected studies series (Farnham: Ashgate, 2011); repr. from *Antichthon* 24 (1990). Tarrant does not explicitly make the distinction between mythemes and beliefs, and he somewhat unconvincingly characterizes myths as "detailed investigation[s]" (p. 22) that serve to impart knowledge rather than true opinion. However, in his discussion of the myth of Theuth and Thamus (*Phaedrus* 274e–275c), he does differentiate between "the historical truth" of the myth and "the truth of its message" (p. 23). Socrates explicitly plays down the importance of the former and highlights the latter. Tarrant also points to *Meno* 81e, where Socrates, treating the (reincarnational) theory of recollection much like a myth, affirms he believes in it, and to 86b, where the philosopher refuses to commit himself to any of its details (p. 27).
[92] The possibility of being born as a woman or an animal in the *Timaeus* illustrates the difficulty of always knowing precisely where the border between a mytheme and a belief lies. But in any case I think Plato wants to convey the belief that one's conduct affects one's next life.
[93] Subsections 2.4.5 (pp. 120–122) and 3.1.3 (pp. 143–47), respectively.

though closely related themes have been discussed.[94] Fully explicit positions, with the doctrine being named, are not to be found.[95] Closest comes a study by Wilfried Eisele who implies that Philo speaks of reincarnation by stating—based on, interestingly, *Somn.* 1.138—that souls incarnate more than once.[96] However, he errs in writing, "Der Abstieg

---

[94] The issue is absent in Paola Graffigna, "The Stability of Perfection: The Image of the Scales in Philo of Alexandria," in *Italian Studies on Philo of Alexandria*, ed. Francesca Calabi; Studies in Philo of Alexandria and Mediterranean Antiquity 1 (Boston: Brill, 2003), 131–46, pp. 136, 145; Sarah Pearce, *The Land of the Body: Studies in Philo's Representation of Egypt*; WUNT 1.208 (Tubingen: Mohr Siebeck, 2007), 121, 126, 291; Adam Kamesar, "Biblical Interpretation in Philo," in *The Cambridge Companion to Philo*, ed. Adam Kamesar (Cambridge: Cambridge University Press, 2009), 65–91, p. 85; Termini, "Philo's Thought," 108; Carlos Lévy, "Philo's Ethics," in *The Cambridge Companion to Philo*, ed. Adam Kamesar (Cambridge: Cambridge University Press, 2009), 146–71, p. 164. Thus the readers of *The Cambridge Companion* get no inkling that Philo has been suspected of endorsing the doctrine, and the same applies to two other recent collections of essays: *Philo of Alexandria and Post-Aristotelian Philosophy*, ed. Francesca Alesse; SPhA 5 (Leiden: Brill, 2008) and *Reading Philo: A Handbook to Philo of Alexandria*, ed. Torrey Seland (Grand Rapids: Eerdmans, 2014). Another kind of omission leading to the same result is that a scholarly monograph of more than five hundred pages with the title *Jewish Views of the Afterlife*, which does discuss reincarnation in Judaism (Paull Simcha Raphael, *Jewish Views of the Afterlife*, second edition [Lanham, MD: Rowman & Littlefield, 2009], 314–24) and even calls it, "after the twelfth century ... as kosher to Judaism as Mogen David wine" (p. 314), fails to include any mention of Philo whatsoever. Or, an analysis of Photius's charges against Clement of Alexandria (and in passing of those levelled against Origen as well, *Bibl.* codd. 109 and 8, respectively) of believing in reincarnation, in its discussion of the background against which Clement's position on the doctrine should be analyzed, simply states that "reincarnation seems not to appear as a theological option" in Philo (Piotr Ashwin-Siejkowski, *Clement of Alexandria on Trial: The Evidence of "Heresy" from Photius' Bibliotheca*. VCSup 101 [Leiden: Brill, 2010], 125).

[95] Annegret Meyer, *Kommt und seht: Mystagogie im Johannesevangelium ausgehend von Joh 1,35–51* (Würzburg: Echter Verlag, 2005), 314 says some souls "sehnen sich nach der Erde und dem Körper, sie verharren dort," but the reference is only to *Somn.* 1.138 and not 1.139 and the meaning of "remaining" is not spelled out. On 1.139 Meyer says that other souls "fühlen sich eingesperrt; sie zieht es nach Ablauf des irdischen Lebens wieder hinauf in die Höhe des Geistes." Reddoch, "Dream Narratives" has already been mentioned (see n. 50 on p. 16).

[96] Wilfried Eisele, *Ein unerschütterliches Reich: Die mittelplatonische Umformung des Parusiegedankens im Hebräerbrief*; Beihefte zur Zeitschrift für die neutestamentliche Wissenschaft und die Kunde der älteren Kirche 116 (Berlin: de Gruyter, 2003), 212–13:
Einen Hinweis darauf [that the not fully pure souls begin their vertical motion with a descent], den man allerdings leicht übersieht, gibt zweitens auch das πάλιν in [*Somn.* 1.138]: Ein Aufstieg findet erst statt, nachdem sich die betreffende Seelen *wieder* von der Erde und den Körper getrennt haben (αἱ δ' ἀνέρχονται διακριθεῖσαι πάλιν). Sie haben also offenbar davor schon einmal getrennt von diesen existiert und sind dann erst herabgestiegen, um sich mit ihnen zu verbinden.
(Emphasis added.) He also speaks of "mehreren zeitlich aufeinanderfolgenden Bewegungen" (p. 212), meaning the descents and ascents of souls.

einer unkörperlichen Seele kann in jede Art von Körper erfolgen, darin unterscheidet sich Philon nicht von Platon." The reference is to *Timaeus* 42a–c, a section where reincarnation also as animals is part of Plato's scheme.[97] Eisele points to the creatures of land, water and fire mentioned in *Gig.* 7–11, but this does not justify his claim. Although Philo introduces these creatures by saying, "the universe must be animated (ἐψυχῶσθαι) through and through," the land, water and fire animals, as well as the stars, are presented as static classes: each element has its *own* creatures (§7). There is no indication that a soul may move from one class to another.

Runia's work discussed in the previous subsection has been used by other scholars in analyses of Philo's thought also in regard to reincarnation. A recent example is the study of John T. Conroy, Jr. on Philo's use of the notions of the death of the soul and the transformation into animal form.[98] Conroy states,

> David Runia has convincingly shown that Philo has transformed the Platonic transmigration of souls into a hierarchy of being, with humans who properly utilize their minds to contemplate the heavenly realities as being superior to animals whose necks are so formed that they view primarily the things of the earth.[99]

There are several problems in Conroy's argumentation of which I will concentrate on those related in some relevant way to reincarnation. He says that in Philo the *death of the soul* means a transformation into a beast and that this is an ontological change linked with the destruction of the mind and not a metaphor.[100] But it has to be emphatically denied that the death

---

[97] As was discussed, the human mind cannot incarnate as an animal which does not have νοῦς. See above, n. 75 and text on p. 21.
[98] John T. Conroy, "'The Wages of Sin Is Death:' The Death of the Soul in Greek, Second Temple Jewish, and Early Christian Authors" (Ph.D. diss., University of Notre Dame, 2008) and "Philo's 'Death of the Soul': Is This Only a Metaphor?" SPhA 23 (2011): 23–40.
[99] Conroy, "Death of the Soul," 36 and "The Wages of Sin," 82. He gives as the reference "Runia, *Philo and the* Timaeus, 305." This is not the 1986 work but Runia's original dissertation ("Philo of Alexandria and the Timaeus of Plato" [Ph.D. diss., Free University of Amsterdam, 1983]). The page number should be 303 (~ *Philo and the* Timaeus, 348) rather than 305.
[100] Conroy, "Death of the Soul," 34, 37. Here it becomes apparent that despite Conroy's reference to Runia, their positions differ markedly. Runia sees Philo converting Platonic reincarnation into *allegory*—e.g., "loss of control over the irrational parts of the soul and the body" (see above, p. 23). No ontological change is involved. If Conroy's analysis were accurate, the expression "utterly beastly mind (my tr. for θηριωδέστατος νοῦς)" at *Agr.* 46 would be quite anomalous. Albert C. Geljon and David T. Runia in *On Cultivation* (Leiden: Brill, 2013), 143 rightly do not claim it is but instead remark that "[t]he intellect becomes savage when it loves the *body* and the *passions*" (emphasis added). This is the same as the death of the soul; cf. Philo's main text on this death at *Leg.* 1.105–108: the

of the soul is a case of "only the irrational soul continu[ing] to *exist.*"¹⁰¹ The death of the soul is an ethical or existential concept that characterizes the state of a morally degraded soul. The mind is, to be sure, affected by the soul's death. It loses its ruling position, and this enables the lower parts of the soul to freely realize their sensual tendencies whereby they are pronouncedly dead in an ethical sense. But the mind's *existence* is unaffected.¹⁰²

As to the doctrine of reincarnation itself, Conroy does not seem to be fully aware of many of its manifestations in Plato or elsewhere in Greek literature. Consequently, he does not recognize the echoes of those manifestations in Philo. For example, he does not acknowledge that the notion of changing into animal in Philo form derives from the description of the process of reincarnation in *Timaeus* 42c.¹⁰³ Other such echoes are the term σύνοδος used about the coming together of body and soul in connection with the latter's death in *Leg.* 1.106, the "σῶμα σῆμα problem" (i.e., body as the tomb of the soul), the chariot parable in the *Phaedrus* and the use by Plato of the verb μεταβάλλω in describing the changes of the soul in the cycle of reincarnation.¹⁰⁴ It is also incorrect to use the term "metempsychosis" of the *non-*reincarnational change "from a human soul into a beast's soul."¹⁰⁵

Despite these critical observations, Conroy has a definite point in suggesting that "Philo intends 'immortality' to mean the actual continuation of the soul in existence after it is separated from the body" and that

---

soul is entombed in both the *body* and the *passions*—hardly against its will but rather because of its love for them. See below, subsection 2.1.4 dealing with the causes of incarnation, especially causes 1 (pp. 46–48) and 8 (pp. 57–70).

¹⁰¹ Conroy, "Death of the Soul," 26; emphasis added.

¹⁰² If the occasional references to the mind's "death" (e.g., *Plant.* 147,, *Her.* 52, *QG* 1.75) were understood to mean its annihilation, we would be left wondering why Philo has practically nothing to say of souls whose highest part has been amputated. An isolated case is *Spec.* 3.99 where both the change into animal form and the loss of the intellect (but *not* the death of the soul) are connected to *insanity*. Conroy does note that the mind "makes its home elsewhere" (and thereby *continues* to exist), but he does not comment on how this relates to his idea of the rational part of the soul becoming a corpse.

¹⁰³ Yet this Timaean text is quoted in Conroy, "The Wages of Sin," 81 and connected to the hierarchy of being. For the close parallels in Philo, see below, subsection 2.4.5 (p. 120). In "Death of the Soul," 37, Conroy dissociates "transformation from human to beast" in Philo from the myth of Er in the *Republic*.

¹⁰⁴ Conroy, "Death of the Soul," 28–29, 33, 33–34, 38–39, respectively. For these, see below, n. 197 on p. 57 for σύνοδος; pp. 57–64 for the death of the soul; pp. 93, 171–172 for the *Phaedrus*; and above, p. 23 for μεταβάλλω.

¹⁰⁵ Conroy, "Death of the Soul," 40. Given his emphasis on the verb μεταβάλλω, this word may have been meant to be metabolē.

because immortality "is not a mere metaphor but implies something ontologically, so those whose souls are said to die, do so in more than in a merely metaphorical manner."[106] However, instead of affirming that the transformation from human to beast "has nothing to do with [Platonic] metempsychosis,"[107] it is more appropriate to conclude that the amount of circumstantial evidence is sufficient for the possibility that Philo accepted reincarnation to be among the alternatives explored.

---

[106] Idem, 36–37. In his view this means an ontological change, in mine, an existential one.
[107] Idem, 37.

CHAPTER TWO

THE INDIRECT EVIDENCE

In this chapter Philo's position on the doctrine of reincarnation is approached through indirect evidence. The accounts that follow are not meant to be exhaustive in other respects, for their main purpose is to clarify and bring to one place such features of Philo's thought which I will repeatedly refer to afterwards, selected aspects that are instrumental in establishing his position on reincarnation.

In the first three sections the question as to whether there is, in principle, a niche for reincarnation in Philo's thought is explored: The answer to this question is sought by first examining Philo's anthropology (2.1) where issues addressed include how the human being is constituted and why the soul or mind incarnates in the first place. Subsequently, his individual eschatology and soteriology (2.2) is discussed, the focus being on how salvation is achieved, and, in particular, what *failing* to be saved means. Both sections also frequently discuss the ethical implications of Philo's views.[108] Then (section 2.3), the issue addressed is that while nowhere does Philo explicitly denounce transmigration, in certain passages he expresses views that might be interpreted as contradicting it. The task is to assess the impact of such texts on the possibility of his endorsing reincarnation. In the fourth section the approach is a little different: Philo's use of Greek, chiefly Plato's, reincarnational concepts, images and terminology is examined (2.4). The chapter ends with a summary of the conclusions that can be drawn (2.5).

2.1 *Anthropology*

2.1.1 *Dualism*

For the present study, the most fundamental feature of Philo's views of the human being during her earthly life is the notion that while she consists of soul and body, this is *not her essential condition*. Instead, the body is something in which the soul only temporarily resides. This residence is, for Philo, very often a highly regrettable state: "the body [is a] baneful corpse

---

[108] By "ethical implications" I mean the values and goals which (should) determine how one lives one's life.

to which [the soul is] tied" (*Leg.* 1.108; similarly *Leg.* 3.74, *Migr.* 21, *Somn.* 2.237, al.).

Philo uses many different images to illustrate "[t]he duality of body and soul [which] is one of the cornerstones of [his] thought."[109] The most important ones are the following:

- The body is a container or dwelling of the soul (e.g., *Opif.* 137; *Det.* 163; *Deus* 150; *Ebr.* 124; *Migr.* 93, 197; *Somn.* 1.26; *Praem.* 120–121; *QG* 2.27, 4.94).
- The body is the soul's garment; the soul should become naked of it (e.g., *Leg.* 2.22, 2.55; *Cher.* 31; *Post.* 137; *Gig.* 53; *Deus* 56; *Fug.* 110; *Somn.* 1.43; *QG* 1.53, 4.1, 78).
- The body is a foreign land and the earthly life a mere sojourning (e.g., *Cher.* 120; *Agr.* 64–65; *Migr.* 28; *Conf.* 77–78; *Her.* 239–240, 274; *Mut.* 38; *Somn.* 1.46, 1.181; *Praem.* 117; *QG* 3.10, 3.11, 3.45, 4.74, 4.178). Egypt is the foreign country *par excellence*, and it is also the central biblical symbol of the body in Philo.[110] Thus also the deeper meaning of the exodus from Egypt is the migration from the body (*Migr.* 14). As it happens, the Passover has much the same meaning.[111]
- The body is the soul's grave (e.g., *Leg.* 1.108; *Deus* 150; *Migr.* 16; *Somn.* 1.139; *Spec.* 4.188; *QG* 1.70, 2.69, 4.75, 153).[112]
- The body is the soul's prison (*Leg.* 3.42; *Ebr.* 101; *Migr.* 9; *Her.* 68, 85; *Somn.* 1.139).
- The body is a river (*Gig.* 13; *Her.* 315; *Conf.* 66; *Somn.* 1.147, 2.109; *QG* 4.234).[113]

2.1.2 *Pre- and Post-existence of the Soul*

Above, the *pre- and post-existence* of an incorporeal part of the individual was noted to be one of the essential characteristics of reincarnational belief systems.[114] Generally speaking, this part may be called the soul or spirit or it may be some vital energy.[115] It should be noted that there is one

---

[109] Runia, *Philo and the* Timaeus, 262.
[110] Pearce, in her monograph (*The Land of the Body*) on this very subject, characterizes this as "a symbolism which dominates Philo's interpretation of Egypt and all things Egyptian in the Pentateuch" (p. 85). The symbolism occurs mainly in the *Allegorical Commentary*.
[111] See below, pp. 116–117.
[112] For this and the following notion, see below, subsection 2.4.4 (pp. 119–20).
[113] See subsection 2.4.2, pp. 114–17. Examples of the body being symbolized also by the *sea* will also be discussed below.
[114] See p. 6.
[115] In the present study, the question as to whether in Philo it is the mind or the entire soul that possibly reincarnates is not crucial, as the goal is to establish if he accepted the

exception to the necessity of pre-existence: this condition does not necessarily apply to a soul's first embodiment. A logical consequence is that denial of pre-existence in a distinct case does not automatically mean refuting the idea in general.

The notion that the soul inhabits the body temporarily, as just discussed, is directly related to the pre- and post-existence of the soul. In Philo this idea takes a consistent pattern: the soul will eventually return to where it came from. Let us take a few examples.[116]

In *Gig.* Philo explains that some the souls have ended up in bodies.

> [D]escending into the body as though into a stream [they] have sometimes been caught in the violent rush of its raging waters and swallowed up; at other times, able to withstand the rapids, they have initially emerged at the surface and then soared back up to the place whence they had set out. (*Gig.* 13)

In *Conf.* Philo tells us why all those whom Moses calls wise are sojourners who do not make the foreign country of the body their home but return to the heavenly region:

> So when they have stayed awhile in bodies, and beheld through them all the sense-perceptible and mortal things, they again return to where they first started from. (*Conf.* 77–78)

In *Somn.* Philo states that the intellect

> forsook its heavenly abode and came into the body as into a foreign land. But the Father who gave it birth ... will take pity on it and loose its chains, and escort it in freedom and safety to its mother-city. (*Somn.* 1.181)

When speaking of the earthly life as sojourning, Philo does not always spell out the scheme in full and separately mention the soul's existence both before and after the earthly visit, but these are implied by the image itself. In *Abr.* Philo comments on the restraint shown by Abraham while mourning Sarah's death. He had learned from "holy books" that

> death is not the extinction of the soul but its separation and detachment from the body and its return to the place whence it came. (*Abr.* 258)

Explaining the meaning of Abraham's own departure "to his fathers" (Gen 15:15) in *QG*, Philo writes,

---

doctrine in any form. Nonetheless this issue also receives some attention because of its connection to the question of what reaching salvation entails. See below, pp. 40, 85–90.

[116] All five passages quoted are discussed in more detail below.

> Clearly this indicates the incorruptibility of the soul, which removes its habitation from the mortal body and returns as if to the mother-city, from which it originally moved its habitation to this place. (*QG* 3.11)

Philo's belief in the soul's pre- and post-existence must be considered abundantly clear. Yet doubts have also been expressed. David T. Runia writes that "mostly [Philo] regards the soul as being created by God at man's birth (cf. *De cherubim* 114)" and that Philonic passages that speak of pre-existence or even reincarnation "represent an aspect of Middle Platonist doctrine which Philo does not regard as entirely unacceptable, but which he has not bothered to integrate fully into his thought."[117] Runia mentions one passage to be compared to his view (*Cher.* 114).[118] There Philo asks several questions about the soul, *inter alia*: "Do we at some time get it as our own?[119] Before our birth? But then we ourselves did not exist." Just before this passage, however, Philo explicitly defines himself as "consisting of soul and body" (§113); the combination obviously could not exist before the body did.[120]

It is not clear on which grounds Runia considers Philo's integration of the notions mentioned deficient. He refers to Richard Baer who, whilst he thinks Philo never harmonized the idea of pre-existence with "the far more usual Genesis account of man's creation," does admit that "Philo accepts the Platonic doctrine of the pre-existence of the soul."[121] Baer, for his part, refers back to James Drummond who writes about "two unharmonized types of thought."[122] The first one is that Philo "readily embraced" the pre-existence of the soul.[123] But, writes Drummond,

> when he speaks of the creation of man, and the communication to him of the divine Spirit, this doctrine totally disappears, and he follows the Scriptural statement that God breathed into man a breath of life.[124]

---

[117] Runia, *Philo and the Timaeus*, 347–48.
[118] But he himself mentions (ibid.) *Plant.* 14, *Conf.* 77–82, *Her.* 282–83 and *Somn.* 1.139 as passages speaking about pre-existence.
[119] For the grounds of this translation of mine, see n. 488 on p. 153.
[120] Furthermore, Philo also says "we will not be" after death (§114), and yet goes on to describe post-mortem events in which the soul takes part. There are thus no grounds for concluding that he is denying either pre- or post-existence here. See subsection 2.3.1 and especially section 3.2 for a more detailed discussion of this passage.
[121] Richard A. Baer, *Philo's Use of the Categories Male and Female*, ALGHJ 3 (Leiden: Brill, 1970), 86.
[122] Drummond, *Philo Judaeus*, 2.277.
[123] Idem, 1.336.
[124] Idem, 2.277.

There are several problems with this statement. First of all, the whole paragraph where Drummond discusses this question is devoid of references to Philo's treatises. Second, Drummond here in fact paraphrases and quotes the *biblical* text: the creation of the first man and God's breathing into him the breath of life; we hear nothing of Philo's *interpretation*. We need, then, to assume that Drummond means that if the soul is breathed in, it is not pre-existent *qua* soul.

It may first be noted that in purely logical terms there need be no contradiction between the individual soul's pre-existence and the creation of the human *species* through a special act of creation.[125] For is this not what Plato, in effect, does in the *Timaeus* with regard to the immortal part of the soul?[126] However, Philo also refers to Gen 2:7 with regard to the *individual*. In *Opif.* he writes,

> [Moses] says that the sense-perceptible and individual human being has a structure which is composed of earthly substance and divine spirit, for ... the soul obtained its origin from (γεγενῆσθαι ... ἀπ') nothing which has come into existence at all, but from the Father and Director of all things. What he "breathed in" was nothing else than the "divine spirit"[127] which has emigrated here from that blessed and flourishing nature for the assistance of our kind, in order that, even if it is mortal with regard to its visible part, at least with regard to its invisible part it would be immortal. (*Opif.* 135) [128]

---

[125] This relates to the exception from the necessity of pre-existence as a prerequisite for reincarnation noted above (p. 32).

[126] See 41d. Admittedly, there is the difference that in the Timaean account *all* souls are created at once through the initial act of the demiurge; these then go on to incarnate and reincarnate (41e–42d).

[127] I enclose this expression in quotation marks as I regard it as a probable allusion to Ex 31:3 and/or 35:31. These are the only verses in the Pentateuch where πνεῦμα θεῖον occurs (there are only two further instances in the LXX, Job 27:3, 33:4). Note that in *Leg.* 3.95–96 Philo combines Ex 31:2–3 and Gen 1:27: the name Bezalel refers to the "the shadow of God", i.e., the Logos. These verses are used in the same context in *Plant.* 18–27 as well ("divine spirit" at §18, Gen 1:27 at §19, clear allusion to Ex at §23, quotation at §26). Cf. also *Her.* 57, *Det.* 86.

[128] Translation Runia, except for the last word, ἀθανατίζηται, which he renders, "would be immortalized." LSJ gives *Opif.* 135 and 154 as examples of the verb's meanings (in passive) 'to become or *be immortal*' (my emphasis). Cf. *QG* 4.166 where the meaning *must* be the latter. Furthermore, the possibility that the highest part in the human being was *originally mortal* is contradicted in the immediate sequel:
> Sharing (ἐστι μετέχοντα) in both to the extent necessary, [the human being] has come to existence (γεγενῆσθαι) as a creature which is mortal and at the same time immortal, mortal in respect of the body, immortal in respect of the understanding.

But it does seem that in *Opif.* 77, 154 Philo uses the verb ἀθανατίζω to mean *becoming* immortal. For a brief discussion of Philo's concepts of immortality and the losing and regaining thereof, see the next subsection.

Philo speaks here of the soul's "origin," and we cannot press his words to imply that once it has come into existence it can incarnate only once. We can compare the quotation above with *Opif.* 69, "on that single mind of the universe, as on an archetype, the mind in each individual human being was modelled," and find a similar idea despite the different biblical basis.[129] I suggest that these passages are representative of *one* strand in Philo's multi-faceted interpretation of the account of the creation of the human being where both Gen 1:27 and 2:7 are seen to refer to the *divine origin* of the human mind or soul. Examples of this strand include, e.g., *Her.* 231, where Philo, after quoting the verse, states, "And thus the mind in each of us ... is an impression (τύπον) at third hand from the Maker" (i.e., an image of the image of God), and *QG* 1.50 where he simply says, "the mind is a divine inbreathing." In the same vein, Philo calls the soul (*Leg.* 3.161) or mind (*Somn.* 1.34) a divine fragment and justifies this with Gen 2:7, "He breathed into his face a breath of life."[130] The same verse acts as the proof text also in *QG* 2.59 where we read, "the divine spirit is the substance of the rational [part of the soul]." Explaining the Genesis verse itself in *QG* 1.4 Philo says that the "moulded" human in question "obtained a soul[131] when God breathed life into his face." The divine origin of the soul or mind does not preclude pre-existence and reincarnation.

I argue elsewhere that Philo's most extensive exegesis of Gen 2:7 in *Leg.* 1.31–42 is almost entirely *universal* and not protological: the main implications of Philo's allegorizations are soteriological.[132] For instance, in 1.31–

---

[129] Runia's comment (*On the Creation*, 226) that "this formulation speaks about the relation between God and the human being, but tells us nothing about who or what was actually created on the sixth day" seems to emphasize the universal aspect of Philo's statement. However, I think there is also a protological side to it, because the divine-human relation is presented as that of a model and a copy; the event of *making* the copy is implicit.

[130] The notion of the souls being divine fragments has been ascribed to the Stoics (Diog. Laert. 7.143), but it seems to be of older provenance; cf. the criticism of the idea by Epicurean Velleius in Cicero's *De natura deorum* 1.27.

[131] Marcus: "a spirit," but the Armenian word used here, hnqh (*hogi*), "renders both ψυχή and πνεῦμα" (Marcus in PLCL Suppl. 1.145), and in *QGE* the former, in fact, "more frequently" according to Ralph Marcus, "The Armenian Translation of Philo's *Quaestiones in Genesim et Exodum*," *JBL* 49.1 (1930): 61–64, p. 64; see also Paola Pontani, "Saying (Almost) the Same Thing," in *Studies on the Ancient Armenian Version of Philo's Works*, ed. Sara Mancini Lombardi and Paola Pontani; SPhA 6 (Leiden: Brill, 2011), 125–46, pp. 135–40. Aucher: "animam;" Mercier: "une âme;" QGUM: "einen Geist."

[132] See my "'Call Him Earth:' On Philo's Allegorization of Adam in the *Legum allegoriae*," in *Where Are You, Adam? Papers from the Conference in Åbo, Finland, in August 2014*, ed. Antti Laato and Lotta Valve; Studies in the Reception History of the Bible 7 (Åbo: Åbo Akademi University & Winona Lake: Eisenbrauns, forthcoming).

32 the "breath of life" quite clearly gives what Philo calls the "earthly human/mind" characteristics that belong to the "heavenly human/mind."[133] The "breath" does not mean the mind, because the latter is the recipient of the former (1.37) which enables it to "soar so high as to grasp the nature of God" (1.38). Thus here as well there is no contradiction with the pre-existence of the soul.

2.1.3 *The Structure of the Soul and the Location of Corruption within the Human Being*

Philo's anthropology is more complex than simply the equation *soul + body = human being*. The soul has its own structure which may be relevant for establishing the compatibility of Philo's views with reincarnation: When an individual who does not meet the criteria for salvation dies, what will happen to the *imperfection* in him/her—which in all likelihood may have much to do with a possible new incarnation? Where does it reside: in the mind, the lower parts of the soul or the body?

For the present purpose it is not necessary to delve into the various ways in which Philo divides the soul into parts; the most usual divisions are an eight-fold, two different three-fold models and a two-fold one.[134] The important thing to note is the general rule: the leading part, the mind, is rational, the rest, irrational. The mind is also the only thing in us that is indestructible (*Deus* 46); of the other parts Philo speaks of as "the mortal portion of our soul" (*Fug.* 69, drawing on *Timaeus* 69c–e; also *Ebr.* 70 and *Migr.* 18; cf. *Her.* 52). In this context it is helpful to distinguish between at least three senses of immortality in Philo and explicate their relationship with corruption in an ethical sense.

---

[133] The salvific and heavenizing effects of the "breath of life" in *Leg.* 1.32 have been noted in earlier research; see especially Pascher, *Η ΒΑΣΙΛΙΚΗ ΟΔΟΣ*, 127–31; Karl-Gustav Sandelin, "Die Auseinandersetzung mit der Weisheit in 1. Korinther 15" (ThD diss. Åbo Akademi University, 1976), 31–35 and Gerhard Sellin, *Der Streit um die Auferstehung der Toten: Eine religionsgeschichtliche und exegetische Untersuchung von 1 Korinther 15* (Göttingen: Vandenhoeck & Ruprecht 1986), 104–5. But these scholars still maintain that *also the creation* of the "earthly human" is at stake in in Philo's allegorization of Gen 2:7 in *Leg.* 1. I find very few signs of this, the clearest protological statement being that God "created (ἐδημιούργησεν) no soul barren of virtue" (1.34).

[134] I.e., mind, five senses, speech and the organ of reproduction (Stoic—e.g., *Det.* 168); mind, speech, senses (simplification of the previous—e.g., *Cher.* 113); reason, spirited part, appetitive part (Platonic—e.g., *Conf.* 21); and finally, reasoning and unreasoning (also in Plato—e.g., *Congr.* 26). There are others as well; see, e.g., the Index of PLCL Suppl. 2, s.v. Soul for *QGE*. See also Billings, *Platonism of Philo*, 47–53.

1. Immortality juxtaposed with the body: A human being during the earthly life is a *combination* of mortal and immortal (e.g., *Opif.* 135) and mortal *as such*. Even the most virtuous of men, Moses, "bec[a]me immortal" in this sense upon leaving the "mortal life" in the body (*Mos.* 2.288).
2. Juxtaposed with the Philonic concept of the death of the soul, i.e., life dominated by vice. This is a *state* of the soul: a dead soul is *existentially* so (in ethical terms, that is). Salvation means (real) life (e.g., *Leg.* 1.108), and a never-ending one at that (e.g., *Somn.* 1.139), i.e., immortality.[135]
3. In absolute terms: Neither of the foregoing senses, however, mean that the highest part of the human soul is not *ontologically* indestructible all along (e.g., *Congr.* 97). Thus a "dead" soul is *not* immortal at the existential level, though at the same time it (or at least the mind) *is* immortal ontologically.[136]

Thus, although the mind is the soul's rational, highest, immortal and even divine part, this does not mean it is infallible and incorruptible in a moral sense.[137] The idea of the mind's having to choose good or bad and its being torn in opposite directions is a recurrent idea in Philo,[138] and so are the mind's degraded state[139] and its purification or other betterment[140] all the way to perfection.[141] But it seems that the mind's degradation is a result of the influence of the soul's lower parts and, especially, of the passions and the pleasures *through* these parts. The exegesis of Gen 27:43 is a representative example regarding the senses:

---

[135] If Philo is found to endorse reincarnation, senses 2 and 3 are connected by the fact that reaching immortality means, quite literally, to cease from dying (life after life).

[136] Conroy, "Death of the Soul," 25 assumes immortality is not inherent in the soul, this being "[t]he immediate implication" of *Opif.* 154 where "the soul is immortalized" through reverence for God. He fails to note that in §135 the human being is created immortal with regard to the intellect in sense (3) above. He also refers to *QG* 1.10 and 1.51 (as "*QG* 51"). These are clear cases of sense (2) and do not warrant Conroy's claim that "souls are not 'naturally' immortal" (*ibid.*). Sense (2) is the one of least resistance also in *Opif.* 77, 154. See n. 128 above.

[137] The mention in *QE* 2.96 of the mind's being "inerrant," as all corresponding praising thereof, should be taken to refer to what it is ontologically and potentially.

[138] E.g., *Leg.* 3.189, *Sacr.* 137, *Ebr.* 8, *Her.* 84, *Congr.* 84, *QG* 4.159.

[139] E.g., *Leg.* 2.102; *Cher.* 116, *Agr.* 46, 83, 89; *Conf.* 21, 126; *Migr.* 62; *Mut.* 172; *Somn.* 2.237; *Spec.* 1.214–215, *QG* 1.50, 4.165.

[140] E.g., *Congr.* 110, *Somn.* 1.84, *Mos.* 1.190, *Spec.* 1.269, *QG* 4.46, *QE* 1.4.

[141] E.g., *Leg.* 2.91, 3.140, 3.244; *Sacr.* 7; *Det.* 65; *Post.* 97; *Agr.* 42, 159; *Plant.* 94; *Migr.* 214, 223; *Fug.* 213; *Somn.* 1.213, 2.234; *QG* 3.18, 4.30, 4.35; *Virt.* 189. For some reason the notion of reaching perfection seems to be chiefly restricted to the *Allegorical Commentary* and the *Quaestiones*.

> Excellently well does [Rebecca] call the journey to the senses [i.e., Haran] a flight; for the mind proves itself indeed a runaway, whenever it forsakes the objects of intellectual apprehension (τὰ ... νοητά) which are proper to it, and turns to the opposite array of the objects of sense-perception (τῶν αἰσθητῶν). (*Migr.* 209)

If we look at Philo's exegesis of the curses pronounced on Eve and the serpent in Gen 3:13–14 in *Leg.* 3.59–68, we find that even the senses may be considered innocent, simply reporting as they are to the mind what sense objects there are to report. But "the snake tricked me," says Eve; "pleasure ... artfully falsifies [the object], representing as something advantageous that which is of no benefit at all," comments Philo (3.61). This does not mean, however, that sense-perception with its "false opinions" is, in practice, free from censure (see also, e.g. *Her.* 71).[142]

In another passage we get the impression that a certain kind of mind may not be an unwilling victim of the senses and pleasures:

> But there is a different (type of) mind [than those represented by Noah and Moses] which loves the body and the passions and has been sold in slavery to that chief cateress of our compound nature, Pleasure. (*Deus* 111)

As the image of being a slave hints, more than a question of absolute evil this is one of right rulership. "[B]ut when irrational sense gains the chief place [from the mind], a terrible confusion prevails" (*Leg.* 3.224). The lower parts of the soul and the body need to be kept under the control of reason. Philo writes in *Sacr.*:

> Surely to those who can reason it is a prouder task than kingship to have the strength to rule ... over the body and the senses, and the belly, and the pleasures below the belly, and the other passions and the tongue and in general all our compound being (συγκρίματος). (*Sacr.* 49)

What is the role of the body, then? Runia has noted, "The passivity of the body entails that the real conflict in man takes place between the rational and irrational parts of the soul."[143] This certainly looks likely given how Philo illustrates the soul–body relationship.[144] But can this understanding be upheld in light of passages like *Leg.* 1.105–106 where Philo, in highly ethical terms, warns about the possibility that the body rules the soul? The context is the exegesis of Gen 2:17b, the consequences of eating from the tree for knowing good and evil: "you shall die by death." This involves, Philo says, the "destruction of virtue" and a situation where "the body,

---

[142] Quoted on p. 88.
[143] Runia, *Philo and the Timaeus*, 262.
[144] See above, p. 30–31.

which is the worse, rules (κρατοῦντος), and the soul, which is the better, is ruled (κρατουμένου)" (1.106).

My response is that in the last analysis Philo does not really consider the body an *agent*. In *Leg*. 1.105–108 Philo operates under the crude dichotomy of body and soul, the separation of which is the definition of physical death (see also, e.g., *Leg*. 2.77, *Plant*. 147, *Abr*. 258; from Plato, e.g., *Phaedo* 67d). And when *the ethical dichotomy of good and bad is superimposed on the anthropological of soul and body*, there is simply no other alternative but that the material body becomes the representative of evil and the immaterial soul that of good.[145] I will henceforth call this scheme "*double dichotomy*." In *Leg*. 1 "the death of the soul" denotes life dominated by evil, which is why the body is said to rule. Double dichotomy is at work also in *Leg*. 3.69 where "[T]he body ... is wicked and a plotter against the soul;" similarly *Leg*. 3.191, *Mut*. 174, *Her*. 243. It is already found in Plato; e.g., the whole *Phaedo* is based on this approach. And *Leg*. 1.106 perhaps echoes *Phaedo* 80a where we read, "When the soul and the body are joined together, nature directs the body to serve (δουλεύειν) and be ruled (ἄρχεσθαι), and the soul to rule (ἄρχειν) and master (δεσπόζειν)."[146] Plato does not explicitly

---

[145] Gretchen Reydams-Schils, "Philo of Alexandria on Stoic and Platonist Psycho-Physiology: The Socratic Higher Ground," in *Philo of Alexandria and Post-Aristotelian Philosophy*; ed. Francesca Alesse (Leiden: Brill, 2008) 169–95, p. 173 says that for Philo the "the struggle between soul an (sic) body ... appears to carry the day" over against the tripartition of soul (or any other division thereof) and reiterates this by stating (p. 175) that the soul–body dichotomy is "much more important than any distinction among the soul's faculties and/or parts." However, she does not consider the question as to whether the body can in a meaningful way be said to participate in a "struggle" against the soul. It is close to the truth that the soul/body dualism appears almost on every page of Philo (p. 187) but I think this does not have all the consequences which Reydams-Schils says it has. For example, it is strained to speak (p. 188) of "the struggle between soul and body" in *Mut*. 33 where the body is "a menace to the soul;" the body is not an active fighter but instead a passive *obstruction* for the virtuous aspirations of the soul (e.g. §36: "absolute happiness is impossible to one who is bound to a mortal body"). Likewise, in *Gig*. 12–15, 30–31, which Reydams-Schils also appeals to, the body is not an agent in any way on a par with the mind. It is characterized as a river, a dead thing (§§ 12-15), the "foundation of ignorance and scorn" and a burden (§§ 30–31). Granted, Philo utilizes imagery from the *Phaedrus* (and the *Timaeus*), but does the fact that "Philo leaves out the image of the soul's charioteer and his two horses" represent his "subtly moving away from Plato's account of passion as a conflict between different soul parts" (pp. 187–88)? Be that as it may, it does not follow that he has aimed at making the body an active agent. As I see it, the soul–body dichotomy is chiefly related to the *orientation* of the individual: Heaven or earth? Things of the soul or goods of the body (*Mut*. 173)?

[146] Cf. *Timaeus* 34c, where Plato says the same with regard to the makeup of *the cosmos*; he uses the word "mistress" (here δεσπότις) about the soul as does Philo in *Cher*. 115, *Sacr*. 72, *Spec*. 1.269, *Prov*. 2.17 and *QE* 1.19. NB. All my references to *Prov*. are to the Greek portions surviving in Eusebius; I use the PLCL numbering used also in the PhI and TLG,

call the body evil but "most like the human and mortal and multiform and unintellectual and dissoluble and ever changing" (80b). Yet the thought is close, if we think of the consequences Socrates attributes to the body-loving life: it is the bodily residues (so to speak) hanging on to the unphilosophical soul that draw it back after death and make it reincarnate (81c).

Philo's references to the evil in the body can thus be seen to reflect a Phaedonic inspiration, for the double dichotomy of that dialogue stands in contrast with the *Timaeus*, *Phaedrus* and *Republic*. Philo does not usually speak in quite the same terms as Plato about the soul's bodily "contamination" that is "heavy" and has become "part of its nature" and remains so after death (81b–c). But there are a few passages curiously reminiscent of such an idea. For instance, in *Det.* the answer Joseph receives when searching for his brothers, "they have departed *from here*" (Gen 37:17), is correct, says Philo, because what is being pointed to is

> the bodily mass, showing that all who maintain a toilsome contest for the winning of virtue quit the earthly region and are resolved to mount the skies, carrying in their train no bodily deficiencies. (*Det.* 27)

Cf. also *QG* 2.61, where Philo speaks of the soul of a wicked person (apparently) in the afterlife: "the evils with which it has grown up [are] in a certain sense its members and grow together with it."[147]

Thus it can be concluded that even if we could not say that Philo held the irrational parts of the soul to be the root cause for evil within the individual, it seems that they are where evil first gains a foothold—not in the body or the mind. This raises an intriguing question: is it possible that just as the soul should seek escape from the body, the mind should try to become free from the rest of the soul?

Such an event indeed seems to be connected with the death of Moses, whereby God "resolved his twofold nature of body and soul into a monad (εἰς μονάδος ἀνεστοιχείου φύσιν), transforming his whole being into a most sun-like mind" (*Mos.* 2.288).[148] Following Philo's own terminology, I will

---

not Aucher's, despite the problems involved; see Maurizio Olivieri, "Philo's *De providentia*: A Work Between Two Traditions," in *Studies on the Ancient Armenian Version of Philo's Works*, ed. Sara Mancini Lombardi and Paola Pontani; SPhA 6 (Leiden: Brill, 2011), 87–124, pp. 94–96.

[147] See below, pp. 83–85 for a more detailed discussion of *QG* 2.61.

[148] Against this description it is hard to see how Goodenough, "Philo on Immortality," 105 could arrive at his views that "the incarnation of Moses did not imply the 'mixture' Philo sees in all other men . . . . Unlike Moses, the ordinary man finds at death his 'mixture' dissolved." Cf. *QE* 2.29 (ex. Ex 24:2), where Moses's going up means that "the prophetic mind becomes divinely inspired and filled with God" whereby "it becomes like

henceforth call "*monadization*" the salvific phenomenon whereby *the human soul's becoming pure mind through dismissal of its other constituent parts.*[149]

Could incomplete monadization have the same kind of role in Philo as the bodily contamination does in Plato? This is really a soteriological issue, which is why further discussion thereof is postponed.[150] On a more general level, however, it may be stated that active striving for ridding the mind of the influence of the lower parts of soul, especially the senses—and by extension, sense pleasures—has a fundamental role in Philo's thought.

In our present context we may approach the phenomenon of monadization from another viewpoint. For in harmony with the notion encountered above that the soul will finally return to where it came from we can examine whether the mind's incarnation is for Philo part of, or preceded by, a reverse process, "demonadization." There are, in fact, a number of passages in Philo where something like this is discussed. For instance, in *Cher.* 57–58 Philo tells us that before the mind "met" sense-perception it was devoid of it: "For there was a time when Mind neither held converse with sense-perception nor had it, but a great gulf divided it from associated interdependent things," i.e., the sense objects.[151] There is a similar account in *Leg.* 2.24, but now Philo is quick to point out that sense-perception came into being when Adam, the mind, was *asleep*. He allegorizes this to signify that the sleep of the mind (i.e., its relinquishing its dominant position) means wakefulness of the senses (a condition in which the human being is susceptible to the lure of the passions) and *vice versa* (2.25–30, 49–50; similarly, e.g., in *Her.* 257).

What then about the third part of the soul, speech? The Paradise story does not provide Philo with a *topos* to which to attach speech, and thus in

---

the monad," and "he who is resolved into the nature of unity" comes near to God; "he is changed into the divine, so that such men become kin to God and truly divine." The plural implies the description is applicable not just to Moses (let alone his death) but generally to minds that can be deemed to have progressed to the stage of being "prophetic."

[149] I do not claim that this concept captures exactly what in Philo's view happened to Moses when he died, as Philo does not discuss the parts of the soul here, and he mentions also the body.

[150] See below, subsection 2.2.2 on p. 85–90. I want to briefly note the remote similarity between the concept of monadization and the Platonist idea of *double death*: "one death in which soul is separated from body, the other in which mind is separated from soul (put to highly effective use by Plutarch in the myth of *De facie quae in orbe lunae apparet* (*Mor.* 943A ff.)," as Runia (*Philo and the Timaeus*, 331) describes it; see also Hermann S. Schibli, "Xenocrates' Daemons and the Irrational Soul," in *CQ* New Series 43, no. 1 (1993): 143–67, pp. 156–61. Runia continues, "There is no trace of this theory in Philo," and here I must disagree.

[151] It is noteworthy that Philo presents this as a rather deplorable state (§§ 59–60).

practice sense-perception gets the task of representing the whole irrational side of the soul.[152] With regard to the next logical step in demonadization, incarnation, it can only be lamented that the part of *Leg.* containing Philo's exegesis of Gen 3:21, God's making the tunics of skin for Adam and Eve, has not survived, for in *QG* 1.53 Philo explains that the tunics mean the body:[153] "It was necessary[154] that the mind and sense should be clothed in the body," and this happened "of necessity" and "straightway."[155]

In *Somn.* there is a description where the mind's encounter with the senses and its incarnation do not seem easily distinguishable. Interpreting God's words in Gen 28:15 ("I will bring you back to this land"), Philo writes:

> For excellent would it have been for the intellect to have remained in its own keeping and not have left its home for sense-perception; but, failing

---

[152] In fact, Philo says this directly: "The irrational portion of the soul is sense and the passions which are the offspring of sense" (*Leg.* 2.6; implied also in 3.111). There does not seem to exist Philonic passages concerning demonadization involving *speech* as a part of the soul.

[153] Jean Bouffartigue, "La structure de l'âme chez Philon: terminologie scolastique et métaphores," in *Philon d'Alexandrie et la langage de la philosophie. Actes du colloque international organisé par le Centre d'études sur la philosophie hellénistique et romaine de l'Université de Paris XII-Val de Marne*, ed. Carlos Lévy (Turnhout: Brepols, 1998), 59–75, has (pp. 64–65) drawn attention to Porphyry's (d. c. 305) also using the term δερμάτινος χιτών in the same sense in *De abstinentia* 1.31.13–15, 2.46.4–5 (Bouffartigue gives 1.31.3 and 2.46.1). He thinks it is not impossible that Philo's brainwave has reached Porphyry.

[154] Marcus "proper," but the Armenian is պարտ (*part*), for which NBHL gives χρέος as well as ὀφείλημα + cognates; MI δεῖ 10 and χρή 5 times. Aucher: "oportebat;" Mercier: "il fallait;" QGUM: "es war nötig." The NBHL is a more than 2200-page, 2-volume Armenian dictionary which also contains Greek and Latin equivalents drawn from the work of the so-called Hellenizing School (fl. ca. 570–730) of Armenian translators by the Armenian Mechitarist monks in Venice in the 19th century. The School's translations include, in addition to Philonic and Pseudo-Philonic treatises, works by, e.g., Irenaeus, Porphyry, Iamblichus, Aristotle and Pseudo-Aristotle, Plato, Cyril of Alexandria and Gregory of Nyssa. Among the Mechitarists, J. B. Aucher (M. Awgerean) was responsible for the first two editions (and translations to Latin) of Armenian Philo, and he had a key role in the incorporation of the work of the Hellenizing School in the NBHL (Abraham Terian, "Syntactical Peculiarities in the Translations of the Hellenizing School," *St. Nersess Theological Review* 13 [2008]: 15–24, p. 15 n. 2; repr. from *First International Conference on Armenian Linguistics: Proceedings: The University of Pennsylvania, Philadelphia, July 11–14, 1979*, ed. John A. C. Greppin [Delmar: Caravan, 1980]).

[155] The interpretation of the tunics as the body is repeated at *QG* 4.1; cf. *Cher.* 58 where the bodiless condition of the mind at the moment preceding the creation of the senses is stated ("had no contact with body"). There is a tension between *QG* 1.53 and 1.4, 8 where Philo speaks of the "moulded human" of Gen 2:7 as already "consist[ing] of soul *and body*" (1.8). However, my observations on how Philo derives both protological and universal allegories from protological texts (see especially the discussion on causes 8 and 9 of incarnation, pp.57–79) makes me think it is unnecessary to declare this a contradiction.

> that, it is well that it should return to itself again. But perhaps in these words he also hints at the doctrine of the incorruptibility of the soul; for, as we said a little before, it forsook its heavenly abode and came into the body as into a foreign land. (*Somn.* 1.180–181)

The appropriateness of the intellect's coming into contact with the senses is gravely questioned here, and the establishment of the contact is depicted in terms of movement, not of the structure of the soul. Furthermore, the process is in practice equated with embodiment. From the viewpoint of demonadization this means that the actual focus is on incarnation, as it in any case also means contact with the senses.[156]

To sum up the discussion on demonadization: what the examination shows is that Philo can present the mind's coming in contact with sense-perception and the soul's entering a body as two distinct, or at least distinguishable, things. This, for its part, reinforces the possibility that for Philo the reverse phenomena, leaving the body as well as the soul's irrational part, may also be distinct and occur separately, and that both may be necessary for achieving final salvation. This will be returned to in section 2.2.

At the outset of this subsection the question was raised, what is the location of imperfection within the individual: the mind, the lower parts of the soul or the body? We have seen that none of these is free from corruption, although it is the irrational part of the soul that is the most susceptible to evil. The ultimate problem here is, I think, this: why can even the mind be degraded? This problem is ultimate because of the mind's position as the most important part of the soul. The fatal development is the rise of passions and the desire for pleasure, which result when the mind comes in contact with the objects of sense through sense-perception. In our analyses so far we have not encountered a clear explanation from Philo as to why all this takes place, but more light will be sought to this question in the next subsection as we look at the matter from a slightly different angle and try to understand Philo's view as to why the mind incarnates in the first place.

Nevertheless, we are already in a position to say that the role of the body in the fall and rise of the mind is comparable to the physical world at large:

---

[156] It is noteworthy in this context that at times Philo also elsewhere more or less identifies the body with the senses; the interpretation of Haran in *Somn.* is generally in this vein (see, e.g., 1.41–46; similarly also, e.g., *Migr.* 187). Had Philo seen "in-sensication" and in-carnation as one and the same thing, however, he could not have written what he did in *Leg.* 2.24 and *Cher.* 58–60.

it is the *venue* for the mind's struggle.[157] And in spite of the language of double dichotomy, it is a *passive* role. So although we must, in our attempt at establishing Philo's position on reincarnation, pay special attention to the soul's relation to the body, we do well to also keep a close eye on the former's irrational part.

2.1.4 *Why Does the Mind Incarnate?*

As we have seen, in Philo's thought the body is not the soul's real home: incarnation should be a mere visit. On the other hand, it is also portrayed as a prison term.[158] These two alternatives bring out well the fact that Philo's characterizations of the mind's embodiment are not always easy to reconcile with each other. Is incarnation voluntary? For instance, the quote from *Conf.* 77–78 above implies that once enough has been seen, the souls go off back to heaven.[159] This does not match well with being a prisoner. However, we can note that in the *Conf.* passage Philo is speaking of the sages, but this observation does not entirely clarify the picture: Do some souls come here of their own will and some forced? Or do all come out of necessity but only the wise are allowed to depart at will? Do the wicked *want* to remain or are they always *confined* to do so? What does it mean not to be able to exit the body? Does not physical death bring freedom?

Philo is far from explicit about such matters, which is why the answers need to be gathered from small pieces. Given this state of affairs, we cannot—at this point—give any fixed chronology for the soul's journey. When examining the causes of incarnation we must therefore keep in mind that the original incarnation may have had some cause other than the possible subsequent ones, if the latter are, e.g., the result of a soul's becoming enticed by the enchantments of the corporeal environment. In protological terms this means that the temporal and causal relationships between the original incarnation and an original fall are an open question. The five causes enumerated by Winston to be discussed deal with the original incarnation. But they will be assessed in terms of how well they could explain *re*-incarnation, i.e., serve as driving forces of rebirth. Four further causes are identified in the discussion below and examined in like manner after which a summary of all nine is presented.

---

[157] A good example is the close identification of the expression "earthly region" (ὁ περίγειος χῶρος) and the body in *Det.* 27 (above, p. 40).
[158] See above, pp. 30–31.
[159] See p. 32.

Five Original Causes of Incarnation According to Winston

We start with David Winston's presentation of "the causes of the soul's fall" in Philo.[160] He enumerates five causes and correlates four of them with reasons given by two Middle Platonists, "Albinus" (i.e., the author of *Didaskalikos*, now generally acknowledged to be Alcinous)[161] and Calvenus Taurus (see Table I).

Table I. The Causes of the Soul's Incarnation in Three Thinkers According to Winston.

Philo	**Alcinous** (*Didaskalikos* 25.6)	**Calvenus Taurus** (Iamblichus *De anima* apud Stob. 1.49.39.44–53)[162]
1. Souls are "lovers of body" (φιλοσώματοι) (*Somn.* 1.138).	Love of body (φιλοσωματία).	
2. Souls are "unable to bear the satiety (κόρος) of divine goods" (*Her.* 240).	The soul's wantonness (ἀκολασία).	
3. Even terrestrial things should "not be without a share in wisdom to participate in better life" (*QG* 4.74).	The will of the gods.	To afford a manifestation of the divine life, for it is the will of gods to reveal themselves through the pure life of souls.
4. Some souls "enter into mortal bodies and quit them again at certain fixed periods" (*Plant.* 14) or are "selected for return according to the numbers and periods determined by nature" (*Somn.* 1.138).	Souls are "awaiting their numbers" (Winston)/ "following their turn in a numbered sequence" (Dillon) (ἀριθμοὺς μενούσας).	The completion of the universe.
5. The soul descends "in order that it might be akin to created beings and not be continuously and completely happy" (*QG* 4.74).		

---

[160] Winston, *Logos and Mystical Theology*, 34–36. That the *original* cause is meant is implied by Winston's beginning his discussion with Plato's "explanations for the soul's entry into the cycle of reincarnation."
[161] See Dillon, *Alcinous: The Handbook of Platonism* (Oxford: Clarendon, 1993), ix–xiii. In the TLG the treatise is found under Albinus. Dillon makes the same connections between Alcinous and Taurus (pp. 156–157) as Winston but does not consider Philo.
[162] The passage is given as "Stob. 1. 378. 25 ff. Wachs." in Dillon, *Alcinous*, 156.

Cause 1: Love of Body
With regard to the first cause the correlation between Philo and Alcinous is the least problematic. However, it must be asked why and how a soul would become a lover of the bodily life *before* its incarnation. This question is not discussed at all by Plato in the *Phaedo* in which the adjective φιλοσώματος originates (68b).[163] In that dialogue loving the body is the main driving force that *maintains* the cycle of reincarnation; such love is less understandable as the *original* cause of the soul's entering the corporeal life.

Dillon presents interesting comments on the immediate sequel of the mention of body-love in *Did.* 25.6 where immortal souls "pass through many bodies" and Alcinous states that "body and soul, after all, have a certain affinity (πως οἰκειότητα) for one another, like fire and asphalt."[164] Referring to a similar image of fire and naphtha in Porphyry's *Ad Gaurum* 48.26–28 Dillon writes about Alcinous's simile that

> it would imply that when a soul in the course of its peregrinations through the universe comes into a certain degree of proximity to body [i.e., an embryo], it must spring towards it and ensoul it, and this would happen without any forethought on the part of the soul in question, but simply as a natural reaction. Embodiment is thus a necessary consequence of the arrangement of the universe, and not a fault to be imputed to soul.[165]

Somewhat similarly, Porphyry refers (49.1) to the magnetic stone's ability to draw iron as another comparable phenomenon in his discussion on the ensoulment of the embryo. But are we dealing with the first, original incarnation, or with reincarnation? Embodiment as "a necessary consequence of the arrangement of the universe" (Dillon) would as such qualify as the original cause, but not as a driving force of rebirth without further assumptions, because mere necessity would entail no criteria for the release from reincarnation. Necessity may also be too far-reaching an interpretation of Alcinous's "body-love" and "affinity" which could well be understood as factors maintaining reincarnation. Alcinous explains body-love as the affinity between body and soul, which resembles that between fire and asphalt. If this last image can be interpreted in the light of Por-

---

[163] See the detailed comments on *Somn.* 1.137–139 below in subsection 3.1.2.
[164] Dillon, *Alcinous*, 157 says that οἰκειότης refers to "a sort of natural affinity ... , or weakness, for embodiment" rather than to wilfulness.
[165] Dillon, *Alcinous*, 158. In the TLG the *Ad Gaurum* is under "pseudo-Galenus" and the passage is 11.2. On the authorship, see James Wilberding, *Porphyry*: To Gaurus On How Embryos Are Ensouled *and* On What is in our Power (London: Bristol Classical Press, 2011), 7–10; there is a "virtually universal consensus" (p. 10) the author is Porphyry.

phyry's—the idea being that naphtha can catch fire even at a distance—we are approaching Philo's description in *Somn.* 1.138 that the incarnating souls are "closest to the earth and lovers of the body."[166]

If we look at the context of Philo's reference to *loving the body* in *Somn.* 1.138, we see that the body-loving souls' incarnation and physical death are followed by their return motivated now by their having become *used to mortal life*. What is the relationship between the two reasons for descent? We can note that in *Somn.* 1.139 as well as in *Ebr.* 101 the concept of mortal life is presented in parallel with the body. Similarly, the physical death of Moses at *Mos.* 2.288 is connected with leaving the mortal life, and also in an unidentified Greek fragment from *QE* (no. 15 in PAPM, 21 in PLCL) Philo makes a tight connection between "the bodily mass" and "the life of the mortals." Hence it seems that we are in fact entitled to understand the concept of mortal life more or less interchangeably with the (life in the) body.[167] It follows that Philo does not in *Somn.* 1.138–139 present *two* reasons for incarnation but *one*; loving the body and having become used to mortal life are more or less the same thing, and we can equate the two descents in *Somn.*[168] This gives added credibility to the alternative that body-love should be seen to be based on previous experience of the incarnate state.

In Philo's exegesis of Gen 3:22 (but here referring to Adam's transgression) in *QG* we get a glimpse of what kind of role the desire for mortal life (and thus also love of body) might have played in the beginning:

> Now while (the human) mind was pure and received no impression of any evil deed or word, it had secure enjoyment of that which led him to piety, which is unquestioned and true immortality. But after he began to turn to wickedness and to hurl himself down thereto, desiring mortal life, he failed to obtain immortality. (*QG* 1.55)

The end result of the disobedience by Adam, motivated by zeal for pleasure, is also called "psychic death" by Philo at *QG* 1.51.[169] This important

---

[166] The interpretation of Porphyry's simile is by Wilberding, *Porphyry*, 69.
[167] The fact that in *Contempl.* 13 the mortal life is believed (!) to be over *during* the earthly life does not prevent us from doing so; Philo does not adopt that opinion himself.
[168] The French translator of *Somn.*, Pierre Savinel, performs this identification in his Introduction. See below, n. 475 on p. 148. It is noteworthy that in *Fug.* 62 the association of mortal life and the earth as a region of the universe is very close. This is no wonder, if the body is closely associated with both the world (above, p. 44) and the mortal life.
[169] Marcus: "spiritual death," Aucher: "mors spiritualis." But the Armenian word used is a derivation of the word hnqh (*hogi*) and can, indeed should, be translated with reference to the Philonic concept of the death of the *soul*. So QGUM, "der seelische Tod." Mercier somewhat inconsistently translates "la mort spirituelle" but writes in a footnote, "ψυχικός."

concept is explained at some length at the end of the first book of *Leg.* (1.105–108), where too the consequence of the transgression is interpreted as the death of the soul. Philo gives an interesting characterization of this death, which, on the one hand, seems to represent the transgression itself ("decay of virtue"), but on the other, the punishment received as a consequence ("the penalty-death"). What connects this to the causes of incarnation is the mention in 1.106 that the soul's death means the "coming together (σύνοδος)" of body and soul. We will return to this aspect below when *incarnation as a punishment* is separately discussed as the eighth possible cause of incarnation in Philo.[170]

As for *QG* 1.55, the mind's turning to wickedness and its desire for mortal life do not receive an explanation. In 1.51 Adam's giving himself to earth is mentioned twice. Analyzing this phenomenon would take us too far from reviewing the causes presented by Winston. We will come back to it when we discuss cause no. 9, the *corporealization of the mind*.

Cause 2: Inability to Bear the Satiety of Divine Goods

Winston's view is that Philo is in *Her.* 240 speaking of incarnation, although only migration to earth is directly mentioned.[171] This is in harmony with the conclusion reached above that in Philo the physical world and the human body are comparable "locations."[172] The connection between Philo and Alcinous is weaker than with the previous cause. Alcinous's "wantonness" seems to refer to more wilful immorality, and thus be more related to the idea of punishment than to the kind of involuntary inability we find in *Her.* 240.

---

[170] See below, pp. 57–70. Causes 6 and 7 are related to Winston's nos. 3 and 5; all four stem from *QG* 4.74.

[171] The whole sentence runs in Greek,
πάσης οὖν βαρυδαιμονίας ἀναπεπλῆσθαι νομιστέον ἐκείνας, αἵτινες ἐν ἀέρι καὶ αἰθέρι τῷ καθαρωτάτῳ τραφεῖσαι μετανέστησαν, τὸν θείων ἀγαθῶν κόρον οὐ δυνηθεῖσαι φέρειν, ἐπὶ τὸ θνητῶν καὶ κακῶν χωρίον γῆν.
I would translate this as
These [souls] must be considered full of misery, who, although reared in the air and the purest ether, migrated to the place of the mortals and the wicked, the earth, having become unable to bear the excess of the divine good things.
For κόρον οὐ δυνηθεῖσαι φέρειν cf. Esth E:3 (LXX Göttingen; 8:12c Rahfls) τόν τε κόρον οὐ δυνάμενοι φέρειν ("not being able to deal with prosperity") and see Philo's use of the phrase in mundane contexts *Agr.* 48, *Abr.* 135 and *Mos.* 2.13. The two last occur after a partial quotation of a fragment of Menander (724 Kock): "the greatest cause of human ills are good things, too much of good things" (my tr. for ἀρχὴ μεγίστη τῶν ἐν ἀνθρώποις κακῶν ἀγαθά, τὰ λίαν ἀγαθά).

[172] See p. 43.

But why are some souls unable to cope with God's abundant good? Winston's translation where souls are "unable to bear" etc. (similarly Yonge) is inaccurate in its stationariness, because the verb form (οὐ δυνηθεῖσαι) in question is an aorist, and thus we should be able to take it as a reference to a punctual and completed event to the effect "ceased being able to." Colson's "the good things of God bred in them an intolerable satiety" is better in this respect but blurs the inability. Thus the second cause seems to be some kind of change of these souls as a result of which the divine realm turned out to be too good for them. As far as I know this explanation occurs only here in Philo, and the words θεῖος, ἀγαθός and κόρος make no joint appearance in the TLG corpus before him. What is nevertheless clear is that this second cause is much more plausible as the (or an) original cause of the soul's incarnation than as a force that keeps the cycle of reincarnation turning.

Cause 4: Periods and Numbers as Determinants of Incarnation

It seems appropriate to deal with Winston's third and fifth causes together, as they both come from *QG* 4.74. But we will first take a brief look at the fourth cause, numbers and periods.[173] Winston's statement that the "emphasis on numbers and periods implies that the incarnation of souls is part of the mathematical structure of the universe" is easy enough to agree with. But as was the case with the first cause, this one too would be more natural as a factor affecting ongoing reincarnation; this time, however, rather by *regulating* the technicalities, notably the durations of lives and the periods between them, than as actually causing re-embodiment. It can also be noted that in both Philonic passages (*Plant.* 14 and *Somn.* 1.138) the (numbers and) periods are related to the *discarnation*, not incarnation, of souls.[174] Alcinous's "awaiting numbers" probably refers to something similar but is too brief for us to ascertain.[175] Taurus's "completion of the universe" is not related to periods of time but most probably has another referent, *Timaeus* 41b. [176]

---

[173] The passages from *Plant.* and *Somn.* which Winston refers to will be analyzed in more detail in subsection 3.1.2 below.

[174] Winston uses Whitaker's translation for *Somn.* 1.138 ("selected for return according to the numbers and periods determined by nature"); a more appropriate translation would be, "having again been separated (from the body) according" etc. See 3.1.2.

[175] Dillon's "following their turn in a numbered sequence" or even "waiting for their number to come up"—(*The Middle Platonists*, 34, 156) go some way from being a translation towards being an explanation—somewhat too specific at that, given the paucity of information available.

[176] "For three mortal kinds still remain ungenerated; but if these come not into being, the Heaven will be imperfect."

Cause 3: Terrestrial Things' Sharing in Wisdom and Cause 5: The Souls' Being Akin to Created Beings

If we look at the exegesis of Gen 23:4 in *QG* more broadly and not just the part quoted by Winston, we find that more than two causes are readily identifiable (6–7 below):

> Why does (Abraham) say, "I am a stranger and sojourner among you?" But does not every wise soul live like an immigrant and sojourner in this mortal body, having (as its real) dwelling-place and country the most pure substance of heaven, from which (our) nature migrated to this (place) by (6) a law of necessity? Perhaps this was in order that it might (7) carefully inspect terrestrial things, (3) that even these might not be without a share in wisdom to participate in a better life, or in order (5) that it might be akin to created beings and not be continuously and completely happy. (*QG* 4.74)

We will first examine (3) and (5) together and then (6) and (7) separately. As for the *third cause*, what is the wisdom necessary for participation in a better life? What is meant with a better life? How do terrestrial things have a share in wisdom that helps them attain such life?[177] Despite the obscurity of the text, any similarity to Alcinous's blunt "the will of the gods" can be only found via Taurus's "will of gods to reveal themselves through the pure life of souls." Yet the points of contact remain few; only the notion of something heavenly or divine finding an expression on earth can be seen in both Philo and Taurus.

Some more light is thrown on the passage if we can take *Det.* 86 as speaking of the same thing. There it is said that God "stamped on the invisible soul the impress of Itself, to the end that not even the terrestrial region (ὁ περίγειος χῶρος) should be without a share in the image of God." The parallelism is reduced by the absence in *QG* 4.74 of any direct reference to the creation of the human being, but in any case the *QG* passage is quite protological.[178] Furthermore, the passages have in common the

---

[177] Méasson, *Du char ailé de Zeus*, 354–55 sees in the background of *QG* 4.74 both the *Phaedrus* and the *Timaeus* but notes that the idea of the wise soul's incarnating in order to foster wisdom in earthly things is alien to the latter dialogue. Instead, Méasson links this idea to the "rayonnement du sage, source d'élévation morale et de bonheur pour ce qui l'entoure," which she sees as a frequent theme in Philo. She refers to *Somn.* 1.176–178, where, however, none of those benefitting from the uplifting influence of a worthy person correspond to earthly things in general.

[178] Cf. *Opif.* 135 (ex. Gen 2:7): "What he breathed in was nothing else than the divine spirit which has emigrated here from that blessed and flourishing nature for the assistance of our kind." The theme of assistance appears also in *Leg.* 1.34, *Gig.* 27 and *Her.* 58–61, all of which discuss the "spirit" of either Gen 2:7 or Ex 31:3, *Her.* also Gen 1:27, which is not far in *Leg.*, either. See the discussion on the relationship between the pre-

reference to the divine expansion even to the earthliest recesses of the cosmos. In *QG*, this takes place through the "wise soul's" migration into the midst of terrestrial things. As its home is "the most pure substance of heaven," the migration may not have been entirely voluntary, but this is not explicitly stated. However, this viewpoint is more clearly included in the expression "law of necessity," to be discussed as cause (6), to which the "will of the gods" mentioned in the parallels Winston proposes is in fact closer. Overall, cause (3) can be classified as a possible *original* cause of incarnation, but by itself it would be arbitrary as a driving force of reincarnation: there would be no obvious criteria for salvation.

What can be said of *fifth cause* is that it seems teleological, but the *telos* envisaged, lack of continuous and complete happiness of the soul, is awkward. The mention of "be[ing] akin to created things" may give us a clue, however. It surely refers to corporeal things, and we are thus dealing with some kind of degradation, as also the lack of complete happiness implies. *Fug.* 59 (ex. Lev 10:2) gives indirect support by describing a reverse process: Nadab and Abihu are said to "receive an incorruptible life in exchange for mortal existence, and be translated from the created to the uncreate." It is thus probably not wide of the mark to identify the becoming like created things of *QG* 4.74 with entering the mortal life.

One possible aspect of this entry may be the mind or soul's becoming *earthly* in some way, which is not very far from becoming akin to created things. In *QG* 1.51 and *Leg.* 3.252 Philo comments on Gen 3:19, God's words to Adam about returning to earth: "because he did not remain uncorrupted ... , he gave himself wholly over to the earth" (*QG*); "is he not now ranked with things earthlike and chaotic?" (*Leg.*).[179] But since the *corporealization of mind* along these lines is quite a specific notion that does not exactly match what Philo is saying in *QG* 4.74, I will deal with it separately as cause no. 9. But it may already be noted that *if* causes (5) and (9) can be taken together to refer to something like an originally uncorrupted and wise soul which, after entering the earthly sphere, identified itself with it and the body and was trapped in these, cause 5 would qualify both as the original and a recurrent cause of incarnation. Furthermore, looking at the matter from the viewpoint of the teleology in *QG* 4.74, it seems that

---

existence of the soul and Philo's interpretations of the biblical accounts of the creation of the human being, above, p. 33–36. It is worth noting that in *Leg.* 1 the "breath of life" and Paradise are both intimately linked with virtue and *wisdom* referred to in *QG* 4.74 (see *Leg.* 1.31–62 and my "Call Him Earth").

[179] Cf. *QG* 2.61: "the souls of those who act impiously imitate the mortal body in being corrupted."

according to Philo such a "fall" was *meant* to take place.[180] Was the mind thus destined to find out that lasting happiness cannot be found in the corporeal and earthly things? This would constitute a tolerable logic for the teleological unhappiness, one that could be added to the scheme drafted above. Such finding out is in fact close to cause 7, as we shall see.

Other Possible Causes of Incarnation

Cause 6: Law of Necessity

This cause comes closer to the "will of gods" of Alcinous and Taurus than cause no. 3. As an *explanation* both the will of gods and law of necessity are quite devoid of content. The idea of inevitability, while far from proving that Philo is operating within a reincarnational framework, is a noteworthy feature shared by proponents of the doctrine.[181] See, e.g., the proem by Empedocles quoted below, which features both necessity and gods; *Timaeus* 41e–42a where one of the "laws of destiny (νόμους τοὺς εἱμαρμένους)" is that souls are originally "by virtue of Necessity (ἐξ ἀνάγκης) ... implanted in bodies" and Diog. Laert. 8.14 which says Pythagoras was the first "to declare that the soul, bound now in this creature, now in that, thus goes on a round ordained of necessity (κύκλον ἀνάγκης)."[182] In particular, however, the "law of necessity" brings to mind Socrates's allegory of the soul in the *Phaedrus*: in 248c the falling to the earth of souls is stipulated by θεσμός Ἀδραστείας, for which "law of necessity" would not be a mistranslation.[183]

---

[180] Runia (*On the Creation*, 369) thinks that for Philo "this development was inevitable, it seems" at least in *Opif*. Similarly p. 363. Philo says in *Opif*. 151, "But, since nothing is stable in the world of becoming and mortal things necessarily undergo reverses and changes, the first human being too had to enjoy some ill fortune."

[181] Cf. J. B. Aucher's footnote to precisely this notion in QG 4.74 in *Philonis Judaei Paralipomena Armena* (1826; repr. Hildesheim: Weidmann, 2004), 303:

> Beware that you do not believe the error, established in Philo, of the Platonists and Origenists about the soul [having been] expelled from heaven into the fortified prison of the flesh, the symbolic expression of which covers many circumlocutions, in particular Adam's deplorable fall from the happy position of the earthly paradise.

(My tr. for "Cave, ne Platonicorum, vel Origenistarum errorem de anima caelitus depulsa in carcerem carnis in Philonem stabilitum credas, cujus symbolica dictio multos in se anfractus continet, maxime deplorabilem casum Adam de felici statu paradisi terrestris." I thank Outi Kaltio for help with the translation.)

[182] For Empedocles, see p. 137.

[183] Fowler renders, "a law of Destiny." Cf. Aeschylus, *Prometheus vinctus* 936, where Smyth translates οἱ προσκυνοῦντες τὴν Ἀδράστειαν σοφοί as "Wise are they who do homage to Necessity."

Philo refers directly to the necessary nature of the mind's (or soul's) union with the body also elsewhere. We have already noted this in *QG* 1.53.[184] In *QG* 4.29 the starting point is Gen 18:33, Abraham's returning to his place after God had spoken to him. Philo explains that this means that the God-possession of "one who is begotten and brought into being" is bound to be limited in duration and followed by the return to oneself. What he then says is quite interesting from the viewpoint of the necessity of incarnation. I cite it from Mercier's French which makes more sense than Marcus's English:[185]

> [C]ar à l'âme qui est dans le corps, il est impossible de persévérer avec constance sans qu'il arrive aux pieds de chanceler, mais il est obligé que l'intellect le plus pur et le plus lumineux se mêle parfois à ce qui est mortel en raison des nécessités. C'est ce que (l'Ecriture) a dit en parabole par l'échelle céleste; elle a dit que non seulement les anges montaient, mais aussi qu'ils descendaient. (*QG* 4.29)

In spite of the differences between the translations, the main purport seems clear: there was no choice, the mind *had to* experience a union with "the mortal (element)." This element is probably the body mentioned in the preceding sentence, but as we saw above, Philo calls also the irrational parts of the soul mortal.[186] He may be referring to both.

The unavoidable nature of embodiment is more suitable as the original cause of incarnation than as a driving force of rebirth for the same reason as with some of the earlier causes: no criteria for exiting the cycle can be derived from it.

Cause 7: The Careful Inspection of Terrestrial Things
To recall, our text for cause no. 7 in *QG* 4.74 runs as follows: "Perhaps [the migration to this (place)] was in order that [the soul] might carefully inspect terrestrial things." The observation of both worlds (sense-perceptible and noetic), often in the form of an ascent from lower to more exalted things, is a notion which the reader of Philo meets in many places and also

---

[184] See p. 42.
[185] Marcus's translation runs,
> For it is impossible for the soul to remain permanently in the body when nothing slippery or no obstacle strikes its feet. But it is necessary that the most pure and luminous mind should be mixed with the mortal (element) for necessary uses. This is what is indicated by the heavenly ladder, (where) not only an ascent but also a descent of the angels is mentioned.

[186] See p. 36.

in several variations.¹⁸⁷ However, its link with the original cause of the soul's incarnation is nowhere as clear as in *QG* 4.74.

The key word in the Armenian text is այցելութիւն (*ayc'elut'iwn*), for which NBHL gives ἐπισκοπή and ἐπίσκεψις. Nowhere in his extant writings does Philo seem to be saying exactly the same about terrestrial things, but the following description of the mind's progress is comparable (although broader):

> Next it enters upon the consideration (ἐπίσκεψιν) of itself, makes a study of the features of its own abode, the things of the body, sense-perception and speech and comes to know, as the phrase of the poet puts it, "All that existeth of good and ill in the halls of thy homestead." (*Migr.* 195, quoting Hom. *Od.* 4.392)

The gradual progress will lift the mind from everything sense-perceptible all the way to "the contemplation (ἐπίσκεψιν) of Him that is" (*ibid.*). The early stages of that development are described in *Somn.* 1.55–56, where, as in *Migr.*, Abraham's moving from Chaldea to Haran (the land of the senses in Philo) is discussed: "hold an inspection (ἐπίσκεψαι) of eyes, ears, nostrils, and the other organs of sense ... . Before you have made a thorough investigation (καλῶς ἐπεσκέφθαι) into your own abode, is it not an excess of madness to examine that of the universe?" Thus it is warranted to take Philo's reference in *QG* 4.74 to getting to know the physical world as also implying the advancement thereafter to the noetic cosmos.

The main biblical lemma of *QG* 4.74, Gen 23:4 ("I am a sojourner and stranger among you") is used as a secondary lemma in Philo's long exegesis of Gen 11:2, the settling in Shinar of the builders of the tower of Babel, at *Conf.* 60–82.¹⁸⁸ This comes at §79, but let us first look at the context of §§ 77–82. For Philo the settling (verb κατοικέω) symbolizes the fools' *permanent* stay in sin. This is contrasted with the mere sojourning (παροικέω) of "all whom Moses calls wise" who do not intend to colonize the earth after leaving heaven. Instead,

> they are used to leaving home for the terrestrial nature on account of their love of seeing and learning. So when they have stayed awhile in bodies, and beheld through them all the sense-perceptible and mortal things, they again return to where they first started from, regarding the heavenly place

---

¹⁸⁷ For different kinds of accounts of this sort, often involving the aspect of self-knowledge and often also connected to the ascent of the soul, see, e.g., *Opif.* 69–71, *Leg.* 3.97–100; *Conf.* 77–78; *Migr.* 13, 88, 184–195, 216–220; *Fug.* 46–47; *Somn.* 1.52–60; *Abr.* 57–58, 68–88; *Spec.* 1.36–38, 44, 2.44–45, 52, 3.1–2; *Praem.* 26, 41–43; *Contempl.* 10–12; *QG* 1.6, 4.21.

¹⁸⁸ We already had a brief look at §§ 77–78 on p. 32.

as their fatherland, in which they live as free citizens, and the terrestrial one, in which they had sojourned, as a foreign country. (*Conf.* 77–78)[189]

From the viewpoint of the central problem of this study, the expression "used to leaving home for the terrestrial nature" is highly interesting. A reference to repeated incarnations cannot be ruled out.[190] This is, however, neither logically necessary nor provable on philological grounds.[191] But with regard to cause no. 7 of incarnation, we can say that the explanation in *Conf.* 77–78 is broadly in accord with that in *QG* 4.74: heaven is in both the soul's real country from which it comes down in order to see the earthly things. In *QG* Philo connects this study trip to the *necessity* of the descent, while in *Conf.* the actual reason for incarnation is "love of seeing and learning (ἕνεκα τοῦ φιλοθεάμονος καὶ φιλομαθοῦς)." The *Conf.* passage may not be generally applicable, as it discusses sages, but hints in the direction of involuntariness may be seen in the sequel: "Jacob ... laments his stay in the body (§80)" and Moses "alienate[s] himself from it" (§82). These quotes are from the section where Philo adduces secondary biblical lemmas about Abraham (Gen 23:4), Jacob (Gen 47:9), Isaac (Gen 26:2–3) and Moses (Ex 2:22) in support for his thesis of the sages' negative attitude towards prolonged incarnation. As the first one is connected to *QG* 4.74 through the lemma, we shall look at it, together with its prelude, more closely:

> To the traveller abroad the land which sent him forth is still the mother to whom also he yearns to return. Therefore, reasonably will Abraham say to the guardians of the dead and stewards of the mortals when rising from the

---

[189] Mostly my translation for εἰώθασι δὲ ἕνεκα τοῦ φιλοθεάμονος καὶ φιλομαθοῦς εἰς τὴν περίγειον φύσιν ἀποδημεῖν. ἐπειδὰν οὖν ἐνδιατρίψασαι σώμασι τὰ αἰσθητὰ καὶ θνητὰ δι' αὐτῶν πάντα κατίδωσιν, ἐπανέρχονται ἐκεῖσε πάλιν, ὅθεν ὡρμήθησαν τὸ πρῶτον, πατρίδα μὲν τὸν οὐράνιον χῶρον ἐν ᾧ πολιτεύονται, ξένην δὲ τὸν περίγειον ἐν ᾧ παρῴκησαν νομίζουσαι.

[190] According to Jean-Georges Kahn (PAPM 13, 161) Philo in *Conf.* 75–83 seeks to secure "sur les bases bibliques la philosophie platonicienne et pythagoricienne de l'âme." The grounds he gives for this somewhat sweeping statement are fairly meagre the main point being the notion of the soul's migration from its heavenly homeland to the earth and back. He refers to the *Phaedrus* and, surprisingly, also to the *Phaedo* (but not to the *Timaeus* which in my view is closer). Kahn also says the word παροίκησις means "la migration des âmes" in Plotinus—in whose case it means *trans*migration, but he does not explicitly mention the doctrine or comment Philo's relation to it.

[191] The verb ἔθω, 'to be accustomed,' does indeed refer to something recurrent, but we have an example in *Hypoth.* 11.13 that although the event is repeated, it is each time experienced by a different individual: "The old men too ... regularly close their life (τὸν βίον εἰώθασι καταλύειν) with an exceedingly prosperous and comfortable old age." The possible non-Philonic authorship of this work—suggested most recently by John Barclay, *Flavius Josephus: Translation and Commentary, Vol. 10: Against Apion* (Leiden: Brill, 2007), 353–55—is not relevant in this context.

dead life and vanity, "I am a sojourner and stranger among you." (*Conf.* 78–79)

The biblical passages involved are clearly not the sources for Philo's idea of the sages' eagerness to learn about and see the things on earth. We will have to look for it elsewhere. An apposite passage where, despite its belonging to a different Philonic genre, the ideas of *Conf.* 77 are partially paralleled and elaborated is the following:

> For to make a study (σκοπεῖν) of God and the Universe embracing all that is therein—both animals and plants, and of the noetic archetypes and also of the sense-perceptible objects based on them, and of the good and evil qualities in every created thing—shews a disposition which loves to learn (φιλομαθῆ) and see (φιλοθεάμονα) and is really philosophical. (*Spec.* 3.191)

What is the context and how do God and the intelligibles come into the picture? The immediate starting point is the law in Ex 21:26 about the consequence of knocking out the eye of a servant, from which Philo is lead to extolling sight as the best sense, conducive as it is to philosophy. This notion can inform our examination of cause 7.[192] It has obvious implications for the possible salvific effects of the visionary ascent—the first step of which is the inspection of the terrestrial things. But was, as we already asked, the mind destined to find out that happiness cannot be found in corporeal things?[193] Philo does not say this in so many words, but this would certainly fit our observations. The thought is not far in *Somn*:

> When they have thoroughly learned in all its details the whole study of sense-perceptions, [those in quest for prudence] claim it as their prerogative to advance to some other greater object of contemplation, leaving behind them those lurking places of sense-perception. (*Somn.* 1.59).

Ultimately, these Abraham souls "attain to an exact knowledge of Him Who in reality is" (1.60).[194]

---

[192] The connection of sight and philosophy is based on *Timaeus* 47a–c and recurrent in Philo. Colson at *Spec.* 3.185 refers to *Opif.* 54, *Abr.* 164 and *Spec.* 1.339; Runia, *On the Creation*, 201 to *Opif.* 69–71, 77–78; *Congr.* 21; *Abr.* 57–58, 156–164; *Spec.* 3.184–192 and *QG* 2.34.

[193] Above, p. 52.

[194] As this passage well exemplifies, it is clear that despite using expressions related to sight (as here: θεώρημα), touch (*Ebr.* 152) and taste (*QG* 4.234) Philo does not in his descriptions of mystical contemplation mean that physical sense-perception is involved. Scott D. Mackie, "The Passion of Eve and the Ecstasy of Hannah: Sense Perception, Passion, Mysticism, and Misogyny in Philo of Alexandria, *De ebrietate* 143–52," *JBL* 133, no. 1 (2014): 141–63, pp. 145–6 refers to "feminine, sensual tactility [which] probably also extends to [Hannah's] visual apprehension of God" and to "her sensual body cooperat-[ing] perfectly with her masculine mind as she attains the *visio Dei*." I find nothing in the

It is interesting to note that of the causes discussed so far, the inspection of terrestrial things—including the advance to "greater objects of contemplation"—is the first which would qualify both as the original cause (or purpose) of the mind's incarnation and as a driving force of reincarnation.[195] For such a task seems to be one that could be continued through many incarnations. Reaching the highest levels, noetic things and God, would be a plausible prerequisite of salvation.

Cause 8: Incarnation as a Punishment: Death of the Soul
Above we saw that in *Leg.* 1.107 Philo speaks of *punishment* in the same context as the soul's incarnation.[196] To recall, he is characterizing the death of the soul in the context of the biblical warning about the punishment from eating the forbidden fruit (Gen 2:17). Importantly, Philo says that this death *is* the union (σύνοδος) of soul and body (1.106).[197] He then uses as its synonym the concept of "penalty-death (θάνατος ὁ ἐπὶ τιμωρίᾳ)" (twice in 1.107). The protological context of the biblical passage in question (Gen 2:17) might make us think that we are dealing with the *original*

Ebr. section (or elsewhere in Philo) to support these claims. The cost of interpreting the bodily changes of the mystic depicted in *Ebr.* 147 not as side effects but as "cooperation"— i.e., ignoring that the text gives no grounds for such an interpretation and assuming that Philo in one place reverses his all-pervasive ethos of the incompatibility of everything corporeal with the mind's noetic aspirations—is far too high. Philo is not depicting a female mystic; "Hannah" is the *explanandum*, "soul filled with grace" (§§ 146, 149) is the *explanatio*.

[195] In *QG* 4.74 this cause is hierarchically under cause no. 6, the law of necessity. Thus we might weave them together along the lines, "it is the law of necessity that each soul go through the process of learning to know the various spheres of reality, advancing from the lowest, earthly ones to the highest, divine ones."

[196] See p. 48.

[197] Whitaker translates Philo's σύνοδος ἀμφοῖν, "a meeting of the two in conflict," taking σύνοδος in its sense 'meeting of two armies' (used by Philo at *Migr.* 63). The verb κρατέω too can be used about being victorious in a conflict. While Philo may be alluding to a military confrontation, I suggest that his point is not merely to say that the relationship between soul and body is antagonistic. Zeller, "Life and Death," 23 (n. 13) says Whitaker with his battle imagery overlooks the fact that σύνοδος was "[a] technical term for the union of soul and body in Platonic tradition" and gives two examples: Alcinous, *Didaskalikos* 25.2: "as death is the separation (διάκρισις) of the soul from the body, so life is the union (σύνοδος) of soul—which obviously had a previous existence—with body;" and Plotinus 1.7.3: "if life is the union of soul and body and death their dissolution, the soul will be able to undergo both" (my tr. for εἰ σύνοδος μὲν ψυχῆς καὶ σώματος ζωή, θάνατος δὲ διάλυσις τούτων, ἡ ψυχὴ ἔσται ἀμφοτέρων δεκτική). Both authors define σύνοδος as *life*, just as it is for Philo "[life] of wickedness" (1.107), and both Alcinous and Philo contrast σύνοδος with διάκρισις. A further commonality is that at the end of 25.1 Alcinous states that "it is soul's nature to rule." Philo would agree, although he is depicting the opposite case. He is clearly swimming in a river of Platonic and Platonist tradition here.

reason for the soul's embodiment. This, however, is clearly not the case. For after the biblical citation Philo immediately notes the contradiction that despite the threat of "dying by death" the first couple not only does *not* die but even procreates. He distances himself from the biblical narrative by moving to the universal level (1.105): "What, then, is to be said to this? That death is (ἐστί) of two kinds, one that of the human in general, the other that of the soul in particular." It is important to acknowledge that this present-tense declaration is in no way dependent on the acute events unfolding in the orchard. Thus the context in which Philo wants to place his audience is one where both deaths occur. Therefore the penalty-death too—"decay of virtue" (1.105)—is something that happens to a soul which is *already incarnate*. It follows that the allegory in 1.105–108 is to be taken as universal.[198]

The section does *not* tell us how Philo envisaged the original fall to have taken place. Its sole link to the protological account in Genesis is the exegetical inspiration Philo derives from the expression "die by death." But the picture is not quite clear yet. How can an incarnate soul be joined to a body, when it dies the death of the soul? That virtue decays and vice prevails are easy to comprehend and even becoming entombed in the body (1.108) can be understood as qualitative change taking place in the mode of embodiment: it *becomes* an entombment and also (1.107) a penalty—as if the gates of the corporeal realm were locked behind the soul's back and the sojourning became a settling. But by defining the death of the soul as the union of soul and body, Philo also defines it, as it were, as physical birth. These concepts operate on different levels: whether

---

[198] If Philo's interpretation of "dying the death" in *Leg.* 1.105–108 were taken as protological, we would have to conclude that in Philo's view Adam and Eve might have died either physically or psychically. It would follow that, unlike in *QG* (1.53, 4.1), in *Leg.* Philo did *not* interpret the making of the tunics of skin in Gen 3:21 in terms of incarnation but instead held that embodiment had already taken place by the time the punishments for the transgression were meted out (3:19). While this is possible in principle, then the question is raised whether we should be able to find in *Leg.* also a protological interpretation of some verse which Philo considered to symbolize the soul's incarnation. The most natural candidate, Gen 2:7 is out of the question. As already noted (see above, p. 35), Philo's allegorization of that verse in *Leg.* 1.31–42 is essentially universal; he also explicitly says (1.32) that the mind has not yet entered the body. The only other verse that I can think of for such an interpretation is Gen 3:7 where Adam and Eve "made loinclothes for themselves" after their sin. Gen 3:1b–8a was covered in the now lost original second book of *Leg.*, but we do possess Philo's quotation of and a brief comment on 3:7 in *Leg.* 3.55. There we find no reference to incarnation, but it has to be noted that Gen 3:7 is now a *secondary* biblical lemma; Philo's interpretation of it as a primary lemma may have been something else—as is exemplified by the completely divergent allegorizations of Gen 2:7 at *Leg.* 1.31–42 and 3.161.

the *soul* is living or dead is an existential or ethical matter, and thus strange to be linked with the union, a physical event—all the more so since Philo has just denied its connection with the ordinary death.

There is a word in 1.106 that may help us out of this dilemma: Before calling the soul-death σύνοδος Philo says that it is "*almost* (σχεδόν)[199] the antithesis of the death which awaits us all." Assuming this is not superfluous, we gain some additional freedom of interpretation: the undoubtedly close link between the soul's death and the coming together of body and soul is something else than a strict equation. What I suggest is that the death of the soul means moral corruption that has incarnation as its *result*. Given the previous conclusion that an already embodied soul is being spoken of, *re*-incarnation is implied. Whether or not this interpretation can be deemed feasible will be assessed at later points in this study.[200]

There is a very interesting parallel to the mention of penalty-death of *Leg.* 1.107 among the spurious fragments of the fifth-century BCE Pythagorean philosopher Philolaus: "The ancient theologians and seers also give witness that on account of certain penalties the soul is yoked to the body and is buried in it as in a tomb."[201] Huffman gives as parallels Plato, *Gorgias* 493a and *Cratylus* 400c; Athenaeus *Deipnosophistae* 4.157c (4, 45 Kaibel) and Aristotle fr. 60 = Iamblichus *Protrepticus* 8 (47.21 ff. Pistelli)—but not *Leg.*, although Philo has the precise combination lacking in the other parallels of the soul's being both punished and entombed ("in passions and wickedness of all kinds," 1.106; "in the body as in a sepulchre," 1.108). Except for the *Gorgias*, the idea of the earthly life as a punishment is present in all.[202]

---

[199] Whitaker: "practically."

[200] The next occasion for this arises when we come to the actual biblical punishment foreseen in *Leg.* 1.105–108 at the end of the third book of *Leg.*, discussed in connection with our ninth potential cause of incarnation.

[201] Fr. 14 DK, from Clement of Alexandria, *Strom.* 3.17.1, tr. Huffman for μαρτυρέονται δὲ καὶ οἱ παλαιοὶ θεολόγοι τε καὶ μάντιες, ὡς διά τινας τιμωρίας ἁ ψυχὰ τῶι σώματι συνέζευκται καὶ καθάπερ ἐν σάματι τούτωι τέθαπται. Regardless of the fragment's inauthenticity (for which see Carl A. Huffman, *Philolaus of Croton: Pythagorean and Presocratic* [Cambridge: Cambridge University Press, 1993], 404–6) Philo may have been acquainted with the text. We know that he was familiar with texts attributed to Philolaus, since he mentions him by name in *Opif.* 100—although there too the genuineness of the views attributed to Philolaus is questionable; see Runia, *On the Creation*, 273, 275, 298–300. Earp PLCL 10.469 mentions three references to parallels in Philolaus: at *Cher.* 26, *Somn.* 1.30 and *Spec.* 4.188. The last one is an interesting parallel to *Leg.* 1.105 ff (see below, p. 141), and Earp's reference is to the fragment above.

[202] According to Fritz Graf, "Text and Ritual: The Corpus Eschatologicum of the Orphics," in *The "Orphic" Gold Tablets and Greek Religion: Further Along the Path*, ed. Radcliffe G. Edmonds III (Cambridge: Cambridge University Press, 2010), 53–67, p. 58, the notion that "our life is [a punishment of the soul] would presuppose reincarnation." In *Gorgias*

Similarly to the pseudo-Philolaus fragment, Aristotle says it is "an inspired saying of the ancients." Athenaeus's account, citing Clearchus the Peripatetic, names a Pythagorean called Euxitheus as the source of this idea, whereas in *Crat.* Plato attributes it to the Orphics—unlike the notion of being buried whose proponents are not named:

> some say [the body] is the tomb (σῆμα) of the soul, their notion being that the soul is buried in the present life.... But I think it most likely that the Orphic poets gave this name (sc. σῶμα), with the idea that the soul is undergoing punishment for something; they think it has the body as an enclosure to keep it safe, like a prison, and this is, as the name itself denotes, the safe (i.e., σῶμα < σώζω) for the soul, until the penalty is paid, and not even a letter needs to be changed. (*Crat.* 400b–c)

In the *Gorgias* Socrates says (in a context suggesting a reference to Pythagorean doctrines),

> In fact I once heard one of our sages say that we are now dead, and the body is our tomb, and the part of the soul in which we have desires is liable to be over-persuaded and to vacillate to and fro. (*Gorg.* 493a)[203]

The ideas of punishment and entombment are thus not new, and we get an idea of the circles where they were current. However, parallels do not enable us to decide the important question of how plausible it would be to assume that whenever Philo speaks of the soul's death, he is at the same time also speaking of a punitive incarnation.

Nowhere else is Philo equally explicit on the embodiment being a penalty as in *Leg.* 1.106–107, but the idea is implied in many passages elsewhere. The next place where Philo explains the death of the soul is *Leg.* 2.77–78 (ex. Num 21:5–6). The death is caused by the pining by "our" soul's lower part "for the dwellings in Egypt, that is, in the corporeal mass" and by "immoderate indulgence in pleasures." It will last as long as the soul "fails to repent and acknowledge its change/turning." In purely logical terms, this condition disconnects the termination of the death of the soul from the physical one. The latter seems not relevant; repentance is needed, and this also implies there has been some "crime" to repent and also that the soul's death is a penalty for it. But, also logically, there is nothing here to indicate that remorse must come while the soul is still embodied. But what would make the soul repent in the afterlife? I am not aware of

---

493a, only the comparison of the body to a tomb is made. For this notion, see below, p. 119.

[203] Graf (*ibid.*) states that "reincarnation thus seems present" here because of "the σῶμα σῆμα doctrine."

any substantial evidence to suggest that Philo believed in some form of purgatory.[204] Thus the death of the soul is probably restricted to the state of being incarnate only and thus possibly to being in the cycle of reincarnation, if that is what Philo believed in, and since its cessation is dependent on repentance, then obviously there will need to be more than one incarnation in many cases.

This could be what is meant by the sequel, for in *Leg.* 2.80 Philo, continuing the use of first person plural, says our souls are "unable to strip off our bodies." This comes close to seeing incarnation as a penalty. A similar idea with a clearer reference to punishment appears also in the third book of *Leg.*:

> for it is not possible for the one whose abode is in the body and the mortal race to attain to being with God; this is possible only for him whom God rescues out of the prison. (*Leg.* 3.42)

It would be strained to think that in these passages Philo is speaking of something essentially different, although they are not identical in idea. In *Leg.* 3.42 Philo chooses to emphasize God's gracious role, where as in *Leg.* 2.82 Philo says a soul can mend its state of death by looking "with clear vision on self-mastery and God." Merely becoming "enamoured of endurance and self-mastery" will not do, for many such souls (2.83) "do experience the might of God and receive the turning to the lower way."[205]

We examine two more passages from *Leg.* They are linked by vocabulary to Philo's explanation of the death of the soul at the end of *Leg.* 1. After praising a saying of Heraclitus, "We live their death and have died to their life,"[206] Philo writes,

---

[204] We might imagine some sort of education being given to departed souls with the purpose of making them see their error. But this would be pure speculation which, in my view, could not be supported by anything Philo has written. Reincarnation would require fewer assumptions.

[205] This is a good example of how our view on Philo's position on reincarnation affects our reading his texts. If we *knew* he endorsed the idea, it would be most natural to take the last phrase as a reference to it. If we are certain he did no such thing, the phrase appears somewhat more vague, a reference to pride going before a fall. The notion that some of those who seek high things are swept down again because of their arrogance or other ineptitude is mentioned by Philo in several passages (e.g., *Agr.* 169, *Migr.* 171, *Somn.* 1.44, *QE* 2.40).

[206] Ζῶμεν τὸν ἐκείνων θάνατον, τεθνήκαμεν δὲ τὸν ἐκείνων βίον is Philo's formulation. Cf. Heraclitus fr. 62 DK: ἀθάνατοι θνητοί, θνητοὶ ἀθάνατοι, ζῶντες τὸν ἐκείνων θάνατον, τὸν δὲ ἐκείνων βίον τεθνεῶτες. According to Mansfeld, "Middle Platonist Cento," 145 this is not about souls but the four elements being transformed into each other. He bases this on fr. 36 DK (66 Marc.) and arrives (p. 146) at the conclusion that Philo in *Aet.* 111 presents a "Platonist" interpretation of both fragments which is "linked up with the cycle of

now, when we are living, the soul is dead and has been entombed in the body as in a sepulchre; whereas, should we die, the soul lives forthwith its own proper life, and is released from the body, the baneful corpse to which it was tied.[207] (*Leg.* 1.108)

Here the punitive aspect is implied by the happy release, but 1.108 intimately belongs to the train of thought about the penalty-death of the soul begun at 1.105.

In 3.71–72 the imagery is different: a soaring mind, on the one hand, and one still under the spell of mortal things, on the other, are compared, respectively, to a philosopher and a body-loving athlete. The former will take care not to be "hurt by an evil thing, a very corpse, tied to it." This last phrase warrants seeing an intentional connection between *Leg.* 1.105–108 and 3.69–74. The context of the text in *Leg.* 3 is Er's being put to death by God for his wickedness (Gen 38:7). His name means 'leathern,' and "the body, our leathern bulk ... is wicked and a plotter against the soul, and is even a corpse and a dead thing" (3.69).[208] Furthermore, "it is not only now that God slays Er, nay, but the body was a corpse to begin with" (3.70). That the soul's life with this carcass is nothing but a punishment is not spelled out but implied by the latter's being so heavily denounced by God and, importantly, by Philo's use of one of the verbs of his own coinage, νεκροφορέω: "we are each of us nothing but corpse-bearers" (3.69); "[w]hen then, O soul, wilt thou in fullest measure realize thyself to be a corpse-

---

reincarnation and transmigration."—The majority of scholars consider *Aet.* a genuine Philonic treatise; see, e.g., James Royse ("The Works of Philo", 56) who refers to David T. Runia, "Philo's *De aeternitate mundi*: The Problem of Its Interpretation," in *VC* 35 (1981): 105–51). Philo's authorship is denied by Samuel Sandmel (*Philo of Alexandria: An Introduction* [New York: Oxford University Press, 1979], 76) and Roald Skarsten ('Forfatterproblemet ved *De Aeternitate Mundi* i Corpus Philonicum' [Ph.D. diss., University of Bergen, 1987]). Runia's comment on Skarsten's thesis, "[b]ecause Philo makes so much use of source material in this treatise, however, detailed linguistic comparisons may well come up with misleading results" (in "The Text of the Platonic Citations in Philo of Alexandria," in *Studies in Plato and the Platonic Tradition: Essays Presented to John Whittaker*, ed. Mark Joyal [Aldershot: Ashgate, 1997], 261–91) is relevant but does not amount to debunking the Norwegian scholar's findings, which are now available in English in Kåre Fuglseth, "The Reception of Aristotelian Features in Philo and the Authorship Problem of *De Aeternitate Mundi*," in *Beyond Reception: Mutual Influences between Antique Religion, Judaism and Early Christianity*, ed. David Brakke, Anders-Christian Jacobsen, and Jörg Ulrich; Early Christianity in the Context of Antiquity 1 (Frankfurt am Main: Peter Lang, 2006), 57–67, esp. pp. 61–63. I have no position on this question which is not of decisive importance in the context of this study.

[207] The living and dying in this passage have usually been understood in a literal sense. For reasons as tho why this is not feasible, see below.

[208] This is one of the rare cases of Philo's explicitly presenting the body as an active, evil agent (ἐπίβουλος). But it follows directly from the biblical text and is to be viewed as an example of double dichotomy (see above, p. 39).

bearer?"[209] (3.74). Dieter Zeller, among others, sees in the background the Etruscan practice reported by Aristotle of "chain[ing] their captives face to face with corpses."[210] In fact, Aristotle presents this information in precisely the fragment which Huffman adduces as a parallel to the pseudo-Philolaus fr. discussed above. The context is quite similar to Philo's in *Leg.* 1.105–108. Aristotle says,

> the soul is undergoing punishment [and] our life is chastisement for great sins. For the yoking of the soul to the body is very like something of this sort. For just as they say that the Etruscans often tortured captives by binding corpses (νεκρούς) face to face with the living, matching each part to each part, so the soul seems to have been stretched through the body and fastened to all the sensory organs of the body. (Fr. 60 Rose)[211]

Reading *Leg.* 1.108 and 3.71–72 together, it seems very natural to assume a correspondence between the philosopher who ignores the evil corpse bound to him and is not hurt by it (3.72) and the soul released from precisely the same nuisance (1.108). This close equivalence is of great interest, for it serves to clarify 1.108 where it is somewhat abruptly stated that the event of death brings liberation: "should we die, the soul lives forthwith its own proper life." These words describe the free soul, and based on 3.72 they mean a "philosopher" soul, i.e., *not* a morally dead one.[212]

---

[209] Conroy's claim in "Death of the Soul," 33 that the verb refers to "the body carrying something dead, a corpse of the rational soul" is completely misinformed. There is no doubt that the verb refers to the soul's carrying the body and not *vice versa*: "the soul rais[es] up and carr[ies] without toil the body which of itself is a corpse" (*Leg.* 3.69). Similarly in *Leg.* 3.74, *Agr.* 25, *Somn.* 2.237, *QG* 4.77 and elsewhere. See also LSJ; Méasson, *Du char ailé de Zeus,* 318; Runia, *Philo and the* Timaeus, 262; "Verba Philonica, ΑΓΑΛΜΑΤΟΦΟΡΕΙΝ, and the Authenticity of the *De Resurrectione* Attributed to Athenagoras," in *VC* 46.4 (1992): 313–27, pp. 320–21; Pearce, *The Land of the Body*, 110; Geljon and Runia, *On Cultivation*, 118.

[210] Quotation from Zeller, "Life and Death," 48. See also Mansfeld, "Middle Platonist Cento," 140 and David T. Runia, "Verba Philonica," p. 321.

[211] The ways of referring to this text vary considerably. Mansfeld, "Middle Platonist Cento," speaks of *Protr.* fr. 10 b Ross. In the TLG the fragment quoted by Huffman is Aristotle's *Protr.* frr. 106–107 in Düring's edition *and* Iambl. *Protr.* 47.21–48.9. I omit the first part of section 106 Düring.

[212] Cf. the athlete's attitude in 3.72: he "refers everything to the well-being of the body, and lover of the body that he is, would sacrifice the soul itself on its behalf." It is plainly impossible to reconcile this kind of character with being released from a "baneful corpse," for he knows of no such thing. I am not aware of evidence to suggest that Philo thought that physical death as such raises all souls from their death (see below, subsection 2.3.2, pp. 106–8). Yet it should be mentioned that another "*interpretative paraphrase*" (Mansfeld, "Middle Platonist Cento," 145; emphasis original) of the "Heraclitean oxymoron" (idem, passim) seems to feature just the idea I am denying in Philo: Sextus Empiricus *Pyrrhoniae hypotyposes* 3.230 (given by Mansfeld as Heraclitus fr. 47 [d³] Marc.):

Indeed, if we look closely we find that the expression "should we die" means dying to the life dominated by vice: "now (νῦν μέν), when we are living, the soul is dead ... ; whereas, should (εἰ δέ) we die, the soul lives forthwith its own proper life." The *dying* meant here is the opposite of our *living* as dead souls. We have no basis for assuming these concepts do not operate on the same level; they must both concern living and dying in an *ethical* (and not physical) sense, explaining which has been Philo's whole point since 1.105.[213] In 1.108 he specifically discusses dying to the life of wickedness (1.107) which is even said to be the only kind of life which the dead soul *is* alive to (τὸν δὲ κακίας [βίον] ζῇ μόνον, 1.107). Thus it is the only kind of life it *can* die to. We should also note that just as Philo defines the the soul's own death (ἴδιος θάνατος) in 1.106 as becoming entombed in passions and wickedness and as the coming together of body and soul, its own life (ἴδιος βίος) is in 1.108 defined as its dying to the life of wickedness and the release from the body. Cf. *Gig.* 14, where Philo states that this kind of salvific dying concerns those correctly philosophizing souls that emerge from the river of the body and fly back to God: they "practice dying to the life in the body." And as if to confirm the relevance of this statement for the interpretation of the *Leg.* passages under consideration, Philo in *Gig.* 15 calls the body "that corpse which was our birth-fellow (τὸν συμφυᾶ νεκρὸν ἡμῶν)."[214] The dead soul has to die again in order to undo its death.[215] Then, its proper life will follow.

Heraclitus says that both living and dying are present in both our living and being dead: for on the one hand, when we live, our souls are dead and entombed in us, and, on the other, when we die, the souls are revived and living.
(My tr. for ὁ δὲ Ἡράκλειτός φησιν, ὅτι καὶ τὸ ζῆν καὶ τὸ ἀποθανεῖν καὶ ἐν τῷ ζῆν ἡμᾶς ἐστι καὶ ἐν τῷ τεθνάναι· ὅτε μὲν γὰρ ἡμεῖς ζῶμεν, τὰς ψυχὰς ἡμῶν τεθνάναι καὶ ἐν ἡμῖν τεθάφθαι, ὅτε δὲ ἡμεῖς ἀποθνήσκομεν, τὰς ψυχὰς ἀναβιοῦν καὶ ζῆν.) As Mansfeld notes, Sextus's "interpretation, blended with his paraphrase, is the same as Philo's." On the *literal* level it is so much so that it is untenable to think both authors have independently arrived at so similar a wording in their interpretation of a saying of Heraclitus (which they, nevertheless, quote in a very different form). The utilization of a common tradition is the likeliest explanation.
[213] *Pace*, e.g., Geljon & Runia, *On Cultivation*, 118–19; Peter Schäfer, *The Origins of Jewish Mysticism* (Tübingen: Mohr Siebeck, 2009), 161, and Zeller, "Life and Death," 45, 47.
[214] A fuller quotation is found below, p. 132.
[215] There is a total of three different *events* of dying in *Leg.* 1.105–108: (1) physical death, (2) that of the soul and (3) dying to the corporeal life. The first two also represent *states* of being dead, and the body's being a corpse is a third one. Quite understandably, the result of dying to the corporeal life is not referred to by Philo as a *state* of death (with an exception in *Post.* 39 where it is called θάνατος—not necessarily to be understood as a state, but in any case immediately identified with ἀθάνατος ζωή). Conversely, the body's being dead is not preceded by any event of death, for it is a corpse to begin with.

There are thus clear connections between the death of the soul and incarnation as a punishment. In a number of passages Philo speaks of another specific kind of penalty of the soul or mind—its *banishment*—in ways that also seem to refer to its incarnation. For instance:

> Moses, lamenting over those who had become exiles from the garden of virtues, implores ... that the people endowed with sight be planted in on the spot whence the earthy mind, called Adam, has been banished (πεφυγάδευται). This is what he says (Ex 15:17–18): "Lead them in, and plant them in the mountain of your inheritance." (*Plant.* 46)

Let us approach this passage by first asking, *whence* and *whither* the banishment takes place. In the passage cited, the penalty is deportation from *virtue*. We note the connection to the end of *Leg.* 1 where Philo speaks of a "decay of virtue" (1.105) and "d[ying] to the life of virtue" (1.107). He does the same at the beginning of *Leg.* 3 where, inspired by Adam and Eve's hiding from God following their disobedience, he speaks of the bad person as an "exile from virtue" (3.1) who "is in banishment (πεφυγάδευται) from the divine company" (3.7). In *Leg.* 3 and *Plant.* Philo does not discuss *where* the exiles end up, but we find in *Congr.* information that seems relevant. Although at the surface Philo is now one step removed from the Paradise account, numerous links to, *inter alia, Leg.* 3.1–2 and *Plant.* 46 reveal he is thinking of it, too. Philo is discussing here the name of Eliphaz, Esau's son, which he says means "God hath dispersed me:"

> And is it not true that when God scatters and disperses the soul and ejects it with contumely from His presence, unreasoning passion is at once engendered? The understanding which truly loves God, that has the vision of Him, He "plants in" [and enables it to reach] the acquisition and enjoyment of virtue. (57) That is what Moses prays in these words (Ex 15:17), "Lead them in, and plant them in" ... On the other hand, He banishes (φυγαδεύων) the unjust and godless soul from himself to the furthest bounds and disperses it to the place of pleasures and lusts and injustices (εἰς τὸν ἡδονῶν καὶ ἐπιθυμιῶν καὶ ἀδικημάτων χῶρον). That place is most fitly called that of the impious (ὁ δὲ χῶρος οὗτος προσφυέστατα ἀσεβῶν καλεῖται), but it is not that mythical place in Hades. For the true Hades is the life of the bad, a life of damnation and blood-guiltiness, the victim of every curse (πάσαις ἀραῖς ἔνοχος).[216] ... [Based on Deut 32:8 it may also be said that] He drove away all the earthly characters ... and made them homeless and cityless,[217] scattered in very truth... . So then the bad person begets vice by his legitimate wife and passion by his concubine... . The bodily nature is the

---

[216] An apparent reference to "all the imprecations (πάσας τὰς ἀράς) of th[e] covenant" in Deut 29:20.
[217] Cf. *Leg.* 3.2: "the bad person is cityless and homeless ... unfit to dwell in the city of virtue." Esau is here used as a symbol.

concubine, and we see that through it passion is generated, for the body is the region of pleasures and lusts (ἡδονῶν γὰρ καὶ ἐπιθυμιῶν χώρα τὸ σῶμα). (*Congr.* 56–59)

Here it is obvious that the banishment to the "place of the impious" is a penalty. Philo most probably took this appellation from the pseudo-Platonic *Axiochus* (371e), where it is used for the underworldly place of punishment in the afterlife.[218] It seems warranted to regard Philo's references to Hades and Tartarus as carrying a punitive connotation, unless there is evidence to suggest otherwise. Strikingly, in *Congr.* the real *locus* of the punishment is the physical body (§§ 57, 59).[219] The dispersion, as well, is linked with the body via passion and the symbol of the concubine (§§ 56, 59). The concubine in question is Eliphaz's, Timna, whose name ('tossing faintness') symbolises the drowning of the soul in bodily passion (§60).

I think that the accounts in *Plant.* and *Congr.* can be read together, because they are connected by the themes of sight, virtue and banishment, as well as Ex 15:17 which Philo quotes nowhere else. But is this the original banishment? In *Plant.* it is the "earthly mind," in *Leg.* 3.1, the "wicked person," i.e., "one unable to take part" in virtue, who is expelled, and in *Leg.* 3.7 too Philo takes the matter to a universal level in speaking of "the bad person" who "is in banishment (πεφυγάδευται again) from the divine company." In *Congr.* Philo uses similar language when recounting how the unjust and godless soul is banished from God to the body.[220] In none of these texts are there signs that Philo is engaged in *protological* allegoriza-

---

[218] In the *Axiochus* the place in question is precisely that *mythical* Tartarus in the house of Hades which Philo dismisses in *Congr.* 57 and where the never-ending punishments of the Danaids, Tantalus, Tityus, Sisyphus etc. are carried out, so we might even see a comment here to the author of *Ax.* This Platonist dialogue about death contains no explicit mention of reincarnation. Only two extreme options are presented for the souls' post-mortem fate the better one being that those "whom a good daemon inspired in life go to reside in a place of the pious" (εἰς τὸν τῶν εὐσεβῶν χῶρον οἰκίζονται, 371c). Cf. *Fug.* 130–131: μετοικισάμενοι . . . εἰς τὸν . . . εὐσεβῶν χῶρον.—Hades is equated with the life of the bad also in *Somn.* 1.151; similarly *Her.* 45. Note also that Egypt is called the "land of the impious" at *Mos.* 1.96, while it is perhaps Philo's most important symbol of the body in the Bible—admittedly mostly within the *Allegorical Commentary*, but see in *Abr.* 103 and *Ios.* 151.

[219] This is why the latter part of Goodenough's ("Philo on Immortality," 89) statement that "there can be no spacial banishment from a non-spacial God, and 'Hades,' the 'place' of that banishment cannot be spacial" is inaccurate. He refers to *Congr.* 56–57 only; the almost identical expressions used about Hades and the body seem to have escaped him.

[220] The "region of pleasures" of *Congr.* 57, 59 has one more occurrence in Philo, in *Post.* 26—again as a characterization of the body. Looking at *Post.* 26–32 we note that the "standing" nature of God and the Abraham-soul are presented in opposition both to the body of pleasures and the Hades of passions, which further reinforces the connection between these two locations in Philo's thought.

tion, but this in itself does not preclude the possibility of the mind's incarnation having been originally a punishment in his thought.

Cher. has another occurrence of the notion that the consequences of the transgression in Paradise, as presented in Genesis, are interpreted in terms of deportation to "the land of the impious." Although Philo in §1 quotes Gen 3:24 with its reference to Adam being thrown out of Paradise, he again ignores the protological context and starts discussing the difference between the verbs used in 3:23 (ἐξαποστέλλω, 'send forth') and 3:24 (ἐκβάλλω, 'drive away'). The former does not preclude returning, but he "who is driven out by God is subject to eternal banishment (ἀίδιον φυγήν)." Philo further writes,

> But to him who is weighed down and enslaved by that fierce and incurable malady [of wickedness], the horrors of the future must needs be undying and for all time: he is thrust forth to the place of the impious (εἰς ἀσεβῶν χῶρον), there to endure misery continuous and unrelieved (ἄκρατον καὶ συνεχῇ). (*Cher.* 2)

One would like to ask Philo what he meant by "eternal exile" in what we may regard as the body—but in fact that question would contain a fallacy, a false reading. For when Philo speaks of "eternal banishment," he is still elaborating on the *explanandum*, not yet presenting his *explanatio* quoted above.[221] Prior to Philo the concept of "eternal banishment," ἀίδιος φυγή, is used almost exclusively by Dionysius of Halicarnassus as a law term.[222] It is similar to the italicized part in "[f]or to him who is not as yet firmly in the grip of wickedness it is open to repent and return to the virtue from which he was driven, as *an exile returns to his fatherland*" (§2) in that it presents a parallel from the physical world.[223]

---

[221] The former element corresponds to what Runia (in "The Structure of Philo's Allegorical Treatises: A Review of Two Recent Studies and Some Additional Comments," *VC* 38 [1984]: 209–256, p. 230), referring to Valentin Nikiprowetzky (in "L'Exégèse de Philon d'Alexandrie dans le *De Gigantibus* et le *Quod Deus*," in David Winston and John Dillon, *Two Treatises of Philo of Alexandria: A Commentary on De Gigantibus and Quod Deus Sit Immutabilis*; BJS 25 [Chico, CA: Scholars Press, 1983], 5–75) has called an "initial observation" used by Philo to "break open" the text before embarking on his allegorical interpretation. See also Runia, "Further Observations on the Structure of Philo's Allegorical Treatises," *VC* 41 (1987): 105–138, pp. 122–23.

[222] E.g., "Marcius Coriolanus, the man who had been accused of aiming at tyranny [had been] condemned to perpetual banishment" (*Ant. Rom.* 8.1.2).

[223] As I see it, the structure of *Cher.* 1–2 as a whole is as follows. Excluding the biblical quotation, it consists of six parts beginning with (1) νῦν μέν, (2) πρότερον δ'; (3) ὁ μέν, (4) ὁ δ'; (5) τῷ μέν, (6) τὸν δέ. The second, third and fifth concern him who is "sent forth," the first, fourth and sixth him who is "driven out." The first two parts move purely at the level of the story in Genesis. The third and fourth operate jointly on the biblical and a "physical," i.e., real-world level: [3)]"He who is sent forth (biblical) is not thereby prevented from

It is noteworthy that Philo mentions the difference between the two types of exile only with regard to the possibility of return. Nothing points to the place of exile being different, and it is here we start finding more connections to passages examined above. The one who returns in *Cher.* 2 has been driven from *virtue* (cf. *Leg.* 3.1; *Plant.* 46) and so seems to be a dead soul (cf. *Leg.* 1.105, 107). That *repentance* is needed for the return is in harmony with *Leg.* 2.78. But what about those who have caught the "incurable malady"? That does sound quite final, but I would, nonetheless, hesitate to declare that in *Cher.* 2 Philo is speaking of eternal damnation. That the horrors are "undying (ἀθάνατα)" can also be understood to mean that "impiety (ἀσέβεια) is an evil that cannot come to and end ... . It is in life as we know it that it is 'deathless' (ἀθάνατον)" (*Fug.* 61; cf. the "deathless evil" at *Det.* 178). As for the horrors being "for all time (μέχρι τοῦ παντὸς αἰῶνος)," we should also remember the meaning of αἰών as 'lifetime;' cf. "the whole length of life (ἅπαντα τὸν αἰῶνα)" at *Mut.* 185. The problem with an underworldly (note the allusion to the *Axiochus*) eternal damnation is that Philo nowhere expresses an unquivocal belief in such a thing, whereas we have an explicit rejection in *Congr.* 57.

In *QG* we have another affirmation by Philo that the real meaning of the mythical inferno is the human body. In his exegesis of Gen 27:39 Philo writes that God

> does not permit the mind to be emptied and bereft of an excellent and most divine form when it descends into an earthly body, to (the rivers of) desires, Acheron and Pyriphlegethon, for these are the true Tartarus,[224] but

---

returning (physical)" and 4)"he who is driven out by God (biblical) is subject to eternal banishment (physical)." Here ends the "initial observation." The fifth part quoted above contains a combination of allegorical (repentance and return to virtue) and physical (the exile's return to fatherland), while the last one (the indented quotation above) is purely allegorical. We thus have the biblical level involved in parts 1 to 4, the physical in 3 to 5 and the allegorical in 5 and 6. To me this looks like an intentional structure where the physical parallels act as a bridge between the biblical and allegorical levels. To be more precise, the bridge is significant only in the case of the one *sent forth*: the allegorical interpretation in part 5 (repentance as the prerequisite of return) is based on the physical elaboration in 3 (the possibility of return), whereas the allegory in part 6 (enslavement by incurable malady) clearly builds on the allegory of part 5 and functions as its antithesis. The physical elaboration in part 4 (eternal banishment of the one cast forth) plays a lesser role with the verb ὑπομένω being the only direct connection between parts 4 and 6.

[224] "[T]o (the rivers) of desires, Acheron and Pyriphlegethon:" my tr. for the OL, "in Acheronte et Puriflegetonte concupiscentiarum." I am following Françoise Petit, *L'ancienne version latine des Questions sur la Genèse de Philon d'Alexandrie*, TUGAL 113–14 (Berlin: Akademie-Verlag, 1973), 1.93, 2.157 in preferring the Latin here to the Armenian which Marcus translates, "and is burned by the necessities and flames of desire." According to Petit, the Armenian translator has not recognized the proper names of the rivers of

he permits it to spread its wings sometimes and to behold heaven above and to taste that sight. For there are some who through gluttony, lechery and over-indulgence are always submerged and sunken, being drowned by passion. (*QG* 4.234)[225]

The body is identified with "the true Tartarus." This, together with the reference to desires, makes this passage related in thought to *Congr.* 57, 59. The point seems to be that the suffering implied is self-induced, and so the punishment is again not clearly distinguishable from the crime.[226] But here the exposition has a pronouncedly Platonic flavor. The juxtapositioning of the body and the named rivers is an apparent allusion to the *Timaeus*, and the salvific role of flying and "tast[ing] that sight" come from Socrates's speech about the soul's "idea" in the *Phaedrus*.[227] The last sentence creates many connections to other parts of Philo's *oeuvre*. We may note that Marcus in PLCL *ad loc.* assumes the original Greek for "submerged and sunken" to have been καταποντοῦνται καὶ καταδύονται, for which he refers to *Agr.* 89: owing to the force of the passions and injustices (ἀδικημάτων), "the mind, becoming waterlogged, is submerged; and the bottom to which it is submerged and made to sink (καταποντοῦται καὶ καταδύεται) is nothing else than the body, of which Egypt is the figure."[228] This certainly looks like a description of incarnation, and although there is no (solid) underworld here, the force of injustices seems to imply a penalty; we may recall that in *Congr.* 57 "the land of the impious" was also the place of injustices (ἀδικημάτων). It is noteworthy that the biblical lemma in *Agr.* (Deut 17:16) speaks of *returning* to Egypt.

Tartarus (see *Od.* 10.513). But on the following clause I disagree with her. The OL reads, "Haec sunt enim tarterea Idumea," which she prefers on the grounds that the Armenian translator has also not recognized the Greek Ἐδώμ but has confused it with ἔτυμος ('true'). Philo mentions Edom, so Petit, because of the biblical lemma, Isaac's blessing to Esau whose descendants were to settle in that land. While this is plausible in itself, I find the suggested confusion strained and think that it may now be the Latin translator who has not been up to the job—the OL is, after all, "très mauvaise" and characterized by "l'absence de toute méthode" (Petit, *L'ancienne version latine*, 1.13). And the Armenian translator *has* recognized the well-known biblical name of Edom not too far back in *QG* 4.171 (and there the OL has "Edom," not "Idumea").

[225] Marcus in PLCL "in passion," but յախտից (*yaxtic*) is the agent of the sentence. Cf. Mercier's translation in PAPM: "les passions les font couler."

[226] Cf. *Leg.* 1.107 (above, p. 48).

[227] Cf. *Tim.* 43a and see below, subsection 2.4.2 on p. 114–17; *Phaedrus* 246c, 247a, 248a–c, 249a, d. Philo may also be alluding to Socrates's description of the Tartarean watercourses and souls' journeys in and along them in *Phaedo* 112–114.

[228] My translation. See below (p. 84) for a critical assessment of the verbal connection assumed by Marcus and (pp. 182–85) for a fuller discussion on *Agr.* 88–89.

To sum up the discussion on cause 8: There are Philonic texts that speak of the mind's entering the body as a penalty. There are indications that in Philo's view the first incarnation as such is not a punishment but part of the divine plan, and that it is only *re*-incarnation that is of punitive nature (thus also, *e.g.*, the *Timaeus*). Tartarus, Hades and "the land of the impious" are expressions used by Philo about the soul's place of banishment to point explicitly to the body and also to the sensual way of life of the wicked.

Cause 9: The Corporealization of the Mind
In our discussion of cause no. 1, connections were noted between loving the body, desiring mortal life, death of the soul and Adam's dedication to the earth. The further analysis of the issue of where these originate was postponed until now. Likewise, the potential link between becoming akin to created things (cause no. 5) and the mind's becoming earthly in some manner was not pursued in that context. It is now time to turn to these questions. In distinction to incarnation I will call the phenomenon whereby *the mind (or soul) orientates towards, and desires to experience, the world of matter in general and a physical body of its own in particular*—the "*corporealization of the mind.*"

The most important scriptural basis for understanding Philo's view of corporealization is contained in Gen 3:19: Adam's returning to the earth. We begin with his exegesis of that verse in *QG*:

> What is the meaning of the words, "Until you return to the earth from which you were taken?" For the human being was moulded not only from the earth but also from the divine spirit.
> First, it is evident that the earth-born creature was compounded out of earth and heaven. And because he did not remain uncorrupted but made light of the commands of God, turning away from the best and most excellent part, namely heaven, he gave himself wholly over (ὅλον αὑτὸν προσένειμεν in the Gk. fr.) to the earth, the denser and heavier element. Second, if he had been desirous of virtue, which makes the soul immortal, he would certainly have obtained heaven as his lot. Since he was zealous for pleasure, through which psychic death is brought about, he gives himself back to earth; accordingly Scripture says, "For you are earth, and to earth you will depart." Thus earth is the beginning and end of the evil and vile person, heaven of the virtuous person. (*QG* 1.51)

The *quaestio* invokes the anomaly that Adam is said to have been taken from the earth, as if in his entirety, whereas in Gen 2:7 there was also another ingredient, the divine breath—for Philo, the soul (*QG* 1.4).[229] The

---

[229] On the reception of *soul* in *QG* 1.4, see above, n. 131 and text on p. 35.

solutio is, in effect, that Adam's soul has upon its death become so earthlike that it will return to the earth with the body. But the soul's return to the earth must be something other than the body's, which is disintegration.[230] Let us list the salient points and see what remains to untangle:

- The reason for what takes place is the act of disobedience prompted by Adam's zeal for pleasure.
- That act marked Adam's turning towards the earth and dedication to it. This was tantamount to the death of the soul and the reason for the characterization of Adam as earth and his departure thereto.
- This could have been avoided, and heaven would have been Adam's lot, if his desire had been directed towards virtue instead of pleasure.

It is important to note that the first two points mean that *the transgression and corporealization are two sides of the same coin*. The crime here was the disobedience; its direction and contents were earthly and motivated by pleasure.[231]

Two questions do not receive satisfactory answers above: Since immortality would only have followed in the case of his making a correct choice, was Adam originally mortal? And, what does it mean that the bad person has the earth for both his beginning and end, and the good one, heaven? With regard to the first question, my view is that we have here a very good example of the mixing of protological and universal elements. The whole passage has the air of protology, but the statements "virtue ... makes the soul immortal" and "through [pleasure] psychic death is brought about" are universally true to Philo and in no way dependent on the fact that the context of the biblical verse is protological. If dashes or parentheses had been invented by Philo's time, he might well have enclosed these two universal (present-tense) statements in the middle of protological ones (in aorist) within them. Near the beginning of the *solutio* Philo says the earth-born human did not *remain* uncorrupted (ἀδιάστροφος in the Greek fr., lit. 'incapable of turning'), and so we should probably understand the passage to the effect that Adam failed in maintaining his original immortality, but we all can reach it through virtue.

---

[230] Cf. *QG* 2.61 where Philo discusses precisely this point. For a quotation, see below, p. 83.

[231] *Opif.* 151–152 directly speaks of sexual pleasure, but we cannot take that as a *direct* parallel because of the different nature of the genre to which it belongs.

Regarding the second question it may first be noted that connecting the last sentence of QG 1.51 to what precedes it is not straightforward: that the soul's end is dependent on its actions is understandable enough, but how can its *beginning* change according to whether it makes the right or the wrong choice? One option would be to assume that the ellipsis in the end is to be spelled out as "earth is the beginning and end of the evil and vile person, while heaven is *the end* of the virtuous person." Yet this would be arbitrary—and impossible to reconcile with the view that "the human being [was made] also from the divine spirit." One simply has to conclude that the "beginning" meant here is something that *followed* the choice. This means that not only are the beginning and end of the evil and the virtuous person different, but also that these *concepts* applied to them in a different sense. I suggest that the last sentence should be understood in the following way:

(1) The *bad* person has the earth as his *beginning* because the Bible says so: "you were taken" from the earth. The problem that this is not true of the soul is the point of the whole *quaestio*; whether we find Philo's answer plausible need not concern us now. That the earth is his *end* as well likewise stems from the biblical text, "you return to the earth" and "to earth you will depart." Philo does not explicate what he means by the return of *the soul* to the earth. Written by a Platonist, it brings reincarnation to mind, and we have already seen that QG 1.51 is central to Winston in his view of reincarnation in Philo.[232] However, its evidential value is limited by the absence of a reference to either afterlife or recurrence.[233] Yet the connection to the *death of the soul* must be borne in mind. QG 1.51 should, in any case, be added to the cumulative evidence in favor of Philo's endorsement of the doctrine.

(2) What Philo says of the *virtuous* person is in no way dependent on his biblical lemma but reflects his general views: the pre-existence of the soul or mind and its return to the divine realm upon salvation.[234]

Based on both QG 1.51 and the previous discussion of incarnation as a punishment it is possible to draft the journey of the soul to be tested

---

[232] See above, subsection 1.4.2, p. 19.
[233] I cannot see why the translations in PLCL, PAPM and QGUM all *add* an expression denoting recurrence to the sentence preceding the second biblical quotation: "he *again* gives himself back to earth," "il est rendu *de nouveau* à la terre;" "kehrt er zur Erde *wieder* zurück"—cf. Yonge's "he again gives himself over *a second time* to the earth" from Aucher's sound Latin, "terrae se rursum tradidit." Neither the Greek fr. (τῇ γῇ προσενεμήθη) nor the Armenian text (երկրի անդրէն հատուցանէ [*erkri andrēn hatucʿanē*]) contains such accentuation of the return.
[234] See above, p. 31.

against Philo's views expressed in other passages particularly with regard to the stage of the corporealization of the mind. My sketch includes the following six stages:

(1) incorporeal existence with God;
(2) incarnation;
(3) corporealization and transgression;
(4) reincarnation until the prerequisites of salvation are met;
(5) liberation from the life in the body; and,
(6) eternal incorporeal existence with God.

When a *virtuous* soul is said to start and end with heaven (*QG* 1.51), that covers the whole span (1) to (6) with the exception that it may perhaps skip stages (3) and (4).[235] But when a *wicked* mind begins and ends in the earth, that has to do with phases (3) and (4) only; it is neither incarnate nor wicked in (1) and (6) and, although incarnate, not yet wicked in (2); stage (5) is the turning point.

This kind of schematization runs the risk of too large an extent of simplification and a harmonization of statements that are not meant to teach a clear system. Yet if we remain open to the model's possible shortcomings and are prepared to revise or abandon it if necessary, it has its place in the search for greater understanding.[236]

After this discussion it is very interesting to turn to Philo's other interpretation of Gen 3:19 as a primary lemma in *Leg.* 3.251–253. This section is relevant for the main question of this study in general, but also regarding corporealization of the mind in particular, because Philo is a little less taciturn here. Our focus will mainly be on the middle part of the section which in Whitaker's translation—to which I below propose certain changes—runs,

> And how long is [the miserable life of the fool] to be? "Until," He says, "thou shalt turn back into the earth, from which thou wert taken." For,

---

[235] *Conf.* 77–78 (see p. 54 above) suggests that at least the best sages manage to visit the earthly sphere without compromising their integrity. It should be noted that Philo typically describes the heaven (or the ether) as the soul's starting point (e.g., *Her.* 240; *QG* 3.10, 45), which is not the same as God—explicitly mentioned as the origin of the mind in *Opif.* 135 and *Abr.* 258. These statements, the definition of salvation used in this study and the general symmetry in Philo's view of the soul's journey (see above, section 2.1.2) justifies the formulation of stage (1) above, but the model should not be pressed in this respect.

[236] One open question in Philo's eschatology is whether there is room for some kind of *original sin* in the Christian sense or whether each soul goes through the stages independently.

> having forsaken the wisdom of heaven, is he not now ranked with things earthly and chaotic? How then he turns back yet further, we have to consider. But perhaps what he means is of this kind, that the foolish mind has indeed always turned back from the right principle, but has been taken not from the sublime nature but from the more earthly substance, and, whether staying still or in movement, is the same and devoted to the same interests. (*Leg.* 3.252)

For our present specific topic the key statement is, "is he not now ranked with things earthlike (τοῖς γεώδεσι) and chaotic?" We will first consider this and then its surroundings. Finally, the applicability of the six-stage model will be assessed.

Who is being spoken of? The subject of the sentence has to be supplied from 3.251: "the fool," which is one of Philo's epithets in *Leg.* for the wicked soul represented by Adam. The first adjective "earthlike" is fairly natural for such a "mind striving to attain the objects of sense," as it is characterized in 3.251. But how is it that the mind is only "now (νῦν)" earthlike, even though Philo has been speaking of the "earthly human" and "earthlike mind" ever since *Leg.* 1.32, and why is the human moulded in Gen 2:7 called "earthly" or "earthlike" already in *Leg.* 1.31–32, when neither incarnation nor corporealization has taken place? Furthermore, why is the entity called an earthy or earthlike "mind"? To take this last question first, the short answer is: because those are Philo's own terms for the *corporealized mind*.[237] As for the previous one, the question presupposes that *Leg.* consists of Philo's protological allegory which follows the narrative and chronology of Genesis. This assumption is false.[238] Given the way he works with the universal allegorization of the biblical text, there is nothing to prevent him from discussing in *Leg.* 1 a notion whose biblical basis will only fully come to light in *Leg.* 3.[239] In 3.252 the immediate point triggering the reference to the fool's earthlikeness is the word "earth" in the biblical lemma cited, but Philo may also be anticipating the more direct expression in the same verse, "for you are earth" (cf. 3.253).

We next need to examine the reason and meaning of the fool's return to the earth as well as their connection to his being "earthlike." Forsaking

---

[237] This will hopefully become obvious below. See also the article mentioned in the next note.
[238] See Yli-Karjanmaa, "Call him earth."
[239] The fool is also "ranked with things ... incohesive," as I would translate ἀσύστατος here. I take it in this sense because I see it as a reference back to the characterization of "matter" in *Leg.* 1.31 as σπόρας, 'unconnected.' Cf. *Timaeus* 61a, where Plato speaks of loose earth as ἀξύστατος, and *Fug.* 148 (ex. Ex 2:12) where Philo calls sand σπόρας. For a detailed analysis of this connection, involving also *Leg.* 3.36–39, 52, see my "Call him earth."

"the wisdom of heaven" must be a reference to the transgression, but I doubt it merely serves to point out that the commandment of God was breached. Instead we may compare it with the only other occurrence of οὐράνιος σοφία in *Leg.*, in Philo's exegesis of Gen 2:8:

> [Moses] has already made it manifest that the sublime and heavenly wisdom is of many names; for he calls it "beginning" and "image" and "vision of God;" and now by the "planting" of the "pleasaunce" he brings out the fact that earthly wisdom is a copy of this as of an archetype. (*Leg.* 1.43)[240]

It is noteworthy that in 1.45 Philo, without changing the subject, makes a slight change of vocabulary and speaks of God's "sow[ing] and plant[ing] earthly virtue into the race of mortals" and says later in 1.79 that "God sowed in the earthborn [human] (τῷ γηγενεῖ) good sense and virtue."[241] Given the reference to the earthly mind at 1.33 as γηγενής and the intimate connection of the breath of life to *virtue* in 1.34-35, we have good grounds for seeing the heavenly wisdom and virtue connected both to the Paradise and the breath of life. We are thus dealing with the soul's forsaking virtue (and thus becoming dead; see cause no. 8) and wisdom. This, in it itself, may be understood either protologically or universally.

Next, Philo turns to the biblical reference to "(re)turning" and asks how is it possible that he "turns back yet further" (Whitaker), or rather, "turns himself yet around" (ἔτι ἀποστρέφεται)? He apparently takes the "forsaking" of wisdom as the *first* turning, and his wonderment at the second one implies he is not thinking of physical death.[242] Philo switches from active to medio-passive which introduces a slight change in meaning, and in the sequel where the verb is used in the perfect tense with a direct object, the change becomes quite significant: "the foolish mind has indeed always *been facing away from* the right principle (ἀπέστραπται ... τὸν ὀρθὸν λόγον)."[243] Further, it is "devoted to the same interests (ἐφιέμενός τε τῶν αὐτῶν)," as

---

[240] My use of quotation marks aims at distinguishing the biblical *explanandum* from Philo's *explanatio*. The first three words are enclosed in them also in PLCL. The two first seem to be references to (Philo's lost exegesis of?) Genesis 1:1 and 26-27, and the third one possibly to the repeated formula "and God saw that it was good."

[241] Whitaker at 1.45 renders τῷ θνητῷ γένει "*for* the race of mortals," but my interpretation is defended by 1.79 and the connection to the breath of life (see below).

[242] I understand the logic to be: since the fool has already turned the wrong way, does not another turn bring him to the right direction? And yet this cannot be, because Philo finds this second turn negative as well. Note the similarity to the problem discussed above at 1.105 (p. 58): how does the incarnate soul incarnate still further?

[243] "The right principle" is mentioned in *Leg.* at *1.45-46, 92-93*; 3.2, 80, 106, 147-148, 150, 168, 222, 251, 252 and used interchangeably with *virtue* in practice in all these passages the most explicit ones being printed in italics. Note especially that at 1.45-46 Paradise, virtue and the right principle are all identified with each other.

Whitaker obscurely renders. This expression picks up "the mind striving to attain the objects of sense (ἐφιέμενος τῶν αἰσθητῶν)" of 3.251. So the fool's "return to the earth" ends up meaning the corporealized mind's state of facing towards the objects of sense and away from virtue.

But how should the temporal dimension be understood? Philo's reading of the time limit in Gen 3:19 is μέχρι ἀποστρέψεις εἰς τὴν γῆν, whereas the LXX has ἕως τοῦ ἀποστρέψαι σε εἰς τὴν γῆν.[244] Why does Philo bother to make this change—which opens up the possibility that not "until" but "as long as" is meant—only to suppress the whole idea of timing the return with his "has indeed *always* been facing away" from virtue?[245] In any case there is a problem with Whitaker's translation "until," because Philo so strongly associates the verb ἀποστρέφω with shunning virtue, and to say anything reminiscent of the painful life of the fool lasting *until* he turns away from virtue would be absurd. Does Philo want to hint at reincarnation by rewriting the biblical sentence so that it can be understood to mean, "as long as you return to the earth?"

The future indicative (ἀποστρέψεις) is rare with temporal conjunctions, "because that tense does not usually make clear the difference between action continuing and action simply occurring in the future" (HWS §2398). The HWS almost entirely ignores the future in its treatment of the indicative in its "summary of the constructions of ἕως and of other words meaning both *so long as* and *until.*"[246] The only mention of the future is in a

---

[244] The four Greek fragments of *QG* 1.51 that Petit in PAPM 33 ad loc. cites all agree with the Septuagint here, which does not guarantee that this is the reading Philo found in his Bible. Gen 3:19 is not cited with μέχρι (or ἄχρι) replacing ἕως by anyone else, so this reading seems to be peculiar to Philo. Peter Katz, *Philo's Bible: The Aberrant Text of Bible Quotations in Some Philonic Writings and its Place in the Textual History of the Greek Bible* (Cambridge: Cambridge University Press, 1950) omits Philo's version here. Apparently he does not even consider it a quotation, although it is clearly presented as one (φησίν), and the rest of the sentence is directly from the LXX.

[245] Herbert Edward Ryle, *Philo and Holy Scripture, or the Quotations of Philo from the Books of the Old Testament* (London: Macmilan, 1895), 19 n. 19 implies the change is made because the verse is quoted "in answer to the question μέχρι τίνος;" but this is not convincing. As to the nature of the change, I think (*pace* Gregory Sterling, "Which Version of the Greek Bible Did Philo Read?" in *Pentateuchal Traditions in the Late Second Temple Period: Proceedings of the International Workshop in Tokyo, August 28–31, 2007*, ed. Akio Moriva and Gohei Hata; JSJSup 158 [Leiden: Brill, 2012], 89–128, p. 110) that Philo's version is *less* literal than the LXX—which has an infinitive just like the Hebrew (עַד שׁוּבְךָ).

[246] When the meaning is "so long as" (§2422), the indicative is used if "the action of the temporal clause denotes definite duration," wheras when "until" is meant (§2425), the indicative is used "of a definite ... action." These are not extremely informative definitions, because whether it is the duration or action which is definite is precisely the question here. Cf. what Smyth says in §2398 about the future tense in temporal clauses: "when used [it] refers to definite time." The example given for this is Demosthenes 19.262 (*De*

note in §2425: "Of a future action the future is very rare." Thus we need to predominantly rely on observations of *Philo's* usage. The general rule proves to be that when he has the indicative, "as long as" is meant, while "until" is expressed with ἄν + subjunctive.[247] I have found but few exceptions to this, and these are not directly relevant for *Leg.* 3.252.[248] Therefore, on grammatical grounds, one must consider the alternative "as long as" to be the more likely.[249] This makes the suspected hint at transmigration seem probable, and the sentence should be understood to mean that the fool's agony will last as long as he returns to the earth. This is, without contradiction, followed by the classification of the foolish mind as earthly and its having forsaken the wisdom of heaven.[250]

The final remark of *QG* 1.51—dealing with the beginning and end—also has a counterpart in *Leg.*[251]

> And that is why he goes on to say, "For you are earth, and to earth you will depart," which amounts to what I have already said. It signifies this also, "thine origin and thine end are one and the same, for thou beganst from

---

falsa legatione), "beware lest you discern the wisdom of my words too late, when you have lost the power of doing what you ought (ὅτ' οὐδ' ὅ τι χρὴ ποιεῖν ἕξετε)." That the time is "definite" thus means its being defined by the losing of the said power.

[247] For the indicative ("as long as") see, e.g., *Opif.* 151; *Leg.* 1.82, 2.70, 3.195; *Sacr.* 3; *Deus* 3, 134; *Plant.* 97; *Ebr.* 98; *Somn.* 1.119. For the subjunctive with ἄν ("until"), e.g., *Leg.* 2.39, 78, 86, 3.14; *Det.* 128; *Somn.* 1.122, 152; *Decal.* 87.

[248] There are rare cases such as those in *Post.* 132 and *Deus* 173 where ἕως is coupled with indicative aorist to mean "until" in a reference to the past.

[249] Two further considerations suggest Philo made an intentional amendment: (1) Independently of the change in *meaning* introduced, the alteration of both ἕως to μέχρι and the substantivized infinitive to a finite verb form is difficult to explain as accidental given the fairly close adherence to the LXX elsewhere in *Leg.* (2) The words in question are in Genesis spoken by God. If this had any impact, we can, even *a priori*, be certain that it was in the direction of *more* deliberation on Philo's part rather than less.

[250] Thus the biblical lemma does not belong exclusively to the *explanandum*, because Philo gives it an interpretative touch with his reformulation, and a significant one at that.

[251] Very brief comments can here be offered about the statement that the fool "has been taken not from the sublime nature but from the more earthly substance (γεωδεστέρας ὕλης), and, whether staying still or in movement (μένων δὲ καὶ κινούμενος) is the same" in *Leg.* 3.252. First, when the statement about "more earthly substance" is viewed against 1.31, 42, 88, it becomes clear Philo is simply referring to what he has been saying all along, "There are two types of humans" (1.31) and that what he is saying applies to the earthly one. (2) The specification, "whether staying still or in movement" is most naturally understood to mean something like "the foolish mind is the same regardless of whether or not it is at any given moment engaged in *active* pursuit of sensual things." For examples in *Leg.* see especially 3.34 but also 1.29; 2.40, 44, 100; 3.94, 222. As to why the foolish mind's staying still is presented here as inconsequential (and not laudable), cf. *Migr.* 148: "with [unstable persons] there is nothing praiseworthy even in their taking a turn to the better course; for it is the result not of judgement but of drift."

earth's decaying bodies, and into them shalt thou again come to thine end."
(*Leg.* 3.253).

Philo first harmonizes the two statements in Gen 3:19 about earth being the destination of Adam by declaring that his explanation of the first also applies to the second. But he also has two new points to make. The first one, although rather obvious in one sense, has significant implications in another: the equivalence of earth and decaying bodies. Here either sense objects in general or human bodies in particular must be meant. Both are decaying, and the word σῶμα is used in both senses in *Leg*. The question of which are meant has only a limited significance, for as was noted, the body and the physical world with its sense-perceptible bodies play a similar, passive role with respect to the soul in Philo.[252] The second new aspect is the reinforcement of a *dynamic* understanding of the return, for which the renewed reference to Adam's movement furnishes an opportunity. He is thus saying that the corporeal world is the fool's beginning and end—exactly the same idea as in *QG* 1.51.[253]

Given the high degree of similarity between *Leg.* 3.252-253 and *QG* 1.51, it comes as no surprise to find them fitting the six-stage model of the soul's fall and rise in the same way.[254] Both passages contain a blend of protological and universal allegory in that they describe the universal consequences, present in all imperfect souls, of their corporeality which is, ultimately, a state with protological roots.[255] If the model is accurate, corporealization is something that happened, or happens, to the already incarnate mind, and it therefore qualifies as a driving force of reincarnation, but is not the original cause of incarnation. This has the support of both *Leg.* 1.105-108, where the incarnate soul dies and is said to experience a union with the body, and *QG* 1.53, where Philo says the clothing of the mind and sense in the "skin tunics" (the body) took place "straightway," without any transgression, as if this had been part of the plan all along. Thus incarnation seems not to be originally a penalty—quite to the contrary, for it takes place "in order that His handiwork might first appear worthy of the divine power" (*ibid.*).

That Philo in *QG* 1.53, in his exegesis of Gen 3:21, ignores the transgression should alert us to the fact that we should not assume Philo is

---

[252] See p. 44.
[253] See above, p. 73.
[254] Cf. p. 73. The exception is the absence of the virtuous person in the former.
[255] The available evidence does not allow us to say whether the model applies to all souls collectively or to each soul individually. Thus the protologicality involved may also be either absolute (referring to the beginning of time) or relative (referring to the beginning of the existence of an individual soul). Cf. n. 236 on p. 73.

unfolding a running, protological allegory which follows the order of events in Genesis. In *Leg.* too there are examples of Philo's explaining away the chronology, e.g., the statement that the mind and the senses are "in actual time ... equal in age" (*Leg.* 2.73) despite Adam's being created before Eve. Universal allegory is entirely independent of the sequence of the biblical narrative, and it is also possible that Philo did not feel bound by that order even in his own *protological* chronology; he may have decided to follow the Timaean one: incarnation first (42a), failure to live justly and reincarnation second (42b). But this is very difficult to ascertain, first and foremost because the parts of *Leg.* which contain the interpretations of eating the forbidden fruit and the making of the skin tunics appear not to have survived. From what we have, it seems Philo held that incarnation was unavoidably the lot of humankind from the beginning, while the abandonment of virtue was rather a likely consequence of the corporealizing conditions than a logically inevitable development.[256]

It is worth noting that now that the punishments for the transgression are discussed in the biblical text, Philo does not make much use of the vocabulary he applied when interpreting in *Leg.* 1.105–108 the penalty of "dying by death," foreseen in Gen 2:17. Perhaps this should not even be expected given that the biblical terminology is now different. However, my earlier conclusion that the punitive coming together of body and soul happens to the already incarnate soul fits well in the six-stage model. Incarnation (stage 2) turns into reinarnation (4) through the mind's shunning virtue (3). Causes 8 and 9 are thus mutually compatible.

After this examination of cause no. 9 it is warranted to take a new look at what Winston writes about the earth's being the beginning and end of the wicked (*QG* 1.51), the "eternal death" awaiting those who live like Cain (*Post.* 39) coupled with the "deathless evil" and "ever dying" (*Det.* 178) and the endless series of reincarnations as the fate of the incurably wicked. What the above discussion has made clear is, I think, that we do not need to take the earth's being both the beginning and the end as a vicious circle from which there is *no* escape. It is also not mandatory to understand the death in *Post.* 39 as ever-lasting; the word ἀΐδιος has also more limited senses.[257] As for *Det.* 178, the idea seems to me to be that this world will never be free from evil.

---

[256] Cf. our brief discussion and Runia's comment on this subject above, p. 52.
[257] E.g., in Aristotle, *Politics* 1285a8 and 1317b41 kingship and magistracy, respectively, are each ἀΐδιος, held "for life" in Rackham's translation. LSJ gives these examples under the meaning 'perpetual.'

Summary of Nine Potential Causes of Incarnation in Philo

Table II (p. 81) summarizes the above discussion on what reasons for the mind's incarnation can be extracted from Philo's writings. Regarding the *original* cause of incarnation it seems that the evidence for some kind of fall in the pre-incarnate state is sparse (cause 2, inability to bear the heavenly abundance). Embodiment of souls seems to have been part of God's plan in Philo's view; causes 6 (law of necessity) and 7 (inspection of terrestrial things), which can be seen as representatives of this idea, are, furthermore, reconcilable with each other. Causes 3 (helping terrestrial things to share in better life via wisdom) and 5 (becoming akin to created things for the purpose of unhappiness) can, with some reservations, be included.

It is significant that in our examination of no less than three causes, i.e., nos. 1 (love of body), 8 (incarnation as punishment) and 9 (corporealization of the mind) it was found that the suitability as a cause of incarnation is good, but not as the original reason of incarnation. This result in itself points in the direction of reincarnation. Furthermore, these causes can easily be seen as being different aspects of the same chain of events.[258] The corporealization of the mind and the original transgression belong together and involve the desire for bodily pleasure and for mortal life; they are also related to the idea of incarnation as a punishment, both as the death of the soul and as the banishment to the body.[259] Cause 5 too can be seen to fit in, but is perhaps best understood as a combination of causes 7 and 9.

Finally, it may be noted that the combination of the original and recurrent causes found feasible above forms a coherent whole. That cause 7 is marked as "good" also in the latter column illustrates well the souls' situation: the inspection of "all the sense-perceptible and mortal things" (*Conf.* 78) should not become a permanent stay but rather remain a sojourning and lead to progressively higher spheres, ultimately God.

---

[258] As described by the six-stage model, p. 73.

[259] In other words, φιλοσώματος can be added along γεώδης/γήϊνος νοῦς as an authentic Philonic appellation for the corporealized mind. Indeed, these all appear in *Leg.* 1.31–33.

Table II. Summary of Nine Potential Causes of Incarnation in Philo.

Cause	Key passages	Suitability as the cause of incarnation	
		originally	recurrently
1. Love of body	Somn. 1.138–139, QG 1. 55	poor	good
2. Inability to bear the heavenly abundance	Her. 240	good	poor
3. Helping terrestrial things to share in better life via wisdom	QG 4.74	possible	possible
4. Numbers and periods	Plant. 14, Somn. 1.138	poor*	poor*
5. Becoming akin to created things, unhappiness	QG 4.74	possible	possible
6. Law of necessity	QG 4.74, 4.29	good	poor
7. Inspection of terrestrial things	QG 4.74, Conf. 77–79, Spec. 3.191, Somn. 1.59–60	good	good
8. Punishment	Leg. 1.107–108, 2.77, 80, 3.69, 74; Plant. 46; Congr. 56–59; Cher. 2; QG 4.234	poor	good
9. Corporealization of mind	QG 1.51, Leg. 3.252–253	poor	good

* Likely role: regulator, not cause of incarnation.

2.2 Afterlife and Salvation

2.2.1 The Fate of the Imperfect

Explicit speculation on the hereafter is not one of Philo's main concerns. Termini's statement that Philo "spiritualizes the very notions of life and death, and minimizes the importance of physical death" is valid.[260] In my view the background for this minimization lies in the view that the details of afterlife do not in themselves determine the way in which the life on earth should be lived. In his thought the orientation must in any case be away from the corporeal and towards the divine; this brings happiness, its

---

[260] Termini, "Philo's Thought," 108. For an example of this spiritualization, see Fug. 55 ("some people are dead while living, and some alive while dead"). Similarly, e.g., QG 1.70. Also the ideas of the death of the soul (above, pp. 57–64) and practising death (below, pp. 122–24) belong under this rubric.

opposite, misery. This is sufficient for Philo to be able to justify his ethical standards.

This is not, however, the entire picture, for the above does not mean that Philo had no concept of afterlife; nor does it follow that he had no view of what the misery resulting from body-oriented life leads to *post mortem*, nor that he was uninterested in these issues. But for some reason, when he expresses his thoughts of what follows the death of a "wicked" person, he usually does so quite sparingly and inexactly.

Philo's most direct descriptions of the post-mortem events will be dealt with separately in the next chapter. In addition, accounts and expressions that might be seen to be in harmony with an anti-reincarnational stance are discussed in section 2.3. What remains the task in the remainder of this section is to review some of the few passages that are found between these two poles, passages where Philo, while not being explicit, nevertheless reveals views regarding afterlife that have implications for our quest for his position on reincarnation.

One such view is that there seem to be post-mortem punishments in store for the wicked. When dwelling on the question of what was the fit penalty for the fratricide perpetrated by Cain, Philo states that killing the murderer was not the solution, for it

> is a human thought, entertained by a person who has no eyes for the great court of justice. For people think that death is the termination of punishment but in the divine court it is hardly the beginning. (*Praem.* 69)[261]

The "divine court" can be taken as the equivalent of God,[262] which makes this statement quite pregnant. Nonetheless this does not tell us what kind of sentences are passed in the hereafter. An interesting piece of relatively specific information on the afterlife of the wicked can be found in *QG*, in the exegesis of Gen 9:6, "As for the one who sheds a human's blood, in return for this blood shall he be shed."[263] Philo's answer regard-

---

[261] In *Praem.* 70–73 Philo explains Cain's punishment—living in a perpetual state of dying—literally, as if passed on a single individual, whereas in the *Allegorical Commentary* he treats Cain in this context (Gen 4:15) as a symbol of "folly" (*Det.* 178), "depravity" (*Conf.* 122) and "impiety" (*Fug.* 60); and compares him to Scylla, the "deathless evil" of *Odyssey* 12.118 (*Det., Fug.*).

[262] Perhaps self-evidently so, but see also *Virt.* 171–74 (ex. Num 15:30) where this is made explicit. *Spec.* 4.34 and *Prov.* 2.35–36 are similar.

[263] The NETS has "it" instead of "he," but Philo's version is more in keeping with the rather confused rendering in the LXX (ὁ ἐκχέων αἷμα ἀνθρώπου ἀντὶ τοῦ αἵματος αὐτοῦ ἐκχυθήσεται) of the original Hebrew ("Whoever sheds the blood of man, by man shall his blood be shed," JPS).

ing the meaning of this passage, preserved in Armenian, is, in its entirety, as follows.

> There is no error in this text but rather a sign of emphasis, for, says (Scripture), he himself shall be shed like blood who sheds blood; for that which is shed flows out and is absorbed and does not have the power of consistency.[264] And by this (Scripture) indicates that the souls of those who act impiously imitate the mortal body in being corrupted, in so far as each of them is wont to seem to suffer corruption. For the body is dissolved into those (parts) out of which it was mixed and compounded, and is again resolved into its original elements. But the cruel and wicked[265] soul is tossed about and sunken by its intemperate way of life and by the evils with which it has grown up, (which are) in a certain sense its members and grow together with it. (*QG* 2.61)

Is it possible to read the above as an elaboration of what the returning to the earth of *both* body and soul means: the former faces a dissolution to its elements, the latter is "tossed about" and "sunken"? There is no Greek fragment for *QG* 2.61. The Arm. has յածեալ (*yaceal*) for "tossed about" and հեղեղատեալ (*hełełateal*) for "sunken." Mercier translates the former in PAPM as "se roule;" the Armenian verb (յածեմ/յածիմ [*yacem/yacim*]), has senses related to, agitation, circulation and wandering. The Greek equivalents given by NBHL are partly exceedingly rare in Philo, but there are a few with a sense related to wandering and going round that are a little more frequent.[266] For հեղեղատեմ (*hełełatem*) NBHL gives κατακλύζω only.

There is similarity here to *QG* 4.234 (a passage whose verbal connection to *Agr.* 89 was referred to above).[267] The intemperateness of the soul's way of life in QG 2.61 corresponds to those who "through gluttony, lechery and over-indulgence are always submerged and sunken" in 4.234.[268] Furthermore, in the latter a verb cognate with հեղեղատեմ (*hełełatem*) appears in

---

[264] The Arm. has գոյութեան (*goyut'ean*), i.e., rather 'substance,' 'essence,' 'nature' etc. Mercier: "de sa substance;" Aucher: "vim substantiae." There is one case of known equivalence of this word in Philo, with οὐσία (the Greek frs. actually have οὐσιώδης) in *QE* 2.45 (not 1.45 as MI states).

[265] Marcus translates "labouring" but suspects that the word in the Greek original was μοχθηρός or πονηρός.

[266] Ῥέμβω (zero occurrences in Philo), καταρρεμβεύω (0), ρεμβεύω (1), ῥέμβομαι (0), πλάζομαι (πλάζω 15), περιάγομαι (περιάγω 13), ἐμπεριπατέω (14).

[267] See p. 69.

[268] In *QG* 2.61 "intemperate" is անառակ (*anařak*) for which NBHL gives ἀκόλαστος, and there is a known case (*QG* 4.204) where the word used for "lechery" in QG 4.234, ճակաճանութիւն (*čakačanut'iwn*), renders ἀκολασία. Cf. *Post.* 156 where returning to Egypt, "the refuge of a dissolute and licentious (ἀκολάστου) life" is discussed; see Appendix 1, p. 251.

a similar context. To recall, Marcus assumes the Greek for certain souls' being "submerged and sunken (ընկղմին և հեղեղին [ənkłmin ew hełełin])" in *QG* 4.234 to have featured the same verbs as appear in *Agr.* 89: "the bottom to which [the mind overcome by passions and injustices] is submerged and made to sink (καταποντοῦται καὶ καταδύεται) is nothing else than the body." There is a close thematic connection between all three passages: in all the soul that is beset by passions and other evils faces drowning—in the body in *Agr.* 89 and apparently also in *QG* 4.234.[269] Nevertheless, an exact verbal agreement between *QG* and *Agr.* is unlikely. In NBHL, both καταποντίζω and καταδύω (and others) are given for ընկղմեմ (ənkłmem), whereas κατακλύζω alone is given for հեղեղեմ (hełełem).[270] Marcus thus either assumes that καταδύω was translated with հեղեղեմ (hełełem) in *QG* 4.234 only, or, as I think is more probable, he has transposed the verbs in his retranslation into Greek to match their order in *Agr.* In this case the retranslation should be, e.g., καταδύονται καὶ κατακλύζονται.

The meaning of being made to drown *in the body* would fit also 2.61, where, as Marcus notes, "the evils which are parts of the soul somewhat as limbs are part of the body" would well qualify as the added weight that draws the soul back to earth and a new body, to express the matter in Platonic terms.[271] It is also interesting to note in *QG* 2.61 the language of corporealization in the "imitat[ion of] the mortal body."

Very similar vocabulary can be found also elsewhere. E.g., when Philo comments on the fact that Balaam dwells in Mesopotamia, he states that this means

> 'Mid-river-land,' for his understanding is submerged (καταπεποντωμένης) in the midmost depths (βυθῷ) of a river (ποταμοῦ), unable (μὴ δυναμένης) to swim its way upward (ἀνανήξασθαι) and lift its head (ἀνακῦψαι) above the surface. This condition is the rising of folly and the setting (κατάδυσις) of reasonableness. (*Conf.* 66)

There are also several connections, in both words and thought, with the explicit description of incarnation as a descent into and swimming in a

---

[269] The logic seems to be that all souls descend and that while some ascend, others remain sunken.

[270] Just like for for հեղեղատեմ (hełełatem). None of the instances of καταδύω and κατάδυσις that occur in those parts of Philo's *oeuvre* for which there is an Armenian translation has հեղեղ(ատ)եմ [hełeł(at)em] or a cognate.

[271] PLCL Suppl. 1.150, note *i*. Cf. the last sentence with *Phaedo* 81c where the corporeal has become a part of the reincarnating soul's nature (ξύμφυτον). See the quotations below, pp. 92, 123.

river in *Gig.* 13–15:²⁷² in addition to ποταμός and δύναμαι, both passages feature the verbs καταποντόω (as does *Agr.* 89 which also has βυθός) and ἀνανήχομαι. The passages in *Conf.* and *Gig.* can well be read together as pertaining to the same underlying thought, and the link to *Timaeus* 43b further points to the direction that this thought is the incarnation of the soul.²⁷³ Although the account in *QG* 2.61 of the post-mortem fate of a wicked soul is briefer than in *Conf.*, *Gig.* and the descriptions of the soul's entering the body in *QG* 4.234 and *Agr.* 89, it operates with similar vocabulary and images and additionally seems to allude to the *Phaedo*. An explicit statement that a new incarnation awaits it would fit this picture perfectly, but Philo does not say that this is what will happen to it. Nevertheless, it is my judgement that given the connections noted QG 2.61 must be added among the cumulative indirect evidence bespeaking Philo's endorsement of transmigration of souls.

2.2.2 *The Role of Monadization in Salvation*

Philo is more open regarding the afterlife of virtuous souls than that of the imperfect; the nature of the salvation of the former is much less problematic than the post-mortem fate of the latter. One aspect of salvation, however, does require some attention: is it for the *mind* only, or—as might be inferred from certain passages in Philo—can the whole soul be saved?²⁷⁴ In other words, does salvation in Philo's thought require monadization?²⁷⁵ In *QG* 4.242 Philo speaks of "that part [of the soul] which is able to be saved." Studying this matter may not be vital in the search for Philo's stance on reincarnation, but it can prove fruitful in answering the question raised above: can incomplete monadization have the same kind of effect in Philo as the contamination of the soul by the body does in the *Phaedo*, and can it thus act as a driving force of reincarnation?²⁷⁶ Furthermore, this issue has a certain relevance for one of the texts to be discussed in Ch. 30, *Cher.* 114.

---

²⁷² See p. 132 for a quotation.
²⁷³ On Philo's use of the Timaean image, see subsection 2.4.2, pp. 114–17 below.
²⁷⁴ There are passages where a bright future may seem envisaged for the entire soul: *Leg.* 3.141; *Mut.* 123–124; *Spec.* 1.300, 4.141; *Praem.* 62; *QG* 2.11. However, it is my contention that in all these the context is this-worldly. The injunction in Deut 6:5 to "love the Lord your God ... with the whole of your soul (ἐξ ὅλης τῆς ψυχῆς σου) is behind Philo's language at least in the *Spec.* and *Praem.* passages. Thus these passages do not compel us to think the entire soul is saved in Philo's thought.
²⁷⁵ I.e., a salvific transformation of the soul so that only its highest part is left. See the preliminary discussion on and the definition of monadization above, p. 40.
²⁷⁶ See above, p. 41.

When the Philonic corpus is examined from this viewpoint, it turns out that while Philo can speak of the antithetical relationship between the soul's rational and irrational parts in terms of the former's dominion over, or estrangement from, the latter, he can also use stronger language amounting to the elimination of the latter. This variation does not necessarily imply inconsistency, because monadization could be the ultimate stage of a development in which the rational part's sovereignty gradually increases. This is why this subsection focuses on the more radical expressions. I will discuss three notions: assimilation to the monad-like God, the mind's leaving the rest of the soul and its riddance from it.

As to the assimilation to God, it is a goal which Philo warmly embraces in *Fug.* 63 in his explicit quotation from *Theaetetus* 176a–b, including "we ought to fly away from earth to heaven as quickly as we can; and to fly away is to become like God (ὁμοίωσις θεῷ), as far as this is possible."[277] The qualification is not superfluous, for full assimilation seems impossible; cf. the opening sections of *Leg.* 2 in Philo's exegesis of Gen 2:18 where God says, "It is not good that the human being is alone (μόνον)." For Philo the reason is that *being alone* belongs to God (2.1): "God, being One (μόνος), is alone and unique, and like God there is nothing (οὐδὲν δὲ ὅμοιον θεῷ)." In 2.2–3 he further says, "His nature is simple, not compounded" and that "the One God is the sole standard for the 'monad.'" God is characterized in almost identical terms in *Mut.* 184: "the virtues of God must needs be unmixed since God is not compounded but a simple nature." In *Her.* 183 Philo states that God "knows no mixture or infusion and is in His singleness a monad (κατὰ τὴν μόνωσιν μονάδι ὄντι)."[278]

We are left with the problem that while the goal of the soul must be to take its becoming like the monad-like God as far as possible, perfection cannot be reached in this respect, and so we gain no exact view of how far the assimilation *is* possible.[279]

With regard to the mind's leaving the other parts of the soul we first look at this:

---

[277] Admittedly, Socrates only explains this assimilation as becoming "holy, just and wise," but this would not have prevented Philo from seeing the issue in his own way.

[278] Cf. also *Praem.* 40: God's essence is "older than the monad and simpler than the unit" (my tr. for μονάδος πρεσβύτερον καὶ ἑνὸς εἰλικρινέστερον).

[279] Philo's words that "it would not be good that the human being should be alone" (*Leg.* 2.1) should not be pressed to deny the importance of monadization, because they stem directly from the verse being interpreted. And note that in 2.4 he explains that the reason why "for the after-the-image human being (Gen 1:27) it is not good to be alone" is because "he yearns after the image."

> When the soul in all utterances and all actions has attained to perfect sincerity and godlikeness, the voices of the senses cease ... when the understanding goes out from the city of the soul and offers to God its deeds and thoughts. (*Leg.* 3.44)[280]

The leading part of the soul is said to leave the rest of it behind here, but what is Philo talking about, salvation or mystical contemplation? Let us briefly note a couple of points. *Leg.* 3.1–48 is Philo's homily on the bad person's hiding from God (Gen 3:8) and belongs to a subsection (3.39–48) which I would call a parade of prepositional soteriology centered on the preposition ἐκ and its compounds and cognates.[281] The basic thesis is stated in 3.29: "He that flees from his own mind flees for refuge to the Mind of all things" and *vice versa.* Philo states at 3.41 that "it behooves the mind ... to withdraw itself *from* (ὑπεκστῆναι) all:" the body, the senses, the faculty of speech, and "last of all, itself." The end result is described in quite salvific terms at 3.48: "[t]he good person ... returns to the apprehension of the One, thus winning a noble race and proving victor in this grandest of all contests."

The notion of the withdrawal of the mind from the body, senses, speech and, finally, itself occurs in *Migr.* and *Her.* as well. The point of departure in the former treatise is God's exhortation to Abraham in Gen 12:1: "Go forth from your country and from your kindred and from your father's house to the land that I will show you." The idea of the mind concretely exiting the soul is put forward:

> God begins the carrying out of His will to cleanse the human soul by giving it a starting-point for full salvation in the migration out of three "localities" (χωρίων), namely, body, sense-perception and speech. (*Migr.* 2)

Subsequently, however, the notion seems played down:

> The words "Depart out of these" are not equivalent to "Literally sever thyself from them," since to issue such a command as that would be to prescribe death. No, the words import "Make thyself a stranger to them in judgement and purpose; let none of them cling to thee (πρὸς μηδενὸς περισχεθεὶς αὐτῶν); rise superior to them all.(*Migr.* 7)

It should be noted that the identification of a literal interpretation with physical death in §7 means that the context is the earthly life, and thus concretely leaving the lower parts of the soul may only be possible after

---

[280] The latter part is my tr. for ὅταν ἐξελθοῦσα τὴν ψυχῆς πόλιν ἡ διάνοια θεῷ τὰς ἑαυτῆς πράξεις καὶ διανοήσεις ἀνάψῃ.
[281] 3.39–48 has 30 occurrences of these, whereas roughly equal lengths of text before (3.30–38) and after (3.49–57) contain only four and two instances, respectively. The starting point is Gen 15:5 with ἐξήγαγεν αὐτὸν ἔξω; other secondary lemmas with ἐκ follow.

death.²⁸² Later, at §192, Philo chooses another kind of image and speaks of the mind's "having divested itself (ἀποδυσάμενον) of body, sense-perception and speech." This comes after he has in §§ 190–191 described the foretaste of the salvific "migration hence" that one can experience during sleep and contemplation. To regard monadization as part of salvation in *Migr.* 2, 192 would not in my mind be far-fetched; §7 and §§ 190–191 could be seen as describing preparatory stages that can be achieved during the life in the body.

In *Her.* Philo "interviews" an understanding that has obeyed God's command in Gen 12:1:

> "I migrated from the body," she answers, "when I had ceased to regard the flesh; from sense, when I came to view all the objects of sense as having no true existence, when I denounced its standards of judgement as spurious and corrupt and steeped in false opinion, and its judgements as equipped to ensnare and deceive and ravish truth away from it place in the heart of nature; from speech, when I sentenced it to long speechlessness, in spite of all its self-exaltation and self-pride." (*Her.* 71)²⁸³

Here again the departures seem to be of the less concrete variety we saw in *Migr.* 7. To the quitting of the triad of body, senses and speech Philo again adds the task of leaving oneself (*Her.* 69, 74, 85); i.e., dedicating one's powers of thinking, purposing and apprehending to their giver, God. This can be seen as speaking against a concrete separation, although Philo nowhere specifies what he thinks God will do with this gift.

We now turn to the most tangible expressions amounting to the mind's riddance from the lower parts of the soul. In *Migr.* 200 Philo speaks of souls from which the irrational element has not yet been eliminated (ἐκτετμημέναι);²⁸⁴ they still have sense-perception's gang hanging on to them (ἐφελκόμεναι).²⁸⁵ In *Fug.* 90–92 Philo derives the exhortation to strive for what looks like monadization from Ex 32:27, where the sons of Levi are instructed, "and each one kill his brother, and each one his neighbor, and each one the one nearest to him." This means that "the soul rid itself

---

²⁸² Cf. the description of Moses's death in *Mos.* 2.288 (above, p. 40).
²⁸³ Connecting deception and sense-perception has both a biblical—Gen 3:13: "[t]he snake tricked me," i.e., the serpent (pleasure in Philonic allegory) deceived Eve (the senses)—and a Platonic model: cf. *Phaedo* 83a, "the eyes and the ears and the other senses are full of deceit (ἀπάτη)" wherefore philosophy "urg[es the soul] to withdraw (ἀναχωρεῖν) from these." See also *Abr.* 88: "the mind did not remain forever deceived (ἀπατηθείς) nor stand rooted (ἔστη) in the realm of sense-perception."
²⁸⁴ A reading adopted by Wendland for MSS. δὲ κεκτημέναι; one MS. also has τὸν λόγον instead of τὸ ἄλογον. These make no sense.
²⁸⁵ A probable allusion to *Phaedo* 65e where Socrates says that none of the senses should be "dragged along" (verb ἐφέλκω) with thinking to disturb one's reason.

(ἀποβαλούσης) as I have said, of that neighbor of our rational element, the irrational" and "the intellect sever and banish from itself (διοικίσαντος καὶ διαζεύξαντος) ... the word of utterance." Philo describes the purpose of this:

> All this is to the end that reason may be left alone, destitute (ἔρημος) of body, destitute of sense-perception, destitute of utterance in audible speech; for when it has been thus left, it will live a life in harmony with such solitude, and will render, with nothing to mar or to disturb it, its glad homage to the Sole Existence. (*Fug.* 92)

The parallel exegesis in *Ebr.* 70 presents the same interpretation: "We shall dissever (διαζεύξομεν) the passion-loving and mortal element from the virtue-loving and divine."

In *Leg.* 3.127–140, commenting on Lev 8:29 ("Moses took the breast"), Philo uses verbs we already encountered in *Migr.* 200 and *Ebr.* 69. Importantly, he now makes a distinction between Aaron and Moses in that the former is only able to *control*, with reason, the spirited element of the soul (θυμός located in the breast), whereas the latter is able to "cut off" (ἐκτέμνω, ἀποκόπτω), "remove" (ἀφαιρέω) it (or the passions) entirely.[286] Cf. also, e.g., *Cher.* 31 and *Praem.* 26 where similar language appears.

To conclude: Philo uses variable language about phenomena which point to the direction of monadization. It cannot be established with certainty if the definition of monadization (a salvific event, the human soul's becoming pure mind through dismissal of its other constituent parts) is fulfilled. But if we take another angle and look at the end of the journey of the soul, salvation as the incorporeal life with God, if it is Philo's view that the lower parts of the soul still survive, they are surely of little or no consequence. Yet this in itself does not enable us to answer the question of whether incomplete monadization could act as a driving force of reincarnation. But if we loosen our criteria and look more broadly at the

---

[286] There are a total of thirteen occurrences of these three verbs in *Leg.* 3.128–140. Ismo Dunderberg, "Judas' Anger and the Perfect Human Being," in *The Codex Judas Papers. Proceedings of the International Congress on the Tchacos Codex Held at Rice University, Houston, Texas, March 13–16, 2008*, ed. April D. DeConick; NHMS 71 (Leiden: Brill, 2009), 201–21 on p. 210 contrasts this elimination with Plato's psychology, where "the irascible element (θυμικόν) was a *necessary* part" (emphasis original) of the soul. But in Plato and Philo alike the soul's lower parts are mortal (see above, p. 36) and thus not necessary in the ultimate sense. Cf. 4 Macc where one of the favorite ideas is that "pious reason is absolute master of the passions" (1:1). But the human "passions and habits" were planted in us by God (2:21), and so "no one of you can eradicate anger from the soul" (3:2); "reason is not an uprooter of the passions but their antagonist" (3:5). But here no identification is made between the passions and the passionate part of the soul.

importance of the mind's absolute rulership over the other parts of the person, the answer should be given in the affirmative.

2.2.3 *The Driving Forces of Reincarnation and the Prerequisites of Salvation in Plato: A Comparison with Philo*

The existence of *driving forces of reincarnation* is here regarded as the second essential characteristic of reincarnational belief systems.[287] In other words: what is it that makes souls reincarnate? These forces also determine *the prerequisites of salvation*, i.e., the preconditions for the process to come to an end. Keller distinguishes between three regulators of rebirth: (1) karma, the doctrine of action and consequence: the debt incurred by one's undesirable actions must be paid off; (2) the individual's attitude towards a precise body of doctrines; (3) progress towards divine perfection.[288] I would like to add two further criteria, (4) the attainment of certain esoteric knowledge or wisdom and (5) divine grace.

Karma is not confined to Indian religions, and the idea itself is simple and by no means entails reincarnation. It is present in Greek philosophy, Judaism, and early Christianity, e.g., in the metaphor of reaping what one has sown.[289] Grace is at the other end of the spectrum, for it entails the idea that other criteria need *not* be entirely fulfilled. The intervening three criteria are less clearly distinguishable from each other; depending on the definition of perfection, (2) and (4) could also be seen as elements of (3).

This subsection focuses on a comparison between Plato and Philo in the context of the former's descriptions of reincarnation.[290] The rationale is that we have Plato's driving forces for reincarnation on a plate, which may offer us a convenient short-cut to find the trail of Philo's: First, a brief review of Plato is carried out in order to see what his prerequisites of salvation and driving forces of reincarnation (both called *factors* below) are. Subsequently, Philo and Plato are compared in order to find out what Philo has to say about these factors.

---

[287] See p. 6. The first one, the pre- and post-existence of the soul was discussed above in subsection 2.1.2 (p. 31–36).
[288] Keller, "La réincarnation," 28–33.
[289] E.g., Plato, *Phaedrus* 260c–d, *Republic* 615a; Aristotle, *Rhetorica* 1406b10; Prov 22:8, Job 4:7–8; Gal 6:7–9.
[290] The comparison largely ignores Platonist interpretations which may have influenced Philo. The question is neither uninteresting nor unimportant, but it is not crucial for the present study given the scoping of the research task (see 1.2.2).

Plato

Of all the dialogues that mention reincarnation the *Timaeus* (esp. 41e–42c, 90b–92c) and the *Phaedo* (esp. 80e–83e, 107c, 113d–114c) stand out as containing the most explicit accounts of the reasons why souls have to be reborn and of what they should do in order to free themselves. In the *Timaeus* Plato describes how, after being implanted in a body, the soul becomes subject to

> (T1) firstly, sensation that is innate and common to all proceeding from violent affections; secondly, desire mingled with pleasure and pain; and besides these, fear and anger and all such (emotions) as are naturally allied thereto, and all such as are of a different and opposite character. And if they shall master these they will live justly, but if they are mastered, unjustly. (*Tim.* 42a–b)

Just life, then, consists of mastering the passions, pleasures and pains. Plato continues by explicating how this mastering conditions the process of reincarnation:

> (T2) And he that has lived his appointed time well shall return again to his abode in his native star, and shall gain a life that is blessed and congenial; but whoso has failed therein shall be changed into woman's nature at the second birth; and if, in that shape, he still refraineth not from wickedness he shall be changed every time, according to the nature of his wickedness, into some bestial form after the similitude of his own nature. (*Tim.* 42b–c)

Here living "well" clearly continues the idea of living "justly" (mastering one's affections) as the prerequisite of salvation.[291] Plato then describes how a soul can get out of the cycle of rebirth in which it is subject to continual change:

> (T3) nor in his changings shall he cease from woes until he yields himself to the revolution of the Same and Similar that is within him, and dominating by force of reason that burdensome mass which afterwards adhered to him of fire and water and earth and air, a mass tumultuous and irrational, returns again to the semblance of his first and best state. (*Tim.* 42c–d)

The "revolution of the Same and Similar" can, in a simplified way, be understood as the rational principle within the soul, and it is precisely that capability that must be used for controlling both the passions and the

---

[291] The equivalence of the two adverbs is explicit in *Crito* 48b. Similarly *Republic* 618e.

body.²⁹² We have thus come full circle, back to the root cause of the affections and injustices: life in the body.

In *Tim.* 90e–92b Plato lists the negative qualities of men which cause them to be born in what he regards as lower forms of life (women and animals): cowardice, life unjustly lived, lightmindedness, vain trust in physical sight, neglecting philosophy and the inspection of the heavenly nature caused by following the wrong part of the soul, thoughtlessness, stupidity, impurity, error, ignorance. The whole dialogue ends in a summary of what determines souls' direction in their transmigration towards either deeper rootedness in reincarnation or freedom from it :

> (T4) Thus, both then and now, living creatures keep passing into one another in all these ways, as they undergo transformation by the loss or by the gain of reason and unreason (νοῦ καὶ ἀνοίας). (*Tim.* 92b–c)

In the *Phaedo* the setting is different, Socrates, Cebes and Simmias's conversation about the immortality of the soul. There are, nevertheless, many features in common with the *Timaeus*. The most relevant section (80e–83e) is too long to quote in full, but a few representative samples may be offered. Socrates characterizes the reincarnating soul:

> (Ph1) when it departs from the body it is defiled and impure, because it was always with the body and cared for it and loved it and was fascinated by it and its desires and pleasures, so that it thought nothing was true except the corporeal, which one can touch and see and drink and eat and employ in the pleasures of love. (*Phaedo* 81b)

The corporeal here refers to the objects of sense and pleasure. The soul's yearning after them is connected with its aversion to everything intellectual and philosophical (81b). The impure soul

> (Ph2) is weighed down by [the corporeal] and is dragged back into the visible world ... [and as regards such souls,] through the desire of the corporeal which clings to them they are again bound to a body. (*Phaedo* 81c, e)

The preconditions of salvation are described as follows:

> (Ph3) And no one who has not been a philosopher and who is not wholly pure when he departs, is allowed to enter into the communion of the gods, but only the lover of knowledge. It is for this reason, dear Simmias and Cebes, that those who philosophize correctly refrain from all bodily desires

---

²⁹² For Philo's use of both the heavenly revolutions and the circuits of the mind of the *Timaeus*, see Runia, *Philo and the* Timaeus, 208–15, 276–78. Philo recycles part of the vocabulary of *Tim.* 42b–c in a passage that has also thematic links to it, *Virt.* 205; see Yli-Karjanmaa, "Philo of Alexandria," in *A Companion to the Reception of Plato in Antiquity*, ed. Harold Tarrant et al. (Leiden: Brill, forthcoming).

and resist them firmly and do not give themselves up to them. (*Phaedo* 82b–c)

Perhaps the most central concept here is *purity*; as seen above, the gist of the argument is that willing association with the body contaminates the soul and thereby leads to the latter's re-imprisonment. Only the philosopher realizes that

> (Ph4) the most dreadful thing about the imprisonment is the fact that it is caused by the lusts, so that the prisoner is the chief assistant in his own imprisonment. (*Phaedo* 82e)

The situation is subsequently summed up and the connection between immortality and reincarnation pointed out as follows:

> (Ph5) For if death were an escape from everything, it would be a boon to the wicked, for when they die they would be freed from the body and from their wickedness together with their souls. But now, since the soul is seen to be immortal, there is no other escape from evil, or salvation, for it than becoming as good and wise as possible. (*Phaedo* 107c–d)

The last notion is in much the same vein as living well or justly in the *Timaeus*. Another term Plato uses similarly is *pious* (ὅσιος) in 113d and 114b. Cf. also *Meno*:

> They say that the soul of man is immortal, and at one time comes to an end, which is called dying, and at another is born again (πάλιν γίγνεσθαι), but never perishes. Consequently one ought to live all one's life in the utmost holiness. (81b)

The apex of this good, wise, just and pious living is exemplified by those "who have duly purified themselves by philosophy:" they are granted permanent freedom from the body (*Phaedo* 114c), i.e., from reincarnation.

The *Phaedrus* contains comparatively little on factors that maintain reincarnation. In what little there is, distinctive of this dialogue are the role of memory and the soul's weight: that souls fall to the earth from the heavenly chariot race has to do with forgetfulness and becoming heavy (248c). Conversely, lightness leads to liberation (249b), and the philosopher is in communion with things divine through memory (249c). In a statement reminiscent of several of our quotations from the *Timaeus* above, Plato mentions the different types of lives (those of a philosopher, king, politician, gymnast, etc.) that reincarnating souls will face, and states:

> (Phdr1) Now in all these states, whoever lives justly obtains a better lot, and whoever lives unjustly, a worse. For each soul returns to the place whence it came in ten thousand years, (*Phaedrus* 248e)

for the soul's wings do not grow back before that time has elapsed—excepting

> (Phdr2) the soul of him who has been a guileless philosopher or a philosophical lover (of boys). (*Phaedrus* 249a)

Thus in both the *Phaedrus* and the *Phaedo* (Ph3) philosophy plays a role, undoubtedly very similar to that of reason in the *Timaeus* (T3).

Plato also does not say much in the *Republic*. There is a reference to the "inevitable evil caused by sin in a former life (ἐκ προτέρας ἁμαρτίας)" in 613e. In addition, in the myth of Er's visit to the hereafter (614b–621b) there is a mention that the post-mortem division of souls into those that go under the earth and those that go up to heaven (between lives) is based on whether they have been just or unjust (614c). Socrates's brief concluding statement about how permanent salvation may be achieved reflects ideas already encountered in especially the *Timaeus* and the *Phaedo*: The tale by Er

> will save us if we believe it, and we shall safely cross the River of Lethe, and keep our soul unspotted from the world... . [A]nd so we shall hold ever to the upward way and pursue righteousness with wisdom always and ever, that we may be dear to ourselves and to the gods both during our sojourn here and when we receive our reward. (*Rep.* 621c)

Finally, the *Laws* presents what might be called an extremely literal case of having to reap what one has sown. The subject is murder:

> Concerning all these matters, the preludes mentioned shall be pronounced, and, in addition to them, that story which is believed by many when they hear it from the lips of those who seriously relate such things at their mystic rites, that vengeance for such acts is exacted in Hades, and that those who return again to this earth are bound to pay the natural penalty—each culprit the same, that is, which he inflicted on his victim—and that their life on earth must end in their meeting a like fate at the hands of another. (*Laws* 870d–e)

To sum up the main features of the quotations above I have drawn up the following simplified diagram about the factors in Plato's thought which determine whether a soul will remain in the cycle of reincarnation or be liberated from it. The main areas concern the *orientation* of the soul, its *state* and its relation to exercising its *rational faculties*.

THE INDIRECT EVIDENCE

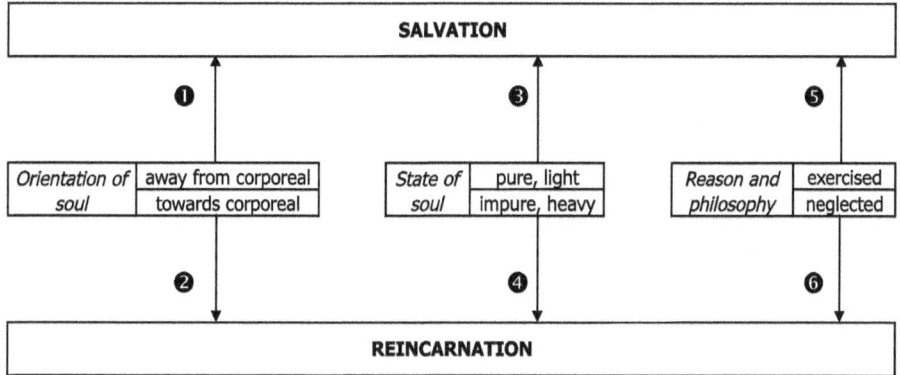

Figure 1. Aggregated Factors Leading the Soul to Reach Salvation or to Reincarnate in Plato.[293]

Philo

In what follows I will deal with what Philo says about those factors we saw to be Plato's central prerequisites of salvation and driving forces of reincarnation. In particular the *states* these factors lead the soul into will be examined.

Mastering the Passions, Senses and Body by Reason, Philosophy and Wisdom

There is a large body of passages that could be cited here. For the present purpose I have attempted to choose examples that exhibit language and ideas that are as close to Plato as possible. We start with *QE* 2.51, where Philo states that in order to be able to *see God*, which is the "great benefaction" granted to the "*rational* race," the mind has to prepare itself by "excising desires, pleasures, griefs, fears, follies, injustices and related evils." In Philo the notion that this salvific struggle should be led by *reason* (here only implied but see, e.g., *Leg.* 3.137, *Migr.* 67, *Virt.* 113) follows directly from the fact that all of life should consist of following its voice, which tells the difference between good and evil (*Congr.* 81, *Somn.* 1.110–111, *Abr.* 256). This belongs intimately together with one of the most central themes of Philo's whole *oeuvre*, his insistence on the necessity that

---

[293] Interactions *between* the factors in the middle part are omitted for clarity. In the orientation section, the "corporeal" stands for the body, the senses and sense objects as well as the soul's affections (passions, desires and pleasures). Reason and philosophy accommodate wisdom. Living well, justly, piously etc. is not shown separately; these may be thought of as top-level terms that cover all the various factors that lead to salvation.

the divinely rational highest part of the soul should always be in charge and keep the lower parts under control.[294]

In *Post.* 101 Philo brings in philosophy, saying it is the *road to God* to be followed by those who are willing to reject "the soft enchantments of pleasure" in their "study of what is good and fair." In *Gig.* 13–14 and *Plant.* 24–25 correct philosophy, together with practising death (i.e., dying to the bodily life) is presented as the prerequisite for a whole set of salvific events or states: the soul's liberation from the body, its *returning to where it came from, immortality* (so also *Opif.* 77) and *inheriting God.* [295]

Philo makes no consistent distinction between philosophy and wisdom. Sometimes he outright identifies them (*Ebr.* 49), while at other times he presents philosophy as the instrument for attaining wisdom (*Congr.* 79). Wisdom (σοφία or φρόνησις)[296] is a means to salvation very much in the same way as philosophy: it leads to overcoming the passions (*Leg.* 3.131, *Spec.* 2.147), *controlling the body* (*QG* 4.75), inheriting God (*Sobr.* 56–58) and immortality (*Fug.* 97, *QG* 4.46, *QE* 1.15). The relationship between philosophy/wisdom and purity is not clearly causal in one way as in *Phaedo* 114c.[297] These factors simply belong together in a way that is usually not analyzed (e.g., *Leg.* 1.77, *Deus* 22, *Ebr.* 100–103, *Congr.* 132, *Mut.* 208–209, *Decal.* 58). In some passages purity is the precondition (*Cher.* 49–50, *Prob.* 3–4), in some, rather, the result (*Mut.* 124, *Abr.* 100, *Spec.* 1.269, 2.147). The opposite of wisdom is folly (ἀφροσύνη; see *Somn.* 2.198) which brings the soul to ruin, yokes it to the passions (*Leg.* 3.193) et cetera.

---

[294] Cf. subsections 2.1.3 and 2.2.2 above. As Runia, *Philo and the* Timaeus, 265 puts it, the mind "can incline to either virtue or vice, depending on how [it] reacts to the assaults of sense-perception and the pernicious influences of the passions (*Leg.* 2.53, 64). This moral contest is precisely parallel to what Plato envisages at [*Timaeus*] 42b2" (the mastering or being mastered in quotation T1 above).

[295] The same combination is attested in *Phaedo* 64a, 67e, 80e–81a. The goals served by philosophy are thus in agreement in Plato and Philo. More on practising death below (2.4.6, p. 122).

[296] In *Praem.* 81 Philo relates σοφία to "the service of God" and φρόνησις to "the regulation of human life," but from our present perspective the difference is not crucial; both are conducive to the orientation towards the incorporeal. In *Fug.* 194–195 they are treated as equivalents.

[297] See above, p. 93.

Purity

In his exegesis of Deut 10:9 (God will be the allotment of the tribe of Levi) Philo connects the rejection of earthly things and reaching God with purity:

> for in reality the mind, which has been perfectly cleansed and purified, and which renounces all things pertaining to creation, is acquainted with One alone, and knows but One, even the Uncreate, to Whom it has drawn nigh, by Whom also it has been taken to Himself. (*Plant.* 64)

Purity leads to the soul's meeting with God also through its *becoming a house of God* in *Sobr.* 62 and *Cher.* 98–107. Other benefits of purity with more or less direct implications for salvation include immortality (*Her.* 239) and shedding the irrational parts of the soul (*Migr.* 67). Purification leads the soul to meet God also in *Somn.* 1.147–148, where Philo says that God himself "walks in the understandings of those who have been purified to the utmost" whereas angels come to "the soul which is still borne along in the body as in a river," i.e., to "those who are still undergoing cleansing and have not yet fully washed their life defiled and stained by the body's weight"—a combination of Plato's reincarnational images from the *Timaeus*, the *Phaedo* and the *Phaedrus*.[298]

An example of how Philo connects purity with overcoming bodily passions is found in *Her.* where he tells us who it is that is entitled to inherit the divine and immaterial things:

> the recipient of inspiration from above, of a portion heavenly and divine, the wholly purified mind which disregards not only the body, but that other section of the soul which is devoid of reason and steeped in blood, aflame with seething passions and burning lusts. (*Her.* 64)

Philo mentions the overcoming of passions as a result of purity also in, e.g., *Cher.* 95, *Abr.* 223 and *Spec.* 1.259–260. Other consequences include *freedom from sense objects and earthly things* (*Her.* 185), *rising to heaven* (*Her.* 239), elimination of bad thoughts (*Ebr.* 28, *Mut.* 239–240) and receiving hidden knowledge (*QG* 4.35). *QG* 4.195 mentions that the purified soul is drawn away from the customary lures towards knowledge and toil whereby it can stop its "going about in a low-lying place." An interesting passage is *QE* 2.45 where Philo says that "not even the purest understanding"[299] can ascend to

---

[298] The river image is from *Timaeus* 43a; for the latter quotation cf. extracts Ph1–2 above (p. 92) and *Phaedrus* 248c, where, however, it is the soul that is heavy (see below, 2.4.7). Cf. Wis 9:15: "For a corruptible body burdens the soul."

[299] So (καθαρωτάτης) in the Greek fragment; Marcus translates the Armenian սրբագոյն (*srbagoyn*) accurately as "holiest."

God. I take this to be a reference to *God's salvific grace*. We have already seen God's decisive role in freeing the soul from the prison of the body in *Leg.* 3.42.³⁰⁰ *Ebr.* 145 echoes the same thought: "For without divine grace it is impossible either to leave the mortal things, or to stay for ever among those immortal." Cf. also Philo's interpretation of God's words in Ex 3:6 ("I will be with thee"):

> [B]ut the seeking of God, best of all existencies, incomparable Cause of all things, gladdens us the moment we begin our search, and never turns out fruitless, since by reason of His gracious nature He comes to meet us with His pure and virgin graces, and shews Himself to those who yearn to see Him. (*Fug.* 141)³⁰¹

The notion of God's decisive role in salvation occurs decidedly less often in Plato, but it is not entirely absent. In *Phaedo* 67a Socrates says that all unnecessary dealings with the body are to be avoided "until God himself sets us free (ἀπολύσῃ)."

Summary of the Common Features

The examination performed shows that although the details vary, all the relationships present in Plato are also found in Philo.³⁰² Everything Plato says about the reasons why souls must be repeatedly incarnated and the means they can employ to avoid this is also found in Philo in reference to either going away from or progressing towards salvation. This in itself is a highly significant fact which in our context of investigating the evidence for and against Philo's accepting the idea of reincarnation would certainly be seen as reasonable grounds for initiating "prosecution" in the case.³⁰³

---

³⁰⁰ See p. 61.
³⁰¹ Similarly *Abr.* 79: "when the soul came into His presence, [God] did not turn away His face, but came forward to meet him and revealed His nature, so far as the beholder's power of sight allowed." See also, e.g., *Leg.* 2.104; *Post.* 43, 154; *Ebr.* 145; *Migr.* 25, 124; *Her.* 60, 273; *Somn.* 1.152; *QG* 4.47. In *QG* 2.12 God's grace seems to be the lot of one enjoying sensual pleasure; however, this seems more like God giving the soul a good *start* on the road to salvation; cf. *Deus* 76. That salvation may come unexpected (*Migr.* 25) or without supplication (*Her.* 186) is not in contradiction with its being granted only to those already making progress, neither is the fact that ultimately everything is God's grace, including the soul's very existence (*Deus* 107, *Her.* 58, *Mut.* 222). Philo also points out that although it is easy for God to give, it is not necessarily possible for humans to receive (*Mut.* 218).
³⁰² See Figure 1 on p. 95.
³⁰³ Fortunately, our "trial" will not require any such weighing of partial evidence, not to mention any judgemental valuation of Philo's views. Instead, we continue the search for all relevant information and will arrive at our "verdict" in due course.

Tables III and IV list examples of appropriate passages in both authors and specify the *effects* of the factors in Philo. The first table deals with the means of achieving salvation, the second with the reasons for failing to reach it.

Table III. Passages in Plato and Philo Illustrating the **Salvific** Relationships in Figure 1 (p. 95) and the Resulting States in Philo.

Relationship	Plato	Philo passages; resulting effects
1 INCORPORE-ITY → SALVATION	T1–T3, Ph3	*Leg.* 3.137, *Migr.* 2, *Ebr.* 69–72: salvation *Gig.* 14, *Somn.* 1.139, *QG* 2.69: incorporeal life *Mut.* 81–82, *QE* 2.51: seeing God *Post.* 101, *Plant.* 64: reaching God *Gig.* 13–14: return to starting point, immortality, inheriting God *Her.* 64: inheriting divine things
3 PURITY + LIGHTNESS → SALVATION	Ph3, *Phaedo* 114c	*Cher.* 98–107, *Plant.* 64, *Sobr.* 62, *Somn.* 1.147–148: reaching God *Her.* 64: inheriting divine things *Her.* 239: immortality *QG* 4.46: elevation to wisdom, salvation through changing the mortal life to immortal *QG* 4.195: being drawn away from the customary and raised to the greatness of virtue
5 REASON + PHILOSOPHY → SALVATION	T3, *Tim.* 92c, Ph3, Ph5, *Phaedo* 114c, Phdr2	*Leg.* 3.153–159: "Passover" from the passions, endurance, self-mastery *Gig.* 13–14: incorporeal life, return to starting point, immortality, inheriting God *Post.* 101: reaching God *Plant.* 24–25: being borne upward, becoming enamoured of happy natures that dwell on high

Table IV. Passages in Plato and Philo Illustrating the *Anti-Salvific* Relationships in Figure 1 and the Resulting States in Philo.

Relationship	Plato	Philo passages; resulting effects
2 CORPOREAL-ITY → NO SALVATION	T1–T3, Ph1–Ph2, Ph4	*Opif.* 152: exchanging immortality and happiness for mortality and misfortune *Leg.* 1.105–108, 2.77; *Det.* 70; *Agr.* 98; *Fug.* 113; *Mut.* 96; *QG* 4.46, 51, 152 etc.: *death of the soul*: becoming entombed in passions and wickedness (+ coming together of body and soul as a punishment in *Leg.* 1) *Leg.* 3.47: inability to search God *Migr.* 152–155: going circle-wise for a long time, delay in escape from the body *Somn.* 1.138–139: returning after death to the mortal life *Gig.* 15: "sinking beneath the stream" in the body–river *QG* 4.111: being "altogether kept back and shut in, planted and rooted in the earth with heads bent down"
4 IMPURITY + HEAVINESS → NO SALVATION	*Tim.* 92b, Ph1–Ph2	*Opif.* 158: being thrown down and tripped up *Cher.* 52: birth of the inner Cain[304] *Det.* 167–169: punishment (ever dying, §178) *Gig.* 31: inability to look at the revolving heavens, having the neck pulled down and standing rooted to the earth *Somn.* 1.147: continuing to be "borne along in the body as in a river" *Spec.* 4.114: being pulled down, strangled and overwhelmed with fleshly elements *QG* 2.57: impure passions threaten the soul with death *QG* 3.52: inability to be saved *QG* 4.195: going about in a low-lying place
6 NEGLECT OF REASON + PHILOSOPHY → NO SALVATION	T1+T3, *Tim.* 91e, *Phaedo* 81b, Ph3	*Leg.* 3.193: becoming yoked to the passions *Cher.* 10: expulsion from virtues with no chance of return *Gig.* 15: "sinking beneath the stream" in the body–river *Post.* 73: death of the soul *Somn.* 2.198: being forced down from the height and ruined to the uttermost extremes

It is clear that not all of the beneficial effects in Table III necessarily mean final and full salvation, i.e., permanent incorporeal life with God. Instead, steps towards it are also represented. However, distinguishing between these alternatives is not necessary, since our interest is primarily directed at the relationships in Table IV and the question, *What are the effects of the Platonic causes of reincarnation in Philo?* If Philo endorsed the doctrine, the

---

[304] Earp summarizes Philo's Cain symbolism in PLCL 10.295–96 (where references to passages can be found): Cain symbolizes, *inter alia*, "the self-loving principle," being "occupied with the lower, mortal, earthly level of life" and "dead to the life directed by virtue." In *Det.* 70 Cain is connected with the death of the soul.

answer is easy to give, assuming that the authors see the driving forces similarly. If he did not, then strictly speaking the question falls outside the scope of this study whose purpose is to find out Philo's position on the tenet. As we have already seen in our examination of the indirect evidence, several items in the *effects* column of Table IV are reconcilable with reincarnation. Many others are discussed below; the response will, however, need to wait until we have the results of Chapter 3.

2.3 *Does Philo Rule Out Reincarnation?*

This section continues the exploration of whether the necessary prerequisites exist in Philo's thinking for him to have adopted the idea that souls reincarnate. The focus is now on statements that might be thought to preclude reincarnation. Nowhere does Philo explicitly state that each soul incarnates only once; hence we are dealing with *indirect* evidence. Yet he presents certain ideas which may imply this, and these need to be examined given the opinion of several scholars that the hints at reincarnation found in Philo represent something the Alexandrian did not in his heart endorse or mean.[305]

2.3.1 *Pre-existence of the Soul Questioned?*

As seen above, Philo's belief in the pre-existence of the soul has been doubted on the basis of the following passage:[306]

> Whence came the soul, whither will it go, how long will it be our mate and comrade? Can we tell its essential nature? Did we at some time acquire it as our own?[307] Before birth? But then there was no "ourselves" (ἀλλ' οὐχ ὑπήρχομεν). (*Cher.* 114)

Philo is clearly denying "our" existence before birth here, but what exactly does he mean? This passage was already briefly dealt with and the conclusion was reached that it cannot be used for denying the pre-existence of the soul in Philo's thought.[308] But let us delve in the matter a little deeper. From whose viewpoint is Philo talking here? He separates himself from the soul in asking if it was given as a possession, and in §115 too he talks about its knowing and leaving "us." But he does not identify himself with the

---

[305] See 1.4 above.
[306] See above, p. 33 for Runia's view.
[307] The translation is Colson's with the exception of this sentence, ποτὲ δὲ καὶ ἐκτησάμεθα αὐτήν; for which see below, n. 488 on p. 153.
[308] Above, p. 33.

body, either, as just before the quotation he asks, "[w]here was my body before birth and whither will it go when the soul has departed (μεταστάντος <ψυχῆς>)?"³⁰⁹ This question is preceded by an anthropological statement (§113): "I am formed of soul and body, I seem to have mind, faculty of speech, sense, yet I find that none of them is really mine."³¹⁰

It is difficult to make a consistent whole out of all this, in particular because it is unclear who or what the "I" of the text is. It is neither soul or body, and it cannot be the leading part of the soul, mind (ὁ νοῦς), either, as the Philonic mind would never say, "the soul knows us, though we know it not" (§115). Nor is it credible that some undefined internal observer within the human being occurs only here. Looking at the matter from a viewpoint of rhetoric may shed more light on it. The section *Cher.* 113–119 is concerned with reiterating the point, first introduced at §57, that nothing in the universe is ours, that everything is just a loan from God, the real owner of all that exists. The section can be further divided into five subsections: Philo uses the first person plural in the first (§113), third (§§ 114–115) and fifth (§§ 117–118), the first person singular in the second (§§ 113–114) and fourth (§§ 116–117); §119 has neither.

Much of §§ 114–117 consists of elaborating the anthropological statement of §113: body, soul, mind, speech and sense perception are each mentioned again. All the others are dealt with by Philo as being "mine" (§§ 114, 116–117), but the soul is "ours" (§§ 114–115). My impression is that the soul is what Philo identifies himself the most with: he speaks of the body, mind, speech and senses as if from the soul's viewpoint, but at §§ 114–115 he does not seem to want to conduct the discussion along the lines, "Let me discuss my soul;" instead, he switches to a collective mood, "Let us discuss our souls." In §115 Philo says the soul will leave us at death and we cannot stop it as it "affords no grip or handle to the body;" instead, "when it will, it will ... depart." This represents the viewpoint of those who are left behind at death: of the body and of "us" others. This is how we typically witness death: there is nothing we can do about it, "press ... as we may." This analysis reinforces the earlier conclusion that the phrase "there was no 'ourselves'" does not amount to denying the pre-existence of the soul.³¹¹

---

³⁰⁹ For the grounds of my conjecture here, see below, n. 490 and text on p. 154.
³¹⁰ Colson "reason" instead of "faculty of speech"—inconsistently, for when Philo in the sequel (§§ 116–117) again goes through νοῦς λόγος αἴσθησις he adds τὰ φωνῆς ὄργανα to the middle term; Colson then translates λόγος as "utterance."
³¹¹ As already noted (n. 120 on p. 33), Philo seemingly also denies its post-existence with his "we ... shall be no more"—and yet "we" subsequently rush to regeneration. *Cher.* 114 is the subject of a detailed analysis in section 3.2.

Philo continues the train of thought of *Cher.* 113–119—nothing in the universe is ours—with this puzzling statement:

> For each of us has come into this world as into a foreign city, in whose affairs he had no share before birth (πρὸ γενέσεως), and having arrived he sojourns (παροικεῖ) [here] until he has exhausted the appointed span of life. (*Cher.* 120)[312]

In this explanation of Lev 25:23 ("the land is mine, because before me you are guests and resident aliens (προσήλυτοι καὶ πάροικοι)") Philo compares the universe to a city. He continues by emphasizing that God is its only citizen: the wise are sojourners, while the fools are mere outcasts (§121). The adverbial "before birth" is part of the city metaphor, but whereas the concepts of city, citizen, sojourner and outcast all readily have a counterpart (i.e., world, God, sage and fool, respectively), "before birth" is both hard to fit in the metaphor and difficult to interpret. After all, how *could* one participate in the affairs of a city before one is born?[313]

The most likely option is that Philo is being inaccurate. It is reasonable enough to assume he simply meant to include "before" in the city metaphor which would then turn into "before birth" in the interpretation: just like a sojourner has had nothing to do with the affairs of a foreign city before entering it, we have had no part in the affairs of this world before birth. If this is accepted, does the statement preclude the idea of reincarnation? It does not, because in this metaphor God is the only citizen in any case, i.e. the only one managing the city's affairs: no soul *can* have participated in "politics" regardless of any temporal considerations. This in fact makes the reference to previous absence superfluous; the rank of sojourner alone is decisive. What the notion of absence seems to stem from is revealed by the words Philo uses, "alien" (lit. 'incomer': ἐπηλύτης < ἐπέρχομαι) and "sojourner" (πάροικος)—cf. the προσήλυτοι καὶ πάροικοι of the LXX. The words themselves carry the connotation of entrance and, by implication, of prior absence. The inclusion of "before birth" is thus probably an adaptation to the terminology of the metaphor, derived from the Leviticus passage: we *enter* the world, and that we do from the state in which we were before we were born.

---

[312] Colson's translation has been modified somewhat to make it more literal. The word "foreign" (ξένην) is Cohn's conjecture; the MSS. have κενήν, καινήν. The latter could be correct but this does not affect the sense.

[313] Except in a previous incarnation. This does not seem a relevant alternative, however, for it would require that Philo is making a distinction between cities in which one has lived as a citizen in an earlier life and those where one has not.

A different kind of statement meets us in *Spec.* 3.84. Philo comments on the death penalty to be passed on murderers (Gen 9:6, Ex 21:12 and elsewhere). Although there are some textual problems, the thought seems to be that those who take another's life deserve "myriads" of deaths themselves, *although only one is possible.*[314] Here again, an anti-reincarnational interpretation is not convincing, since the fact that Philo does not consider a plurality of *death penalties* for a single person possible does not mean that he must also have thought that there can be no plurality of *lives*, either. In Plato, in fact, we have a very similar statement, just before one of his references to reincarnation.[315] Yet it is undeniable that were reincarnation for Philo a doctrine to be openly discussed, this would have been an apposite context to state that the consequences of one's evil actions may extend to next lives as well.[316]

When explaining the commandment to honor one's parents Philo repeats several times the idea that parents in having children bring into existence something that was previously non-existent. *Prima facie* the interpretation mentioned above—that the individual person is the combination of body and soul and therefore does not exist before birth—could apply here, but the passages must first be examined closely. They are *Decal.* 111 and *Spec.* 2.2, 225, 229, 243 and 248.

The central terminology is contained in the expressions, used of the parents, "those who bring from non-existence to existence (οἱ ἐκ τοῦ μὴ ὄντος εἰς τὸ εἶναι παραγαγόντες)" and "the causes of life (οἱ τοῦ ζῆν αἴτιοι)." The first one is not used by other authors before Philo, but he himself uses a similar wording about God in, e.g., *Mos.* 2.100 "He brought into being what was not (τὰ μὴ ὄντα ἤγαγεν εἰς τὸ εἶναι)."[317] The second expression is

---

[314] For the textual problems, see PLCL 7.528–29, 635. For the thought, cf. *Spec.* 3.90, where the same idea is reiterated.

[315] *Laws* 869b: "so that if 'to die a hundred deaths' (πολλάκις ἀποθνῄσκειν) were possible for any one man, that a patricide or a matricide, who did the deed in rage, should undergo a hundred deaths (θανάτων πολλῶν) would be a fate most just." What *is* held possible by the Athenian is, as we already saw, reincarnation (870d–e; see the quotation on p. 94).

[316] There are many other places as well where a mention or reincarnation would have been appropriate, if Philo believed in it. These include, e.g. *Ios.* 125–130 where Philo equates physical death with the "death" of the infant when it changes into a child, that of the child upon becoming a boy etc. A statement to the effect that the process then starts over in the next life would have been natural. Yet we cannot argue *e silentio*, particularly as there are also other possible explanations for Philo's reticence, most notably that of reincarnation being an esoteric teaching.

[317] Similarly 2.267, *QG* 2.13b; cf. *Spec.* 4.187. Note the difference: the parents are only co-creators, παραγαγόντες. Thus Folker Siegert's retranslation to Greek in *Philon von Alexandrien: Über die Gottesbezeichnung „wohltätig verzehrendes Feuer"* (De Deo): *Rückübersetzung des Fragments aus dem Armenischen, deutsche übersetzung und Kommentar*, WUNT 46 (Tübingen:

used by several authors before Philo, e.g., by Plato in *Cratylus* 396a about Zeus in relation to humans and in 399d about the soul in relation to the body—a notion elaborated by Aristotle in *De anima* 415b.

As the commandment is almost the sole context in which this idea occurs,[318] reasonable weight may be laid on the fact that Philo has a specific reason to present it. In *Decal.* 106–107 Philo describes the commandment to honor the parents as "the last of the first set in which the most sacred injunctions are given and it adjoins the second set which contains the duties of human beings to each other." This is because

> parents by their nature stand on the border-line between the mortal and the immortal side of existence ... the immortal because the act of generation assimilates them to God, the generator of the All. (*Decal.* 106)

Philo reiterates this in *Spec.* 2.224. He is invited by the occasion to reinforce this argument by using similar vocabulary about the parents as he does about God.

Furthermore, there are two other factors that weaken the case for taking Philo's words to mean a denial of the pre-existence of the soul. First, the references to God's bringing the non-existent into existence do not mean that Philo believed in creation of the world *ex nihilo*.[319] Rather he endorsed the existence of passive primal matter (*Opif.* 8–9, 21–22; *QG* 1.55). Analogously, the terminology used about the parents does not mean that the *constituents* of the new individuals—the soul and the elements of the body—had no prior existence. Second, given Philo's numerous references to ignorant and pleasure-seeking common people, the notion that parents in general are semi-divine has to be qualified considerably.[320] The certain artificiality of the emphasis on the parents' high standing is also indicated by the fact that parents are in reality no different from everyone else: Philo says about humans in general that we are a mixture of human and divine (*Opif.* 135, *Mut.* 184).

However, it is not only the parents that are spoken of by Philo in a manner that may raise doubts concerning his endorsement of the idea of

---

J. C. B. Mohr, 1988), p. 29, of the description of *God's* activity at the end of *Deo* 7, ἐκ μὴ ὄντος εἰς τὸ εἶναι παραγωγή, is suspect. He refers to *Opif.* 81 cited by NBHL s.v. nṣ (oč), but there the subject of the action is the *humankind*.

[318] In *Deus* 117–119 he refers to the reproduction of animals and humans and calls this, with some reticence, "the process by which things are drawn and journey *so to speak* from non-existence to existence (ἀγωγὴ καὶ ὁδός τίς ἐστιν ἐκ τοῦ μὴ ὄντος εἰς τὸ εἶναι)."

[319] I agree here with Runia, *On the Creation*, 253.

[320] For instance in *Spec.* 2.231 Philo characterizes the voting "mob" of the cities as "always so reckless and devoid of circumspection." See also, e.g., *Ebr.* 198; *Sobr.* 20; *Her.* 76; *Congr.* 27; *Abr.* 147; *Ios.* 59; *Virt.* 10; *Praem.* 24; *Prob.* 23; *Contempl.* 20; *Prov.* 2.31; *QG* 4.8; *QE* 2.34.

the pre-existence of the soul. The other party as well, children, are sometimes referred to in a similar way. Let us first see what he has to say about Abraham's receiving in his trance a message which contains the promise, "[t]hen in the fourth generation they shall be brought back here" (Gen 15:16). Philo elaborates on this in *Her.* 293–299.[321] These words are, in their deeper meaning, meant "to bring before us the thought of the complete restoration of the soul," and this leads to the notion of the "generations" of the soul. Philo calls the age of childhood from birth to seven years "the first generation of the soul" (§295) during which the child

> possesses only the simplest elements of the soul, a soul which closely resembles smooth wax and has not yet received any impression of good or evil, for such marks as it appears to receive are smoothed over and confused by its fluidity. (*Her.* 294)

In other words, small children do not have in their souls any marks of previous experiences, and if they seem to receive them (after birth—note the present-tense γράφεσθαι) these are not permanent.[322] In my view it is not plausible to use this passage for advancing the possibility of Philo's having denied reincarnation on the grounds of his observations of children. In Plato, forgetting the pre-natal experiences is part of the picture (*Republic* 621a), whereas linking children's early inclinations with their previous lives is not. The fluidity of children's nature as such has no implications from the viewpoint of rebirth.

2.3.2 *Freedom at Death?*

In *Cher.* 120, discussed above, the duration of the sojourning was expressed as exhausting "the appointed span of life." While this does not seem to signify much more than "we live until we die," there are other passages in Philo that contain a similar idea and link it with something additional so that the result seems more *final* than in *Cher.* In *Migr.* 133 Philo, meaning Abraham, says that if he "finishes the race of life without stumbling, when he has reached the end (πρὸς τὸ τέλος ἐλθών) he shall obtain crowns and prizes as a fitting guerdon." A similar reference to the completion of life

---

[321] *QG* 3.12 contains a somewhat different interpretation with no direct reference to the soul.

[322] In *Prob.* 159–160 Philo describes souls that are not yet "driven by desire" nor "establishe[d in] freedom" in a manner that is in broad agreement with the *Her.* passage but with only a passing metaphorical reference to physical age. In *Spec.* 3.119 he calls infants "most innocent" (ἀκακώτατοι), but as the context is the appropriateness of the death penalty for baby-murderers, any qualification based on the infant's soul having possibly committed some offence in a previous life would in any case have been misplaced.

occurs in *Deus* 75, where Philo says that everybody makes errors; "there is no man who self-sustained has run the course of life from birth to death without stumbling."[323] These examples have the aorist tense accentuating the aspect of completion.

Do these statements amount to references to the one and only incarnation? There are several uncertainties. Receiving "prizes" after a good life and finishing the course of life are not in logical conflict with there being several lives. *Migr.* 133 is the stronger candidate to mean permanent liberation from earthly life; the high prizes may mean salvation. However, generalizing this to all souls is not an option, since Philo is talking about Abraham in this instance.[324]

Somewhat similarly, Philo calls death the end of "our troubles" or "everything in life" etc., e.g., in *Abr.* 64, 230; *Ios.* 129; *Spec.* 2.95. These statements could, in principle, reflect a view according to which there is only one life. Yet this cannot be ascertained on the basis of these statements themselves. If taken to mean anything more than the end of an individual's earthly existence, in the particular body in question, they are problematic. If "everything in life" comes to an end, is there life after death? If death means the "'end' of all ills" (*Abr.* 230, *Spec.* 2.95), will it be so also for the wicked souls—salvation without punishment? No, it will not be so; such an idea is irreconcilable with Philo's thought, and let us remember *Praem.* 69: "people think that death is the termination of punishment but in the divine court it is hardly the beginning."[325]

In *Abr.* 255–259 Philo recounts Abraham's conduct upon Sarah's death. The restraint the patriarch shows in his mourning is attributed to the teaching of wisdom that

> death is not the extinction of the soul but its separation and detachment from the body and its return to the place whence it came; and it came, as was shown in the story of creation, from God. (*Abr.* 258)

The quotation echoes the themes of the *Phaedo* regarding the soul's continued existence after the demise of the body; the terms χωρισμός and διάζευξις occur in both thinkers in characterizing the separation that takes place at death (see 67d, 88b).

Philo's reference to "the story of creation" points very probably to *Opif.* 135 where Philo says, "the soul obtained its origin from nothing which has come into existence at all, but from the Father and Director of all

---

[323] Philo uses the notion of "unstumbling life" more generally to signify stability without the notion of completion in *Sacr.* 63, 123; *Post.* 22; *Plant.* 49 and *Spec.* 4.167.
[324] Cf. *Her.* 283 where Abraham's soul is said to have risen to the ether after death.
[325] See above, p. 82, for a brief discussion of this passage.

things."³²⁶ Runia comments on the mixed mortal–immortal nature of the human being (mentioned by Philo at *Opif.* 135) by stating that at death the "immortal soul can rejoin the heavenly realm (e.g. Moses at *Mos.* 2.288)."³²⁷ However, as was just discussed, this applies to the virtuous only. Moses is *sui generis*; Sarah, too, can definitely not be taken as a representative of ordinary people for whose salvation physical death cannot suffice.³²⁸

Somewhat similar to the passages about the soul's return to God are those in which Philo says death means the beginning of the soul's "proper life." In *QG* 4.152, in the context of Gen 25:8, Philo says: "the death of the body is the life of the soul, since the soul lives an incorporeal life of its own."³²⁹ But again it is Abraham's soul that is Philo's starting point, and while the sequel shows that the statement applies to the virtuous more generally, it is not universally applicable. There are also other passages where Philo—in one way or another—narrows down a statement on a good *post-mortem* fate so that it applies to the virtuous only (*Her.* 276; *Migr.* 189; *QG* 1.16, 3.11).³³⁰

To conclude: while physical death can be characterized trivially as the end of all ills for any soul, the question that is our main concern now is not thereby answered: is the ensuing liberation temporary or permanent? The prospect of permanent freedom looms for the virtuous—but not for all.

---

³²⁶ On the relationship between *Opif.* and *Abr.*, see Runia, *On the Creation*, 2.
³²⁷ Runia, *On the Creation*, 327.
³²⁸ Goodenough, "Philo on Immortality," 87 n. 5 fails to note this in his statement about *Abr.* 258, "at death the soul returns to God." Likewise, his comment about *Her.* 282–283 (p. 89 in the same article) reveals a lack of attention to the fact that the soul returning to the ether is none other than Abraham's.
³²⁹ No Greek fragment survives for this part of QG 4.152. Marcus retranslates: "ἴδιον ἑαυτῇ τῆς ψυχῆς ἀσώματον βίον διαγούσης vel. sim." The saying of Heraclitus (see above, n. 206 on p. 61) is quoted here too.
³³⁰ Kenneth A. Fox, "Paul's Attitude Toward the Body in Romans 6–8: Compared with Philo of Alexandria" (Ph.D. diss., University of St. Michael's College, Toronto, 2001) delineates, in his account of Philo's attitude towards the body, a path of development that ends in "the [mind's being at death separated] from the body, [whereby] the body is dissolved (διαλύω, *Somn.* 1.26), and the mind returns to its 'father's house' (*Somn.* 1.256), the intelligible world of immortality" (p. 255). While true for the virtuous, this account ignores the question of what happens after death to those who have *not* "become [pupils] of the Practiser and learn[t] to use weapons and engage in wrestlings against passion and vainglory" (*Somn.* 1.255).

2.3.3 *Predestination of the Wicked?*

In *Mut.* Philo presents a view which seems to indicate that some souls are wicked from the beginning. If this means that some souls have been created permanently wicked and others good, there is little room for evolutionary reincarnation for the former.

> And the greatest gift is to obtain Him for our Architect (τὸ αὐτοῦ λαχεῖν ἀρχιτέκτονος), Who was also the Architect of the whole world, for He did not form the soul of the bad (φαύλου μὲν γὰρ ψυχὴν οὐ διέπλασεν), since wickedness is at enmity with Him, and in framing the intermediate one He was not the sole agent ... Surely then he is a man of virtue to whom God says "I am thy God," for he obtained God alone for his maker without the co-operation of others. At the same time Moses teaches us here by implication the doctrine which he so often lays down that God is the maker of the wise and good only (μόνων ἀγαθῶν καὶ σοφῶν δημιουργός ἐστιν). (*Mut.* 30–32)

One wonders if the idea of God as "the maker of the wise and good only" really occurs "often" in Moses, or in Philo's exegesis of the Pentateuch. I am not aware of any such passage. This anomaly is, I think, indicative of the fact that *Mut.* 30–32 is a medley of several Philonic notions that do not elsewhere occur so abruptly combined, and that this is the reason for some of the oddities of the passage that result in difficulties in recognizing the ideas presented for what they are.[331] However, this is not the place for their full analysis, and we will concentrate on what it means to "obtain Him for our Architect" and what can be made of God's being the maker of the good only.

A key question is whether Philo means that the gift of obtaining God as one's architect is one which a soul either receives, or does not receive, *initially*, at its coming into existence, or if a soul can obtain it *post factum*. To understand what Philo is saying, we need to start from *Mut.* 18, where Philo begins his discussion of God's words to Abram in Gen 17:1 ("I am your God") by asking: "Which indeed amongst all this multitude of created things does not have Thee for its God?" None, he answers, because the Existent indeed *is* "Creator and God" of the world.[332] He explains that that

---

[331] E.g., Colson in a note on the word "often" takes that expression as a reference to "the other texts where God says 'We,'" for which he refers to *Conf.* 16 (should be §169), as well as to Gen 48:15–16 as interpreted in *Conf.* 181. The section *Conf.* 169–182 includes the notion about the role of God's powers in the creation of the human soul and the idea that the punishment of the wicked is the business of powers lower than God (ex. Gen 48). It does not speak of God's being the creator of virtuous souls only.

[332] Based on *Mut.* 27, I use "the Existent" in the sense in which the word "God" usually appears in this study, because the latter is now reserved for the special meaning Philo has in mind (see below).

is not the point: God is speaking of "human souls which do not deserve to be cared for" (*ibid.*)—this is what is meant when souls *whose* God the Existent is *not* are discussed. There are two notions in the background. First, the distinction which Philo makes in several treatises between the epithets God (θεός; the beneficent or creative power) and Lord (κύριος; the sovereign one).[333] At §24 he uses a trichotomy reminiscent of the quotation above: "it is His will that the bad person should be ruled by the Lord" whereas "the one who progresses should be benefited by Him as God;" but "the perfect should be led by Him as Lord and benefited by Him as God."

The second notion behind the Existent's not being the God *of* everyone is that God cannot be the *possession of* anyone: "God is a human's to be his glory and assistance"(*Mut.* 26). This is a very pregnant declaration, because here we have the yardstick against which it can be assessed to which degree God is *someone's*. Thus it follows that "the words 'I am *your* God' are used by licence of language and not in their proper sense. For the Existent considered as existent is not relative" (§27). However, the potencies of the Existent "are in some cases spoken of as in a sense relative, such as the kingly and the beneficial, for a king is a king *of* someone and a benefactor the benefactor *of* someone" (§28). Philo continues by making a point that is decisive for our present inquiry: "Akin to these two is the *creative* potency called God" (§29).[334] Therefore, Philo's words "He did not *form* the soul of the bad" refer to *God*, as distinct from the Lord, and mean the same as "He is not the *God* of the bad." We already know the reason: because the wicked are the constituency of the *Lord* (§24). Thus the idea that some souls were created originally bad, so apparent at first glance, vanishes before our eyes.

2.3.4 *Agnosticism Regarding the Hereafter?*

If it can be shown that Philo had a sustained uncertainty about what happens to souls after death, it is very unlikely that he firmly believed that souls reincarnate. He does admit that certain ultimate things, such the reason God spoke in plural in Gen 1:26, or the essence of the mind or soul, are not comprehensible to humans (*Opif.* 72, *Leg* 1.91, *Mut.* 10, *Somn.* 1.31). Yet this does not prevent him from presenting "probable conjectures [that seem] plausible and reasonable" (*Opif.*).

---

[333] See, e.g., *Leg.* 1.95, *Plant.* 86, *Deus* 110, *Abr.* 121, *Mos.* 2.99.
[334] From this point onwards Philo refers with "God" to the creative activity of the Existent with "θεός being derived from τίθημι," as Colson notes *ad loc.* The same idea appears in, e.g., *Conf.* 97, 137; *Abr.* 121; *Mos.* 2.99.

As a result of a close reading of the Philonic corpus I have come to the conclusion that while Philo has no explicit and systematic teaching of the hereafter, he does not express explicit agnosticism about it, either. He is cautious, and he may also be deliberately vague. It is my impression that he says much less than he thinks.

2.4 *Platonic Reincarnational Terminology and Imagery in Philo*

Philo did not shy away from using concepts, images and terminology which Plato uses in reincarnational contexts.[335] This use is copious, which in itself is noteworthy in the context of this study, for although nowhere in his surviving works does Philo go so far as to quote entire, explicit descriptions of the actual event of reincarnation in Plato, the material examined in this section comes *from within* such descriptions or their immediate vicinity. Philo knew this, and it is evident that the references to Plato were not placed in his works with the idea that they will *not* be found or their contexts recognized.[336]

A few words are first in order about Philo's implicit criticism or correctives of Plato, for they demonstrate his independence. Runia's view that it is not appropriate to think that "Philo shows the tendency to follow slavishly the dictates of his Platonist sources and the interpretations they offered" is applicable to Plato too.[337] As previously mentioned, Runia lists "instances of independence of mind and doctrinal divergence in relation to both Platonic text and Platonist interpretation" in his study on Philo's use of the *Timaeus*.[338] While the grounds for including in this list Philo's

---

[335] The word "Platonic" in the section title is a simplification: Plato (or Socrates or Timaeus) may not in all or even most of the cases be the *original* source of this language. The notions of the body as a grave or a prison are good examples, as has already been discussed (above, pp. 58–62). It is evidently possible that Plato also in other cases functions as a mediator of earlier, traditional ideas or images even if he makes no mention of it.

[336] Runia, *Philo and the* Timaeus, 66: "[n]aturally Philo expected his utilization of the *Timaeus* to be recognized." Similarly *On the Creation*, 229: "The words καὶ πάλιν πτηνὸς ἀρθείς would have been sufficient for Philo's readers to recognize that he was going to avail himself of the *topos* of the 'flight of the soul (or mind).' This motif is best-known from Plato's myth in the *Phdr*." Likewise J. Leopold, "Philo's Vocabulary and Word Choice," in David Winston and John Dillon, *Two Treatises of Philo of Alexandria: A Commentary on De Gigantibus and Quod Deus Sit Immutabilis*; BJS 25 (Chico, CA: Scholars Press, 1983), 137–40, p. 138 (referring to *Gig*. 31, 61 and *Deus* 2, 135): "Philo's allusions to Plato's poetic phrases and images from Socrates' 'dithyrambic' second speech in [*Phaedrus* 244a-257b] would have been readily recognized and appreciated by his audience."

[337] Runia, *Philo and the* Timaeus, 512.

[338] Idem, 512–13. See above, n. 77 on p. 22.

"rejection" of reincarnation remain unconvincing, there is no reason to doubt the existence of the phenomenon itself.

I do not think that in Philo's eyes Plato was a serious competitor for Moses in the degree of the *inspiredness* of his writings; it is unimaginable that Philo's habit of referring to the biblical text as sacred could have been applied by him to Plato's dialogues.[339] In other respects the comparison between Moses and Plato is more difficult. One could perhaps say that Moses provided the faultless, basic *framework* for Philo and what he wanted to say, while Plato (as well the Stoics, also others) supplied a considerable share of the actual *contents* with which, utilizing the extensive freedom of maneuver allowed by his allegorical method, Philo filled that framework. Philo examined the Pentateuch word by word with utmost care. This is worlds apart from his way of using Plato: direct quotations are relatively rare.[340] Instead, Philo takes over major ways of thinking, but the use of the Platonic text is realized in bits and pieces.

Philo did not consider Plato infallible, and our Alexandrian exegete was capable of sharply denouncing what the Athenian philosopher had written. Admittedly this only happens once in Philo's extant *oeuvre*, in *Contempl.* 57–64, where the symposia described by both Xenophon and especially Plato are attacked. The main subject of Philo's scathing remarks is pederasty, denouncing which seems much more important for him than accurately reading what Plato had written.[341] But he is clear to make a distinction between the written and the writer, for he calls both authors "men whose character and discourses showed them to be philosophers." Thus the criticism is directed towards their "describ[ing the symposia] as worthy to be recorded, and surmising that they would serve to posterity as models of the happily conducted banquet" (§57), but even this is left implicit. Nonetheless, Philo's adamantly negative view of pederasty becomes very clear to the reader.[342] This enables us to make a highly illuminating comparison between Philo's utilization of Plato's reincarnational vs.

---

[339] Colson's "considerable doubt" (PLCL 9.16) concerning the appellation in *Prob.* 13, "the most holy Plato (τὸν ἱερώτατον Πλάτωνα)," adopted in PCW, is sound. This is the reading of one MS. only, the others have λιγυρώτατον, which can be shown to make much sense in the context of Philo's quotations from the *Phaedrus* in §§ 8, 13. For the details, see Yli-Karjanmaa, "Philo of Alexandria."

[340] For an analysis of Philo's quotations from Plato, see David T. Runia, "The Text of the Platonic Citations." There are 23 instances of the word Plato and its cognates in the *Corpus Philonicum*, more than half of which are in the three philosophical treatises (*Prob.*, *Aet.*, *Prov.*), none in the *Allegorical Commentary*. Socrates is named eight times.

[341] See Colson's note, *ibid.* p. 521.

[342] Explicit denouncements of homoerotic behavior are found also in *Abr.* 135–136 and *Spec.* 2.50, 3.37–42.

pederastic passages. The former is abundant and the subject of this whole section, whereas examples of the latter are very rare; I can only name *Gig.* 13-14 as a passage worth noting in this respect. There the souls' returning to their starting point, their correct philosophizing and their practicing the dying to the bodily life are discussed.[343] Philo utilizes here both the *Phaedrus* (248e-249a) and the *Phaedo* (67de, 80e). We already saw that in the former passage Plato speaks of the soul's return to its starting point and refers to the possibility of shortening the duration of reincarnation through guileless philosophy or philosophical pederasty.[344] Quite apart from how seriously Plato meant this to be taken, *Gig.* 13-14 does not disprove my position. It is a single case best understood as Philo's turning a blind eye on pederasty in a context where he has other things in mind to address. He makes his stance clear elsewhere and does not have to worry about being suspected of approving the practice.[345]

2.4.1 *Being Bound to a Mortal Body*

We begin with Plato's words in *Phaedo*:

> But, I think, if when [a soul] departs from the body it is defiled and impure, because it was always with the body and cared for it and loved it and was fascinated by it and its desires and pleasures ... [such souls] flit about until through the desire of the corporeal which clings to them they are again bound to a body (πάλιν ἐνδεθῶσιν εἰς σῶμα). (*Phaedo* 81a-b, e)

Plato also uses ἐνδέω + σῶμα later in the dialogue with reincarnation implied (91e-92a) when Socrates returns to his argument "that learning is recollection and that, since this is so, our soul must necessarily have been somewhere before it was bound to a body (πρὶν ἐν τῷ σώματι ἐνδεθῆναι)." Another important passage is *Timaeus* 44b: "so often as the soul is bound within a mortal body (εἰς σῶμα ἐνδεθῇ θνητόν) it becomes at the first irrational" (also 43a, 44d, 69e).

From the viewpoint of the present study, Philo's single most interesting use of this expression occurs in *Somn.* 1.138: those incorporeal but body-loving souls that are closest to the earth "are bound to mortal bodies (ἐνδεθησόμεναι σώμασι θνητοῖς)." This comes particularly close Plato's word-

---

[343] For a quotation, see below, p. 132.
[344] See above, quotations Phdr1-2 on p. 93.
[345] This would be contingent on the chronology of his writings, if we (wrongly, I think) assumed that his position's being known was wholly dependent on his *literary* output. As for other Philonic passages, in the estimation of some scholars Philo refers to the time periods of *Phaedrus* 249a in *Somn.* 1.138 and its parallels (see above, n. 50 and text on p. 16) but I consider this unlikely (see below, pp. 136-38).

ing in *Tim.* 44b, as does *Mut.* 36: "absolute happiness is impossible for one who is bound to a mortal body (θνητῷ σώματι ἐνδεδεμένον)." Other examples include: "bound as we are to a body (ἐνδεδεμένους σώματι)" in *Leg.* 3.151 and "bound to a corruptible body (ἐνδεδεμένος σώματι φθαρτῷ)" in *Virt.* 74. Similar phrases occur in *Leg.* 2.22; *Conf.* 92, 106, 177; *Her.* 274; *Ios.* 264 and *Spec.* 4.188.[346]

Plato's expression seems to have been considered an apposite description of the human condition on earth and in the body by Philo. It points to the involuntary character of incarnation, both regarding the state of being in the body and the prospect that becoming permanently liberated is not that simple.

2.4.2 *The River Metaphor*

The Platonic text behind this image is *Timaeus* 43a–d. It is too long to quote in full, but let us take an example that connects with both the previous expression, the soul's being bound in the body, and the following one, paying back the elements at death. The context is the carrying out of the Demiurge's command (41d) to the "young gods" (42d) to fashion the bodies and lower parts of the soul of the mortal creatures:

> They took the immortal principle of the mortal living creature and ... borrowed (δανειζόμενοι) from the Cosmos portions of fire and earth and water and air, as if meaning to pay them back (ἀποδοθησόμενα) ... and thus they constructed out of them all each several body, and within bodies subject to inflow and outflow they bound the revolutions of the immortal soul. The souls, then, [were] thus bound within a mighty river (ποταμὸν) [and they] neither mastered it nor were mastered, but with violence they rolled along ... the flood (κύματος) which foamed in (κατακλύζοντος) and streamed out (ἀπορρέοντος), as it supplied the food, was immense. (42e–43b)

As has been noted in previous scholarship, "[t]his Platonic image [of the engulfed soul] is one of Philo's favourites."[347] At this point, I have little to add, and, like Runia, I see little point in "pil[ing] up examples."[348] Such examples have already been mentioned in this study and more are referred to later on, and in Ch. 4 I will try to assess the overall significance of this

---

[346] Neither Billings, *Platonism of Philo*, nor Runia, *Philo and the Timaeus*, notes Philo's use of this Platonic phrase. Méasson, *Du char ailé de Zeus*, 285 notes the link between *Somn.* 1.138 and *Phaedo* 81e.
[347] Runia, *Philo and the Timaeus*, 260–62; see also Billings, *Platonism of Philo*, 70–71 and Méasson, *Du char ailé de Zeus*, 176–92.
[348] Runia, *Philo and the Timaeus*, 260. But see the Topical Index s.v. soul, drowning of.

symbolism. Instead, I present a few selected observations regarding Philo's use of the image and scholars' comments thereupon.

Given the focus of the present study, the most important application of the river metaphor is *Gig.* 13, an explicit description of the incarnation of pre-existent souls who have "descend[ed] into the body as though into a river."[349] Runia notes that the river image "is used in a large number of different contexts and configurations" so that in addition to the body it also symbolizes the sense objects and the passions, and even the world of wickedness more generally.[350] While this is true as such, I would not (and I do not claim that Runia does) emphasize the *difference* between these symbolical meanings given their overall affinity in Philo's thought; pleasures and evil deeds can be added to the list (*Agr.* 88, *Conf.* 30). These all inevitably belong to the life lived on earth and in the body.

I do not agree with Méasson when she says that the image of the submerged soul is used in a description of incarnation only "[u]ne fois" (i.e., at *Gig.* 13).[351] *Agr.* 88–89 is another passage where the image is used in connection with a reference to the soul's entering the body, as we have already seen: "and the bottom to which it is submerged and made to sink is nothing else than the body."[352] Méasson's view is that this is a description of the danger posed by the passions to the *already incarnate* soul, but it does not seem adequately grounded.[353] Runia, too, lists *Agr.* 89 among passages where he says the river stands for the stream of passions.[354] However, as Philo speaks of "the passions and evil deeds blowing against the unstable soul," their role is rather that of a storm wind, whereas the water represents the body. Runia is correct in stating that this is not a pure application of *Tim.* 43 but a combination thereof with the image of sailing.[355]

---

[349] The close parallelism between *Gig.* 6, 12–15, *Plant.* 14 and *Somn.* 1.138–141 will be discussed in subsection 3.1.2.
[350] Runia, *Philo and the* Timaeus, 260–61.
[351] Méasson, *Du char ailé de Zeus*, 191 n. 177.
[352] See pp. 69, 83. A fuller treatment of this passage will be given below, pp. 182–83.
[353] Méasson, *Du char ailé de Zeus*, 191. She implies that passions would not be a menace to a discarnate soul, whereas I think they are a most apposite driving force for reincarnation, which she does consider to appear in Philo (see below, p. 147).
[354] Runia, *Philo and the* Timaeus, 260.
[355] Idem, 261. Here in fact I would suggest also another Platonic model, *Republic* 611e, where it is discussed "what [the soul] might be if it ... were raised ... out of the depths of this sea in which it is now sunk (ἐκ τοῦ πόντου, ἐν ᾧ νῦν ἐστί)," i.e., its life on earth. This is part of Socrates's comparison of the soul with the sea-god Glaucus with shells, sea-weeds and rocks having attached themselves to him—this being a metaphor of the soul "marred (λελωβημένον) by communion with the body" (611c–d).

Another applied form of the river metaphor is very important: Philo's understanding of Passover. As described by Colson in his note to *Spec.* 2.145, the point of "the ordinary explanation of Passover ... is disguised in the LXX:" the connection between the Hebrew verb פסח and the noun פסח is in no way reflected in the Septuagint, and Philo takes the meaning of Πάσχα to be διάβασις, 'crossing over.' One of of the best explanations of what needs to be crossed over from is the following:

> But to those who are accustomed to turn literal facts into allegory, the Crossing-festival suggests the purification of the soul. They say that the lover of wisdom is occupied solely in crossing over from the body and the passions, each of which overwhelms him like a torrent (ἐπικλύζει χειμάρρου ποταμοῦ τρόπον), unless the rushing current (φοράν) be dammed and held back by the principles of virtue. (*Spec.* 2.147)[356]

In *QE* 1.4 Philo states: "And there is still another Passover of the soul beside this, which is its making the sacrifice of passing over from the body; and there is one of the mind, (namely, its passing over) from the senses."[357] This rings like a description of monadization, and that Passover is a salvific event for Philo is well illustrated in *Sacr.*:

> For we are bidden to keep the Passover, which is the passage from passions to the practice of virtue ... . For it is no mortal passage, since it is called the Passover of the Uncreate and Immortal one. (*Sacr.* 63)[358]

That the body is not always mentioned but the passions are (e.g., *Leg.* 3.165, *Her.* 255, *Congr.* 106)—with or without some other related hindrances of the soul's progress such as evil deeds or things of the senses—makes no great difference, as in any case the Passover is about getting out of *Egypt*, the land of the body. The suitability of the Timaean image is accentuated by Philo's repeated references to the *river* or *stream* of the passions (e.g., *Leg.* 2.103, 3.14, 18, 172; *Conf.* 30, 70; *Fug.* 91). *Somn.* 2.109 crystallizes the whole imagery by speaking of the soul's being "flooded (κατακλυσθέν) and drowned by the streams which the Egyptian river of passion, the body, pours forth (ῥέων) unceasingly through the channel of all the senses."

---

[356] A brief reference to Passover as crossing over from passion is found also in *Her.* 255.
[357] Heinemann, noting the connection between *QE* 1.4 and *Spec.* 2.147 says in a note to the latter in PCH 2.148 that in *QE* the Passover takes place "durch die Ekstase." However, as discussed shortly, the Passover and the Israelites' exodus from Egypt are very much the same thing for Philo, and I find it very improbable that Philo's statements about the Passover refer to temporary moments of ecstasy. Permanent liberation from the body is surely meant.
[358] Cf. Philo's words in *Gig.* 14 which I have used as the definition of salvation, p. 5.

The close link between Passover and the exodus is illustrated by two references to the exhortation in Ex 12:11, "And you shall eat it with haste —it is the Lord's pascha," in *Migr*. First, Philo says that Moses

> bids them with haste (μετὰ σπουδῆς) to sacrifice the Passover (τὸ Πάσχα), which means 'a passing over,' to the intent that the mind with resolute purpose and unfailing eagerness may carry out both its passing away from the passions without turning back, and its thanksgiving to God its Saviour, Who brought it forth into liberty when it looked not for it. (*Migr.* 25)[359]

As Colson then notes at §151, Philo refers to the same verse when, in his account of how "when we were abandoning Egypt, all the bodily region, [our 'ensnaring and flattering element,' represented by Lot, was] checking our zeal to be gone (τῆς περὶ τὴν ἔξοδον σπουδῆς)." One could summarize that if the body–river is the problem, the Passover–exodus is the solution.[360]

2.4.3 *Paying Back the Elements at Fixed Periods*

The relevant passage from the *Timaeus* (42e) with its key verbs δανείζω and ἀποδίδωμι was already quoted under the previous point. Reincarnation is an essential element in the anthropology of the *Timaeus*, and so the borrowing of elements is naturally meant to happen separately for each successive body that the soul inhabits. This, however, is no hindrance for Philo's using the notion a few times.[361]

In *Post.* 5 (ex. Gen 4:16) Philo says of the dead: "the loan (δανείσματος) which was lent (δανεισθέντος) to each person is repaid (ἀποδιδομένου), after longer or shorter terms (κατὰ προθεσμίας ἀνίσους)." Likewise, in *Her.* he states,

> [E]ach of us ... borrow[s] (δανεισάμενος) small fragments from the substance of each [element], and this debt he repays (ἐκτίνει τὸ δάνειον) when the appointed time-cycles are completed (καθ' ὡρισμένας περιόδους καιρῶν). (*Her.* 282)

The Timaean original does not contain any reference to periods of time at this point. But Dillon has drawn attention to the fact that not only Philo

---

[359] Cf. the salvific crossing of the river Lethe in *Republic* 621c (above, p. 94).

[360] In §20 Philo even adds the word "Hebrew" to the list of those describing this solution: Joseph is said to have been proud of "being a member of the Hebrew race, whose wont it is, as the name 'Hebrew' or 'Migrant' indicates, to quit the objects of sense-perception and go after those of Mind."

[361] See the discussion in Runia, *Philo and the* Timaeus, 259–60. In addition to the passages dealt with below, he examines *Decal.* 31 and *Aet.* 29. In both, only borrowing is mentioned.

but also Alcinous in his *Didaskalikos* adds such a reference to his explication of *Tim.* 42e–43a (*Did.* 16.1): the gods "borrowed (δανεισάμενοι) certain portions from primal matter for fixed periods (πρὸς ὡρισμένους χρόνους), with a view to returning (ἀποδοθησόμενα) them to it again."³⁶² Noting the parallelism with *Her.*, he calls this "hardly a significant addition," but for our purposes it is interesting. It is not likely that the two authors have both ended up adding the time periods independently. Instead, we are probably witnessing the influence of a harmonizing Middle Platonist interpretation. This is also the view of Dillon who states that the expression may have been "borrowed by the scholastic tradition from such a passage as *Phaedo* 107e"—where ἐν πολλαῖς χρόνου καὶ μακραῖς περιόδοις denotes the duration of the time period between incarnations. He states the obvious limitation that this possibility is uncertain, but we can carry on our inquiry a little further. Plato mentions time periods in the context of reincarnation also elsewhere in the dialogues *Phaedo* and *Phaedrus*, but the problem with these as models for Philo and Alcinous is that they are not speaking of the duration of a single human life in the body, which is what our authors are writing about.³⁶³ In the *Republic* the words in 617d by Lachesis to the souls that are being sent to new lives are more to the point: "this is the beginning of another death-bringing period of mortal generation."³⁶⁴ But perhaps the likeliest source for the Platonist harmonization, I suggest, is found within the *Timaeus* itself:³⁶⁵

> For, in truth, the constitution of these creatures has prescribed periods of life (τεταγμένους τοῦ βίου γίγνεται χρόνους) for the species as a whole, and each individual creature likewise has a naturally predestined term of life (εἱμαρμένον ἕκαστον ἔχον τὸν βίον). (*Tim.* 89b)

What is interesting is that Philo seems to be drawing on the same tradition also in *Somn.* 1.138 and its parallel at *Plant.* 14, when he uses similar temporal expressions about the timing of physical death.³⁶⁶ The borrowing of the elements is not mentioned in these, but there is a reference at *Somn.* 1.137 to the number of souls equalling that of the stars (from *Tim.* 41d; this too occurs in *Did.* at 16.2), which reinforces the assumption of the

---

³⁶² Dillon, *Alcinous*, 26, 137.
³⁶³ In *Phaedo* 108c Plato has ἕως ἂν δή τινες χρόνοι, in 113a, τινάς εἱμαρμένους χρόνους in a similar context. In the *Phaedrus* we have what might with good reason be called reincarnational periods that are certainly "fixed," 3,000 or 10,000 years (248e–249a). But these have the same problem as *Phaedo* 107e.
³⁶⁴ My tr. for ἀρχὴ ἄλλης περιόδου θνητοῦ γένους θανατηφόρου.
³⁶⁵ Note also that in 42b Plato writes about "appointed time (τὸν προσήκοντα χρόνον)." See quotation T2 on p. 91.
³⁶⁶ See below, pp. 136–38.

interpretative tradition of the *Timaeus* as the context where the addition originated.

As is the case with the other expressions examined this section, borrowing and paying back the elements is not a concept that necessitates reincarnation; it functions well without the tenet. It is, nevertheless true to say that Philo is content to utilize one more reincarnational Platonic notion in the form he learnt it from a reincarnational Platonist tradition.

2.4.4 *The Body as a Grave and a Prison*

Philonic passages featuring the image of the body as a *grave* have already been listed and the most relevant Greek models for the image cited and discussed.[367] *Phaedrus* 250c can still be added, as Philo refers to this text in a few places.[368] Here the connection to the tenet of our concern is more direct, for Plato says souls were originally, before the onset of reincarnation, "not entombed (ἀσήμαντοι) in this which we carry about with us and call the body, in which we are imprisoned like an oyster in its shell." The closest mention of reincarnation is at 249b which discusses the passing of souls into animal bodies and back to human ones.

With regard to Philo, one thing is worth highlighting: if the body is called the tomb of the soul, the idea that *the soul is dead* is implied. *Leg.* 1.105–108 brings this out in very clear terms.[369] This does not work quite as definitively in the other direction, but the idea is not far off. If we are allowed to combine both ideas, the prevalence of the notion of the body as a grave is significantly more widespread in Philo than if we count only those passages where he explicitly speaks of entombment.[370]

The notion regarding the body as a *prison* was already encountered above in *Cratylus* 400c as an Orphic one, and the lust-induced imprisonment in *Phaedo* 82e was also quoted.[371] In the former, reincarnation is not mentioned but seems implied, in the latter it is of key importance. In

---

[367] See above, pp. 31, 58–62.
[368] At least in *QG* 1.70 and an unidentified fr. of *QE* (no. 15 in PAPM; no. 21 in PLCL).
[369] See the discussion on incarnation as a punishment above, p. 57–70.
[370] The notion of the death of the soul occurs often in the *Allegorical Commentary* and the *Quaestiones* but is rare in Philo's other genres. More than fifty passages can be listed (including references to the "destruction" of the soul): *Leg.* 1.76, 105–108, 2.77–78, 82–83, 87, 3.52, 113; *Cher.* 51; *Det.* 49, 70, 74–75; *Post.* 39, 45, 73–74; *Agr.* 98, 100, 163–164, 171; *Plant.* 37, 44–46, 122, 147; *Conf.* 122; *Her.* 52–53, 290; *Fug.* 55–56, 78, 113; *Mut.* 95–96; *Somn.* 1.150–151, 2.70, 234–235; *Abr.* 55; *Spec.* 1.345; *Praem.* 159; *Prob.* 75–76; *QG* 1.33, 45, 51, 56, 70, 75, 2.9, 22, 23, 57, 4.46, 152, 235, 238, 240.
[371] See pp. 60, 93, respectively. In addition, the notion of the soul's being bound to a body is close; see subsection 2.4.1.

addition, the visible world (*Rep.* 517b), Tartarus (*Phaedo* 114b, *Gorgias* 523b), and Hades (*Gorgias* 525c) are called a prison by Plato. Of these, the first one can be considered reincarnational if read in the light of the concluding myth of the dialogue, whereas in the *Gorgias* rebirth is not explicitly mentioned at all. In *Phaedo* 82e Plato's word is εἰργμός, which Philo does not use; the related word εἱρκτή is used by him about the body in *Her.* 68, 273 and *Somn.* 1.139.[372] In the other passages Plato uses δεσμωτήριον, as does Philo a total of 18 times, explicitly of the body in *Leg.* 3.42, *Ebr.* 101, *Migr.* 9, *Her.* 85 and *Somn.* 1.139. The prison can also be one "of the passions," as in *Deus* 111, with no significant change in meaning. Philo's use of this image mostly reflects the idea that living in the body is confining and the exit from this confinement is not easy. Yet the notion that the prison term is a penalty for a crime is a significant undercurrent in his thought, as we discovered when examining incarnation as a punishment.

2.4.5 *Changing to Animal Form*

In *Timaeus* 42c Plato writes that if a soul fails to live justly in human form, in the following incarnation it "shall be changed ... into some bestial form (μεταβαλοῖ ... εἴς τινα ... θήρειον φύσιν)."[373] This image, then, is at the heart of one of Plato's descriptions of the process of reincarnation itself. The notion of human souls being born in animal bodies is worked out in more detail at the end of the dialogue (91a–92c).

Philo is the first known author to reproduce this phrase. In *Spec.* 3.99 individuals who suffer from "delirium and insanity and intolerable frenzy" are said to lose the rational part of their soul and be changed "into a beastly nature (μεταβέβληκεν εἰς θήρειον φύσιν)."[374] Usually, however, the image is used in connection with moral deficiency and not problems of mental health: the souls of those who charge interest have been "altered into savagery and the nature of wild beasts" (*Virt.* 87), and those who care neither for their neighbours nor God "would seem to have been transformed into the nature of wild beasts" (*Decal.* 110). Moreover, as already mentioned, earlier in the latter treatise (§80) Philo says that the Egyptian

---

[372] εἱρκτή appears as an appellation of the body in the pseudo-Platonic *Axiochus* at 374d.
[373] See a fuller quotation (T2) on p. 91.
[374] This is the only occurrence of the adjective θήρειος in Philo; elsewhere he uses a genitive structure (εἰς θηρίων φύσιν).

worshippers of animals have their "souls transformed into the nature of those creatures" and "seem beasts in human shape."³⁷⁵

The image is found in *QG* as well: in 4.133 there is a passing reference to "some men of the crowd" being "in no way distinguishable from beasts in human form," but there is also this intriguing characterization of Cain (ex. Gen 4:15):

> he is proscribed not only by his parents but also by the whole human race, counting him a genus peculiar and separate from the rational species, like one driven out and a fugitive, and one transformed into the nature of beasts. (*QG* 1.76)

It is almost as if Cain was discussed as an individual who, because of his crime, actually lost the rational portion of his soul and was changed into an animal (cf. *Spec.* 3.99 just discussed).

Above, Runia's thesis that some utterly wicked people have become like animals (i.e., they have "los[t the] control over the irrational parts of the soul and the body," and that this is *also their punishment*) was briefly discussed. This seems to be the reason why Platonic reincarnation and Philonic allegory in Runia's view produce "the same result."³⁷⁶ Of the above examples in *Decal.* 80 the image seems to emphasize the laughability of the people meant, in *QG* 4.133, *Virt.* 87 and *Decal.* 110 rather their despicability, *but* in the last one there is a punitive aspect also involved: these people "have been convicted" in two courts: the divine and the human (§111). However, Philo does not say that it is the change they have undergone that is their penalty; instead, their animality continues to be referred to as an image of their degradation. They are so low that they should "become tame" (§113) again and "take some beasts for [their] models" (§114), e.g., to learn from sheep-dogs that defend the flock of their master till death. At the very least we can say that while the penal character of becoming like beasts is, to an extent, implied and obvious, it is

---

³⁷⁵ For Runia's comments on §80, see above, p. 23. Billings, *Platonism of Philo*, and Méasson, *Du char ailé de Zeus*, do not mention the close verbal connections just noted. Pearce, *The Land of the Body*, 291 notes the Platonic reincarnational background of this image in *Decal.* 80 and makes the further point that in that passage the notion also represents assimilation to gods (= the animals worshipped). This is certainly true but may be incidental; in any case *Decal.* 80 seems a unique passage in this respect. Pearce is not explicit about the extent to which she sees a Platonic background to the fact that "Philo characterizes certain very wicked states of behaviour—injustice, despondency, and savagery, for example—in terms of wild beasts in human form." Of the passages mentioned above she refers to *Spec.* 3.99 but does not note that the wording is nearly identical with *Tim.* 42c. Additionally, she points to *Abr.* 8, 33; *Mos.* 1.43 and *QG* 4.133 where the same idea is expressed with somewhat different vocabulary.
³⁷⁶ Above, p. 23.

certainly not highlighted by Philo, and so the correspondence with Platonic reincarnation seems to boil down to the resemblance between souls' becoming *like animals* and becoming *animals,* and this in fact does not tell us much about Philo's position on reincarnation in *human* bodies.

But why did Philo choose to use a thoroughly reincarnational metaphor when pointing to utter wickedness? Was this just a handy image that captured both the crime and its ugly consequences in a single package? Or was it a veiled warning that even though being born into an animal body is not an option, the wicked can expect something dreadful in the next life? And, last but not least, why is the image *absent* from the genre which most fully features Philo's allegory of the soul, the *Allegorical Commentary*?[377] These questions will need to be addressed in further research.

2.4.6 *Practising Death*

Plato tells us in *Phaedo* 63e how Socrates, while waiting for his execution, tells his friends who have come to see him in prison: "a man who has really spent his life in philosophy is naturally of good courage when he is to die." This is because

> those who pursue philosophy aright study nothing but dying and being dead (ἐπιτηδεύουσιν ... ἀποθνῄσκειν τε καὶ τεθνάναι) ... the true philosophers and they alone are always most eager to release the soul, and just this—the release and separation of the soul from the body—is their study (μελέτημα) ... the true philosophers practice dying (ἀποθνῄσκειν μελετῶσι). (64a, 67d–e)

The purpose of all this dying is purification from all bodily influences that hinder the soul from reaching truth (64c, 64e–65a, 65c–d, 66a, 66e–67a, 67c–d). A new incarnation is the fate of those who do not practice this mortification, but rebirth can be avoided, if the soul

---

[377] This absence does not mean that Runia is wrong when in, *Philo and the* Timaeus, 309–10 he says that Philo uses the image of wild beasts to describe "the irrational soul ... so often that it virtually loses all imagistic colour"—on a more general level than discussed above also in the *Allegorical Commentary* (*Leg.* 2.9, *Cher.* 70, *Ebr.* 111, *Agr.* 83, *Conf.* 24, *Migr.* 212, *Somn.* 2.267). However, I am not aware of a single instance of Philo's using almost Plato's actual words from the *Timaeus* in the *Commentary. Somn.* 2.54 comes closest in speaking of living in houses because of the protection "from the incursions of wild beasts or of humans worse than beasts (θηριωδεστάτων τὰς φύσεις ἀνθρώπων)." Cf. *Agr.* 46, where Philo speaks of an "utterly savage mind (θηριωδέστατος νοῦς);" Geljon & Runia, *On Cultivation,* 143 comment that "the intellect becomes savage when it loves the body and the passions;" they do not refer to the *Timaeus.* In their comments on somewhat similar expressions at *Agr.* 31, 83 (pp. 127, 177) they refer to other Platonic passages but not to *Tim.* 42c.

departs pure, dragging with it nothing of the body, because it never willingly associated with the body in life, but avoided it and gathered itself into itself alone, since this has always been its constant study (μελετῶσα ἀεὶ τοῦτο)—but this means nothing else than that it pursued philosophy rightly and really practised being in a state of death (τεθνάναι μελετῶσα): or is not this the practice of death (ἢ οὐ τοῦτ' ἂν εἴη μελέτη θανάτου)? ... [But the impure soul] will be interpenetrated, I suppose, with the corporeal which intercourse and communion with the body have made a part of its nature [and which is] burdensome and heavy and earthly and visible. And such a soul is weighed down by this and is dragged back into the visible world. (80e–81a, 81c)

In Philo, we find this expression both in the Platonic form but also in further developments. At its purest it appears in *Gig.* The souls who reach God

> have soared upwards back to the place from whence they started (ὅθεν ὥρμησαν). [They] have given themselves to genuine (ἀνόθως) philosophy, [and] from first to last study to die to the life in the body (μελετῶσαι τὸν μετὰ σωμάτων ἀποθνῄσκειν βίον). (*Gig.* 13–14)[378]

The two reworked versions in Philo are (1) those where the thought is maintained but vocabulary is altered and (2) *vice versa*. An example of the first one is *Det.* 49, where Philo says that "the wise person, when seeming to die to the corruptible life (τεθνηκέναι δοκῶν τὸν φθαρτὸν βίον), is alive to the incorruptible." Very similarly, in an unidentified fragment of *QE* (no. 3 in PAPM, 1 in PLCL) we read, "If a person dies to the mortal life, the same will in exchange live the immortal one, just like someone who never saw begins to see."[379]

Within the second group, quite opposite notions are conveyed. The way in which Philo uses the idea in *Det.* 34 may be termed "Simmian" rather than Socratic: in an outpouring of stupidity put into the mouth of egoists (see §32), the "so-called lovers of virtue" are, in contradistinction to the well-fed who welcome life's pleasures, "almost without exception obscure

---

[378] The connection of *Gig.* 14 to the notion of practising death in the *Phaedo* is noted by Méasson, *Du char ailé de Zeus*, 288 and Winston & Dillon, *Two Treatises*, 242. As an aside it may be noted here *Gig.* 14 has another reincarnational link to Plato. In *Phaedrus* 248e–249a the soul which is freed from reincarnation returns to where it came from (ὅθεν ἥκει) with the aid of practising philosophy guilelessly (ἀδόλως). See quotations Phdr1–2 on p. 93. The variation performed by Philo does not hide his source. So also Winston & Dillon (p. 242) who do not, however, refer to the theme of returning to the point of departure but only to correct philosophizing. Méasson on p. 282 notes both. Ἀνόθως is Philo's favorite for Plato's ἀδόλως or ὀρθῶς as the criteria for practising genuine philosophy, though he does use ἀδόλως as well (*Deus* 22).

[379] My tr. for 'Ἐὰν δὲ ἀποθάνῃ μέν τις τὸν θνητὸν βίον, ζήσῃ δὲ ἀντιλαβὼν τὸν ἀθάνατον, ἴσως δ μηδέποτε εἶδεν ὄψεται.

people ... with a hungry look for a want of food, the prey of disease, in training for dying (μελετῶντες ἀποθνῄσκειν)."³⁸⁰

In *QG* 4.173 Philo uses the notion with the meaning inverted: "truly the life of the wicked man hastens to death every day, reflecting in and training for dying (μελετῶν τὸ ἀποθνῄσκειν)"—now to the life of *virtue*. This inverted notion occurs, with different vocabulary, also in *Her.* 292 (ἀποθνῄσκειν μανθάνοντα) and *Somn.* 1.151 (ἀποθνῄσκειν ἐπιτετηδευκότες).³⁸¹

A case of its own is fragment 7.3 Harris, which will receive a separate discussion in Ch. 3. It reads in part, "Those who have come to understand truth fitly declare sleep to be the practice of death and the shadow and outline of the revival which follows afterwards."

We thus see that the uses by Philo of this Platonic notion vary from being very similar to Plato's to its opposite. Does Philo have in mind something that links these various uses? Assuming his audiences can be expected to have recognized the reference, the one thing that connects the passages is an act of *reminding* the audience what Plato writes in the *Phaedo*. He does not openly say that Socrates's point in practising death is to avoid reincarnation, but we cannot soundly assume that his audience's knowledge of the dialogue excluded this fact. Thus whether Philo intended to allude to reincarnation or not, in practice that (too) is what he did. At this point of our study we are not really able to give a well-founded position on why he wanted to do so.

2.4.7 *Being Weighed Down*

As has already been seen, in *Phaedo* 81c a soul contaminated by the body is after death "weighed down" and "dragged back" to a rebirth in this world: βαρύνεται τε καὶ ἕλκεται.³⁸² This idea has a partial parallel in the *Phaedrus*, where a soul "grows heavy (βαρυνθῇ), and when it has grown heavy (βαρυνθεῖσα), loses its wings and falls to the earth" for three or ten millennia of reincarnation (248c). Thus in these two passages we are again dealing with the actual event of rebirth. Admittedly, in the *Phaedrus* Plato is ostensibly

---

³⁸⁰ Whitaker comments (PLCL 2.493–94):
Here in the mouth of the worldly [the phrase] connotes the wretchedness of the philosopher's [ascetic] life.... Philo is probably thinking here of *Phaedo* 64a, where, when Socrates uses the equivalent phrase ἐπιτηδεύει ἀποθνῄσκειν, Simmias laughs and says, 'that is exactly what my unphilosophical countrymen would say of the philosophers.' It is a good example of Philo's intimate knowledge of Plato.

³⁸¹ It is actually another version of the concept of the death of the soul (see above, p. 57–64), as a result of which "the soul dies to the life of virtue (τὸν ἀρετῆς βίον θνῄσκῃ)" (*Leg.* 1.107; similarly *Det.* 48–49, 70; *Post.* 45; *Somn.* 2.235).

³⁸² See above, p. 123.

speaking of the soul's falling to the earth for its *first* incarnation.[383] However, this is not a crucial difference given that in the subsequent lives heaviness is, despite the predetermined time periods, a determinant in the cycle of reincarnation.[384] A third relevant Platonic passage, *Timaeus* 91e tells us that the land animals are reincarnations of those humans who neglected the study of philosophy and of the nature of the heavens, and because of this their heads point down to earth (see below).

In Philo we find similar expressions used about the incarnate soul's state of being weighed down. A passage in *Gig.* seems to echo all the passages mentioned: souls that

> bear the burden of the flesh, oppressed by the grievous load (βαρυνόμεναι καὶ πιεζόμεναι), cannot look up to the heavens as they revolve, but with necks bowed (ἑλκυσθεῖσαι) downwards are constrained to stand rooted to the ground like four-footed beasts. (*Gig.* 31)

Numerous Platonic, Philonic and also other parallels to *Gig.* 31 have been discussed by scholars.[385] Runia sees here allusions to *Tim.* 90a, d, 92a and the *Phaedrus* myth.[386] He refers to a passage in *Her.* where the common people

> have bent (ἀπονενεύκασι) [their eyes] earthwards; they pursue the things of earth and their conversation is with the dwellers in Hades. [But Abraham] extends his vision to ... the revolutions of heaven. (*Her.* 78–79)

Méasson refers, e.g., to (*Tim.* 91e–92a).[387] However, she does note the influence of all three dialogues in *Gig.* and also adds the musical harmony

---

[383] I think, however, that we cannot press the myth in this respect. After all, nowhere does Plato say that after the required millennia of reincarnation the soul is immune against another fall.

[384] In 249a–b Plato says that those who have been "made light" by justice will spend the time period between incarnations in heaven, the others, in "places of correction under the earth"—before coming together "to draw lots and choose their second life." The scene is thus the same as in the concluding myth of Er in the *Republic*.

[385] In addition to those discussed below, see also Winston & Dillon, *Two Treatises*, 251–52.

[386] Runia, *Philo and the* Timaeus, 347.

[387] Méasson, *Du char ailé de Zeus*, 317. The relevant parts of Plato's text run:
> And the wild species of animal that goes on foot is derived from those who have paid no attention to philosophy nor studied at all the nature of the heavens, because they ceased to make use of the revolutions within the head ... they have dragged (ἑλκόμενα) ... their head down to earth and there planted them, because of their kinship therewith .... On this account also their race was made four-footed and many-footed, since God set more supports under the more foolish ones, so that they might be dragged down (ἕλκοιντο) still more to the earth.

The thought here is, according to Runia, *Philo and the* Timaeus, 349, that "the more foolish the soul, ... the greater the number of supports ... to connect it to the earth."

mentioned in *Republic* 617b–c.[388] She rightly states the difference between the acquired heaviness of the soul in the *Phaedo* and the incorporeal weight of the soul as the cause of the incarnation in the *Phaedrus* as well as the connection of these notions in both Plato and Philo to whether the soul is talked about as an unitary or multi-part entity. She also adds this passage where Philo's vocabulary is slightly different:

> For the natural gravitation of the body (τοῦ σώματος ὁλκή) pulls down (βρίθουσα) with it (συνεφέλκεται) those of little mind, strangling and overwhelming (αὐχενίζουσα καὶ πιέζουσα) them with the multitude of the fleshly elements. (*Spec.* 4.114)

Regarding *Opif*. 158, where "the lover of pleasure is ... burdened and dragged downwards (βαρυνόμενος καὶ καθελκόμενος)," she notes that, strictly speaking, it is not the weight of the *soul* but of the person which Philo is speaking about; yet I think the difference need not be significant, as she points out for *Tim.* 41d–42d.

In other Philonic passages we may note the following: the soul that "leaves the One" is "weighed down and sore pressed (βαρυνομένη καὶ πιεζομένη)" and ends up "under the crushing load (βαρύτατον ἄχθος)" of desires and lusts (*Deus* 14–15); "the whole soul" is "press[ed] and weigh[ed] (βαρύνασαι καὶ πιέσασαι)" by the bodily senses (*Det.* 16); the soul perceives in the camp of the body such sounds of war that "would proceed from those overpressed and weighed down (βεβαρημένων καὶ πεπιεσμένων) by wine" (*Ebr.* 104); the pleasures of the palate "oppress and overload (βαρύνοντα καὶ πιέζοντα)" the senses (*Ebr.* 214). *Leg.* 3.152 is probably corrupt, for there it is the body which is weighed down.[389] The co-occurrence of βαρύνω + πιέζω is conspicuous, and may point to Philo's utilizing a tradition. The combination does not come from Plato; in fact Philo is the first to use either it or the combination πιέζω + ψυχή.

Once again we find Philo utilizing language influenced by Plato's accounts of reincarnation. Given that he nowhere explicitly distances himself from the notion, despite the apparent fact that his audience will surely have recognized his allusions to Plato and their contexts, it is becoming

---

[388] This and the following remarks are from Méasson, *Du char ailé de Zeus*, 317–19.

[389] Philo is speaking of the soul's having "gone forth from the sacred dwellings of virtue." He continues: "It is then that it"—but should the sequel be "turns to the body, the material things that treat it ill and weigh it down (ἐπὶ <u>τὸ σῶμα, τὰς</u> πλημμελούσας καὶ πιεζούσας ὕλας, τρέπεται)," instead of the PCW text "turns to material things which treat the body ill and weigh it down (ἐπὶ <u>τὰς τὸ σῶμα</u> πλημμελούσας καὶ πιεζούσας ὕλας τρέπεται)"? Wendland's comment *ad loc.* for πλημμελούσας: "vix sanum." Yet cf. *Spec.* 1.100 where wine "presses hard (πιεζομένης) upon the soul" and "weighs down (βαρυνομένου) the body."

increasingly difficult to explain his behavior if he did *not* approve of the doctrine of *metempsychosis*.

2.5 Conclusions on the Indirect Evidence

In this chapter we have noted Philo's fundamentally dualistic anthropology which goes hand in hand with his frequent affirmation of the *pre- and post-existence* of the soul or mind. Ultimately, it is the mind whose incarnation we are dealing with, and there are passages in Philo that point to the mind having to rid itself, not only of the body but also of the lower—irrational and mortal—parts of the soul upon being saved, which process, or event, I have chosen to call *monadization*. It is conceivable that if monadization is not complete by or at physical death, this state of affairs can constitute a driving force of reincarnation in Philo.

As to why the mind incarnates, the examination of nine possible causes yielded the probable result that in Philo's view this is simply part of God's plan. The undeniable hints at incarnation being a punishment are not easily interpreted as referring to the original incarnation. Instead, it seems that an original fall happened to the already incarnate soul and that it was directly related to its *corporealization*, i.e., dedication to the earthly and bodily things. If this is accurate, it follows that Philo's references to incarnation as a punishment are references to reincarnation.

Based on the observations made a tentative six-stage model of the soul's fall and rise was drafted. Several mutually compatible causes of incarnation that could act as driving forces of reincarnation were identified. The whole could be characterized by saying that the provisional scheme, which Philo never explicitly spells out, involves the mind's descent from God to the body and the world, its desire for sensual pleasures which leads to its becoming stuck in the earthly life in the cycle of reincarnation and its release and return back to God.[390]

The comparison of Philo's views with Plato's prerequisites of salvation and driving forces of reincarnation confirmed the significant similarity between the thinkers. The three aggregate factors that maintain reincarnation in Plato (seeking corporeal goods, being impure and "heavy," and neglecting reason and philosophy) lead in Philo to consequences that could be veiled descriptions of reincarnation. Yet the nature of these

---

[390] The body and the world play a similar role as the venue of the soul's ethical battle; to the former Philo sometimes applies the appellations of the mythical underworld.

connections to the doctrine is such that only an overall assessment of the cumulative evidence can determine whether or not rebirth is meant.

The assessment of passages that could be seen to contradict the tenet of reincarnation brought up no cases where such an interpretation could be considered the likeliest one; explicit denials of the idea do not exist in Philo, which in itself is a significant fact when we are dealing with a Platonist who does not shy away from using Plato's reincarnational texts. It is warranted to assume that Philo's allusions to Plato's dialogues were not pointless but that he made them knowing his audience would take notice of them and identify the works and the contexts that they pointed to. This recognition is a relevant factor in establishing his attitude towards reincarnation, because it means that the boundaries of his usage of Plato are blurred: things that in the latter's text are interconnected may have been taken for granted by Philo's audience even when he only refers to *some* of them. It is, in my estimation, undeniable that by abstaining from denouncing the doctrine of transmigration while making extensive use of reincarnational concepts, terms and images Philo took a conscious risk of being suspected of endorsing the tenet.

The conclusion concerning the indirect evidence on Philo's position on reincarnation is thus clear. His anthropology would well be able to accommodate the doctrine, as would his soteriology as well as what can be inferred of his individual eschatology. In Philo's thought orientation away from God and philosophy towards the corporeal leads to consequences that are in harmony with rebirth. The totality of the indirect evidence must be considered to be in notable agreement with the idea that souls are repeatedly born in this world to live in human bodies in order to labor towards achieving the purity which, together with God's vital grace, enables them to reach salvation.

CHAPTER THREE

THE DIRECT EVIDENCE

This chapter deals with the four Philonic texts that most clearly seem to refer to reincarnation. In the overview of previous research it was noted that *Somn.* 1.137–139 is actually the *locus classicus* of reincarnation in Philo. It is a comparatively straightforward case for which no other interpretation than reincarnation has been seriously suggested. In the examination of *Cher.* 114 more attention is paid to both contextual and text-critical issues, for the description is much less self-explanatory than the passage in *Somn.* The study of *QE* 2.40 is distinguished from the others by its genre and its having been fully preserved only in Armenian. Textual issues and many Philonic parallels are discussed. 114. Finally, as for fragment 7.3 Harris, the question of authenticity needs to be addressed in addition to hermeneutical and some textual matters. But in spite of these differences, the one question to be answered regarding every text is the same: *is Philo speaking of reincarnation?*[391]

3.1. *Somn. 1.137–139*

3.1.1 *Introduction*

The *De somniis* is the last extant work of Philo's *Allegorical Commentary* on Genesis. Its two surviving books (*Somn.* 1 and 2) deal with the dreams in Gen 28, 31, 37, 40 and 41. The original first book of the treatise has been lost. Although both extant books begin with a classification of dreams, Philo deals with the actual descriptions of the dreams as with any other material in Genesis.[392] Our passage is part of Philo's comments on Gen

---

[391] The nature of the statements in all four texts is such that if reincarnation is meant, it is met with approval.

[392] For example, in *Somn.* 1.2 Philo says that in the second kind of dreams (the subject matter of *Somn.* 1) our mind "mov[es] out of itself together with the Mind of the Universe" and seemingly becomes "possessed and God-inspired" so that it is able to have "foreknowledge of things to come." This has little if anything to do with his interpretation of Jacob's dream about the heavenly ladder (Gen 28:12–15) from which our passage comes. Instead, the explanations of the dream have much in common with both how Philo in *Somn.* 1 comments on the events in Genesis *preceding* the dream (vv. 10–11) and his general agenda, especially the importance of orientating away from everything corporeal. This has not always been seen in the research on *Somn.*: the relationship between the treatise and classical theories of dream interpretation has been over-emphasized and

28:12: "And he dreamed, and see, a ladder set firmly in the earth, whose top was reaching into heaven, and the angels of God were ascending and descending on it." Philo presents four mutually non-exclusive interpretations of this verse in *Somn*. The passage 1.137–139 belongs to a cosmological interpretation where the ladder symbolizes the air (1.134–145); in the others it is the symbol of the human soul (1.146–149), the ups and down of the "practiser's" life (1.150–152); and finally, life in general (1.153–156).

The cosmological interpretation consists of four parts: a general characterization of the air and the invisible souls that inhabit it (1.134–137); the interpretation of the angels on the ladder as human souls (1.138–139); a literal explanation of the angels as mediators between God and humans (1.140–143); and a few comments on the ladder's being firmly set on the earth and on the composition of the moon and the stars (1.144–145). The passage to be examined consists of the second part to which I have added the end of the first part because of an allusion to Plato's *Timaeus*.

3.1.2 *Text, Translation and Commentary*

There are no important text-critical problems with the passage (see below for three minor ones), and I accept all the readings of PCW.[393] I have laid

---

unfounded claims presented about, e.g., Philo's actually "*using* the system of Posidonius . . . for interpreting the dreams of Genesis" (Claes Blum, "Studies in the Dream-Book of Artemidorus" (diss., University of Uppsala, 1936), 68; emphasis added). See also A. H. M. Kessels, "Ancient Systems of Dream-Classification," *Mnemosyne*, 4/22.3 (1969): 389–424; Robert M. Berchman, "Arcana Mundi: Magic and Divination in the *De somniis* of Philo of Alexandria," in *Mediators of the Divine: Horizons of Prophecy, Divination, Dreams, and Theurgy in Mediterranean Antiquity*, ed. Robert M. Berchman; South Florida Studies in the History of Judaism 164 (Atlanta: Scholars Press, 1998), 115–54; Sofia Torallas Tovar, "Philo of Alexandria on Sleep," in *Sleep*, ed. Th. Wiedemann and Ken Dowden; Nottingham Classical Literature Studies 8 (Bari: Levante, 2003), 41–52; Derek Dodson, "Philo's '*De somniis*' in the Context of Ancient Dream Theories and Classifications," *PRSt* 30 (2003): 299–312; and Reddoch, "Dream Narratives." Features that are common to the interpretation of the dreams in *Somn*. and Philo's exegesis of other Pentateuchal material have been rightly seen by Christiansen, *Die Technik*; Eisele, *Ein unerschütterliches Reich*; and Meyer, *Kommt und seht*.

[393] Two manuscripts omit the section entirely. The omission in A and M (both from the thirteenth cent.) begins at the words ἰσαρίθμους ἄστροις at the end of §137 and extends to the end of §139 and thus covers the precise text I am here dealing with. These MSS. belong to different families which are, however, mutually "connected by certain far back errors" (Fred C. Conybeare, "Cohn's Philo," *The Classical Review* 11.1 (1897): 66–67, p. 66; PCW 1.xxxiii–xxxiv). The omission is difficult to explain as a slip and has the air of deliberate censorship—apparently by a scribe who had read the *Timaeus* (see below, p. 133). The motivation is almost certainly the view that reincarnation is discussed.

out the text according to its structure so that the three pairs of opposed expressions can be easily discerned.³⁹⁴

(137) ... οὐ γὰρ μόνος ἐκ πάντων ἔρημος οὗτος [sc. ἀήρ], ἀλλ' οἷα πόλις εὐάνδρει πολίτας ἀφθάρτους καὶ ἀθανάτους ψυχὰς ἔχων ἰσαρίθμους ἄστροις. (138) τούτων τῶν ψυχῶν

αἱ μὲν κατίασιν ἐνδεθησόμεναι σώμασι θνητοῖς, ὅσαι προσγειόταται καὶ φιλοσώματοι, **αἱ δ' ἀνέρχονται**, διακριθεῖσαι πάλιν κατὰ τοὺς ὑπὸ φύσεως ὁρισθέντας ἀριθμοὺς καὶ χρόνους.

(139) τούτων
αἱ μὲν τὰ σύντροφα καὶ συνήθη τοῦ θνητοῦ βίου ποθοῦσαι παλινδρομοῦσιν αὖθις,
αἱ δὲ πολλὴν φλυαρίαν αὐτοῦ καταγνοῦσαι
δεσμωτήριον μὲν καὶ τύμβον ἐκάλεσαν τὸ σῶμα,
φυγοῦσαι δ' ὥσπερ ἐξ εἱρκτῆς ἢ μνήματος ἄνω κούφοις πτεροῖς πρὸς αἰθέρα ἐξαρθεῖσαι μετεωροπολοῦσι τὸν αἰῶνα.

(137) ... For so far is air from being alone of all things untenanted, that like a city it has a goodly population, its citizens being imperishable and immortal souls equal in number to the stars. (138) Of these souls

some, those that are closest to the earth and lovers of the body, are descending to be fast bound in mortal bodies, while **others** are ascending, having again been separated (from the body) according to the numbers and periods determined by nature.

(139) Of these last **some**, longing for the familiar and accustomed ways of mortal life, hurry back again, while **others**, pronouncing that life great folly, **call** the body a prison and a tomb **but escaping** from it as though from a dungeon or a grave are lifted up on light wings to the ether and range the heights for ever. ³⁹⁵

In what follows next I examine the expressions that I have deemed to shed the most light on what Philo is talking about here. This is not meant to be a general commentary but a specific one: its purpose is to critically verify the preconception that I admit having: Philo describes here the phenomenon of reincarnation.³⁹⁶

---

³⁹⁴ The words printed in bold type serve the same purpose and are not meant to indicate which Greek and English expressions correspond to each other.
³⁹⁵ Tr. Whitaker in PLCL with modifications—of which one may be mentioned: his rendering of διακριθεῖσαι πάλιν as "being selected for return" in §138 is strange. While something like "being again distinguished" could be possible, if we only looked at the words in question, it would make no sense in context. See below, p. 136.
³⁹⁶ From this aim it follows that if a phrase of Philo's is found to have a close connection with a certain reincarnational text by someone else, no attempt is made to map out the whole history of its use. This is especially warranted as concerns Plato's works, which we know Philo knew so well.

However, before we proceed we must introduce two other texts that are clearly parallel to the one under consideration and which are probably ultimately derived from, or influenced by, a common source, *Gig.* 6–15 and *Plant.* 14.[397] The following excerpts may taken for the present purpose (more extracts will appear later):[398]

> *Gig.*: (6) ... Those whom the philosophers designate "daemons," Moses is accustomed to call angels. These are souls that fly in the air... . (12) Now some of the souls have descended into bodies, but others have never deigned to associate with any of the parts of earth... . (13) The former, however, descending into the body as though into a stream have sometimes been caught up in the violent rush of its raging waters and swallowed up, at other times, able to withstand the rapids, they have initially emerged at the surface and then soared back up to the place whence they had set out. (14) These, then, are the souls of the genuine philosophers, who from first to last practice dying to the life in the body in order to obtain the portion of incorporeal and immortal life in the presence of the Uncreated and Immortal. (15) But the souls that have sunk beneath the stream are the souls of the others who have had no regard for wisdom. They have surrendered themselves to unstable and chance concerns, none of which relate to our noblest part, the soul or mind, but all are related to that corpse which was our birth-fellow, the body.

> *Plant.*: (14) ... In the air He made the winged creatures perceived by senses, and other powers besides which are wholly beyond apprehension by sense. This is the host of the bodiless souls. Their array is made of companies that differ in kind. We are told that some enter into mortal bodies, and quit them again at certain periods ... while others, endowed with a diviner constitution, have no regard for any earthly quarter ... [i.e., those whom] the Greek philosophers call heroes, but whom Moses ... entitles "angels."

What Philo says of angels in *Somn.* 1.140–141 is quite similar to the accounts in *Gig.* and *Plant.* The essential point to note now is that in all three versions the souls occupying the air are divided into two types: those that incarnate and those that do not. We now turn to examining the reincarnational connotations of key expressions in *Somn.* 1.137–139.

---

[397] The partial parallel in *Conf.* will be dealt with below. A further one is found in *QG* 4.188; it mentions the incarnation and release (explicitly at death) of souls, the case of never incarnating souls as well as the fact that Moses calls the daemons angels. Apart from mentioning the stars in a close but somewhat vague connection with the angels, it brings nothing new to the picture (there is a quotation below in n. 418, p. 136). Finally, *QG* 4.29—although it clearly does not belong to this series of parallels—may be mentioned as the only other extant text by Philo where the ladder of Gen 28 is commented on. The notion of the necessity of incarnation in that passage was already noted (p. 53), and some brief remarks are presented below (p. 135).

[398] See Eisele, *Ein unerschütterliches Reich*, for a synoptic comparison between *Somn.* 1.133–145, 1.146–149 and *Gig.* 6–18; *Plant.* 11–14 is also discussed.

its citizens being imperishable and immortal souls equal in number to the stars ([ἀήρ] ἀφθάρτους καὶ ἀθανάτους ψυχὰς ἔχων ἰσαρίθμους ἄστροις): To take the last part first, Philo here quotes from *Timaeus* 41d, where the Demiurge, after mixing the appropriate material, "divided it into souls equal in number to the stars (ψυχὰς ἰσαρίθμους τοῖς ἄστροις)." Runia comments that seeing the air as "a flourishing city, populated with immortal souls" whose number is astronomical

> is an obvious attempt to systematize the doctrine of the *Timaeus* in relation to further data on demons and incorporeal souls in the *Symposium, Republic, Phaedrus* and *Epinomis*. The souls created by the demiurge are sown onto the planets *and* the earth (41e4-5, 42d4-5), so that it is natural to deduce that in the process of reincarnation there must be a continual procession of incorporeal souls in the air (cf. also *Phaedo* 81c–d).[399]

The characterization of the souls as imperishable and immortal is clearly an ontological statement and not in contradiction with their living the mortal life. As part of our efforts to delineate Philo's individual eschatology, it is important to note that here we have Philo's clear words that also the unvirtuous souls are immortal.[400]

What is the background of the notion that the souls inhabit the air? It is hardly just the *Phaedrus* as Billings suggests.[401] Runia's proposal seems plausible in that by "systematizing" certain texts by Plato(nists) such a result may be reached. Yet it seems that the idea may be older, as will be shortly seen. It is worth noting that we find similar notions in circles that espoused the tenet of reincarnation. One example is a Platonist with "Pythagorean sympathies," Xenocrates.[402] It seems clear that he considered souls and daemons one and the same thing (frr. 236, 237).[403] He also

---

[399] Runia, *Philo and the* Timaeus, 254. On his views on Philo and reincarnation more generally see above (1.4.3, pp. 20–25), and in *Somn.* specifically, below (p. 144).

[400] See the discussion on the concept of immortality in Philo above, p. 36. As for mortal life as an appellation for life in the body, see p. 47 above.

[401] Billings, *Platonism of Philo*, 41–42. He seems to locate the pre-earthly life of souls in 247a–b in the air, although Plato's text speaks about the heaven (246e).

[402] Dillon, *The Middle Platonists*, 35. Xenocrates was the second post-Platonic leader of the Academy. His precise views are uncertain, mediated as they are largely through Plutarch and not always distinguishable from his. See Dillon, *The Middle Platonists*, 26–32; Hermann S. Schibli, "Xenocrates' Daemons," pp. 146–49, 155–58.

[403] This may reflect older (Pythagorean) usage. Empedocles and possibly also Philolaus used the word δαίμων to mean what was later called ψυχή (fr. 115 DK; see Huffman, *Philolaus of Croton*, 330–31). The idea that at least a virtuous human being becomes a daemon after death occurs in Euripides (*Alcestis* 1003). Plato extends this to the living good in *Cratylus* 398b–c while calling the principal part of the soul by that name in *Timaeus* 90a.

seems to have equated the air with Hades (fr. 213) (and both with invisibility, i.e., being ἀειδής).[404] This is in good harmony with the idea that souls dwell in the air between incarnations. Already Plato had called both the soul and Hades invisible in *Phaedo* 80d.

Commenting on *Gig.* 8 and *Somn.* 1.135, Méasson aptly notes, "on croirait reconnaître ici un écho de la théorie pythagoricienne recueillie par Alexandre Polyhistor: 'L'air entier est plein d'âmes.'"[405] This quotation (εἶναί τε πάντα τὸν ἀέρα ψυχῶν ἔμπλεων) is from Diog. Laert. 8.32, from Alexander's (first cent. BCE) compendium of Pythagorean teachings which contains also other points of contact with Philo. Alexander says "the soul is invisible (ἀόρατος), and so are its faculties, inasmuch the ether itself is invisible" (8.30); cf. Philo's "the air, too, must therefore be filled with living things, though they are invisible to us, since even the air itself is not visible to sense" (*Gig.* 8).[406] Alexander also states that the souls that fill the air "are called daemons or heroes; these are they who send men dreams and signs of future disease and health." Compare this with *Gig.* 6 and *Plant.* 14 above.[407] The identification of airborne souls with *both* daemons and heroes occurs before Philo, according to Augustine (*City of God* 7.6), in the Middle Platonist Varro (d. 27 BCE).

Based on this cursory survey it seems that the notion of the air being filled with souls is originally, as far as we can trace it, probably Pythagorean. The idea entered Platonism already during the Old Academy, but it seems not to have attained a position of an essential doctrine.[408] It is not, for example, attested in Alcinous's *Didaskalikos*.

to be fast bound in mortal bodies (ἐνδεθησόμεναι σώμασι θνητοῖς): This phrase was discussed above in the section on Plato's reincarnational terminology

---

[404] Dillon, *The Middle Platonists*, 27 says the notion of the sublunary realm as Hades became common in Middle Platonism, and that (p. 178) Numenius said it was "a secret doctrine of Pythagoras that Hades is the whole area between the earth and the Milky Way, which is the abode of souls." Dillon refers to fragments 32, 34 and 35 des Places, but in fr. 35 Numenius identifies Hades with the Milky Way itself.
[405] Méasson, *Du char ailé de Zeus*, 275.
[406] Philo mentions that the soul is ἀόρατος also in *Somn.* 1.136; cf. "beyond apprehension by sense" in *Plant.* 14. This notion is much more commonplace without the mention of the invisibility of the medium.
[407] Similarly *Somn.* 1.141, where the terms "daemons" and "angels" are equated. In *Somn.* there also seems to be a link between angels (i.e., God's *logoi*) and dreams; see 1.70, 190.
[408] Interestingly, we find it also in a post-Philonic Stoic author: Lucius Annaeus Cornutus (1st cent. CE) writes in his *De natura deorum* (or *Compendium of Greek Theology*) that the final recipient of souls is air, or Hades—which is so called because of its being invisible (74.6 in Lang's edition; cf. 5.3).

and imagery in Philo and was found to be frequently used by him.[409] As was noted above, the interpretation that the descending angels represent the involuntary nature of the coming together of body and soul is mentioned also in the only other passage in Philo's extant writings that comments on the dream of the ladder, *QG* 4.29.[410] But there we do not find anything that would reveal whether Philo thought the union to take place just once or several times. The Platonic phrase hints at the latter option. In *Tim.* 44b it is, after all, the description of the very event of incarnation; Philo has just zoomed in on it so tightly that we may lose sight of the fact that reincarnation is meant.

those that are closest to the earth and lovers of the body (προσγειότατοι καὶ φιλοσώματοι): Body-love was already identified as a suitable driving force for reincarnation,[411] whereas the word πρόσγειος does not seem to be part of any tradition of reincarnational language.[412] Here it can probably be taken as more or less synonymous with φιλοσώματος; it is easy to envisage that the weaker the love for bodies, the higher the soul is able to rise between incarnations and *vice versa*.

Φιλοσώματος occurs only in the *Phaedo* before Philo.[413] There Socrates asks if it is not

> a sufficient indication, when you see a man troubled because he is going to die, that he was not a lover of wisdom (φιλόσοφος) but a lover of the body (φιλοσώματος)? And this same man is also a lover of money (φιλοχρήματος) and of honour (φιλότιμος), one or both. (*Phaedo* 68b–c)

---

[409] Subsection 2.4.1, pp. 113–14.
[410] See p. 53. I think it is precisely the theme of involuntariness of the psycho-somatic union that is the bridge between the main biblical lemma of *QG* 4.29 (Gen 18:33) and the secondary one (Gen 28:12), rather than the word τόπος occurring in both the main lemma and Gen 28:11 as suggested by David T. Runia, "Secondary Texts in Philo's *Quaestiones*," in *Both Literal and Allegorical: Studies in Philo of Alexandria's* Questions and Answers on Genesis and Exodus; ed. David M. Hay: BJS 232 (Atlanta: Scholars Press, 1991), 47–79, p. 56. That word plays no role in Philo's exegesis of the secondary lemma. Philo returns to the main lemma at the end of 4.29 and reiterates that "our race . . . is by nature shackled and involved it its needs."
[411] See pp. 46–48.
[412] Yet it may have something to do with the idea of Hades being located in the air: Lucius Annaeus Cornutus characterizes Hades as the "air that is densest and closest to the earth (παχυμερέστατος καὶ προσγειότατος ἀήρ)" (*De natura deorum* 4.17–18; cf. n. 408 above).
[413] In the work *On passions* (4.1.32) spuriously attributed to Andronicus of Rhodes (first cent. BCE) the word φιλοσωματία appears. This is defined there as ἐπιθυμία σώματος εὐθηνίας παρὰ τὸ δέον and thus seems to stem from the Platonic usage.

The opposition of loving wisdom vs. the body is not quite this explicit in the *Somn.* passage, but those who shun the mortal life abandon "great folly." Cf. *Deus* 109–111 where the "body- and passion-loving (φιλοσώματος καὶ φιλοπαθής) mind" is contrasted with the supreme wisdom represented by Moses and Noah, and cast "into the prison (δεσμωτήριον) of the passions." In the *Phaedo*, loving the body (verb ἐράω) is connected with the soul's becoming tainted thereby and its having to reincarnate because of this impurity (81b–e).[414]

having again been separated (from the body) according to the numbers and periods determined by nature (διακριθεῖσαι[415] κατὰ τοὺς ὑπὸ φύσεως ὁρισθέντας ἀριθμοὺς[416] καὶ χρόνους):[417] The μέν–δέ construction makes it inevitable that διακριθεῖσαι stands in contrast with ἐνδεθησόμεναι σώμασι θνητοῖς. Moreover, as Philo uses the verb διακρίνω for the separation of the soul from the body elsewhere (*Leg.* 1.106, *Agr.* 164, *Plant.* 147 and *Conf.* 36), there is no reason to think something else is meant here. The parallel in *Plant.* 14 also has exactly this sense despite the different wording: καὶ κατὰ τινας ὡρισμένας περιόδους ἀπαλλάττεσθαι πάλιν, "and quit [mortal bodies] again at certain fixed periods."[418] Cf. *Her.* 282, already discussed above, where too the timing of physical death is meant: καθ' ὡρισμένας περιόδους καιρῶν.[419]

It seems that Colson assumes Philo is in *Somn.* speaking about reincarnation, for in his note he considers the expression as equivalent to that occurring in *Plant.* and asks,

> Have we an allusion to the three περίοδοι χιλιετεῖς of *Phaedrus* 248 E ff., assigned to the philosophical souls, while the unjust remain on earth for 10,000 years? Compare also *Rep.* x. 617, and the proem of Empedocles quoted by Thompson on the *Phaedrus* passage.[420]

---

[414] See also the discussion on purity above, p. 97.
[415] Omitted by one MS., which is easier to explain as an error than its appearance was it not original.
[416] ὁρισμούς is the reading in one MS. and a correction in another. ἀριθμός appears connected with χρόνος by καί in *Gig.* 56 and *Somn.* 2.112; cf. also *Praem.* 110 where also ὁρίζω is found. ὁρισμός only occurs in *Leg.* 2.63 in an unrelated context; it could easily have been erroneously substituted in *Somn.* because of the influence of ὁρίζω.
[417] See also the discussion of temporal expressions above in subsection 2.4.3 on pp. 117–19. There the influence of an interpretative tradition of the *Timaeus* was noted.
[418] Also in *QG* 4.188 physical death is explicitly meant:
souls are buried in the mortal body [and] are released and separated and removed at death, or ... they have never in any way been bound (to bodies). So also (do) the daemons which the sacred word of Moses is want to call 'angels,' and the stars.
[419] See p. 117. In the same context the corresponding expression with an entirely different vocabulary was also noted in *Post.* 5.
[420] PLCL 5.600.

The reference to the *Republic* is evidently to 617d as already discussed.[421] Empedocles's proem in question runs,

> A law there is, an oracle of Doom (ἀνάγκης),
> Of old enacted by the assembled gods,
> That if a Daemon—such as live for ages (μακραίων)—
> Defile himself with foul and sinful murder,
> He must for seasons thrice ten thousand (τρὶς μυρίας ὥρας) roam
> Far from the Blest: such is the path I tread,
> I too a wanderer and exile from heaven.[422]

Of Colson's references the one to the *Republic* is the most pertinent, for, as Méasson notes on the expression in *Somn.* presently under consideration, "ces durées ne seraient autres que celles de la vie humaine."[423] The *Phaedrus* and Empedocles speak of other, longer, reincarnation-related periods.[424] Yet there seem to be parallels that are more relevant than *Rep*. It was already noted that in *Timaeus* 89b Plato speaks of "prescribed periods of life."[425] But what about the "numbers" Philo speaks of?[426] I find the following passage in Aristotle's *De generatione et corruptione* very helpful in understanding what Philo is saying about them in *Somn.* 1.138:

> and the natural processes (κατὰ φύσιν) of passing-away and coming-to-be occupy equal periods of time (ἐν ἴσῳ χρόνῳ). Hence, too, the times and lives of the several kinds of living things have a number by which they are distinguished (ἀριθμὸν ἔχουσι καὶ τούτῳ διορίζονται): for there is an Order controlling all things, and every time and life is measured by a period (πᾶς βίος καὶ χρόνος μετρεῖται περιόδῳ). (*De generatione et corruptione* 336b9–13)

This sheds light on the little less obvious part of Philo's expression in *Somn.* 1.138, "numbers ... determined by nature." The context is similar to

---

[421] See above, p. 118.
[422] As quoted by Plutarch, *De exilio* 607c. Compare also the statement by Herodotus who at 2.123 speaks of a cycle of three thousand years during which the soul passes through the various kinds of animals until it is born in a human body.
[423] Méasson, *Du char ailé de Zeus*, 286. Incorrectly Reddoch, "Dream Narratives," 203, "the period of time souls must remain aloft before returning to Earth."
[424] Cf. also *Phaedo* 113a, where the souls that (between incarnations) have arrived at the Acherusian lake in Tartarus remain there for "the appointed time" (τινας εἱμαρμένους χρόνους). Similarly 107e, 108c.
[425] See p. 118.
[426] Numbers are always involved in measuring time; cf. Cicero, *Somnium Scipionis* 4 (*De re publica* 6.12): "when your life has completed seven times eight full cycles of the sun; and these two numbers (*duoque ii numeri*), each of which for a different reason is held to be a perfect number, in the revolution of nature (*circuitu naturali*) has fulfilled your destined sum for you."

Philo's in speaking of the duration of life.⁴²⁷ It is beyond the scope of this study to delve into the exact meaning of "number" here, but there is likely to be Pythagorean influence in the background.⁴²⁸ Thus Philo is saying that the phenomenon he describes is regulated by natural laws in which numbers play an important role.

longing for the familiar and accustomed ways of mortal life (τὰ σύντροφα καὶ συνήθη τοῦ θνητοῦ⁴²⁹ βίου ποθοῦσαι): These words and concepts do not have an automatically negative connotation in Philo.⁴³⁰ Passages in which Philo does use the words σύντροφος, συνήθης/συνήθεια and ποθέω in a negative sense similar to the present context include, e.g., the following. Philo says about Lot's wife that she was the one

> who was turned into stone, whom we might call "custom" (συνήθειαν), if we gave her her right name; her nature is hostile to truth, and if we take her with us, she lags behind and gazes round at the old familiar objects (τὰ ἀρχαῖα καὶ σύντροφα) and remains among them like a lifeless monument. (*Ebr.* 164)

In *Spec.* 1 Philo discusses the soul which "has committed whoredom," i.e., "thrown itself into ... passion and soul-sickness and vice:"

> But as for the soul, when by constant familiarity with incontinence (ἀκολασίᾳ συντρόφῳ καὶ συνήθει) it has been schooled into harlotry, what agelong stretch of years (τὶς ἂν αἰών) can convert it to decent living? (*Spec.* 1.281–282)

In *Praem.* 16–18 Philo takes Enoch as representing "one who fled from the insurgency of the body." God's transferring him (Gen 5:24) is explained as a reference to migration (ἀποικία) and change of abode (μετανάστασις), i.e., "flee[ing] from home and country and kinsfolk and friends without a backward glance."⁴³¹ Philo continues: "For the customary is an attractive thing (ὁλκὸν γὰρ ἡ συνήθεια)."⁴³² Here too, one's liberation from the body seems threatened by what one has grown used to in the mortal life. As for the verb ποθέω, in *Leg.* 3.249 Philo explains the fire of Ex 22:6 as a symbol

---

⁴²⁷ Cf. *De gen. et corr.* 337a24: "Time, therefore, is a 'number' of some continuous movement—a 'number,' therefore, of the circular movement."
⁴²⁸ See Aristotle *De caelo* 300a15–17: "some of the Pythagoreans [compose the heaven of numbers; they] make all nature out of numbers (ἔνιοι γὰρ τὴν φύσιν ἐξ ἀριθμῶν συνιστᾶσιν)."
⁴²⁹ Word omitted by two MSS. without radically affecting the sense.
⁴³⁰ For mortal life, see above, p. 47. As for the rest, see *Her.* 234, *Mut.* 219 and *Somn.* 1.71, 111 for examples of positive meanings.
⁴³¹ Note the similarity of the ideas presented with *Migr.* 2 (above, p. 87)—the Greek name of which treatise is Περὶ ἀποικίας.
⁴³² Colson: "For great is the attraction of familiarity."

of the irrational impulse: "for being a searcher after the passions it finds what it wanted (ἐπόθει) to get."

In our search for reincarnational connections of Philo's language, it is warranted to take a closer look at the role of *the habitual* in the soul's journey as seen by Philo and Plato. We start from Philo's exegesis of Gen 26:19 in *QG* preserved in Armenian and Latin only. Philo comments on why the well was in the valley of Gerar. The name is to be interpreted as "sojourn:"[433] A sojourner either adapts to those among whom he resides (symbolized by obstructing the wells, Gen 25:15—see below) or else achieves alienation:

> [T]he digging and cleansing and purifying are an alienation, for the soul is thereby drawn away from the habitual (սովորութեանն [*sovorut'eann*]) toward the depth of the discipline of knowledge ... . Therefore the valley is like a sojourn, for he who yields to the deceptions (պատրանաց [*patranac'*]) of what is habitual is a fugitive and continually goes about in a low-lying place and in a valley-site. But he who is raised above them ascends and is removed to the greatness of virtue. (*QG* 4.195)

It is fairly obvious that Philo is again speaking about "the familiar and accustomed ways of mortal life."[434] That these are on the sensual side of life is rather self-evident but also implied by the word "deceptions."[435] Going around in a low place would fit repeated births on earth, but there is no way to ascertain that that is what Philo means here.

In a noteworthy manner, the habitual frequently constitutes a force which directs the process of rebirth in Plato. In *Republic* 620a he writes: "the choice [of the type of life in the new incarnation] was determined for the most part by the habits of their former lives (κατὰ συνήθειαν ... τοῦ προτέρου βίου)." In *Phaedo* 81e Socrates explains, "And they are likely to be imprisoned in characters (εἰς τοιαῦτα ἤθη) which correspond to the practices of their former life (μεμελετηκυῖαι τύχωσιν ἐν τῷ βίῳ)." He reiterates this in 82a when he rhetorically asks Cebes if "it is clear where all the other souls go, each in accordance with its own habits (κατὰ τὰς αὐτῶν ὁμοιότητας

---

[433] The Arm. word is պանդխտութիւն (*pandəxtut'iwn*) for which NBHL gives, *inter alia*, ἀποικία and παροικία. Different interpretations for the name Gerar are given at *QG* 4.59, 185.

[434] The word սովորութիւն (*sovorut'iwn*) translates ἔθος several times in Arm. Philo (MI: six instances), սովոր (*sovor*) and սովորական (*sovorakan*), συνήθης (three).

[435] Marcus actually translates, "lures," although he notes in MI that պատրանք (*patrank'*) renders ἀπάτη in *QG* 4.228 and *QE* 2.9 (to which add *QE* 2.14). Mercier in *QG* 4.195, "se conformer aux duperies de l'habitude," Aucher, "secundum consuetudinis errorem." See n. 283 (p. 88) and text for the deceitful character of sense-perception in Philo and Plato. Speech, too, another member of the triad to quit (*Leg.* 3.41, *Migr.* 2, *Her.* 69) is deceitful (*Migr.* 12).

τῆς μελέτης)?" The description in *Timaeus* 42c, "he shall be changed every time, according to the nature of his wickedness, into some bestial form after the similitude of his own nature," is in a similar vein. *Laws* 904c is not far, either: "For according to the trend of our desires (ὅπη γὰρ ἂν ἐπιθυμῇ) and the nature of our souls, each one of us generally becomes of a corresponding character."[436]

hurry back (παλινδρομοῦσιν): As was noted in the review of previous research, a statement has been made by Mansfeld about the use of this verb by Philo that it usually "refers to the return to the body."[437] An examination of the relevant passages (Appendix 1) shows him to be correct in the sense that παλινδρομέω almost always indicates a movement of one sort or another from incorporeal back to corporeal things.[438] Reincarnation cannot be ruled out, but it cannot be proven to be the referent, either. What is clear is that Philo has for some reason reserved this verb almost exclusively for indicating the return to the world of bodily things and sense-perception. Why? No explanation seems to be forthcoming from an analysis of the pre-Philonic use of the word;[439] neither do related expressions provide any clues.[440]

Without doubt the most important parallel for the usage of this verb here is that in *QE* 2.40 where "those who do not return from the holy and divine city" (as the Arm. text has it) are referred to. There too it is the verb of the actual event of reincarnation, if indeed this is what Philo means. This text will receive a separate treatment below in section 3.3.

great folly (πολλὴν φλυαρίαν): This is a Platonic expression, see *Symposium* 211e and *Phaedo* 66c. In both it is used in connection with the body: in the former it is presented as desirable "not [to be] infected with the flesh and

---

[436] Of these five passages, Méasson, *Du char ailé de Zeus*, 285 notes *Phaedo* 81e in her discussion on Philo's expressions in Somn. That reincarnation is referred to in the *Laws* passage is not quite as clear as it is in the others. In the notes to his translation Bury assumes it is, and points to *Tim.* 42b ff. The tenet is definitely mentioned in *Laws* 870d–e, quoted above on p. 94.
[437] Mansfeld, "Middle Platonist Cento," 144; see n. 50 on p. 16.
[438] The passages are *Post.* 156, *Migr.* 149, *Congr.* 164, *Fug.* 22, *Somn.* 2.233 and *Abr.* 86. See pp. 251–54.
[439] Out of the 31 instances of the verb that the TLG gives as occurring before Philo, 22 are in the medical corpus of Hippocrates, and the rest are *hapax legomena* in seven writers plus two occurrences in Diodorus Siculus. The *hapax* cases include testimonies by later authors such as Plutarch and Galen.
[440] E.g., πάλιν close to or in compounds of τρέχω δρομάω δρομέω δρομόω; or παλινδρομία παλίνδρομος ἀνατρέχω ἀναδρομή.

color of humanity, and ever so much more of mortal trash (ἄλλης πολλῆς φλυαρίας θνητῆς)," and in the latter "the body fills us with passions and desires and fears, all sorts of fancies and foolishness (φλυαρίας ἐμπίμπλησιν ἡμᾶς πολλῆς)."[441] Cf. also *Phaedo* 67a where "God himself sets us free ... from the foolishness of the body (τῆς τοῦ σώματος ἀφροσύνης)."

Philo uses φλυαρία only seven times. The other occurrences (once with πολλή as attribute, *Prob.* 104) are unrelated to the body. It is worth noting that both quotations from the *Phaedo* above come from a long, imaginary citation by Socrates of what "lovers of wisdom" (φιλοσόφοι, 66b) or those who are "rightly lovers of learning" (τοὺς ὀρθῶς φιλομαθεῖς) say to each other. These terms bring to mind the wise who love learning and are only sojourning in the body (*Conf.* 77–78) and those genuinely philosophizing souls that study to die to the life in the body (*Gig.* 14).[442]

call the body a prison and a tomb but escaping from it as though from a dungeon or a grave (καταγνοῦσαι δεσμωτήριον μὲν καὶ τύμβον ἐκάλεσαν τὸ σῶμα, φυγοῦσαι δ' ὥσπερ ἐξ εἱρκτῆς ἢ μνήματος): The images of the body as a prison or a grave have already been discussed in the context of incarnation as a punishment and Philo's use of Greek reincarnational terminology.[443] Concerning the wording in *Somn.* 1.139, it may be noted that Philo uses τύμβος only three times, the other occurrences being at *Deus* 150 and *QG* 1.70. In each instance the body is meant; in the former the body is "the soul's house, or tomb, or what other name it may be given," whereas *Phaedrus* 250c reverberates in the latter: "the bad persons ... are dead to true life and bear their body with them like a tomb (οἷον τύμβον περιφέροντας in the Greek fr.) that they may bury their unhappy soul in it."[444] Additionally, in *Leg.* 1.106, 108 and *Spec.* 4.188 there are participles of the exceedingly rare verb ἐντυμβεύω which Philo actually seems to have coined for indicating the soul's state of being buried in the body.[445] One is reminded about the play on the words σῆμα and σῶμα, and Philo indeed invokes that in *Leg.* 1.108 and *Spec.* 4.188. Τύμβος as such does not seem to carry any reincarnational connotations.

---

[441] The phrase is used also in *Apol.* 19c where Aristophanes's Socrates talks "a vast deal of other nonsense." The two other occurrences of the expression before Philo are in the *Protrepticus* by Aristotle (fr. 110 1. 4) and in *Ars rhetorica* (8.12.37) which is attributed to Dionysius of Halicarnassus but spurious.
[442] For quotations, see above, pp. 54 and 132, respectively.
[443] See above, pp. 57–64, 119–120.
[444] For *Phaedrus* 250c, see above, p. 119.
[445] After the three occurrences in Philo the next is in Didymus Caecus ("the Blind") followed by only six instances in four writers throughout the middle ages.

Plato uses μνῆμα once in a description of rebirth but apparently in a concrete meaning (*Phaedo* 81c–d).

are lifted up on light wings to the ether and range the heights for ever (ἄνω κούφοις πτεροῖς πρὸς αἰθέρα ἐξαρθεῖσαι μετεωροπολοῦσι τὸν αἰῶνα): Probably the most informative background for the gist of this statement can be found in the *Phaedrus* where the lightness of the soul and its wings are often referred to.[446] There is also another verbal connection to the dialogue, i.e., to 246c where Socrates explains that when "[s]oul, considered collectively ... is perfect and fully winged, it mounts upward (μετεωροπορεῖ) and governs the whole world."[447]

That souls soar to the ether on liberation is not an idea explicitly stated by Plato himself.[448] Yet Philo would have known it from Greek literature in any case.[449] In Philo, reaching the ether (which is more or less the same as heaven) does not represent the final salvation, *followed* as it is

---

[446] See 246a, c–d; 248b–c, e; 249b, d; 251b; 256b, d. In the *Timaeus*, also, the soul "flies away" at physical death (81e, verb ἐκπέτομαι).

[447] Some MSS. read μετεωροπολεῖ instead of μετεωροπορεῖ, but even in the case of the latter verb the degree of reminiscence is very high. According to Méasson, *Du char ailé de Zeus*, 284, Philo's choice of verb echoes *Phaedrus* 246c "[s]ans doute," although here she does not note the variation -πολεῖ vs. -πορεῖ (on p. 334 she does). As for the text, Burnet's, contrary to that of Schanz followed by Fowler, reads πᾶσα ψυχή (without the definite article), thus "every soul," which is more understandable.

[448] The seeds of the idea of the soul's ascension to the ether when it is freed from the body are detectable also in Plato's writings: in the *Phaedrus* the soul rises to the heaven, which is the same as the ether according to the *Phaedo* (109b–110a). Or, in *Phaedo* 69c Socrates says that the one who dies pure will dwell with the gods, and given that the stars, too, are gods (*Timaeus* 41a), or, located in the ether (*Phaedo* 109b), it follows that the pure souls rise to the ether after death. *Phaedo* 109b may also be combined with the virtuous soul's return to its native star (*Tim.* 42b). This is not to say that Plato would consider this kind of harmonizing appropriate, but rather to point out how the rise of such an interpretation in later tradition (see, e.g., *Axiochus* 366a) can be understood in the light of his works.

[449] See *Aet.* 30 for a quotation from fragment 839 Nauck of Euripides. It is cited also in *Leg.* 1.7—without the lines mentioning the return to the ether, but we can safely assume Philo had read them too. Cf. also the same tragedian's *Supplices* 531–534: "Let the dead now be buried in the earth, and each element return to the place from where it came to the body, the breath to the air (πνεῦμα μὲν πρὸς αἰθέρα), the body to the ground." In the Pythagorean *Golden Verses* (timing uncertain) the virtuous soul enters the ether after death, becoming an immortal god (lines 70–71). Ideas implying a comparable vertical movement are attested also within Judaism prior to Philo's time. Cf. Eccl 12:7—"and the dust returns to the earth as it was and the spirit (τὸ πνεῦμα) returns to the God who gave it"—and the Hebrew (but not Greek!) version of the Wisdom of Ben Sira 40:11—"all that is from the earth returns to the earth and what is from on high [returns] on high."

by encountering God (*Opif.* 70, *Plant.* 22).[450] At the end of his cosmological interpretation of the ladder (*Somn.* 1.145), extending from earth *to heaven*, Philo mentions the ether again, now as the substance the heavenly bodies. Nevertheless, the distinction between the returning souls and those who "range the heights for ever" does seem to imply that the latter are permanently saved. The same seems true for a partial parallel to *Somn.* 1.139, a clearly *Phaedrus*-inspired passage in *Spec.* 1:

> For the soul of the lover of God does in truth leap from earth to heaven (πρὸς οὐρανόν) and, having been given wings roams the heights (πτερωθεῖσα μετεωροπολεῖ),[451] eager to take its place in the ranks and share the ordered march of sun and moon and the all-holy, all-harmonious host of the other stars, marshalled and led by the God Whose kingship none can dispute or usurp, the kingship by which everything is justly governed. (*Spec.* 1.207)

The use of συντάσσω ("take its place in the ranks of" above) is indicative of a rather fixed union and points to final salvation. However, the happy lot of the saved does not clarify that of the less fortunate souls. The obvious Platonic overtones do not help us in answering our specific question about rebirth—except at the level of indirect evidence, Philo's not avoiding Plato's reincarnational passages.

3.1.3 *Review of Scholarly Opinions*

In what follows my starting point is that the possibility that Philo is speaking of reincarnation in *Somn.* 1.139 is obvious. I will therefore bypass such discussions of the passage (1.137–139) in scholarly literature that do not address this issue explicitly at all.[452] For scholars that have expressed some reincarnation-related view on the passage but have not actually analyzed its contents, see the section on previous research.[453]

---

[450] Another strand in Philo is that striving to rise to the ether should not be made a goal in itself as it is in Chaldean astrology (*Migr.* 184, *Mut.* 72, *Somn.* 1.54).
[451] Colson: "wings its way on high." The phrase is a reference to *Phaedrus* 246c (ἐπτερωμένη καὶ μετεωροπορεῖ).
[452] Examples are Billings, *Platonism of Philo*, 41; Baer, *Philo's Use of the Categories Male and Female*, 86; Peder Borgen, *Philo of Alexandria: An Exegete for His Time*, NovTSup 86 (Leiden: Brill, 1997), 237 and Meyer, *Kommt und seht*, 314.
[453] Section 1.4, pp. 9–29. These include de' Rossi, *The Light of the Eyes*; Pétau, *Opus de Theologicis Dogmatibus*; Fabricius *Exercitatio de Platonismo*; Elmgren, *Philon av Alexandria*; Christiansen, *Die Technik*; Winston and Dillon, *Two Treatises*; Mansfeld, "Middle Platonist Cento"; Vollenweider, "Reinkarnation"; Eisele, *Ein unerschütterliches Reich*; and Reddoch, "Dream Narratives." All say or imply that reincarnation is meant.

144   CHAPTER THREE

David T. Runia writes that, based on the similarities of *Gig.* 6–11, *Somn.* 1.134–141 and *Plant.* 12–14 with certain passages from Apuleius (died c. 180 CE), Philo's source may well have been some Middle Platonist work but that this remains uncertain.[454] He also writes,

> The entire section Somn. 1.134–141 is clearly derived from an intermediate source, and so there is a good chance that the allusion [to *Timaeus* 41d, "equal in number to the stars," in *Somn.* 1.137] was also located there and that Philo simply took it over.[455]

As we saw above, Runia speaks of the lack of full integration on the part of Philo regarding the idea of the pre-existence of the soul, but he is not clear on the evidence to support this thesis.[456] Our key results in Ch. 2 run counter to this claim, but do not suffice to prove that Philo had in fact integrated reincarnation into his thought world.[457] With regard to *Somn.* 1.134–141 and its parallels, I think that simply copying but not really digesting what he had copied would not fit well the kind of thinker Philo was, one who paid so much attention to textual detail in the Bible. Fortunately, we can, to some extent, test the matter, for it stands to reason that such adoption of material would be reflected in Philo's staying close to the original source so that the ideas are expressed in much the same way each time. Table V examines the occurrence or otherwise of such a phenomenon in the four accounts of the airy souls.

---

[454] Runia, *Philo and the* Timaeus, 229. The passages he names are *De dogmate Platonis* 204 (part of sections 1.XI–XII) and *De Deo Socratis* 137 (~ VIII–IX). However, these deal chiefly with the creatures of the elements and the daemons of the air and do not provide a clear parallel to Philo's reference to the entry of some souls into human bodies and the exit therefrom after a certain period, or reincarnation. It is thus questionable if Philo really is drawing on some source common with Apuleius on *these* topics. Note, however, that at *De Deo Socratis* 150 Apuleius notes that human, incarnated souls, too, can be called daemons and at §154 states that there is another, higher (than human) kind of daemons, always free from the body; this is surely the same, traditional distinction Philo makes between human souls and angels. As for reincarnation, Alcinous, whom Runia also mentions in this context (*Did.* 15.1, 16.1–2) comes closer (cf. also *Did.* 25.6, Table I above, p. 45).
[455] Idem, 254.
[456] Idem, 348. See above, pp. 33–36.
[457] See the conclusions on pp. 127–28.

Table V. The Greek Expressions Used for Some of the Items That Occur in the Accounts of the Souls of the Air in *Gig.*, *Plant.*, *Conf.* and *Somn.* Expressions that have a (nearly) identical counterpart are printed in bold.

	Gig. 6, 12–14	*Plant.* 14	*Conf.* 174, 176–177	*Somn.* 1.138–141
What the souls of the air are called and by whom (in Gig. the description applies to all souls, in the others, to angels only)	οὓς **ἄλλοι φιλόσοφοι δαίμονας, ἀγγέλους** Μωυσῆς εἴωθεν ὀνομάζειν	ἃς οἱ μὲν παρ' Ἕλλησι φιλοσοφήσαντες ἥρωας καλοῦσι, Μωυσῆς δὲ ὀνόματι εὐθυβόλῳ χρώμενος ἀγγέλους προσαγορεύει	**ἀγγέλους** τὰς ψυχὰς ταύτας **εἴωθε καλεῖν** ὁ θεσπιῳδὸς λόγος	ταύτας **δαίμονας** μὲν οἱ **ἄλλοι φιλόσοφοι**, ὁ δὲ ἱερὸς λόγος **ἀγγέλους εἴωθε καλεῖν** προσφυεστέρῳ χρώμενος ὀνόματι
The souls' descent	κατέβησαν, καταβᾶσαι	–	–	κατίασιν
Their connection with the body	ὥσπερ εἰς ποταμὸν, συμφυᾶ	εἰσκρίνεσθαι	(οὐκ) **ἐνδεθεῖσαι**	**ἐνδεθησόμεναι**
Their separation from it	(ἵνα τῆς ἀσωμάτου ... ζωῆς μεταλάχωσιν)	ἀπαλλάττεσθαι	–	διακριθεῖσαι
The ascent	ἀνενήξαντο, ἀνέπτησαν	– [458]	–	ἀνέρχονται, κούφοις πτεροῖς, ἐξαρθεῖσαι
The angels' lot	–	θειοτέρας κατασκευῆς **λαχούσας**	ἀκήρατον καὶ εὐδαίμονα κλῆρον ἐξ ἀρχῆς **λαχοῦσαι**	μειζόνων φρονημάτων καὶ θειοτέρων ἐπι**λαχοῦσαι**[459]
Their aversion for the earthly	οὐδενὶ τῶν **γῆς** μορίων ἠξίωσάν ποτε συνενεχθῆναι	ἅπαντος ἀλογεῖν τοῦ **γῆς** χωρίου	–	μηδενὸς μὲν τῶν **περιγείων** ποτὲ ὀρεχθεῖσαι τὸ παράπαν

More examples could be cited, but these will suffice to show that Philo felt free to omit parts and add others when formulating what he had to say about the souls of the air.[460] Certain notions (the appellations of angels and their lot) are more often expressed in almost identical words than others, which to me amounts to integrating more fixed elements with more flexible ones.[461] Is it believable, then, that while presenting on

---

[458] Cf. *Plant.* 22, cited in Appendix 3, p. 262.
[459] Cf. *Opif.* 84: the "heavenly beings" that are exempt from human rule are described as "hav[ing] obtained a portion that is more divine (θειοτέρας μοίρας ἐπιλαχόντα)."
[460] Cf. also the account in *QG* 4.188 with many small differences (n. 418, p. 136).
[461] Here one wonders if the juxtaposition of the Greek and Jewish appellations of angels, in itself, is not part of a Hellenistic *Jewish* tradition, for it seems to be the most fixed element of all. It is not reflected in the Septuagint.

different occasions the contents of a possible Middle Platonist source in different ways, Philo failed to exercise discretion regarding major tenets (pre-existence and reincarnation) therein, and simply included them in treatises of his own? My answer is negative, but one may reply to this question also by pointing out that in *Plant.* and *Gig.* he did not include reincarnation at all; maybe this is a sign of inadequate integration? In *Plant.* other possible signs of Philo's distancing himself from the source are that no vertical movement is mentioned and the phrase "*we are told*" is included. In *Gig.*, the angels' happy *lot* is not mentioned (although they are "sacred and inviolate" and carry on a "glorious and blameless ministry" in §16), and the image of the body as river and the practising of death, absent in the others, are added.[462] The last points strengthen Plato's presence. But ultimately we will be in a better position to answer the question as to why the souls' return to earth is not mentioned in *Plant.* and *Gig.* only after Philo's position on transmigration has been established.[463]

The matter can and should also be viewed from another angle, however. Assuming, for the sake of argument, that Philo endorsed reincarnation but did not want to talk about it often, we may ask: how would his audience, familiar with his interpretations of the dream of the ladder, have seen the accounts in *Gig.* and *Plant.*? Would they not have noticed the parallelism and perceived them as referring to the same underlying set of ideas as those presented in *Somn.*, i.e., as a reference also to reincarnation? I would argue that what I above wrote about Philo and Plato applies, *mutatis mutandis*, here as well: "the boundaries ... are blurred: things that in [one] text are interconnected may have been taken by Philo's audience for granted [in another] even when he only refers to *some* of them."[464] Thus the absence of reincarnation in *Gig.* and *Plant.* is not quite as incontestable as it might at first seem. In any case, it is worth noting Philo wanted to present varying parts of the scheme of souls and angels in the air as the interpretation of no less than five very different biblical verses. This gives it added weight and highlights the importance of understanding this phenomenon both from the viewpoint of Philo's theology and his exegetical method.

In his review of Méasson's work on the Platonic myths in Philo, Runia writes:

---

[462] The river metaphor is present in another interpretation of the ladder dream, see *Somn.* 1.147.
[463] Another clear conclusion from the data in Table V is the uncontroversial fact that a Greek philosophical tradition lies behind the appellations "daemon" and "hero."
[464] See p. 128.

Somn. 1.134–141, because it appears to imply reincarnation, is a unique and rather troubling text in Philo (cf. D. Winston, *Logos and mystical theology in Philo of Alexandria* (Cincinnati 1985) 36 ff.).[465]

This seems to be another way of expressing the thesis of incomplete integration.[466] The reference is somewhat misleading, because Winston considers it likely that Philo believed in reincarnation. Moreover, in the book referred to Winston does not discuss reincarnation in the *Somn.* passage; he only comments certain expressions in §138 and does not even mention the return to mortal life in §139.[467]

In a later article Runia mentions "esp. *Somn.* 1.139" when he says that "[i]t is far from clear that Philo subscribes to the doctrine of metempsychosis, but there are a few isolated passages which an interpreter could read in this way if he wished."[468] More recently, Runia calls *Somn.* 1.139 "one explicable exception" from the rule that "the doctrine of reincarnation is not found in his writings" since he "cannot accept the Platonic doctrine of reincarnation."[469]

Anita Méasson is clear about her view that reincarnation is precisely what Philo is speaking about in *Somn.* 1.138–139.[470] She sees in the account themes from two of Plato's dialogues. To put it briefly, Philo "(ou mieux sa source)" combines the soul's descent on earth to be buried in the tomb of the body and its reascension to the ether on light wings from the *Phaedrus* and the body-loving soul which, even after death, stays close to the earth

---

[465] David T. Runia, review of Anita Méasson, *Du char ailé de Zeus à l'Arche d'Alliance: Images et mythes platoniciens chez Philon d'Alexandrie*, VC 42 (1988): 290–95, p. 295.
[466] See above, p. 33.
[467] Winston, *Logos and Mystical Theology*, 35. In Winston & Dillon, *Two Treatises*, 237 he does say Philo "envisages reincarnation" in *Somn.* 1.139; see the discussion on Winston's views above in subsection 1.4.2, pp. 19–20.
[468] David T. Runia, "Why Does Clement of Alexandria Call Philo 'the Pythagorean'?" VC 49 (1995): 1–22, p. 20, n. 58. He does mention "even the doctrine of metempsychosis" as one of the conceivable reasons why Clement twice calls Philo "the Pythagorean" (*Strom.* 1.72.4, 2.100.3), but then makes the statement just quoted and refers to his *Philo and the Timaeus*, pp. 346–49, for which see above, subsection 1.4.3, pp.20–25. Jennifer Otto, "Philo, Judaeus? A Re-evaluation of Why Clement Calls Philo 'the Pythagorean,'" SPhA 25 (2013): 115–38 argues that the reason why Clement in two out of four instances of naming Philo calls him "Pythagorean" is the connection between Philo and Pythagorean exegesis and esotericism.
[469] David T. Runia, "Theodicy in Philo of Alexandria," in *Theodicy in the World of the Bible*, ed. Antti Laato and Johannes De Moor (Leiden: Brill, 2003), 576–604, p. 600.
[470] Méasson, *Du char ailé de Zeus*, 284, 286, 287, 290. Yet she considers Philo's words in *Somn.* 1.139 as an *indirect* mention of reincarnation (p. 286): "certaines [âmes] refusent leur libération et reviendront sur leur pas, Philon nous laissant entendre, sans le dire explitement, qu'elles vont s'incarner de nouveau." Strictly speaking, she is right. But Philo really leaves no other options for his interpreter.

because it wants to re-enter a body-prison from the *Phaedo*.⁴⁷¹ I find this analysis accurate, perceptive and unforced. There is, however, one point where Méasson's position is not sufficiently justified. She states that the souls which "are closest to the earth" etc. in *Somn.* 1.138 "descendent pour s'incarner une première fois."⁴⁷² Philo does not say this. Are there any grounds for asserting that these souls are in some way distinguishable from those that, "longing for the familiar and accustomed ways of mortal life, hurry back again" in 1.139? I think not. In making this distinction Méasson assumes Philo here departs from what the *Phaedo* says about souls that are φιλοσώματοι: they, as she herself puts it, "ont fait l'expérience de l'incarnation."⁴⁷³ Méasson's interpretation raises the speculative question, already discussed, as to whether souls that have never experienced the body can love it.⁴⁷⁴ Her view that this is a description of the process of rebirth in fact accentuates the unnecessary nature of her assumption that the first-mentioned souls are incarnating for the first time: it is more natural to think that according to Philo souls whirl in the cycle of reincarnation for as long as they love the body and are liberated once they denounce the bodily life.⁴⁷⁵

So far everything points to the conclusion that regardless of whether Philo in his heart endorsed the idea of reincarnation and whether he wrote about it elsewhere or not, that is what he means in *Somn.* 1.139. And indeed, alternative explanations are extremely rare. We shall conclude this subsection by examining those presented by Wright in his article on Philo's relation to the watcher tradition of 1 Enoch. Wright says *Somn.* 1.139 "presents two possible lines of interpretation," but he actually puts forward three: (1) reincarnation; (2) that the return "back to the tomb of the body" is "a case of possession by an 'evil one,'" i.e., an evil spirit; and, (3):

> In terms of Philo's allegorical method, however, this passage could simply be describing someone who had the opportunity to be purified and return to the community, but chose to continue in pursuit of the pleasures of the flesh.⁴⁷⁶

---

⁴⁷¹ Idem, 285–87. As noted above, the ether is not mentioned in the *Phaedrus*. But see n. 448.
⁴⁷² Idem, 284; also 285–286.
⁴⁷³ Idem, 285.
⁴⁷⁴ See the examination of body-love as a cause of incarnation, pp. 46–48.
⁴⁷⁵ Cf. what Savinel says in the Introduction to his translation of *Somn.* in PAPM 19 (p. 15): "Les âmes des charnels dans leur aveuglement préféront redescendre sur la terre 'se faire lier à des corps mortels' (I, 138)." He thus harmonizes the two mentions of incarnation, as I think is appropriate.
⁴⁷⁶ Archie T. Wright, "Some Observations of Philo's *De gigantibus* and Evil Spirits in Second Temple Judaism," in *JSJ* 36.4 (2005): 471–88, p. 477, n. 21. His article focuses on

Regarding interpretation (2) it may be asked, how Philo's words in *Gig.* 16 should be understood given that he wishes his audience to "put away that most oppressive burden, or superstition." Cf. Colson's rendering the last word (δεισιδαιμονία) as "the fear of daemons or superstition," which reflects also its literal meaning. If interpretation (2) is accepted, Philo must have thought that possession is possible but there is no use worrying about it in advance. But there is no evidence of such a view in Philo, and Wright's own position contradicts it when he says that if Philo knew the watcher tradition, he was probably aiming to write a corrective to it (i.e., *Gig.*) and to speak "specifically against the first century idea that evil spirits are the cause of human suffering."[477] If this is accepted, we have the alternative that *Somn.* and *Gig.* contradict each other over this issue, but as the evidence of Philo's speaking of possession anywhere in his works is nonexistent (Wright mentions only *Somn.* 1.139 as a candidate), alternative (2) should be dismissed.

The mention of Philonic allegory in alternative (3) is somewhat difficult to understand, as this usually means Philo's seeing deeper meanings in the biblical text. Apparently Wright means that Philo's allegorical interpretation is itself an allegory of something else, i.e., the continued pursuit of fleshly pleasures by someone who had had the opportunity of purification and returning to the community. This last expression must then refer to the souls that "are lifted up on light wings to the ether and range the heights for ever." But if this is the case, we must, e.g., assume that Philo has chosen to symbolize rejoining this apparently earthly community with an image of ascending to the ether, and this does not make sense. Of Wright's alternatives, only reincarnation is left.

3.1.4 *Conclusions*

There is no serious alternative to regarding *Somn.* 1.137–139 as a description of reincarnation. The text presents the driving forces of the soul's recurrent captivity in the body as being close to earth, loving the body and "longing for the familiar and accustomed ways of mortal life." This fits very well with our previous results about the causes of incarnation: body-love is explicitly present and the punitive aspect implied by the image of the body as a prison. The mind's habituation to mortal life is a new feature, but recurrent in Plato's descriptions of reincarnation. It in no way contradicts

---

Gig., and he does not take a clear position on which of the three alternatives related to *Somn.* he favors.
[477] Wright, "Observations," 482.

our previous findings, for it can be thought of as the "chronification" of the mind's corporealization. The passage also makes clear the preconditions of liberation, i.e. the realization of the bodily life as folly and the body as a dungeon and a grave. Salvation is presented as an incorporeal and exalted state that lasts for ever, which is a somewhat more modest formulation than the definition of salvation in *Gig.* 14 but cannot be said to be in contradiction with it.

All this makes for an internally consistent whole which is in harmony with Philo's views of the human being and his ethos of turning away from all things corporeal in order to reach the heavenly heights (cf. Ch. 2). It is thus no wonder that the fact that Philo speaks of reincarnation in this passage was seen to mean that he in fact approves the tenet in general.

3.2 *Cher. 114*

3.2.1 *Introduction*

De cherubim is the second surviving treatise in Philo's *Allegorical Commentary*. It deals with the interpretation of Gen 3:24 (§§ 1–39) and 4:1–2 (§§ 40–130). The passage under scrutiny belongs to the second part, the leading subject of which is the figure of Cain. For Philo Cain represents the delusion of the mind that all that it perceives through its senses are its own "possession"—the meaning of the name Cain according to Philo (*Cher.* 52, 68).

From the viewpoint of examining Philo's relation to reincarnation the interesting statement is contained in a short aside on the events after death in §114: Philo states in plain terms that physical death is followed by a "regeneration," παλιγγενεσία.[478] This much is clear from the outset, for in spite of several text-critical problems, the notion of regeneration after death is common to all the variant readings; see Appendix 2. In the review of earlier scholarship it was noted that Bentwich sees here a reference to reincarnation "in accordance with current Pythagorean ideas."[479] He was no doubt aware that Pythagoras is reported to have used the word παλιγγενεσία to refer to the tenet; Plutarch did so too.[480] Plato, while not

---

[478] In distinction to the word "rebirth" which I have used to mean reincarnation, I am using "regeneration" as the translation of παλιγγενεσία in Philo. I have not, however, changed the word in other scholars' translations and comments; as a rule, they translate the Greek term as 'rebirth.'
[479] See above, p. 15.
[480] For Pythagoras, see Servius's *Commentary on the Aeneid*, 3.68: "Pythagoras vero non μετεμψύχωσιν, sed παλιγγενεσίαν esse dicit;" also fr. 8 DK 1. 17. For Plutarch, see, e.g., *De esu carnium* ii, 2.998c. For the history of the use of παλιγγενεσία in the sense of reincarnation,

using the noun, in *Phaedo* 113a refers to reincarnation by a combination of πάλιν and γένεσις and has the combination of πάλιν and γίγνομαι in the same sense in *Phaedo* 70c, d; 72a and *Meno* 81b.[481] This slender contact with the *Phaedo* is reinforced by a fair number Phaedonic elements scattered in *Cher*. If taken in isolation, any one of them may be dismissed as too general or incidental, but cumulatively they, in my view, amount to a subtle but clear presence of the dialogue for anyone sufficiently familiar with it.[482] In that dialogue the "ancient tradition" (70c) of *metempsychosis* has the most prominent role of all of Plato's works. If Philo wished a treatise of his to be read against such a background, that is an interpretative key which, although not decisive for the interpretation of any single detail, should not be overlooked.

Thus in principle *Cher*. 114 could well be a reference to reincarnation: we have here a rare description of afterlife and, as a key term, a word with a track record of denoting reincarnation. Philo chooses not to cast any direct light on the nature of the regeneration; I agree with Burnett that the references to the "initiates" as the audience (*Cher*. 42, 48; cf. 49) warrant the view that "we cannot expect [Philo] to give a complete presentation of

---

see Joseph Dey, Παλιγγενεσία: *Ein Beitrag zur Erklärung der religionsgeschichtlichen Bedeutung von Tit 3, 5*. NTAbh XVII, 5 (Münster: Aschendorffsche, 1937), 13–25.

[481] The last passage was quoted above, p. 93. Plato uses these combinations in a generic manner as well, but in the context of afterlife reincarnation is their only meaning. Dey, Παλιγγενεσία, 14 is sceptical about the link between the combinations and παλιγγενεσία, but I think it is clear that in any case Philo would have seen the connection.

[482] Apart from the notion of regeneration itself, I would list these elements as follows:
– The noetic reality is unchangeable (ὡσαύτως ἔχειν): Cher. 51; Phaedo 79d.
– We are God's possessions (θεοῦ κτήματα): §§ 65, 71, 118–19, 124; 62d.
– The soul is divine (θεῖα): §93; 80a.
– The soul and God/the divine reality are *both* invisible (ἀόρατος): §101; 79b, 80a.
– The soul can be tainted (μιαίνω): §§ 51–52; 81b. (This notion Philo was familiar with also from the LXX: Lev 11:44, 21:1, Ez. 4:14, 44:25).
– Nothing mortal is fit to rule: §83; 80a. (Cf. also Sophocles fr. 755 Radt, Ζεὺς ἐμὸς ἄρχων, θνητῶν δ' οὐδείς, quoted by Philo in *Prob*. 19.)
– The soul rules the body: §115; 80a, 94b, d–e.
– An imperfect soul/mind is a wanderer (πλάνης, πλανάω): §116; 79c–d, 81a. (Also Prov 13:9, Wis 17:1; cf. Isa 21:4, Ps 118:176 LXX).
– An imperfect soul is forced to follow the senses: §117; 79c.
– An imperfect soul is characterized by a deficient νοῦς: §116; 81a; cf. 82b.
– The lyre and its harmony are discussed at §110, 92b–c.
– A purified mind (κεκαθαρμένη διάνοια) may have hope (ἐλπίς) of being approached by God: §§ 106–107; 67b–c. (There may also be a revision of Plato's views intended here. Philo explicitly says being God's slave is "a treasure more precious ... than freedom" whereas liberation from the body by God is what Plato is first and foremost concerned with.)

παλιγγενεσία in this treatise."[483] Philo does not seem to think any explanation is needed. It remains for us who would like to have one to draw it up ourselves.

In what follows, I first present the text of *Cher.* 114 in context and with a translation, accompanied with some structural observations (3.2.2). Then, the interpretation of παλιγγενεσία of *Cher.* 114 in earlier scholarship is discussed (3.2.3). The next two subsections deal with the question of what kind of souls undergo regeneration given the reference to incorporeal things in §114 (3.2.4) and the autonomy of the soul in §115 (3.2.5). Philo's use of παλιγγενεσία elsewhere is then discussed (3.2.6) before the conclusions are summarized and a synthetical understanding of the passage in context offered (3.2.7).

3.2.2 *Context, Text and Translation*

In order that the context of the passage is properly taken into account, we shall first refer back to *Cher.* 108 where Philo cites God's words in a secondary biblical lemma, Lev 25:23, "all the land is mine," as support for his argument concerning God's monopoly on ownership: "in possession (κτήσει) all things are God's, and only as a loan do they belong to created beings." This is the beginning of the train of thought that leads to §114.

Philo characterizes "all things" as created and particular (γενητά, κατὰ μέρος; §109). He emphasizes that God made "these particular things" imperfect so that they would need each other. The result was to be a harmonious universe of interdependence (§§ 110–112).[484] Philo begins §113 by stating that God combined (συνθείς) all things in the manner aforesaid and gave them the use and enjoyment of themselves and each other.[485] He then shifts the focus (until the end of §118) to the individual human being—not as a special case but rather as an example of τὰ γενητά—and makes the already quoted anthropological statement at §113:

---

[483] Burnett, "Philo on Immortality," 449–50. He lists other references to μύσται in the *Allegorical Commentary* as follows: *Leg.* 1.29; *Sacr.* 33, 60, 62; *Post.* 173; *Gig.* 54; *Det.* 61; *Fug.* 85; *Somn.* 2.78.

[484] Both Cohn (PCH 2.200) and Colson (PLCL 1.485) refer to the Stoic background of these ideas, Cohn also to Heraclitus. Philo describes this ideal universe in somewhat contingent terms, and its relation to the real world remains ambiguous. This does not, however, need to concern us in the present context.

[485] An important parallel is *Leg.* 1.26 where τὰ κατὰ μέρος σύγκριματα (which I would render "individual compound things") seems to mean very much the same thing as the compound particulars of *Cher.* 109. See n. 520 (p. 162) for the many connections between *Leg.* and *Cher.*

"I am compounded (συνεστώς) of soul and body, I seem to have mind, faculty of speech, sense; yet I find that none of them is really mine."[486] Thus body and soul as well as mind, speech and the senses are presented as the combined particulars in the case of a human being.

We now reach §114. Philo continues with a set of questions, first about the body: where was it before birth and where will it be after death? He then wonders, where are now the baby, boy, young man, et cetera he once was. He then comes to the soul and asks:[487]

1. πόθεν δὲ ἦλθεν ἡ ψυχή,   Where did the soul come from? *(the past)*
2. ποῖ δὲ χωρήσει,   Where will it go? *(the future)*
3. πόσον δὲ χρόνον ἡμῖν ὁμοδίαιτος ἔσται;   How long time will it be our mate *(the present)*
4. τίς δέ ἐστι τὴν οὐσίαν, ἔχομεν εἰπεῖν;   Can we tell its essential nature?

Philo then proceeds to address the above questions (§§ 114–115) preceding this with a rhetorical question about the soul, "Do we at some time get it as our own? (ποτὲ δὲ καὶ ἐκτησάμεθα αὐτήν;)."[488]

---

[486] See above, p. 102.

[487] The translations are essentially mine. Appendix 2 contains background information for the translation especially with regard to understanding the words σύγκριτοι and ποιοί.

[488] Here is my only deviation from the text of the PCW. Modern editors have read πότε (e.g., Colson: "When did we get it?"), which is how the word is attested in the MSS. I think, however, that it must be taken as indefinite for three reasons. (1) Asking about the *timing* of receiving the soul as one's own would be in contradiction with the emphasis Philo lays in the treatise in general and in § 113–119 in particular on the notion of only God's exclusive ownership. (2) As mentioned, Philo in §113 introduces soul, body, mind, speech and senses as the particulars combined in the human being, and returns to all of them in §§ 114–117. Of both the mind and speech he asks, "is [it] my own possession?" and of the senses he says, "not even of my sense-perception do I find myself master." It would make no sense to assume the soul is the subject of a question, "when did it become our possession?" (3) The structure of § 114–115 necessitates that the question "Do we at some time get it as our own?" introduces the *three* following subsections whose aim is to explore if in any of the divisions of time we may call the soul our possession; Philo simply cannot be aiming at finding out the one in which we *did* receive the possession of our soul. This is also why the aorist ἐκτησάμεθα should be understood as gnomic and translated with the present tense.

1. πρὸ γενέσεως;
   ἀλλ᾽ οὐχ ὑπήρχομεν.
2. μετὰ τὸν θάνατον;
   ἀλλ᾽ οὐκ ἐσόμεθα οἱ μετὰ σωμάτων, σύγκριτοι ποιοί, ἀλλ᾽ εἰς παλιγγενεσίαν ὁρμήσομεν οἱ μετὰ ἀσωμάτων, σύγκριτοι ποιοί.
3. ἀλλὰ νῦν ὅτε ζῶμεν, κρατούμεθα μᾶλλον ἢ ἄρχομεν ...
4. λεπτομερὴς γὰρ αὐτῆς ἡ φύσις ...

Before birth?
   But then we did not exist.
After death?
   But we, individual compound beings who are with bodies shall then exist no longer.[489] Instead we, individual compound beings who are with incorporeals, shall hasten to a regeneration.
And now when we are living,
   we are the ruled rather than rulers ...
For [the soul's] nature is subtle ...

It is worth noting that there is actually a clear symmetrical, chiastic structure in the whole of §§ 113–118 with the discussion of afterlife at its center. Philo starts with the statement that we are only using God's possessions and comes back to it at §118. He then mentions soul and body, as he does in §117. He then refers to the mind, speech and senses in §113 and elaborates on them in §116–117. He asks about the body at the beginning of §114 and mentions it again at the end of §115. In §114 he writes about the soul's departure (verb μεθίστημι), and that of the soul (verb μετανίστημι) in §115.[490] At the center there remain the questions of the soul's origin, destination and nature, presented seemingly as incidental remarks serving to underline the notion that everything is God's.

3.2.3 *Regeneration—Merging into the Divine?*

Cohn (in PCH) connects the passage to mystery cults and speaks of the soul's being reborn in the afterlife to a bodiless existence and becoming united with God. He refers to *QE* 2.46 as a parallel. Colson makes the same reference and assumes that the regeneration in *Cher.* is the second birth of Moses in *QE*, "absorption in the Divine [which] occurs at death."[491] We will now take a look at the *QE* passage together with other similar passages

---

[489] We can recognize here echoes from the pseudo-Platonic *Axiochus*, 365d–e where the evils before birth and after death are said to be of no concern (πρὸ τῆς γενέσεως ... οὐκ ἦς ... μετὰ τὴν τελευτὴν ... σὺ γὰρ οὐκ ἔσῃ). It was already noted above that at *Cher.* 2 Philo avails himself of the expression "the place of the impious" found in *Ax.* 371e (see p. 67). A further commonality with *Ax.* 365e is mentioned below (n. 515).

[490] This is why I think Cohn's conjecture at §114 μεταστάντος <μου> does not stand; ψυχῆς is more likely from the viewpoint of symmetry. Cf. *Det.* 163 where too Philo first uses μεθίστημι and then μετανίστημι of the same event (there moving out of the presence of God). In *Abr.* 47 a third verb, μετοικίζω is also involved.

[491] PLCL 2.485. He also makes two changes in the text with which I disagree; see Appendix 2.

where Philo mentions a new birth or life.[492] The starting point of the *QE* passage is Ex 24:16b where, *inter alia,* "the Lord called Moses on the seventh day from the midst of the cloud." Philo refers to this as "calling above:"[493]

> But the calling above of the prophet is a second birth better than the first. For the latter is mixed with a body and had corruptible parents, while the former is an unmixed and simple sovereign part of the soul being changed from a productive to an unproductive form which has no mother but only a father, who is (the Father) of all. (*QE* 2.46)[494]

Philo goes on to connect this event with the fact that this calling of Moses, i.e. "the divine birth," took place on the seventh day and associates it with "the ever-virginal nature of the hebdomad."[495] In *Mos.* 2.210 Philo equates the hebdomad's motherless virginity with its being "neither bred from corruption nor doomed to suffer corruption," which connects well with the sequel in *QE*: the calling happened on the seventh day in contradistinction to the fact that the original, corporeal (μετὰ σώματος συνίστατο in the Greek fragment) earth-born human was assigned the number six whereas the twice-born is without body and receives the number seven.

"The second birth" of *QE* 2.46 is thus a call to incorruption and incorporeity, a salvific event. Philo speaks about a new life that awaits the good also in *QG* 1.16, 3.11 and 4.169.[496] The viewpoints vary but what is in common is the notion that the second life of the virtuous is one without

---

[492] The "revival" (ἀναβίωσις) mentioned in fragment 7.3 Harris will be discussed separately (section 3.3).

[493] ἡ ἀνάκλησις in the Greek fragment of *QE* 2.46; the LXX has ἐκάλεσεν, but the call did come from the mountain—to which Moses then ascended. The ascension had taken place already at 24:9, 13, 15 and then again in 24:18 with no mentions of descents in between.

[494] The first clause survives in Greek and corresponds to the Armenian. The second sentence of the translation is based on the Armenian with the exception of "an unmixed ... soul" which represents what Marcus in PLCL assumes the original Greek to have been. The Arm. seems corrupt, as it has the genitival relation the other way round: "an unmixed and simple soul of the sovereign."

[495] The virginal and motherless nature of the number seven is a recurring theme in Philo; see, e.g., *Opif.* 100, *Leg.* 1.15 and *Mos.* 2.209–210. For the Pythagorean background of this notion, see PLCL 6.609 and the extensive discussion in Runia, *On the Creation,* 273–75, 298–300.

[496] *Det.* 138 is somewhat less specific but agrees with *QE* 2.46 in preferring a spiritual birth to the physical one: "a hope and expectation of obtaining good things from the only bountiful God ... is, to tell the truth, the only birth (γένεσις) of humans in the strict sense, since those who do not set their hope on God have no part in a rational nature." In our present context we can take the Stoic concept of "rational nature" simply as a reference to things divine.

the body and eternal—which matches the definition of salvation adopted in this study.[497] For instance, in the following passage from *QG* (preserved only in Armenian), Philo states,

> The death of worthy men is the beginning of another life. For life is twofold; one is with corruptible body; the other is without body (and) incorruptible... . The decent and worthy man, however, does not die by death, but after living long, passes away to eternity, that is, he is borne (sic) to eternal life. (*QG* 1.16)[498]

It thus seems possible that the παλιγγενεσία of *Cher.* 114 is a good soul's birth into the divine realm after death. This understanding by Cohn and Colson has dominated later research. Goodenough connects the "reabsorp[tion] ... in the Source" with the return of Sarah's soul at death to God and adds that "Coomaraswamy claims that this is equivalent to the Indian triumph of reabsorption in Nirvana, and he seems to me to be right."[499] Wolfson sees here a reinterpretation of the resurrection of the body as the immortality of the soul.[500] Burnett summarizes his article: "Παλιγγενεσία is the rebirth of the soul into incorporeal existence" and occurs "in any metaphysical or essential way" only after death. It is exclusively "for the virtuous souls."[501] And Termini says, "after death there is rebirth" whereby "God raises the virtuous man to Himself."[502]

But this understanding of the regeneration in *Cher.* 114 leads to problems. Let us first mention Dey who in his religio-historical monograph on παλιγγενεσία criticizes the understanding of *Cher.* 114 by Cohn, Pascher and Dibelius: "Nun ist aber doch παλιγγενεσία als Bezeichnung für die nach dem Tod erfolgende Aufnahme zu einem unkörperlichen Dasein nicht

---

[497] See above, p. 5.
[498] This passage is not far in thought from the soul's reaching its "own proper life [whereby it] is released from the body" (*Leg.* 1.108) through dying to the life of wickedness, i.e., reversing the death of the soul. See above, p. 64.
[499] Goodenough, "Philo on Immortality," 101. He also refers to *Abr.* 258 already discussed; see above, p. 107. He implies this rebirth is only for the good souls, and later (p. 106) claims the soul or mind of the wicked "perishes with the body." But he gives no reference to a passage where Philo says so and ignores the fact that even the "lowest" souls are immortal in *Somn.* 1.137 (above, p. 133). See the discussion on immortality in Philo on pp. 36–37.
[500] Wolfson *Philo*, 1.405. Like Colson, he too refers to the "second birth" of *QE* 2.46 which he considers to be used "in the same sense" as regeneration in *Cher.* 114.
[501] Burnett, "Philo on Immortality," 470. He also characterizes "rebirth" as "the reunion of the soul with the place of incorporeal ideas" (p. 454) with the justification that "[t]he objective of God is to unite (συνθείς) all things of the soul to himself (*Cher.* 113)," but as we saw (p. 152), that is not what Philo means in that passage.
[502] Termini, "Philo's Thought," 109.

erwiesen."⁵⁰³ In the context of our passage, Dey puts forward two other options of understanding παλιγγενεσία: the word "muß als Wiederherstellung verstehen werden, sei es im Sinne der Seelenwanderung ... sei es im Sinne der stoischen Lehre" (i.e., the periodic destruction and regeneration of the world).⁵⁰⁴ The latter option can be excluded.⁵⁰⁵

Dey's remarks mean that if Philo meant salvation with παλιγγενεσία, he was apparently the first one to do so.⁵⁰⁶ Regardless, when we return to *Cher.* and take the context into consideration, this alternative loses all plausibility. As we read the rest of Philo's continuous discussion about the individual, it becomes evident that if taken as a description of the souls of the good, the account of what happens after death is highly anomalous. Continuing his discussion begun in §113, Philo writes:

> Is my mind my own possession? That parent of false conjectures, *that wanderer, the opinionated*, the delirious, the fatuous, and in frenzy or melancholy or senility proved to be the very negation of mind. (*Cher.* 116)⁵⁰⁷

This passage recapitulates ideas Philo has presented throughout the treatise and highlights the continuity of thought that survives beneath the surface. Each of the epithets above has in one way or another been discussed earlier, in particular at §69.⁵⁰⁸ Philo then continues the description of the objectionable state of affairs:

> Not even of my sense-perception do I find myself master, rather, it may well be, its slave, who follows it where it leads, to colours, shapes, sounds, scents, flavours, and the other material bodies. (*Cher.* 117)

The correspondence of §116 with §69 has a continuation in that of §117 with §70, where Philo speaks of the untrustworthiness of the senses as the reason why we cannot claim they are *ours*. He continues in §71 to reiterate once again that all is God's, as he also does in §§ 117–118. It should be

---

⁵⁰³ Dey, *Παλιγγενεσία*, 34 n. 3.
⁵⁰⁴ *Ibid.*
⁵⁰⁵ See
Appendix 2, p. 255.
⁵⁰⁶ The word does later appear in this sense. For example, in Clement of Alexandria's *Protrepticus* 9.88.2 it is a synonym for σωτηρία.
⁵⁰⁷ The italicized words are my tr. for the readings by Cohn; the rest is Colson's, who reads ὁ πλάνης οἰστικος and labels the last word as a conjecture by Mangey. Cohn's apparatus, however, says, "ὁ ante οἰητικός add. Mang." The solution to this seeming contradiction is that while Mangey's body text has οἰητικός without the article, he corrects the text in a note, "Melius οἰστικός ... Vel etiam ... ὁ οἰητικός."
⁵⁰⁸ For false conjectures, see §§ 9, 66, 71; wanderer, §§ 23–24; opinionated, §§ 57, 71; delirious, frenzy and melancholy, §69; fatuous, §75; senility (lit. old age), §§ 68, 75.

noted that in neither §§ 69–71 nor §§ 116–118 can we find any reference to virtuous souls.

Throughout *Cher.* Philo remains faithful to his main biblical lemma. From §40 onwards he sheds light from different angles on the notion of possessing symbolized by Cain. He counters the mind's Cainian delirium (οἴησις) that it owns what it perceives with God's absolute proprietorship. To assume that all of a sudden Philo shifts the focus to virtuous souls and their divine birth after death would have no basis whatsoever in the text. Furthermore, it is doubtful whether a soul could "hasten" directly to salvation by itself.[509] The soul has to toil for its redemption in the Philonic way of thinking, but it does so by trying to live the life of virtue. We must, therefore, conclude that it is the *imperfect* souls (among whom Philo reckons himself) that will be regenerated.[510] This is a crucial conclusion. If it holds, I see no sensible alternative for considering the "regeneration" as a new incarnation.

There is another aspect of *Cher.* 114 that many of its translators have failed to take account of. For example, Colson translates the end of the passage "but shall go forward to our rebirth, to be with the unbodied." This misrepresents the syntax of the Greek, ἀλλ' εἰς παλιγγενεσίαν ὁρμήσομεν οἱ μετὰ ἀσωμάτων ἀσύγκριτοι ἄποιοι. This second οἱ μετά clause must be understood as the subject of ὁρμήσομεν—exactly like the first οἱ μετά clause is the subject of οὐκ ἐσόμεθα—also in Colson's translation ("we who are here joined to the body ... shall be no more"). Burnett's claim that "rebirth consists of the soul *becoming* 'unbodied'" (my italics) is equally unfounded.[511] The text has proved difficult for most of its translators, although I think it is clear enough: the entity that hastens to regeneration is the soul which already finds itself with the incorporeals.[512] But what are

---

[509] See above, p. 98, for a discussion of divine grace.

[510] Note the use of first person plural in §114: *we* hasten to regeneration; the list of negative qualities in §116 concerns "my mind," and also in §117 Philo speaks of himself as the follower of the senses. Given the continuity effected by the use of the first person, there is no reason to assume that §114 and §§ 116–117 describe souls that decisively differ from each other. Philo characterizes himself as imperfect also in *Leg.* 2.91, 3.207; *Her.* 275; *Fug.* 128.; *Mut.* 37.

[511] Burnett, "Philo on Immortality," 453.

[512] So too Dey, Παλιγγενεσία, 34 n. 3: the incorporeal state in *Cher.* 114 is "doch kaum als Ziel und Ergebnis der παλιγγενεσία zu fassen, sondern als Ausgangspunkt." Yonge translates (apparently following Turnebus's reading like Cohn): "we shall then be hastening to a regeneration, becoming in combination with incorporeal beings." Goodenough in *By Light, Light*, 375 (cf. "Philo on Immortality," 101) accepts Colson's emendations and translates, "into the rebirth, by which, becoming joined to immaterial things, we shall become unmixed and without qualities." Cohn translates in the PCH, "zur wiedergerburt gelangen, wo wir mit Unkörperlichen vereinigt sind." Elmgren's 1939 dissertation is

these? Can they be identified, and does such an identification affect our understanding of the regeneration?

3.2.4 *The Incorporeals*

Philo ends §114 by saying, "we, individual compound beings who are with incorporeals, shall hasten to a regeneration." In the translation I have taken ἀσωμάτων as a neuter noun referring to incorporeal things generally —including, possibly, also beings. But in principle it could also be masculine and refer to beings only. If we look at Philo's use of the word elsewhere, we find that he uses it about angels (*Sacr.* 5, *Spec.* 1.66, *QE* 2.13, *al.*), souls (*Plant.* 14, *Conf.* 174, *Migr.* 90, *Somn.* 1.31, *al.*) and ideas, i.e., the noetic cosmos (*Opif.* 16, *Leg.* 1.26, *Ebr.* 99, *QG* 4.8 *al.*). In the three other instances of the word in *Cher.*, Philo calls God "the incorporeal dwelling-place of incorporeal ideas (ἀσωμάτων ἰδεῶν ἀσώματος χώρα)" (§49) and says that God wanted the mind to perceive "not only the immaterial but also material objects (μὴ μόνον τῶν ἀσωμάτων ἀλλὰ καὶ στερεῶν σωμάτων)" (§60) and so gave to it the senses.

But is understanding ἀσωμάτων in the text as referring to the divine, noetic reality reconcilable with the conclusion that those who undergo regeneration are imperfect and have to reincarnate? To answer this question, we take a look at some Philo's references to a forced descent experienced by souls. Although it would not be warranted to simply declare them as descriptions of afterlife, it is now their *possibly* being so that counts. Philo says, for example, that souls that are sent back down may be "enamoured

---

unique in that it presents two different translations in Swedish for the passage, while in no way explaining the differences. The first one, which is apparently later (he refers in its context to the second one but not *vice versa*) is the most accurate I have found, as both of the οἱ μετά clauses are treated as subjects using relative clauses (*Philon av Alexandria*, p. 167, my tr.): "then we, who are united to bodies, shall exist no more; instead we, who are united to incorporeal existence, shall enter rebirth." The second one is preceded by an introduction as if of a previously undiscussed passage. It follows the German translation to a notable degree (p. 170, my tr.): "After death we, who are united to the body, shall exist no more but shall arrive at regeneration whereby we become united to the incorporeal." In connection with the first one Elmgren explicitly identifies the regeneration with transmigration of souls. The French translation by Gorez in the PAPM, following Colson's Greek text, reads, "nous prendrons notre élan vers une nouvelle naissance, parmi les êtres incorporels, non composés, non doués de qualités." It is apparently the taking of one's run-up towards regeneration (and not regeneration itself) that occurs "among" the incorporeal beings, and so Gorez avoids presenting union with incorporeals as a result of the regeneration. This is true also of Mangey's (who read οἱ μετὰ ἀσωμάτων ἀσύγκριτοι without the final ποιοί) "sed incompositi cum incorporeis ad novam nativitatem prodibimus."

of endurance and self-mastery and divested of passions" (*Leg.* 2.83) and even "perfect" (*Agr.* 169), and the descent itself may be a case of the impossibility of "stay[ing] for ever among the immortal" (*Ebr.* 145). At *Her.* 46 Philo states that the "mixed life" between the creation-oriented and God-regarding life is often "possessed and inspired by God, though often pulled back," while in *Somn.* 1.43–44 he says that the soul often frees itself from the body and the senses and that this "unclad movement" enables it to apprehend the noetic things at least temporarily; those who are "balked of the noetic things [are] forthwith swept down to the sense-perceptible ones."

These examples suffice to show that we cannot exclude the possibility that noetic and even divine things are in the hereafter experienced by also those imperfect souls who end up descending. Thus we can take the word ἀσωμάτων in *Cher.* 114 as neuter. However, it seems that the incorporeals should be thought of as also including other souls. Not only does this seem logically possible (there are surely many souls in the hereafter), but it is also interesting to note that in his interpretation of Jacob's heavenly ladder Philo specifically mentions that souls, in their inter-incarnational state, are incorporeal (the air is ψυχῶν ἀσωμάτων οἶκος, *Somn.* 1.135). Furthermore, he does the same thing in two of the parallels to *Somn.* 1.138–143, namely *Plant.* 14 (ψυχῶν ὁ θίασος οὗτος ἀσωμάτων ἐστί) and *Conf.* 174 (ψυχῶν ἀσωμάτων ἱερώτατος χορός).[513] In *Gig.* 6–15 the invisibility of souls (§8) and the incorporeity of God (§14) are mentioned. It is a matter of course that disembodied souls are incorporeal; the fact that Philo nevertheless wanted to mention it in three out of these four mutually connected cases may indicate that the epithet itself was part of the tradition he was giving expression to.

3.2.5 *"The Soul Rules Us"—What Is Wrong Then?*

The conclusion so far is that the souls that experience regeneration are those of the imperfect. Yet there seems to be a potential anomaly. Right after mentioning death and regeneration, Philo continues answering his questions, now regarding the present moment and the soul's nature:

> But now when we are living, we are the ruled (κρατούμεθα) rather than the rulers (ἄρχομεν), known rather than knowing. The soul knows us though we know it not; it lays on us commands (ἐπιτάγματα ἐπιτάττει), which we must fain obey, as a servants obey the mistress (δεσποίνῃ). And when it will (ὅταν

---

[513] In *Conf.* 174, 176–177 not souls generally but angels specifically are meant (not heavenly bodies as claimed by Dillon, *The Middle Platonists*, 435).

ἐθέλῃ), it will claim its divorce with the Chief Magistrate (πρὸς τὸν ἄρχοντα)[514] and depart, leaving our home desolate of life. Press it as we may to stay, it will separate from us (διαλύσεται). For its nature is subtle; it affords no grip or handle to the body. (*Cher.* 115)[515]

We find Philo complaining about soul rule, whereas we would expect him either to praise it or—if I am correct and he is *not* speaking about the virtuous—to bemoan the lack of it.[516] How is this to be understood? Somewhat surprisingly, the viewpoint is that of the *body*. The last two sentences of the quotation above illustrate this by practically identifying "us" with the body. It should be noted that this is in harmony with §113, where Philo says he consists of soul and body. These two represent such particular things put in combination because they need each other as are discussed in §§ 109–112. When the soul goes, the body is left.

Now if the soul is in charge and the body subdued, is Philo not applying his *double dichotomy* and thus depicting a virtuous individual?[517] For two reasons, I do not think he is. The first one is that given the enumeration of the parts of the soul in §§ 113, 116–117 Philo is not operating from the standpoint of pure anthropological dichotomy of body vs. soul. And the second one is that in §115 where only these are mentioned, no ethical

---

[514] Colson "in court," but although Philo is formally following the technical divorce terminology of the Attic orators (PLCL 2.486), he is also referring to God, who in §113 "claimed the sovereignty (κράτος) of all for Himself" and is called ἄρχων in §§ 28–29; in §83 he is ἄρχων καὶ ἡγεμὼν εἷς ὁ θεός. There are thus limits to the soul's autonomy: God has to approve the "divorce" before it can be put into effect.

[515] There are several further connections to the *Phaedo*, especially 80a–d, in this passage. Socrates says, e.g., "When the soul and body are joined together, nature directs (προστάττει) the body to serve and be ruled (δουλεύειν καὶ ἄρχεσθαι), the soul to rule and be master (ἄρχειν καὶ δεσπόζειν)" (80a). In what follows there are several references to the body's being impermanent unlike the soul, e.g., "the body meet[s] with speedy dissolution (διαλύεσθαι) [whereas the soul is] entirely indissoluble (ἀδιαλύτῳ)" (80b). Philo's using the verb διαλύω of the soul is not a sign of disagreement with Plato but an apparent continuation of the divorce terminology (see the previous note and LSJ): the body-soul combination breaks up—just like in *Axiochus* 365e, where the combination is called σύγκρισις (cf. Philo's σύγκριτοι). Moreover, Socrates's words, "if God will (ἂν θεός ἐθέλῃ)" (80d) are worth noting especially since Philo in *Cher.* 118 again refers to the timing of death, "ὅταν θέλῃ," now meaning God directly. Finally, in 80d Socrates describes the soul (in the context of death) as "ha[ving] such qualities and such a nature (τοιαύτη καὶ οὕτω πεφυκυῖα)." This seems best taken as a reference to the soul's individuality in a way comparable to Philo's use of the word ποιός in *Cher.* 114; see Appendix 2, p. 257.

[516] Even though the Greek of §115 has no occurrences of the word ψυχή, there is no doubt that the entity that knows and rules and leaves is the soul, even if ψυχή is already found 64 words before.

[517] For the definition of double dichotomy, see above, p. 39.

considerations are put forward.[518] Hence, the references to the body being ruled and known by the soul in *Cher.* 115 are descriptions of the ontological hierarchy of the two, and ethically neutral as such. They also represent the collective viewpoint from which Philo wishes to discuss the soul, that of those who are left behind when the soul departs, i.e., "the body" and "we" others.[519] It is also good to recall that §115 contains the last two items of Philo's four answers to his own questions about the soul in §114. Philo is saying that in none of the cases is the soul our possession, and he elaborates that in the present moment we cannot command it or even know it. Given the fact that in Philo vice primarily resides in the irrational parts of the soul and virtue in the rational part (when in an uncorrupted state), the mere fact of the soul's rule over the body says nothing of what the balance of power between the parts within the former is.[520] Therefore, *Cher.* 115 gives us no reason to change the conclusion that §114 is about imperfect souls.[521]

---

[518] §114 is a mixed case. On the one hand, only the soul and body are named, but calling the souls in the hereafter "compound" is a reference to their consisting of parts. This (as a potential driving force of reincarnation) would be not be an ethically neutral fact, neither would the imperfect souls' hastening to reincarnate.

[519] See the discussion of Philo's rhetoric in *Cher.* 113–119 above, p. 102.

[520] *Leg.* 2.68–70 is an apposite passage to refer to on the intra-psychic nature of the ethical struggle, since it also has several parallels to *Cher.* 115–117. In both, the theme of one's being able neither to own, command nor know one's mind and senses is pronounced: "By the only true God I deem nothing so shameful as supposing that I exert my mind and senses" (*Leg.* 2.68). Philo continues (2.69): "My own mind the author of its exertion? How can it be? Does it know itself, what it is or how it came into existence?" The rest of the passage mentions several of the mind's degradational states, including ἄνους, μωρία and μελαγχολία. This language is thus partly identical with and in general similar to that concerning the mind in *Cher.* 116. The *Leg.* passage ends with a statement that when the senses rule, the mind is a slave (a thought expressed in *Cher.* 117 as well) and when the mind rules, as it should, the senses are idle (i.e., harmless). *Leg.* is the work immediately preceding *Cher.* in the *Allegorical Commentary*, and there are a considerable number of points of contact between the treatises. For instance, the theme that—contrary to the οἴησις of the soul—only God really possesses (or indeed does) anything, so prominent in *Cher.*, is discussed in *Leg.* 1.49–52, 3.33, 56, 78, 195, 198. Also, Colson in PLCL 1.436 notes that "*Leg.* 3.201 ff. are reproduced in an expanded form in *De Cher.* 79 ff.," and many other direct connections exist.

[521] If anything, the passage confirms this, for there is one probable hint in §115 to imperfection, or indeed, the *death* of the soul. Philo begins, "But now when we are living (ἀλλὰ νῦν ὅτε ζῶμεν), we are the ruled (κρατούμεθα) rather than the rulers (ἄρχομεν)." To me this looks like an allusion to *Leg.* 1.106 where we read, "the body, which is the worse, rules (κρατοῦντος), and the soul, which is the better, is ruled (κρατουμένου)," and to 1.108, where he says, "now, when we are living (νῦν μέν, ὅτε ζῶμεν), the soul is dead." Given Philo's attention to textual detail, I do not think these are a chance similarities. Quite regardless of the facts that in *Cher.* 115 the rulership is inverted and the meaning of living changed, I believe Philo is here reminding his audience of what he said about the death of the soul.

3.2.6 *Philo's Use of παλιγγενεσία Elsewhere*

Our final task before summing up the analysis of *Cher.* 114 is to look at the other occurrences of the word παλιγγενεσία in Philo.[522] The purpose of this examination is to check whether any of these might provide us with some relevant information. We begin with *Post.* 124: "Let us consider what may be called the rebirth of the murdered Abel (τὴν δ' ὥσπερ παλιγγενεσίαν Ἄβελ τοῦ δολοφονηθέντος)." The context is Gen 4:25, the birth of Seth to Adam and Eve. By his use of ὥσπερ Philo indicates he is not using the word παλιγγενεσία in (any of) its strict sense(s), whatever he considered that or those to be.

According to Burnett, "[t]he rebirth of Abel in *Post.* 124, then, simply reiterates the theme of *De Cherubim* that it is God who causes the growth of virtues in obedient souls (*Post.* 127)."[523] This theme occurs in *Cher.* 43–47. However, the context of §114, where παλιγγενεσία is found, is quite different, and Burnett himself admits that "παλιγγενεσία as rebirth of the soul into incorporeal existence is only implied."[524] I am not convinced it is even that.

Philo uses the allegorical meanings already familiar from the earlier parts of the *Allegorical Commentary*: Adam signifies the mind, Eve, the senses. Seth, says Philo, means "watering," for which Philo gives two explanations: when the soul is watered with fresh wisdom, it "shoots up and improves." On the other hand, the mind "waters" the senses, which means that the organs of sense are not the subjects but only instruments of sensation, operated by and serving the mind (§§ 125–127). Philo then begins a long presentation on water quoting Gen 2:6 and declaring that "the word of God waters the virtues." He comes back to Seth in §170. Dwelling on Adam's words, "God has raised up for me another offspring (σπέρμα ἕτερον)" in §§ 172–173 he compares Seth first with Cain (the two are enemies) and then with Abel, to whom "the new offspring (τὸ γέννημα)" is "friendly and akin (συγγενές)." Yet there are important differences: Seth is a beginner, orientated towards creation (πρὸς γένεσιν), Abel, the perfect

---

Nevertheless, the actual *contents* of §115 in themselves apply to all souls and are thus ethically neutral.

[522] PhI lists 13 instances, of which nine are in *Aet.* (for which see above, the end of n. 206 on p. 62).
[523] Burnett, "Philo on Immortality," 467.
[524] *Ibid.*

one reaching towards the uncreated.[525] Seth, now "thirst for virtue" and "the seed of human virtue," will never leave humankind whereas Abel "has relinquished all that is mortal and removed and gone to the better nature."[526]

It is clear that Philo is far removed from discussing Abel and Seth as individuals, and so reincarnation cannot be the issue at stake. The possibility of Philo's meaning that Seth's soul had actually been Abel's would also be anomalous given that the later entity is inferior to the earlier one. Nevertheless, if we assume the *basic* meaning of the word to be reincarnation, precisely the use the word where it could make some sense on one level (the literal) but does not quite fit would have made Philo add the word ὥσπερ. From this point of view, παλιγγενεσία in *Post.* 124 *can* in fact be understood to mean reincarnation. However, the same might be said about the Stoic sense of the word: Abel in a sense gets a renewed existence in Seth. The fact that individual persons act as Philo's starting point might be thought to favor the Pythagorean sense of the word, but as our last example from *Legat.* will show, this is not so clear. The word παλιγγενεσία clearly refers to something positive here, while reincarnation cannot be considered a good thing for the souls to whom it is compulsory. However, if the soul in question is that of a virtuous person, such a specific *case* of reincarnation could be viewed as a good thing.[527] But as the Stoic sense too can be considered a positive one, we really have no criteria to decide between that and the Pythagorean meaning.

---

[525] Philo does find fault with Abel, though: he should have refused the invitation by Cain to come to the plain. Cain represents sophistry which Abel cannot fight with success, lacking as he is in the "arts of speech" (*Det.* 37, *Migr.* 74–75).

[526] In the sequel Philo describes how Seth obtains "growth" (παραύξησις, *Post.* 173–174): ten generations later, Noah arises, another ten later (beginning with Shem, Noah's son), Abraham, and finally after yet another seven generations, the all-wise hierophant, Moses, is born. Philo then shifts the focus back to the individual soul's progress (referred to in §125) and explains:

> Mark the advance to improvement made by the soul that has an insatiable desire to be filled with things that are beautiful, and the unlimited wealth of God, which has given as starting-points to others the goals reached by those before them.

Thus Noah and Abraham start from the point to which Seth and Noah, respectively, had advanced, "and the highest point of wisdom reached by Abraham is the initial course in Moses's training." It is as if Philo was following a soul's development through its incarnations! But it would then be difficult to explain the calling of Seth the "reincarnation" of Abel. Cf. Runia, *Philo and the* Timaeus, 265:

> The birth of Seth is the turning point (*Post.* 124–125, 170–174, exeg. Gen 4:25). The long journey of the improvement and ascent of the soul begins, proceeding via the two patriarchal triads to its culmination in the example of Moses (cf. *Praem.* 10–66).

[527] Cf. above, n. 177 on p. 50.

The next case is *Mos.* 2.65: Abraham as well as the household of Noah "became leaders of the regeneration (παλιγγενεσίας), inaugurators of a second cycle (περιόδου), spared as embers to rekindle mankind" after the destruction of Sodom and Gomorrah and the flood, respectively.[528] Burnett does not really manage to harmonize this passage with his salvific conception of παλιγγενεσία. He admits the passage "does seem to have Stoic overtones" but, nevertheless, wants to show that the word should not be understood in the Stoic sense.[529] However, to me the situation seems to be much simpler than above: humankind was born anew after the devastation, and the sense is a biblically tailored application of the Stoic one.

The last occurrence of the παλιγγενεσία to be examined takes us to *Legat.*[530] Philo includes in this treatise a fictional letter from Herod Agrippa to emperor Gaius in which Agrippa refers to his release by Gaius the imprisonment that had taken place at the behest of the previous emperor, Tiberius:[531]

> You took away the dread of death which was perpetually hanging over me; you quickened (ζωπυρήσας) me when I was dead with fear, you awakened me as though by means of regeneration (καθάπερ ἐκ παλιγγενεσίας ἀνήγειρας). (*Legat.* 325)[532]

The use of ἐκ is somewhat unusual but mentioned in LSJ.[533] The alternative would be to translate "as though from regeneration" in which case παλιγγενεσία would need to be taken as something negative. While the meaning "cycle of reincarnation" would satisfy this condition, this would seem abrupt. Agrippa is simply saying he in effect got his life back when

---

[528] Earlier at 2.60 Philo makes a somewhat narrower statement about Noah: he was deemed fit to be "the beginner of a second generation (δευτέρας γενέσεως) of mankind."

[529] Burnett, "Philo on Immortality," 468–69. He is driven by his goal to forceful *eisegesis*, so much so that he ends up claiming that "rebirth did not occur under Noah, nor is it suggested his preservation was παλιγγενεσία" (p. 469).

[530] Contrary to his stated intention ("Philo on Immortality," 448), Burnett does not discuss the *Legat.* passage.

[531] For the letter's fictionality, see Tom Thatcher, "Philo on Pilate: Rhetoric or Reality?" *ResQ* 37, no. 4 (1995): 215-18, pp. 215–16. There is no mention of a letter in the corresponding passage in Josephus. Instead, Agrippa presents his appeal to Gaius not to install his statue in the temple of Jerusalem (which in Philo follows our quotation) during a banquet (*AJ* 18.297).

[532] Tr. Smallwood except for the last part given in Greek, which she has, "raised me again as if to a second life;" Colson, "as though I were born anew;" Yonge, "raised me up as it were from the dead."

[533] "Of cause, instrument, or means *by* which a thing is done;" cf. Luke 16:9: "make friends for yourselves by means of dishonest wealth (ἐκ τοῦ μαμωνᾶ τῆς ἀδικίας)" (New Revised Standard Version).

saved from the looming execution; it is in that sense that he feels "as though" regenerated.⁵³⁴ This could also be described as using the Stoic sense at the level of the individual: gaining a new life after facing (an imminent) destruction.

Based on the above it may stated that it is within the limits of possible that Philo nowhere else than in *Cher.* 114 applies the word παλιγγενεσία in the sense of reincarnation, although that meaning would make sense in *Post.* 124 and, with significant reservations, in *Legat.* 325. But since the Stoic meaning of the word is in any case impossible in the *Cher.* passage, there is no reason to alter the earlier conclusion that the souls are rushing to a new incarnation.

3.2.7 *Conclusions*

Cher. 114 has been characterized as a "somewhat imprecise and inconsistent" account.⁵³⁵ Its textual features and contents have indeed been difficult for many of its interpreters. We can, however, make sense of the passage by considering it another direct reference to reincarnation. This understanding is first and foremost based on the fact that Philo makes no reference to its being a discussion of virtuous souls; instead, its context in general and the sequel in particular make it entirely unwarranted to assume that Philo is describing souls ripe for salvation. In §116 Philo lists the imperfections of a soul (nominally his own) and in §117 he speaks of (his) craving after material, sense-perceptible objects. Such craving is in full harmony with the causes of incarnation identified as potential driving forces of reincarnation in subsection 2.1.4: body-love and the corporealization of the mind. The soul's explicitly compound character in §114 can be understood as a reference to its incomplete monadization, which is the structural counterpart for its bodily leanings. Thus although the souls are said to be with the incorporeals, they are eager to experience reincarnation. I see no feasible alternative to *metempsychosis* as the meaning of παλιγγενεσία in *Cher.* 114.

The structure of *Cher.* 113–118 is intriguing. The reference to reincarnation is situated at the center of an orderly chiasmus. This undoubtedly highlights the notion—and yet, paradoxically, it is mentioned rather in

---

⁵³⁴ Dey, *Παλιγγενεσία*, 33 calls the words καθάπερ ἐκ παλιγγενεσίας "[ein] formelhafte[r] Ausdruck" but it only occurs twice in the TLG (in addition, there are a few additional ones with ὡς or ὥσπερ), the other one being in Plutarch's *Quaestiones convivales* 722d (= 8.3.5), where the meaning is clearly one of starting over.
⁵³⁵ Termini, "Philo's Thought," 109.

passing with no special emphasis or explanation. While this would be appropriate for an esoteric teaching that is important but not to be explicitly elaborated on, this cannot be proven to be the case.[536] In my view, however, the issue as such has no bearing on whether reincarnation is meant.

On the whole, then, my understanding of what Philo says is as follows. The human souls are part of the universal scheme of interdependence. While in the physical world, they have a need of bodies, and their constituent parts have a need of each other. We own none of these particular things (our bodies, senses etc.), we just use them. Our knowledge about the origin and destination of the soul is limited, and we have no control over our lifespan, of how long our life as the combination of body and soul will last. These combinations come into existence at birth and cease existing at death. However, the soul outlasts the body, and it hastens to a new body, driven by the sensual desires of the more earthly parts of the soul.—I have intentionally formulated the description so as to partly resemble certain passages in Plato's *Phaedo* to reiterate the issue of the dialogue's subtle presence in *Cher.* While a systematic comparison of these two works goes well beyond the present context, we may add the references to reincarnation in both as a common feature to be taken into account in such an analysis.

3.3 *QE 2.40*

3.3.1 *Introduction*

In the *Quaestiones in Exodum*, as its name reveals, Philo goes through the text of Exodus in the form of questions and answers. Two books of *QE* survive covering Ex 12:2–23c and 20:25b, 22:21–28:34 with omissions. *QE* 2.40 is one of those passages in Philo's *Quaestiones* which have been preserved both (apparently) entirely in Armenian and partly in Greek. For the Greek text, which covers the latter half of the passage, we have a single witness, an 11th-century manuscript of the *Sacra Parallela* attributed to John of Damascus (d. 749).[537]

---

[536] Cf. Burnett's observations of the esoteric elements in *Cher.* above, p. 151.
[537] J. Rendel Harris, *Fragments of Philo Judaeus* (Cambridge, MA: Harvard University Press, 1886), xx, describes the MS. as follows:
> The Codex Rupefucaldi is a magnificently written volume of 285 leaves . . . . To my surprise, it is not an uncial MS. at all, but an early cursive . . . dating, as near as I can judge, and in accordance with the tradition of the library, from the eleventh century.

168   CHAPTER THREE

I have used the Armenian text of *QGE* published with a Latin translation by J. B. Aucher in 1826. In addition, I have consulted Marcus's English (PLCL) and Terian's French (PAPM) translation. With the exception of Royse's edition of *QE* 2.62–68 and Paramelle, Lucchesi and Sesiano's edition of *QG* 2.1–7 there is still no critical text of the Armenian *Quaestiones*.[538] Aucher's, mainly based on three MSS., is still the Armenian text used by scholars, although the number of manuscripts known to scholars containing portions of *QGE* has since multiplied.[539] Although no textual variants or uncertainty in the Armenian for *QE* 2.40 is indicated in the above publications, the two language versions differ from each other to an extent, so that textual questions cannot be avoided.

The scriptural basis of our passage is Ex 24:12a, God's command to Moses to ascend to the mountain, and to "be there." In all of Philo's extant works, this is the only passage to refer to that verse. However, the rise to Mt. Sinai is featured in several other Pentateuchal verses which Philo comments on, and, even more importantly, *QE* 2.40 represents two widespread motifs in his *oeuvre*, the *flight* of the soul and its *return*. We have already looked at both themes.[540]

Commenting on the individual expressions in our text is hampered by the uncertainty concerning the original Greek wording. On the one hand, although the Armenian translation is characterized as possessing "extreme literalness" and being "wooden" and "interlinear," there is, in any given passage, no guarantee that no misunderstanding or error has crept in. [541]

The MS. is now called Codex Berolinensis 46 and kept in Staatsbibliothek zu Berlin (shelfmark Phillips 1450). Digital copies can be ordered, and I have done so both for this fragment (fol. 213r) and 7.3 Harris (see 3.4 below).

[538] James Royse, "Philo of Alexandria, *Quaestiones in Exodum* 2.62–68: Critical Edition," in SPhA 24 (2012): 1–68; Joseph Paramelle, Enzo Lucchesi and Jacques Sesiano, *Philon d'Alexandrie: Questions sur la Genèse II, 1–7: Text grec, version arménienne, parallèles latins*; Cahiers d'Orientalisme 3 (Geneva: Cramer, 1984). For more details, see Anna Sirinian, "'Armenian Philo': A Survey of the Literature," in *Studies on the Ancient Armenian Version of Philo's Works* ed. Sara Mancini Lombardi and Paola Pontani; SPhA 6 (Leiden: Brill, 2011), 7–44, pp. 30–31.

[539] Earle Hilgert, "*The Quaestiones:* Texts and Translations," in *Both Literal and Allegorical. Studies in Philo of Alexandria's Questions and Answers on Genesis and Exodus*, ed. David M. Hay; BJS 232 (Atlanta: Scholars Press, 1991), 1–15, p. 9; Sirinian, "Armenian Philo," 33.

[540] For the former, see above, e.g., pp. 32, 53, 142, 142 and 145–147. For the latter, the most important text is *Somn.* 1.139. Other passages mentioned or discussed include *Leg.* 2.83 (p. 61), *Agr.* 89 (p. 69) as well as *QG* 1.51 and *Leg.* 3. 252 (pp. 70–79).

[541] The quoted expressions are from Marcus, "The Armenian Translation," 64; Hilgert, "*The Quaestiones,*" 13 and Terian, "Syntactical Peculiarities," 15, respectively. See Pontani, "Saying (Almost) the Same Thing," 125 for a collection of other, corresponding characterizations, including appreciative ones.

And on the other, although it is fortunate that we do have a Greek fragment containing the half of *QE* 2.40 which is the more interesting from the viewpoint of reincarnation, there is no proof of the integrity of its text (especially since we are depending on a single MS.). Furthermore, the possibility of a greater or smaller degree of paraphrasticality is always present in these fragments. Below, the Armenian and Greek texts are both considered with no *a priori* precedence given to either.

3.3.2 *Texts, Translations and Preliminary Remarks*

I first present an English translation of the Armenian. The sentences of the *solutio*, as punctuated by Marcus (PLCL), are marked with letters *a* to *f*. Sentence *d*, and one expression in *e*, are printed with italics and given my own translation, because I disagree with Aucher's Armenian text. The rest of the translation is Marcus's. Then comes the Greek fragment as printed by Petit (with two corrections) together with my translation.

> **Marcus's tr. of the Arm.** What is the meaning of the words, "Come up to Me to the mountain and be there"? *ᵃ*This signifies that a holy soul is divinized by ascending not to the air or to the ether or to heaven (which is) higher than all but to (a region) above the heavens. *ᵇ*And beyond the world there is no place but God. *ᶜ*And He determines the stability of the removal by saying "be there," (thus) demonstrating the placelessness and the unchanging habitation of the divine place. *ᵈ*For those *in whom the desire (for God) is fickle ascend with the intellect*[542] for a short while upwards, (being) flying ones carried by God, (and) immediately return. *ᵉ*They do not fly so much as they are drawn downward, *(as) it is said,*[543] to the depths of Tartarus. *ᶠ*But those who do not return from the holy and divine city, to which they have migrated, have God as their chief leader in the migration.[544]

---

[542] For my corrections of the Armenian text, see Appendix 3.
[543] Literally "(as) they say." Based on my correction of the Greek (see n. 547), I read ասեն (*asen*) instead of ասեմ (*asem*).
[544] There are no differences in thought between Marcus's English and Terian's French or Aucher's Latin translation that are of consequence in our present context.

170 CHAPTER THREE

The Greek fr. by Petit[545] || ^dἘνίοις ἀψίχορος ἐγγίνεται λογισμός, οἵ πρὸς ὀλίγον ἀναπτεροφορηθέντες[546] || αὐτίκα ὑπενόστησαν, ^eοὐκ ἀναπτάντες μᾶλλον ἢ ὑποσυρέντες εἰς Ταρτάρου φασίν[547] ἐσχατιάς. ^f[Εὐδαίμονες δὲ] οἱ μὴ παλινδρομοῦντες. ||	My tr. of the Greek: ^dIn some the intellect becomes fickle, in those who, after having been again carried by wings for a short while, descended right away, ^enot having flown upwards but rather having been dragged down to the extremes of Tartarus, as they say. ^fHappy are those who do not return.

QE 2.40 has not attracted much scholarly attention. When it is commented on, the subject is usually the non-locality of God or Moses's God-possession, and the question of *returning* is very rarely dealt with.[548] In fact, to my knowledge, the only researcher to have done so is Wendy Helleman. She remarks that the ones who "can [not] continue their flight" appear to be "those which have permanently left the body, and do not return to

---

[545] Petit's sigla in PAPM 33 are as follows: "[ ] : étranger au texte original de Philon. \|\| : omission de la citation par rapport à l'arménien." As for the use of italics, she notes (p. 36), "Là où les sources—et il s'agit surtout des sources secondaires—donnent un texte remanié, l'emploi de caractères italiques signale les éléments moins sûrs."

[546] Petit: πτεροφορηθέντες, an obvious oversight. The prefix is positively present in the MS. Marcus's note *e* in PLCL Suppl. 2.83 makes it probable that the prefix was also present in the Armenian translator's *Vorlage*. PhI, relying on PAPM, repeats the error and makes another one in sentence *e* in classifying ἀναπτάντες, which is the active aorist participle of ἀναπέτομαι, as a form of ἀνάπτω. See LSJ, s.v. πετάννυμι (!): "forms prop. belonging to πέτομαι are ἀνα-πτάς [and] ἀνα-πτάμεναι." The TLG as well classifies ἀναπτάντες as a form of ἀναπέτομαι.

[547] My conjecture. Petit prints φησίν and notes, "φημί legit arm." This 1st-person form appears only thrice in Philo (*Leg.* 3.240, *Mut.* 213 and *Somn.* 1.26), and none of these cases is comparable. We do know that the Armenian translators in many cases rendered λέγω—in the sense of "I mean"—literally with ասեմ (*asem*, found here but see n. 543); see Gohar Muradyan, "The Armenian Version of Philo Alexandrinus," in *Studies on the Ancient Armenian Version of Philo's Works*, ed. Sara Mancini Lombardi and Paola Pontani; SPhA 6 (Leiden: Brill, 2011), 51–85, p. 72. However, here this kind of specification is redundant in contrast to, e.g., *QG* 2.34 and 3.39 where the λέγω/ասեմ structure explicitly includes *what* is "meant" *by what*. While the form φησίν of the Greek MS. is very common in Philo as a reference to the Pentateuchal text, there is now no scriptural referent. My main grounds for reading φασίν is *Legat.* 103: "but shameful deeds, they say, need the depths of Tartarus" (tr. Smallwood for τὰ δὲ αἰσχρά φασιν ἐσχατιᾶς Ταρτάρου [δεῖται])." I suggest that in *QE* 2.40 too "(as) they say" indicates that Philo expected his audience to recognize the expression. Indeed, combinations of Tartarus/Hades and ἐσχατιά/μυχός are attested from Hesiod onwards (*Theogonia* 119); also Euripides *Heraclidae* 218, *Hercules* 608 and Wis 17:13. Philo has three more, *Her.* 45, *Somn.* 1.151 and *Legat.* 49.

[548] It is not discussed by Drummond *Philo Judaeus*, 2.44; Goodenough, *By Light, Light*, 214; Runia, *Philo and the* Timaeus, 165, 333 & *On the Creation*, 229; Termini, "Philo's Thought," 109, 112—all of whom comment on or mention the passage. Goodenough, "Philo on Immortality," 88–89 and Conroy, "The Wages of Sin," 116 merely say the mention of Tartarus in *QE* 2.40 is metaphorical.

earth."[549] This, however, does not for her imply the returners reincarnate.[550] Carl Holladay states on the one hand that Philo endorsed reincarnation and, on the other, that "[t]he final sentence [of QE 2.40] suggests that Philo may be speaking of the flight of the soul at death."[551] He does not, however, say *QE* 2.40 is about rebirth. Joseph Pascher's comments about souls that have begun their ascent but fallen back are ambiguous.[552] Méasson sees behind the passage a combination of Platonic themes; the divinization of the *Theaetetus* and the ascent of the soul of the *Phaedrus*.[553] But she too does not comment on the return of the fickle nor does she, unlike for *Somn.* 1.138–139, mention reincarnation.

In our text Philo does not comment on the literal meaning of the biblical verse but goes straight to the allegory he sees. Thus in his interpretation, which is completely removed from the landscape of Mt. Sinai, the passage is *not about Moses*. The prophet comes down from the mountain later in the biblical narrative, but in *QE* 2.40 the stability of the best souls is sealed while only the fickle ones descend. In Philo's view, the text is about ascending and returning souls; indeed, the latter half of the passage from sentence *d* onwards is written in the plural.

In *QE* 2.40 the primary background of the flight of the soul is, as usual, Plato's *Phaedrus*. Runia has noted that this theme,

> often found in Philo [and] drawn in the first place from the *Phaedrus* myth and immensely popular in Hellenistic times, is that the mind leaves the body and on soaring wing actually joins the harmonious revolutions of the celestial beings.[554]

In *QE* 2.40 the rise of the soul "to (a region) above the heavens" and "beyond the world" emphasizes the connection to the dialogue: cf. Plato's descriptions of where the "real eternal absolute" (247e) is located: "outside of the heaven," in "the region above the heaven" (247c), or in "the outer region" (248a). It is very important for the souls to try and *see* the supercelestial, *nourishing* beauty, "the fitting pasturage for the best part of the soul" (248b–c). To do that they must be able to follow Zeus successfully in

---

[549] Wendy Helleman, "Philo of Alexandria on Deification and Assimilation to God," SPhA 2 (1990): 51–71, p. 69.
[550] This she confirmed to me in an e-mail in January 2012.
[551] Holladay, *Theios Aner*, 139, 162, respectively.
[552] Pascher, *Η ΒΑΣΙΛΙΚΗ ΟΔΟΣ*, 243.
[553] Méasson, *Du char ailé de Zeus*, 214. See p. 86 above for Philo's quotation from the *Theaetetus* on the ὁμοίωσις θεῷ motif.
[554] Runia, *Philo and the Timaeus*, 278; he refers to *Opif.* 70; *Spec.* 1.207, 3.1; *QG* 3.3. In *On the Creation*, 229 he refers also to *Her.* 126, 230; *Det.* 87; *Spec.* 1.37–40, 2.44–46 and *Legat.* 5 as well as to PAPM 15.119 for many other parallels.

the heavenly chariot race (248a–b). Failure leads to reincarnation (248c–e) until a predetermined time has elapsed; it can be shortened by becoming an honest philosopher or a philosophical pederast whereby the soul's wings grow back and the original lightness is regained (249a).[555] Another detail connecting *QE* 2.40 to the *Phaedrus* is that, according to Méasson, behind "hav[ing] God as [the] chief leader" of the Armenian text probably lies the Greek expression μέγας ἡγεμών which Plato uses of Zeus in 246e.[556]

It has been noted that the flight of the soul appears in literature in two forms: in descriptions of afterlife and of mystical experiences (during earthly life).[557] Which is the case in *QE* 2.40? This has implications for what we should think of those who fail. If salvation is meant, the successful souls are by definition discarnate, but what about the returners? If they are embodied, the passage has little to offer to a study on Philo's position on reincarnation. But if there is no difference between the states of embodiment of the two groups, and if those who succeed can indeed be determined to reach salvation, it follows that *QE* 2.40 is to be considered a description of afterlife. In that case it is quite possible that reincarnation is meant. The final judgement will eventually hinge on what is found to be the destination of those who are drawn to "Tartarus."[558]

Thus the question of whether Philo means that some souls reincarnate because of their fickleness becomes divided into two: (1) Have the returning souls been separated from their bodies by physical death? (2) Where are they headed? The questions are interdependent in that the answer to the first one affects the second. For although the mythical underworld quite clearly symbolizes the body in Philo, he also says, "the true Hades is the life of the bad" which is why we must allow for a more general meaning alongside the specific one.[559] However, now that we are discussing *entering* Tartarus, there is a significant difference between coming from a discarnate state or from a temporary state of comtemplation. Thus if the first answer is yes, returning to Tartarus must mean a new incarnation, because

---

[555] For Philo's attitude towards Plato's references to pederasty, see the discussion above, pp. 112–13.

[556] Méasson, *Du char ailé de Zeus*, 214 n. 249. Philo uses this epithet of God in *Opif.* 69.

[557] André-Jean Festugière, *La Révélation d'Hermès Trismégiste*, 4 vols. (Paris: Lecoffre, 1944–1954), 2.442 (*non vidi*) referred to by Runia, *On the Creation*, 229.

[558] I think we are justified to take the fact that those who remain do *not return* as meaning that those who descend *do return*, although Philo does not explicitly say this. Yet we must note that the unsuccessful souls may return *from* on high without necessarily returning *to* where they started the ascent from.

[559] The quotation is from *Congr.* 57. See the discussion of incarnation as banishment, pp. 65–68.

Philo nowhere acknowledges a concrete underworld. But if mental states are concerned, it refers to relapsing into wickedness.

If we look at what grounds the passage itself provides for answering the questions, two things merit attention. First, as far as those who do *not* return are concerned, Philo's expressions are so exalted that the account is certainly one of final salvation: we are told about a holy soul's rising all the way to God and its staying in the "holy and divine city."[560] The ascent of Ex 24 is connected by Philo with incorporeity—not explicitly mentioned in our passage—in *QE* 2.29 (in terms of monadization) and 2.46.[561] However, even though it seems clear that salvation is meant, it does not immediately follow that the returners are discarnate. There are biblical examples that a heavenly ascent or a transference by God may not always be preceded by ordinary physical death. Philo's views of these cases must be examined, for should *QE* 2.40 prove to be such a case, we would also have no grounds for considering the returning souls disembodied.

Second, the internal logic of *QE* 2.40 seems to be that the option of not returning would have been open also for those who end up being drawn to Tartarus, had their fickleness not ruined their chances. We are not told they are predetermined to fall back. If the return is found to be contingent, we can infer that both groups are in the same state as regards incarnation.

It is to these two questions that we turn next: do we have any reason to suspect that the saved souls have not experienced physical death (3.3.3) and is the impression of the contingency of the return correct (3.3.4)? The question of where the returning souls are headed is separately addressed (3.3.5) before conclusions are drawn (3.3.6).

3.3.3 *Final Salvation without Death?*

In order to confirm whether Philo is in *QE* 2.40 dealing with events in the hereafter, we need to look at his interpretations of Enoch's transference and Elijah's being taken up to heaven. The biblical narrative does not

---

[560] Philo in several texts refers to a heavenly or noetic metropolis, city of virtue etc. See, e.g., *Leg.* 3.1–2, *Conf.* 78; *Somn.* 1.46, 181; *QG* 3.11, 4.178. Cf. *Republic* 520c–d where the wise are obliged to descend back to the cave of the ignorant from the "pure city" where they mostly dwell with each other.

[561] For the latter, see above, p. 155. Cf. also *QE* 2.43: That Moses goes up with Joshua (Ex 24:13) is explained as meaning that "the two are potentially one." Philo states that Joshua means "salvation" and asks if "being saved by God [is] more appropriate to anyone else than the inspired soul, in which prophecy resounds."

include physical death in these cases. Philo even speaks of Moses in his exegesis of Gen 5:24:

> First of all, the end of the worthy and holy ones is not death but transference (փոխումն [p'oxumn]) and approaching another place. Second, something very marvellous took place. For he seemed to be rapt away and become invisible. For then he was not found.... [Enoch] is said (to have moved) from a sensible and visible place to an incorporeal and intelligible kind. This gift the protoprophet also obtained, for no one knew his burial-place. And still another, Elijah, followed him on high from earth to heaven ... or, it would be more appropriate and correct to say, he ascended. (*QG* 1.86)

As for Moses, it is clear that his physical death is not being denied here.[562] For Enoch some extraordinary phenomenon seems implied, but his "not death but transference" cannot be interpreted to mean that "worthy and holy ones" never die in the ordinary way. Philo's aim may be to focus all attention to the transference, so much so that physical death loses its significance.[563]

Enoch must be considered the exception and not the rule; deciding whether or not his case should be judged to have a bearing on *QE* 2.40 requires further evidence. A closer examination of *QG* 1.86 in fact brings up relevant observations. For the Armenian word for Enoch's "transference" (both in this passage and the Armenian Zohrab Bible) is of the same root (from verb փոխեմ [p'oxem]) as two words that appear in *QE* 2.40 in a similar context in sentences *c* and *f*.[564] Thus it is worth asking whether Philo envisaged that some highly advanced souls could be saved directly from the body without ordinary physical death like Enoch and possibly Elijah. To me such a notion seems quite un-Philonic, but that is no reason not to examine the issue.

The only other place (*Deus* 136–139) where Elijah is discussed by Philo does not refer to his heavenly journey, so we will briefly review the men-

---

[562] *Pace* Peder Borgen, "Heavenly Ascent in Philo," in *The Pseudepigrapha and Early Biblical Interpretation*, ed. James H. Charlesworth and Craig A. Evans; JSPSup 14; Studies in Scripture in Early Judaism and Christianity 2 (Sheffield: JSOT Press, 1993), 246–68, p. 249: "Moses was taken up to God by means of assumption without death and burial." That the burial-place was unknown does not mean that nothing was buried; "this gift" surely refers to Enoch's *not being found* which Philo takes as analogous to the grave's location not being known. Cf. also *Mos.* 2.291 where Moses "was buried (ἐτάφη) with none present."
[563] See below, p. 206 for such language in *Migr.* 189 and *Praem.* 110.
[564] I.e., "the stability of the *removal*" of the soul, and the "holy and divine city, to which they have *migrated*." Unfortunately, the Greek fr. of *QE* 2.40 contains neither notion. The NBHL gives as Greek equivalents for փոխեմ (p'oxem) ἀλλάττω, ἀλλοιόω, μεταβάλλω, μετατίθημι and μεταλλάσσω.

tions of Enoch. Philo's most systematic discussion of his case is in *Praem.* 15–21. The biblical text says, "he was not found, because God transferred (μετέθηκεν) him." One of Philo's characterizations of the transference is "change of abode (μετανάστασις)" which has a salvific connotation.⁵⁶⁵ In *Abr.* 17–26, 47, where Enoch's transference is also discussed, the event is clearly one of more modest betterment, and "the transferred" is, even after the event, described as "half-wrought" (§47). In any case, in neither *Praem.* nor *Abr.* does Philo bring up the notion of reaching salvation directly from the earthly life without ordinary death.

The last remaining discussion of Gen 5:24 in *Mut.* 34–38 features the most soteriological orientation of all.⁵⁶⁶ The fact that Enoch "was not found" refers, according to Philo, to the rarity of everything really good and the non-existence of a perfect person. The "lover of wisdom" does exist but is

> hidden from us and shun[s] our company. And to confirm this we read that he was "transferred," that is, changed his abode (μεταναστῆναι) and journeyed as an emigrant (μετοικίαν στείλασθαι) from the mortal life to the immortal. (*Mut.* 38)⁵⁶⁷

The last expression is strong enough to be considered a reference to salvation. It is important to note that Enoch is not an individual but represents a "kind (γένος)" (§34) of souls, "the children of discipline" (§33) and thus apparently not a special case in that respect which Philo wants to discuss here. Now too nothing is said that in any way even alludes to a possibility of salvation without death. It is in fact the contrary alternative that is implied, for there are clear links to the description of the physical death of Moses which Philo describes in *Mos.* 2.288 by saying that he "ma[d]e his migration (ἀποικίαν ... στέλλεσθαι) from earth to heaven, and [left] this mortal life for immortality." This connection is further reinforced by the fact that similar descriptions of monadization are found in both *Mut.* 33 and *Mos.* 2.288.⁵⁶⁸

---

⁵⁶⁵ See, e.g., its use in *Migr.* 189 (quoted below on p. 206) and *Gig.* 61 (see p. 208).

⁵⁶⁶ In addition, there is a brief reference at *Post.* 43 where Philo speaks of "those who have been well-pleasing to God, and whom God has translated (μετεβίβασε) and removed (μετέθηκεν) from the perishable (φθαρτῶν) to immortal (ἀθάνατα) races."

⁵⁶⁷ Note the connection to *Somn.* 1.139: leaving the mortal life (see p. 138).

⁵⁶⁸ See above, pp. 40 for *Mos.* In *Mut.* 33 Philo writes of the virtuous that they have "resolved into a single form (εἰς ἓν εἶδος ... ἀναλυθέντες), that of soul, and become unbodied understandings (ἀσώματοι διάνοιαι)." Cf. *Somn.* 1.36 (ex. Ex 34:28, not 24:18 as stated in PLCL) where Philo says Moses "became unbodied" (ἀσώματον γενόμενον) during his 40-day stay on the mountain. This interpretation is an apposite point of comparison to *QE* 2.40 in that it *maintains* the biblical context and allegorizes Moses's fasting only.

Philo thus nowhere makes a point of Enoch's corporeal state at the moment of his transference, let alone of Elijah's being taken up to heaven in his body. So even if Philo originally employed in *QE* 2.40 the verb used for Enoch's transference, μετατίθημι, for the souls' migration, that in itself is not a reason to assume that in the former those who are saved have not died in the ordinary way.⁵⁶⁹

While this conclusion favors the possibility that the *returners* are also discarnate, Philo's account is simply not precise and systematic enough for this to be concluded with certainty. In this respect *QE* 2.40 stands in stark contrast to the way in which *Somn.* 1.138–139 presents a neatly tiered *diaeresis* of souls in different states and also mentions the event of physical death. In order to learn more about the state of embodiment of those who face the plunge to Tartarus we must turn to these poor souls themselves. Can we infer if being saved was in principle possible also for them?

3.3.4 *The Contingency of the Return*

To try and answer the question as to whether reaching God and staying in the divine city would also have been possible for those who are dragged down to Tartarus, it is first of all warranted to examine the structure of the whole passage with regard to these two groups of souls. We can see that Philo switches back and forth between them, and is not simply carried away from the virtuous to their antithesis at sentence *d*; he also comes back at *f*. The groups seem *comparable*—indeed Philo's words amount to a comparison, for in sentence *f* those who are saved are defined in terms of the other group when they are labelled as "those who *not return*." Conversely, what is said about the saved implies that those who *do* return are *not happy* (Gr.) or do *not have God as their leader* (Arm.). Since both language versions contain the transition back to those who do not return, we have no reason to doubt the authenticity of the transition itself.

---

⁵⁶⁹ As already noted (n. 564), the Armenian verb in *QE* 2.40, փոխեմ (*p'oxem*), rendered in sentences *c* and *f* by Marcus and Terian as removal/enlèvement and migration, translates also other Greek verbs in Armenian Philo—e.g., μεταβάλλω in *Leg.* 1.89 and *Abr.* 17. However, based on the fact that in sentence *f* a reference is made to the holy and divine city "*to which* (յոր [*yor*]) [the non-returning souls had] emigrated and been transferred (գաղթեալ փոխեցաւն [*gałt'eal p'oxec'ann*])," *movement* is implied and thus μετατίθημι is more natural. Note that the translations of *QE* 2.40 above on p. 169 do not reveal the presence of the participle of the verb գաղթեմ (*gałt'em*) for which MI gives ἀποικίζω (*QE* 2.49) and μετοικίζω (*Contempl.* 19). For the equivalence of emigration and transference, cf. Philo's words at *Praem.* 17 about Enoch: "By transference (μεταθέσεως) [Scripture] clearly signifies the new home (ἀποικίαν)."

Do we have any way of establishing whether the returners *might not* have ended up in Tartarus or if they *might* have followed God? Although the Greek fragment speaks of the intellect *becoming* fickle, I have, as explained in Appendix 3, come to the conclusion that the beginning of sentence *d* is paraphrastic (cf. Petit's italics), and that originally the text did not speak of such a change during the flight. I also think there is an error of one letter in the Armenian text and that it too did not mention becoming.[570] However, the significance of these considerations in our present context is not clear, and, regardless, both texts tell us that one change does take place: the soar turns into a dive. That this happens for "some (ἐνίοις)" in the Greek fr. seems to refer to contingency; it approaches a qualitative statistical statement to the effect, "there are always bound to be also those who cannot make it."

The Armenian յորս (*yors*; literally, "[those] in whom") at the beginning of sentence *d* does not have the same force.[571] The special characteristics of these souls are the fickleness of their desire for God and their failing to have him as their leader. Nevertheless, they too at first ascend (verb ἀναπέτομαι as in *Phaedrus* 249d, where souls who *love* the beautiful *long* to *fly upward* from the earth), which is an indication that there perhaps was hope to begin with. But it seems that this is all we can extract from the text.

We can, nevertheless, continue our inquiry a little further. Are fickleness and not following God incurable maladies in Philo? If they are not, the question becomes one regarding their "amount" in the souls (of which we are given no information here), and the return is beginning to look quite contingent. To take the latter shortcoming first, having God as one's leader is the result of *progress* in Philo: In *Migr.* 128 he says, "to live agreeably with nature ... is attained whenever the mind, having entered on virtue's path walks in the track of right reason and follows God," and a little later (§131), "[t]o follow God is, then, according to Moses, that most holy man, our aim and object."

Second, such fickleness as in *QE* 2.40 can be considered a form of instability, which is not an incurable evil for Philo. Before Abraham is able to get rid of the unstable Lot, he is described as follows:

---

[570] It is noteworthy that the presence of the participle եղեալ (*ełeal*, from եղանիմ [*ełanim*], 'to become') in Aucher's Arm. text is not directly seen in the translations into English, French or Latin, which I take as a further indication of the syntactical problems it creates. I think the correct word is ելեալ (*eleal*, from ելանեմ [*elanem*], 'to ascend'); see Appendix 3.

[571] Note how close the Arm. is if retranslated to Greek: ἐν οἷς ἀψίκορος πόθος ἐστί. The Vorlage may have had a possessive dative, ἐνίοις ἀψίκορος πόθος ἐστί.

178   CHAPTER THREE

For at present he is but a novice in the contemplation of things Divine and his principles are unformed and wavering. By and by they will have gained consistency and rest on a firmer foundation. (*Migr.* 150)

That the desire and love for God are not an easy thing in Philo's view is also shown by even Moses's having to struggle for sustaining them:

But so unceasingly does [Moses] himself yearn to see God and to be seen by Him, that he implores Him to reveal clearly His own nature (Ex 33:13) in order that he finally partake of true judgement and exchange unstable uncertainty for stablest confidence. Nor will he abate the intensity of his desire (πόθον), but although he is aware that he is enamoured of an object which entails a hard quest, nay, which is out of reach, he will nevertheless struggle on with no relaxation of his earnest endeavour, but honestly and resolutely enlisting all his faculties to co-operate for the attainment of his object. (*Post.* 13)

As a final examination aimed at establishing the contingency or otherwise of the return, we shall look at parallel accounts of returning souls within the *Quaestiones*. There are three such accounts that share important characteristics with *QE* 2.40: *QG* 1.85, 4.45 and *QE* 1.7. It is worthwhile to summarize their central aspects.

Table VI. Descriptions of Return in *QG* 1.85, 4.45 and *QE* 1.7, 2.40. Verbal connections between the *Armenian* texts are indicated with italics, those between existing **Greek** fragments in bold.

Passage	Description of return	What the returners fail in
QG 1.85[572]	"some, after *fickly*[573] tasting excellence and having been given hope of health, again *revert to the same* disease."[574]	incorporeity, pleasing God, excellence; worth and holiness (*QG* 1.86)

---

[572] It is interesting to note that one of the two Greek fragments for this text is in the same MS. as the one for *QE* 2.40 and immediately follows it (f. 213r). The title under which both appear is "Concerning unstable monks who return to evil" (Περὶ μοναχῶν παλιμβόλων, καὶ παλινδρομούντων εἰς κακίαν). The text can be found in TLG under Joannes Damascenus {2934.019} as printed in MPG vol. 96, p. 532.
[573] The Armenian word used in *QG* 1.85, արագայագ (*aragayag*), is not the same as in *QE* 2.40 which has վաղայագ (*vałayag*). But since both վաղ (*vał*) and արագ (*arag*) can mean 'quick' and are combined with յագ (*yag*; NBHL: πλησμονή, κόρος), I consider there to be a verbal connection. MI, referring to *QG* 1.85, indicates արագայագ (*aragayag*) as the equivalent of ἀψίκορος; it does not mention վաղայագ (*vałayag*), for which NBHL too gives no Greek or Latin equivalents.
[574] For "fickly tasting excellence" Marcus has "briefly experiencing uprightness" which is no doubt better English, but my literal rendering attempts to bring out more clearly the connections to the other passages being discussed. The contents of the Armenian version are substantially the same as those of the Greek fragment preserved: Ἤδη τινὲς ἀψίκοροι γευσάμενοι καλοκαγαθίας καὶ ἐλπίδα παρασχόντες ὑγείας, εἰς τὴν αὐτὴν ἐπανέστρεψαν νόσον.

QG 4.45	"many who are, as it were, carried into the port again *go back* from there and are drawn *into the same* harm ... because their withdrawal ... was not carried out with a firm ... *intellect*."[575]	salvation, vision, continence, holiness, purity
QE 1.7	"some who have progressed in virtue **descend/ return** and flee before they have reached the end, for the newly grown power of virtue in the soul is destroyed by ancient error, which after being quiet *for a short while* again returns to the attack with great power"	piety, worthy holiness, virtue, reaching the end
QE 2.40	"those in whom the desire (for God) is *fickle* ascend with the *intellect for a short while* upwards, (being) flying ones carried by God, (and) immediately **descend/***return*"	divinization (of a holy soul), permanent ascent to God, reaching the holy and divine city, following God

Philo uses a rich variety of images to express the same basic idea: for some, at least in certain conditions, permanently reaching the goal is a task too difficult. If we look at the inevitability vs. contingency of the return, we see that in none of the cases is the attempt at progress doomed to fail in advance. In *QG* 1.85 there is "hope of health," and the sentence immediately preceding the quotation runs, "[scripture] praises [Enoch] since he persevered in the same condition of morals and did not again change until the end of his life;" if being stable is laudable, it must be contingent and so must instability. *QG* 4.45 is a clear case: the withdrawal should and thus could have been performed more steadily. In *QE* 1.7 virtue is not strong enough to counter the attack of "ancient error;" hence these souls descend. Thinking that this is the only possible result would be far-fetched given the fact that these souls have already made progress, and here again it is "some" who fail. As for the destination which the returners fail to reach, strictly speaking the only factor common to all four accounts in Table VI is holiness. However, "incorporeity," "the end" and reaching God can well be taken as references to salvation.

Based on the comparability of the two groups of souls, the curability of their error and the parallels featuring contingent returns of souls that cannot reach salvation, the failure of the returners in *QE* 2.40 must not be thought of as inevitable. The most natural setting, by far, for a situation

---

[575] There is no Greek fr. for *QG* 4.45. *Abr.* 47 contains an interesting parallel: Enos (who represents hope) "has *not yet* been able to attain [the excellent], but resembles sailors eager to put into port, who yet remain at sea unable to reach their haven." Note the temporary nature of the non-attainment, expressed also at §7 where Philo calls hope "the *first* step towards the possession of blessings."

where apparently discarnate souls can either be saved or dragged back to the body-oriented life is the hereafter. When we add the fact the Greek fr. contains Philo's favorite verb for returning to the corporeal sphere, παλινδρομέω—which he, furthermore, uses in his *locus classicus* on reincarnation—, the alternative that the returning souls of *QE* 2.40 face reincarnation begins to seem quite likely. However, we must still try to clarify as far as possible the meaning of Tartarus in this passage.

3.3.5 *The Plunge into Tartarus*

Philo's references to Tartarus and Hades were reviewed above, and it was found that he does not consider these to be some underworldly locations.[576] Instead he uses the terms particularly to refer to the physical body but also generally to refer to the life of the wicked. The only other place in either the Armenian or Greek text of *QGE* where Tartarus is mentioned is *QG* 4.234, and there it is explicitly identified with the body, as was seen above.[577] This is not the only feature to connect *QG* 4.234 with *QE* 2.40, for both allude to the *Phaedrus*. In the former God "permits [the mind that has descended into the earthly body] to spread its wings (թևակոխել [t'ewakoxel])[578] sometimes and to behold (հայել [hayel]) heaven above and to taste of that sight (տեսլենեն [teslenēn])." This is an obvious reference to the supercelestial nourishing vision in the myth of the dialogue.[579]

The passages are connected, in addition to Tartarus, other direct links and the *Phaedrus*, also by Philo's exegesis of Ex 24:11b in *QE*: those who in the biblical lemma "appeared in the place of God and were eating and

---

[576] See pp. 65–70.
[577] There are no instances of Hades in the *Quaestiones*. See the quotation of QG 4.234 on p. 68. In the OL there is one additional mention of Tartarus, here too as the opposite of heaven, but the term is used on quite a general level. This is addition no. 10 (ex. Gen 26:34), where Philo presents a short list of opposites to which Esau in his wickedness gives equal value: "light and darkness, black and white, good and bad." Of these opposites the better are "worthy of heaven," the worse, "[worthy] of Tartarus" ("et haec quidem digna caelo, illa tartaro"). See Petit, *L'ancienne version latine*, 1.72–73.
[578] NBHL gives, e.g., πτερύσσομαι. From տև (tew), 'wing.' The Arm. words are given to facilitate the comparison with and also between *QE* 2.39 and 2.40. See below.
[579] Marcus, with his "taste (*sic*) of that sight," does not seem to recognize the reference. Cf. 248a: "the reason for the great eagerness to see where the plain of truth is, lies in the fact that the fitting pasturage for the best part of the soul is in the meadow there, and the wing on which the soul is raised up is nourished by this;" 251b: "the effluence of beauty enters him through the eyes ... and as the nourishment streams upon him, the quills of the feathers begin to grow." Cf. *Mos.* 2.69 where Moses is said to have enjoyed "the better food of contemplation (τροφὰς ... τὰς διὰ θεωρίας)" during his 40-day stay on the mountain. For the links between *QE* 2.40 and the *Phaedrus*, see above, pp. 171–72.

drinking" are said by Philo to have "attained to the face of the Father;" they

> make a migration (զզաղութն [zgałut'n]) to a holy and divine place (սուրբ և աստուածային տեղին [surb ew astuacayin tełin]) (where they) see (տեսանեն [tesanen]) the Master (զզխաւորն [zglxaworn]) in a lofty and clear manner, envisioning (երևութացեալք [erewut'ac'ealk']) God with the keen-sighted eyes of the mind. (*QE* 2.39)

Numerous verbal connections to 2.40 confirm that we have every reason to read the passages together.[580] The tasting of the heavenly sight in *QG* 4.234 finds a counterpart at the end of *QE* 2.39:

> this vision is the food of the soul, and true partaking is the cause of a life of immortality. Wherefore, indeed, it is said, they 'were eating and drinking.' ... [They] did not fail to see (տեսանեն [tesanel]) God become clearly visible, but ... fulfilled (լցին [lc'in]) their great desire (ցանկութիւնն [c'ankut'iwnn]).

With all the above links, we can see that *QG* 4.234 contains some of the key elements present in *QE* 2.39–40: a divine mind's using its wings to taste the divine vision and the descent to the Tartarus of the body.

Given the strength of the *QG* passage as a parallel to *QE* 2.40 I think it is warranted to follow also another track that leads from it to a passage which too has a bearing on whether Tartarus should be taken as an appellation of the body in *QE* 2.40. For Philo says in *QG* 4.234 that some souls "through gluttony, lechery and over-indulgence are always submerged and sunken, being drowned by passion." As discussed above, there are connections both to Plato—notably the image of the submerged soul—and, as Marcus notes, to *Agr.* 89.[581] While the exact verbal agreement suggested by Marcus is unlikely, the passages are linked by the specific image of the soul being drowned in the body by the activity of the passions.[582] It should also be

---

[580] In *QE* 2.40 Philo speaks of "the divine place (աստուածային տեղին [astuacayin tełisn])" and "holy and divine (սուրբ և աստուածային [surb ew astuacayin]) city to which they have migrated (գաղթեալ փոխեցանն [gałt'eal p'oxec'ann])" (see n. 569) and having "God as their chief leader (զխաւոր առաջ [glxawor aṙaj])."

[581] See above, p. 83.

[582] A further but not highly specific commonality between *QG* 4.234 and this section of *Agr.* is that at §101 the "lack of self-control, and gluttony (ἀκρασίας καὶ λαιμαργίας), and all the other practices which immoderate and insatiable (ἀμέτηροι καὶ ἄπληστοι) pleasures ... give birth to" are blamed for "compel[ling the soul] to fall in pits and clefts;" "licentiousness (ἀκολασίαν) finds no road at all." Cf. the gluttony (որկորածտուիւն [orkoražētut'iwn]), e.g., λαιμαργία, lechery (ճակաճանութիւն [čakačanut'iwn], e.g., ἀκολασία) and over-indulgence (շուոյտութիւն [šuoytut'iwn], e.g., ἀσέλγεια) of *QG* 4.234.

noted that that part of *Agr.* to which §89 belongs manifests clear influences of the *Phaedrus*.[583]

Philo's secondary biblical lemma in §§ 84–93 is Deut 17:15b–16a.[584] These verses involve both horses and the theme of *returning to Egypt*, the land of the body for Philo. The allegorical interpretation of the return is the soul's "sinking" to the body. After brushing aside a literal understanding of the verses Philo states that Moses's account

> is concerned instead with the irrational, uncontrolled and disobedient motion in the soul, which it will be advantageous to restrain, lest it return all its people back to Egypt, the region of the body, and by force make it a lover of pleasure and passion rather than a lover or excellence and of God. For, as Moses himself has said, the one who has acquired a multitude of horses must necessarily make his way to Egypt. (*Agr.* 88)

Philo thus declares that the passions pave the way to the dreaded return. We come to the expression whose close equivalent is found in *QG* 4.234, when Philo writes,

> For when a wave, by the force of the passions and evil deeds blowing against the unstable soul which is sailing off the right course, comes rising upon both sides of the soul—mind and sense-perception—as if of a ship, then in all likelihood the mind, becoming waterlogged, is submerged; and the bottom to which it is submerged and made to sink (καταποντοῦται καὶ καταδύεται) is nothing else than the body, of which Egypt is the figure. (*Agr.* 89)[585]

Philo's switching to nautical terminology in §89 is, as Paz has aptly noted, due to his wanting to allude to the thanksgiving hymn of Ex 15—which he

---

[583] In Geljon and Runia's commentary of *Agr.* (*On Cultivation*) §§ 67–123 are the third chapter of the first part of the treatise. In their *index locorum* (where only those passages are mentioned which are cited or discussed in some detail) there are seven references to Plato in the commentary to this section: six to the *Phaedrus* (for §§ 68–72) and one to the *Timaeus*. These are mainly related to Socrates's simile of the soul's two *horses*, because Philo is engaged in explaining the distinction between a horseman and a rider, whereas in *QG* 4.234 his approach to the dialogue is determined by the catchwords *earth* and *heaven* in the biblical lemma.

[584] The text is quoted at §84: "You will not be able to establish over yourself a foreign person, because he is not your brother; for the reason that he will not multiply for himself cavalry, nor will he return the people back to Egypt."

[585] Mostly my tr. for ὅταν γὰρ καθ' ἑκάτερον τοῖχον τῆς ψυχῆς νεὼς τρόπον, τόν τε νοῦ καὶ αἰσθήσεως, ὑπὸ βίας τῶν καταπνεόντων εἰς αὐτὴν παθῶν τε καὶ ἀδικημάτων ἀντιρρεπούσης καὶ κλινομένης ἐξαιρόμενον ἐπιβαίνῃ τὸ κῦμα, τόθ' ὡς εἰκὸς ὑπέραντλος ὁ νοῦς γινόμενος καταποντοῦται. βυθὸς δέ ἐστιν, εἰς ὃν καταποντοῦται καὶ καταδύεται, σῶμα αὐτὸ τὸ ἀπεικασθὲν Αἰγύπτῳ. Close parallels to *Agr.* 89 but without reference to the body are at *Det.* 100, *Post.* 22, *Migr.* 148. For *Agr.* 89 see also p. 69 above. For translating κλινομένης as 'sailing off the right course' cf. κεκλιμένη ναῦς in Theognis *Elegiae* 1.855 referred to in LSJ.

has already discussed and quoted from at §§ 79–82.[586] He connects the drowning of the Pharaoh's cavalry with the Platonic image of the engulfed soul and thus gets a chance to remind his audience that instability in the face of the attack of the passions leads to a violent descent to the body. And as this is a case of turning the soul "back to ... the region of the body" (§88), the possibility of this being a hint at reincarnation must be considered significant even when read independent of other passages.[587]

Returning implies a prior exit from "Egypt," and so does the connection to Ex 15. Is physical death or a contemplative flight meant? The latter alternative is made unlikely by the statement that the soul is still "unstable [and] sailing off the right course." Rather, the description here is reminiscent of the wicked soul's being "tossed about and sunken" in the hereafter in QG 2.61.[588] The idea of a passion-induced descent is also very similar to QG 4.234, where the soul is drowned in the desire–rivers of Tartarus, i.e., the body.

Later in *Agr.* we find a section which is linked to §89 by several notions.[589] §§ 169–178 is a homily on, *inter alia*, the preferability of committing involuntary sins as compared to voluntary ones. First, Philo describes the fate of *voluntary* sinners:

> Many a time even those who have reached perfection have been deemed imperfect because they believed their improvement was due to their own eagerness and not the supervision of God, and so on account of this belief, after having been raised and lifted up (μετεωρισθέντες) to the furthest degree, they fell from very high places into the deepest abyss (εἰς ἔσχατον ... βυθόν) and disappeared. (§169)

The end of §169 tastes very much like being "dragged down to the extremes of Tartarus" in *QE* 2.40. Furthermore, the notion of the falling

---

[586] Yakir Paz, in his review of Albert C. Geljon and David T. Runia, *Philo of Alexandria: On Cultivation: Introduction, Translation and Commentary*, Bryn Mawr Classical Review 2013.10.61 (bmcr.brynmawr.edu/2013/2013-10-61.html) points to the expression κατέδυσαν εἰς βυθόν at Ex 15:5. We may add that the words καταποντίζω/-τόω, τεῖχος and κῦμα appear in 15:4–8 as well as in *Agr.* 89. Cf. also "the wind of your wrath (θυμοῦ)" in 15:8 vs. "the force of the passions and evil deeds blowing against the unstable soul" in §89. I think speaking of the mind and sense-perception in §89 picks up §80 where these are represented by Moses and Miriam in the context of the hymn of Ex 15 sung on the occasion of the successful escape from Egypt.

[587] Geljon & Runia in their commentary on *Agr.* (*On Cultivation*) do not comment on the issue of *returning* to the body (pp. 179, 181).

[588] See above, p. 83–84.

[589] Paz, review of Geljon and Runia, *On Cultivation*, sees an allusion in §169 to Ex 15:5, probably based on the word βυθός, but I think also the "disappearance" in the former is reminiscent of the sea hiding (ἐκάλυψεν) the Egyptians (v. 10).

souls' not relying on God is not far from God's not being the chief leader in *QE*.

Then there are those who sin *involuntarily*, "who have let out all the ropes of piety and, sailing with good speed, have striven to berth in her harbours," are nevertheless driven back to sea by a counter-wind (§174). This, for its part, brings to mind the description of going back from the port in *QG* 4.45.[590] But here the souls are not to blame, "for their lack of speed occurred against their will" (§175). Thus both the voluntary and involuntary sinners have made an *attempt* at reaching the goal—and failed, but for different reasons. The latters' ending up back at sea is clearly contingent and temporary; it is compared to the *almost* inevitable stumbling of runners at §177. The voluntary sinners' ascent, on the other hand, does seem doomed in advance given their self-reliance.[591] But they too have already made considerable progress—"attained perfection"![592]

The lowest abyss, βυθὸς ἔσχατος in §169, should, I think, be read juxtaposed with the accounts in §§ 89 and 174. At §89 the body is explicitly called βυθός. The imagery and vocabulary are (in §174 only partly) different in the later accounts, but there is an accumulation of connections: in §89 to *QG* 4.234 (probably καταποντόω, soul drowned in the body by passion) and in §169 to both §89 (βυθός, ἐξαίρω, allusions to Ex 15) and *QE* 2.40 (the plunge, lowest abyss, lack of God's supervision). In my estimation these passages form a coherent whole on the assumption that both the lowest abyss (§169) and Tartarus (*QE*) are veiled references to the body. Furthermore, the images of the ship, sea and wind connect §174 to §89: the same forces are at play.[593] A factor connecting §§ 169 and 174 is that the love of pleasure, contributing decisively to the drowning in §89, is no longer mentioned whereas progress is. It actually seems the three accounts

---

[590] See above, Table VI on p. 178.
[591] Cf. Philo's calling his own mind "opinionated" in *Cher.* 116, which especially in the context of that treatise signifies the delirious self-sufficiency symbolized by Cain. Geljon & Runia, *On Cultivation*, 254 aptly note in their comments on *Agr.* 169–173, "Philo's idea of the failure of giving honor to God reminds us of his interpretation of the figure of Cain." See above, p. 157.
[592] They still need to "acquire solidity" (see *Agr.* 158–160).
[593] Geljon & Runia (*On Cultivation*, 260) comment on §174 by saying that "[t]his imagery is closely related to the picture of the waves of passions by which the intellect is tossed." Indeed, no other motive to again apply the nautical terminology seems forthcoming than a conscious allusion to §89. It should be added, however, that this time the passions are not part of the picture. (The last appearance of πάθος is at §143 where passions weigh down the sophists.) For §169 cf. *Migr.* 170–171: the lack of God's guidance leads to a fall from the heights. Philo's comment is that it is better "to stay where we are, roaming, with the bulk of mankind, through this mortal life."

are presented in an ascending order of progress. In §174, there is no more talk about sinking; the movement is horizontal and not vertical. These changes are not surprising if we consider that the connotations of βυθός go in two directions, the body (because of §89 if not otherwise) and the underworld. It would not have been a suitable word to use at §174, because Hades and Tartarus are in Philo related to the life of the *wicked*: the underworldly "abyss" would not be an appropriate choice of word to use when talking about those whose salvation is so close as it is in *Agr.* 174–175.[594]

Based on both the internal logic of *QE* 2.40 and the parallelisms with *QG* 4.234 and *QE* 2.39, *Agr.* 89, 169 and the *Phaedrus*, it is my conclusion that Philo's statement about souls being dragged to the extremes of Tartarus is meant as a reference to their ending up in a new incarnation.

3.3.6 *Conclusions*

There is strong evidence that salvation and its alternative are spoken of in *QE* 2.40: permanent existence with God is envisaged for those who do not return from the city of God. Notwithstanding the special cases of Enoch and Elijah in the Bible, Philo does not entertain a notion that a virtuous soul can be saved directly from the body without ordinary physical death. This means that afterlife is being discussed, at least as far as the saved, and thus discarnate, souls are concerned.

There is no evidence to suggest that the saved souls differ from the returning ones in terms of their state of embodiment. Thus if one wants to make such an assumption, one should also acknowledge its extra-textual nature. Furthermore, nothing points to their being predestined to return. On the contrary, several factors bespeak contingency: The two groups are comparable; they *are*, in effect, compared when partly defined in terms of each other—in which connection no difference related to incarnation is mentioned. The descent is preceded by an attempted ascent which means that these souls do not belong to those who do not even try; they have already made some progress. Most of the parallel accounts of returning souls reviewed feature clear contingency.

The probable meaning of Tartarus in *QE* 2.40 is the body. The more general sense, the hideous life of the wicked, follows as well, for although the souls that in *QE* 2.40 are drawn to Tartarus do not belong among the worst, Philo is clearly not expecting them to enjoy themselves. That the

---

[594] Somewhat similarly, Philo also does not use the image of entombment (in the body) of virtuous but still incarnate souls.

body is meant is also likely based on the clear connections (partly via *QE* 2.39) to, and also between, *QG* 4.234 and *Agr.* 89 which both speak explicitly of descending or sinking back to the body.

All this points in the direction of reincarnation, and since we have encountered no evidence to the contrary, it must be the conclusion that transmigration is again being referred to. The driving force might now be characterized as the *lack of devotion* to God: the desire the souls feel for the divine and the degree to which they are willing or able to rely on God's leadership are inadequate. In the Philonic way of thinking the lack of the desire for God goes together with the desire for earthly things and sense pleasures, and so the reason for the descent here is easily reconciled with the earlier results concerning body-love as the main driving force of reincarnation.

As a final—indirect and not decisive—piece of evidence for taking *QE* 2.40 as speaking of transmigration is the fact that it so clearly draws on the reincarnational myth of the *Phaedrus*. The two passages that greatly help us in understanding it, *QE* 2.39 and *QG* 4.234, do likewise. Again, one has to ask: what is the meaning, the significance of Philo's using Plato this way? Assuming that this use carries no message at all is sure to lead to an inadequate and impoverished understanding of what Philo wants to say; to see silence where clues are provided is in fact a form of *eisegesis*.

3.4 *Fragment 7.3 Harris*

3.4.1 *Introduction*

This fragment receives its identification from the fact that it was published by J. Rendel Harris in the collection *Fragments of Philo Judaeus* in a section "Fragments of Philo from the lost fourth book of the Allegories of the Sacred Laws" as the third fragment on p. 7.[595] Harris's collection contains

---

[595] Harris, *Fragments of Philo*. He gives the sources as follows: "Mangey (II. 667) from John Monachus [of Damascus] (= Rup. f. 265[r]); also in Maximus (II. 615) and in Cod. Reg. 923 (f. 342 b) where it is referred to the Allegories of the Law." The text given by ps.-Maximus (seventh to tenth cent.) is also printed in MPG 91 col. 881, i.e., *Loci communes*, sermo xxix, and in Ihm's (2001) grand critical edition of the *Loci* (pp. 621–22). James Royse (*The Spurious Texts of Philo of Alexandria: A Study of Textual Transmission and Corruption with Indexes to the Major Collections of Greek Fragments* [Leiden: Brill, 1991], 163; and "Reverse Indexes to Philonic Texts in the Printed Florilegia and Collections of Fragments," in *SPhA* 5 [1993]: 156–79, p. 175) gives one additional source, the (c. eleventh cent.), published in MPG 136, col. 920 D7–11. The present names of the codices are Berolinensis 46 (Rupefucaldinus in Harris) and Parisinus 923 (Regius); I have examined digital copies of the fragment in both MSS., kept in Staatsbibliothek zu Berlin and

no commentary; for this fragment he prints a reference "Plat. *Phaedo* 81 A." in the margin.

As the text appears in a slightly different form in the sources, a critical text is first drawn up and a translation provided (3.4.2).[596] Then the fragment's degree of "Philonicity" is analyzed in terms of its language (3.4.3). The occurrence in later authors of key features of the fragment is then surveyed to explore the possibility their alluding to, or of one of them being the author of, the fragment (3.4.4). After some tradition-historical observations (3.4.4, 3.4.5) follow reflections on the fragment's contents and different interpretative options (3.4.6) before conclusions are drawn regarding the light the fragment sheds on Philo's position on the idea of reincarnation (3.4.7).

3.4.2 *Text, Translation and Preliminary Observations*

εἰκότως μελέτην μὲν θανάτου,[597] σκιὰν δὲ καὶ ὑπογραμμὸν τῆς αὖθις ἐσομένης[598] ἀναβιώσεως[599] τὸν ὕπνον οἱ τὰ ἀληθῆ πεφρονηκότες ἀπεφήναντο· ἑκατέρων γὰρ ἐναργεῖς φέρει τὰς εἰκόνας.[600] *μεθιστᾷ*[601] *γὰρ καὶ παριστᾷ*[602] *τὸν αὐτὸν ἐξ ὁλοκλήρου.*[603]

Those who have come to understand truth fitly declare sleep to be the practice of death and the shadow and outline of the revival which follows afterwards. For it carries images of both clear. *For it completely removes and sets beside the same one.*

Bibliothèque nationale de France, respectively. In the latter, the last eight letters of the fragment are on the following folio, 343r. For a brief description of Berolinensis 46, see above, n. 537 on p. 167; of Parisinus 923 Harris says (p. vii) that it is "in uncial Greek characters of the ninth century, and adorned with interesting marginal pictures."

[596] Harris only gives the reading printed by Mangey.

[597] The punctuation varies in the MSS.; Parisinus 923 has a full stop, Berolinensis 46 a raised dot here.

[598] ἐσομένης Maximus and Antonius, the rest have ἐπομένης. This could be right, but there is, in practice, no difference in meaning. See below.

[599] ἀναστάσεως in one MS. of Maximus (probably a Christian interpolation). A full stop after this word in Parisinus.

[600] φέρει—εἰκόνας: ἔχει τὰς εἰκόνας μᾶλλον δὲ φέρει in one MS. of Maximus. (Is this the equivalent of "has the images—no, sorry—carries them"? Be that as it may, the variant is inconsequential.)

[601] Circumflex absent in Parisinus 923 (also from ἀληθῆ; present in παριστᾷ). Iota subscripts are not shown either in Parisinus 923 or in Berolinensis 46.

[602] μεθιστᾷ—παριστᾷ: μεθιστᾷ in four MSS. of Maximus (a minority). This omission is explainable as by *homoeoteleuton*.

[603] The italics indicate that I consider the last sentence corrupt or paraphrastic, probably both. See below.

For comparison, Yonge's translation, which is the only one in a modern language I am aware of, is offered:

> Very naturally some who have been wise enough to arrive at correct notions of the truth, have described sleep as a thing to teach us to meditate upon death, and a shadow and outline of the resurrection which is hereafter to follow, for it bears in itself visible images of both conditions, for it removes the same man from his state of perfection and brings him back to it.

The last sentence of the fragment is difficult to understand. It is probably the result of a combination of corruption and paraphrasis. The subject must be "sleep," but I do not see how Philo could say that sleep—or physical death which it is being compared to—could in any way *remove* a soul from "perfection."[604] Now the phrase ἐξ ὁλοκλήρου (ἐξολοκλήρου) has a meaning 'completely,' 'entirely' in Lampe's *Patristic Greek Lexicon*, but it is not attested in the TLG before the 2nd century CE. In the translation I have nevertheless opted for this interpretation as the only way of making some sense of the sentence, which also means that the sentence as it stands is probably by a later hand. I think this is a more likely option than assuming Philo anticipated the use of ἐξ ὁλοκλήρου as 'completely' in one single instance. This cannot, however, be wholly excluded given Philo's linguistic creativity—and one of the earliest instances of the expression in this sense is in Origen.[605]

The forms of the compounds of ἵστημι are an even stronger indication of the un-Philonic origin of the last sentence as it stands. Elsewhere, Philo can manage without the apparently Ionic-influenced -ιστᾷ forms (present active indicative, third person singular).[606] Not a single case is to be found anywhere else in Philo (the same is true, e.g., about Plato; Aristotle has two, Aesop is the first and has several). The LXX has five occurrences, all outside the Pentateuch. Together with the phrase ἐξ ὁλοκλήρου these forms amount to sufficient grounds for considering the last sentence to be by a

---

[604] Furthermore, "brings him back" for παριστᾷ is untenable. With reservations this perhaps could be the meaning if the word was περιιστᾷ. The heading under which the fragment is in Berolinensis 46, "Concerning sleep: That the ecstasy of sleep, with the ensuing recovery, carries a shadow of death and a most clear sign of resurrection (Περὶ ὕπνου· ὅτι σκιὰν μὲν θανάτου, σημεῖον δὲ ἐναργέστατον ἀναστάσεως φέρει ἡ πρὸς ὕπνον ἔκστασις, καὶ αὖθις ἔκνηψις)" is indicative of a perceived antithetical relation between the two verbs. However, that ἔκνηψις—literally 'becoming sober or calm' (LSJ)—should represent resurrection seems forced.

[605] Fr. 57.12–13 in *Fragmenta in evangelium Joannis (in catenis)*.

[606] Actually it is the form ἱστᾷ of the base verb ἵστημι which is Ionic, "ionic koine byz" according to the TLG . The TLG classifies both μεθιστᾷ and παριστᾷ as "attic epic ionic doric koine byz" the only difference being that the latter is "late ionic." The -ίστησι(ν) forms of both verbs are given exactly the same dialect information.

later hand in its present state. The opaque meaning and the awkward syntax also speak of corruption. The last sentence probably does contain *something* of the original text, but its significance is reduced by our having no way of ascertaining what exactly that is.

3.4.3 *Is It Philo?*

Despite the specific lemma in one source and the general one in the others, there is no guarantee that this passages really comes from Philo's exegesis of Gen 3:20–23 (the text whose commentary was contained in the now lost fourth book of *Leg.*).[607] The themes of sleep and death are not discussed there, but given Philo's copious use of secondary and tertiary biblical lemmata from anywhere in the Pentateuch and beyond, this fact is not decisive. And while death is not mentioned within the range of the primary lemmas, *living forever* is (3:22). This surely inspired Philo to dwell on matters of life and death. In fact, out of the eight fragments printed by Harris as coming from the fourth book of *Leg.*, the long fragment 8.1 has been identified by Runia as part of Philo's exegesis of Gen 3:22.[608] There, interestingly enough, Philo quotes as a secondary lemma Deut 30:15, 19, where the choice between life and death is discussed. The two fragments do not, however, belong immediately together. They do not have much in common in terms of substance, nor are they cited in the same sources. One of Harris's fragments of *Leg.* 4 has been identified as spurious (7.1 = Origen, *Commentary on St. John* 19.21, removed by Wendland)[609] and one (6.1) as coming from the lost portions of *QE*.[610] James Royse, who has meticulously investigated the Philonic fragments, has not challenged the label *Leg.* 4 for fr. 7.3 Harris.[611]

As to the vocabulary and grammar of the fragment, I have chosen to go over it word by word as part of my efforts to establish the fragment's genuineness. Starting from the beginning of the text, εἰκότως with 181 occurrences is quite common in Philo. The phrase μελέτη θανάτου comes from Plato's *Phaedo* as indicated by Harris. This notion will be returned to in the next subsection.[612]

---

[607] As a matter of convenience, in what follows I take as my starting point that the fr. is (mainly) genuine; hence the phrases like "elsewhere in Philo" below.
[608] Runia, *Philo in Early Christian Literature*, 30. See also Royse, *The Spurious Texts*, 9.
[609] See Royse, *The Spurious Texts*, 97.
[610] Removed by Petit (PAPM 33) who gives it the number 16. Royse, *The Spurious Texts*, 192, 222.
[611] Royse mentions our fragment in *The Spurious Texts*, 160, 175, 186, 192; "Reverse Indexes," 175.
[612] For an overview of Philo's usage of this notion, see also above, p. 122.

The word σκιά (fifty-two occurrences) is no rarity in Philo, and he uses it to denote a copy or an imitation also elsewhere (e.g., *Conf.* 190, *Migr.* 7–12). The case of ὑπογραμμός is very different. The word is quite rare with a total of only approximately 330 occurrences in the whole TLG beginning with Second Maccabees (2:28) and the New Testament (1 Pet 2:21)—and none in Philo.[613] The situation changes to some extent if we include the base verb ὑπογράφω which has a longer history and wider use. In Philo there are 29 occurrences plus two more of ὑπογραφή. Let us take Philo's exegesis of Ex 31:2–3 as an example:

> The artificer of this fabric was called by the holy word Bezaleel, which is when interpreted "in the shadow of God" (ἐν σκιᾷ θεοῦ). For it is the copies (μιμήματα) of which he is chief builder, whereas Moses builds the patterns (παραδείγματα); for this reason the one drew an outline as it were of shadows (οἷα σκιὰς ὑπεγράφετο), but the other fashioned no shadows, but the existences themselves that served as archetypes (ἀρχετύπους). (*Somn.* 1.206)

This example alone suffices to show that the use of the word ὑπογραμμός in the fragment is, while untypical, undoubtedly possible for Philo. It is worthwhile noting too, that such a synonymic use of σκιά and ὑπογραμμόν/ὑπογράφω cannot be found in the TLG before Philo, and after him only from the fourth century onwards.[614] σκιά as such could be used in a similar manner; see, e.g. Heb 8:5 (with ὑπόδειγμα), 10:1.[615]

Then come εἰμί (6961) followed by αὖθις (122). There are two similar instances in Philo, αὖθις coupled with a future participle of εἰμί, in *Opif.* 67 and *Post.* 117.[616] The former passage is a curious case from the viewpoint of the fragment. Philo has advanced to the fifth day of creation and is saying that despite the chronology in Genesis everything really came about simultaneously:

> But even though everything was constituted together, it was still necessary that the ordered sequence should be outlined (ὑπογράφετο) in an account, because in the future beings would originate from each other (διὰ τὴν ἐσομένην αὖθις ἐξ ἀλλήλων γένεσιν). (*Opif.* 67)

---

[613] Situation in July 2014.
[614] The verb appears in such a context first in ps.-Macarius (*Homiliae spirituales* 47.114), the noun, in John Chrysostom (*In epistulam i ad Timotheum* 62.510.43).
[615] Both the author of the Epistle to the Hebrews (8:5) and Philo (*Leg.* 3.102) use σκιά in their exegesis of Ex 25:40 where it does *not* occur (there is συσκιάζω in 25:20), although in different ways. See Runia, *Philo in Early Christian Literature*, 77–78.
[616] The competing verb ἕπομαι does not appear anywhere in Philo coupled with αὖθις. This is the main reason for my reading ἐσομένης and not ἐπομένης here.

The reference to intra-species generation is needed as Philo justifies the ascending order of creation (from fishes to humans) by appealing to the development in nature, from insignificant seed to full fruition.[617] The notion of "generation from each other" is used by Philo about sexual reproduction also elsewhere (e.g., *Cher.* 54) and about the four elements' changing into each other by, e.g., Aristotle (*Metaphysica* 988b31). But it is also used by Plato in the *Phaedo* in a reincarnational context in 71b, 103c; in the form of γίγνεσθαι ἐξ ἀλλήλων it appears in 71c–d (see next subsection). The *contents* of *Opif.* 67 do not have anything in common with the fragment but I would not rule out a an allusion to it. As for αὖθις, it should be noted that it appears in exactly the same position in *Somn.* 1.139, i.e., to describe the timing of the return/revival. It is also worth attention that the *Phaedo* has the expression αὖθις γίγνεσθαι in 77d and 88a (and also in *Republic* 498d) in the sense 'to reincarnate.'

The general meaning of **ἀναβίωσις** is 'coming back to life.' At first the statistics seem very similar to that of ὑπογραμμός: there are roughly 300 occurrences in the TLG and the first one in the Second Maccabees.[618] The next instances are found in Plutarch; there are none in Philo. Similarly, if the verbs ἀναβιόω and ἀναβιώσκομαι are included, the history starts earlier, from the 5th cent. BCE onwards, with Epimenides, Crates, Pherecydes, Euripides, Plato etc.—but this time the zero in Philo's column remains, which makes the word a *hapax legomenon* in his extant writings. Philo does use the corresponding verb ἀναζάω (= ἀναζωόω) once, in *Somn.* 1.147, where its meaning is positive: God's *logoi* "with the healing of their breath ... quicken into new life (σωτήριον πνέοντες ἀναζωῶσι) the soul which is still borne along in the body as in a river."

After the unproblematic word **ὕπνος** (65) comes **ἀληθής** (317). Philo uses the concept of τὰ ἀληθῆ in the sense of the ultimate verities in *Cher.* 9 (μελέτη τῶν ἀληθῶν) and *Migr.* 76 (ἡ τῶν ἀληθῶν ἐνάργεια). But this is not typical. Rather, Philo likes to speak about, e.g., τὰ νοητά or τὰ θεῖα.[619] Still, the expression τὰ ἀληθῆ is not highly anomalous.

The verb **φρονέω** (69) is no rarity in Philo, and using a participle is usual. But no form of the perfect tense is found elsewhere in his works. For comparison it may be noted that only one out of the 51 occurrences of another verb meaning 'to understand,' κατανοέω, has the perfect in Philo.

---

[617] I do not quite see Philo's logic here. See Runia, *On the Creation*, 211–13, 218.
[618] The meaning in 7:9 is resurrection of the body: "You accursed wretch, you dismiss us from this present life, but the King of the universe will raise us up to an everlasting renewal of life (εἰς αἰώνιον ἀναβίωσιν ζωῆς), because we have died for his laws."
[619] For comparison: Plato uses the τὰ ἀληθῆ (in the accusative) only once (*Rep.* 519b) in the sense discussed here (as also, in the genitive, in, e.g., *Phaedrus* 248c).

Plato, Philo and Plutarch each have only one perfect participle of the verb φιλοσοφέω, Aristotle two.[620]

Philo uses the verb **ἀποφαίνω** 116 times in total. If we take a sample of Philo's usage of the word by looking the instances with the form attested in the fragment (ἀπεφήναντο) and the corresponding singular (ἀπεφήνατο) we see that he can use it to make either negative (*Opif.* 7, *Praem.* 40), fairly neutral (*Plant.* 144) or positive references (*Decal.* 176, *Abr.* 270, *Spec.* 3.119, all concerning a biblical text) to views presented by others.

Ἐναργής and εἰκών are fairly common words in Philo (135 and 120, respectively); they are used together in *Deus* 4, *Mut.* 213 and *Decal.* 101. Somewhat surprisingly, the combination is quite rare and may have some value as a marker of Philo. We will, therefore, dwell on it for a little longer. The TLG has a single pre-Philonic instance of ἐναργής as an attribute of εἰκών, found in Epigram 74 of the poet Posidippus who was active in the Alexandrian court in third cent. BCE. After Philo there is one, surely unrelated, occurrence in Dio Chrysostom, followed by three occurrences in Clement of Alexandria. The combination next appears in the 4th century, once in Methodius, then in non-Christian writings associated with the Byzantine court,[621] and subsequently in church fathers known to have read Philo:[622] these include Gregory of Nyssa (three), Gregory of Nazianzen (two), Basil (two). The numbers increase as we reach Theodoret of Cyrrhus and Cyril of Alexandria, of whose acquaintance with Philo not much can be said.[623] None of the occurrences in later writers can be said to constitute a parallel to the contents of the fragment. However, the trajectory of the usage of these words seems just a little too similar to that of *verba Philonica* to be the result of a mere chance.[624] Thus their appearance can be regarded as contributing, to a small extent, to a cumulative argument in favor of regarding the fragment as either Philonic or authored by a church father who used Philo.

In Philo, neither ἐναργής nor εἰκών is used with **φέρω** (330) anywhere else. Ἐναργής is used with **παρίστημι** (107) thirteen times, as is quite

---

[620] The relevance of this comparison stems from the connection between the two kinds of wisdom, φρόνησις and σοφία (see n. 296 and text on p. 96). Plato's participle will meet us later (p. 205).
[621] Themistius, once; Emperor Julian, twice.
[622] Runia, *Philo in Early Christian Literature*, 243.
[623] Theodoret mentions Philo once, in a "rather trivial" context (Runia, *Philo in Early Christian Literature*, 270); Cyril, never.
[624] Runia, *Philo in Early Christian Literature*, 108 has, upon coining the term, defined these as "words that are common in Philo but found nowhere else in pre-Christian Greek, and that are then taken over by the Church fathers from their reading of Philo's works" and which started spreading in non-Alexandrian Christian authors after Origen.

natural, but none of the occurrences have features in common with the fragment.[625] **μεθίστημι** (10) is rare in Philo.[626] Μεθίστημι and παρίστημι do not occur with a common object anywhere else in Philo. I have found only one occurrence of their doing so in the whole TLG, in the Byzantine historian and statesman Georgius Acropolites's (d. 1282) *In imaginem beatae virginis*, line 13: Μεθιστᾷ καὶ σὲ καὶ παριστᾷ τῷ θρόνῳ, which I would translate, "He transfers you too, and places (you) beside the throne." The subject is the "Word of God" (l. 4, i.e., Christ), and line 13 concerns the post-mortem fate of the believer.[627] There is no reason to assume Georgius is dependent on the fragment.[628] However, his text is very useful in showing what may have fallen off at the end of the fragment's text: a word referring to God, the Logos, the world of ideas etc. in the dative.[629] In this way we can at least imagine that more sense could be made of the last sentence with only a minor addition. However, I have not wanted to adopt any such speculative conjecture in the text.

---

[625] It is perhaps interesting to note that ἐν σκιᾷ and ἐναργῶς are presented as *opposites* in *Leg.* 3.103. Indeed, one may ask if there is a contradiction in the fragment's text when it first says that sleep is the *shadow and outline* of revival and the states that sleep carries an image of revival (too) *clear*. One could think that the former is the others' opinion which Philo wants to formulate a little more strongly with his own comment—if that is what the latter is.

[626] The close relationship between μεθίστημι and μετανίστημι in Philo has been noted above. See n. 490 and text on p. 154.

[627] Cf. the last line (17) where the "I" of the poem asks for "Eden after life."

[628] He does not mention Philo by name, nor does he use *verba Philonica* in his works, unless we count ἀπεικονίζω among them: one pre-Philonic occurrence, 13 in Philo (not 14 as in PhI; *Fug.* 5 belongs to ἀπεικόνισμα), one in Georgius (*Laudatio Petri et Pauli* 23.11). Among the latter's works there is one titled *In Gregorii Nazianzeni sententias*. Gregory at least had a good chance of reading Philo, but the issue has not been much studied; see Runia, *Philo in Early Christian Literature*, 241–43. Direct knowledge of Philo by Georgius as well cannot be excluded, but an actual investigation of the matter falls outside the scope of this study. Yet we can take one example that may or may not reflect Philo's direct or indirect influence. Georgius says of Peter and Paul in *Laudatio* 9.27–29 (my tr.): "Like Enoch they seem transferred (μετατιθέμενοι) and passing over (μεταβαίνοντες) from the earthly (τῶν γηίνων) to the heavenly things, from the transient to the immortal (τὰ ἀθάνατα)." Cf. *Post.* 43 (n. 566, p. 175). There is noteworthy similarity, although "earthly" and "perishable" are not exact synonyms. The only other text I have found where a like idea is coupled with a reference to Enoch is Pseudo-Caesarius, *Quaestiones et responsiones* 214.72–3 (μεθίδρυσις ἐκ φθαρτῆς καὶ ἐπικήρου ζωῆς εἰς ἀθάνατον καὶ ἀταλαίπωρον χωρίον).

[629] Cf. the παρά + dative structure in the definition of salvation (n. 12 on p. 6). For two examples of the use of παρίστημι with a dative in a salvific context, see in 4 Macc 17:18: "they now stand before the divine throne (τῷ θείῳ νῦν παρεστήκασιν θρόνῳ) and live the life of the blessed age" and 1 Cor 8:8: "Food will not bring us close to God (οὐ παραστήσει τῷ Θεῷ)."

The adjective ὁλόκληρος is not very rare in Philo (66). Its usual meaning comes close to 'perfect'; in no less than thirty of its occurrences it is tightly connected with either παντελής or τέλειος. In the Philonic corpus ὁλόκληρος does not elsewhere appear connected with either the preposition ἐκ (or ἀπό) or the verbs μεθίστημι or παρίστημι.

On the whole, the fragment's vocabulary cannot be said to affect the evaluation of its authenticity strongly in either direction; it is partly typical, partly atypical. Yet in addition to this information we ought to have some knowledge about how much the frequencies of words usually vary in Philo. While any thorough assessment of this kind is beyond the scope of this study, a random sample of nine passages, each containing twenty verbs, adverbs, nouns, pronouns or numerals (like the fragment), was analyzed for word frequencies.[630] The corpus out of which the samples were taken using the random number generator of a spreadsheet programme comprised *Leg.* 1–3, *Cher.*, *Sacr.* and *Det.*, i.e., roughly 30,000 words both before and after the fragment's assumed position in Philo's *oeuvre*. The results are presented graphically in Figure 2.

The *y* axis is logarithmic because of the wide variation, from 1 for the *hapax legomena* to 4617 (αὐτός) to 6961 (εἰμί).[631] The diagram shows, e.g., that for *Sacr.* 21 the *average* frequency of the words is 158. The bars show the smallest and largest frequencies, and for Sacr. 21 these were 3 (βάδισμα) and 1814 (ψυχή). Note that because of the logarithmic scale, the absolute lengths of the bars cannot be compared with each other.

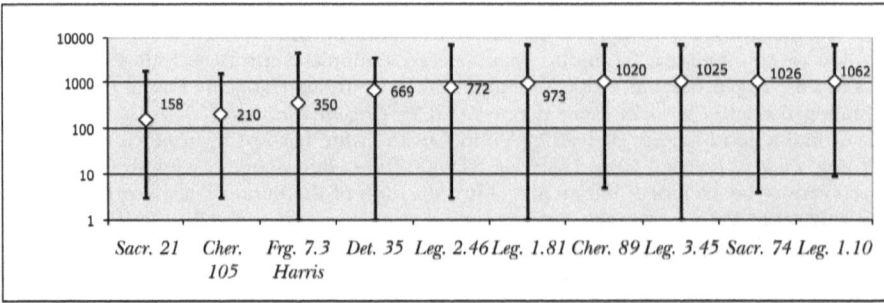

Figure 2. The Mean (the Numbers), Minimum and Maximum (the Bars) Frequencies in Corpus Philonicum of Words that Occur in Nine Random Passages Plus the Fragment.

---

[630] I have included the last sentence of the fragment. Any of its words may come from Philo.

[631] The words that occur only once in Philo are τετράστιχος, σάρδιον and τόπαζος in *Leg.* 1.81, ἀνεμιαῖος and εὐσάλευτος (a probable *verbum Philonicum*) in *Leg.* 3.45, σοφιστεύω in *Det.* 35 and ὑπογραμμός and ἀναβίωσις in the fragment.

The major result is that the fragment does not stand out; its word frequencies fit well within the wide variation. Three other passages also include the only occurrences of words, *Leg.* 1.81 no less than three. Unfortunately, the PhI does not contain any statistics that could easily have been produced and presented in tabular form; what, for instance, is the number of words that occur only once, in total and by treatise?[632]

With regard to the *hapax* words, it should be noted that four out of eight belong to families of cognate words that Philo uses more frequently: the root of ἀνεμιαῖος, ἄνεμος, appears 16 times; εὐσάλευτος is a very rare word with only ten occurrences in the whole TLG, but Philo uses the verb σαλεύω 16 and the noun σάλος 19 times; in addition to σοφιστεύω, σόφισμα σοφιστεία σοφιστής σοφιστικός occur 90 times in total; and, as seen above, the words ὑπογράφω/-γραφή are used 31 times.

An interesting case from the viewpoint of the fragment is *Leg.* 1.81. It shows that the reason for the use of very rare words can lie in their use in another text. The *hapax legomena* τετράστιχος, σάρδιον and τόπαζος appear within a biblical *quotation* (Ex 28:17).[633] Philo could have repeated any of the words also in his exegesis, and they would then have a clear intertextual referent. Given Philo's different way of using the Platonic text—the philosopher is very rarely *explicitly* quoted but borrowings and allusions abound—we may say ἀναβίωσις as well has a clear intertextual referent of which we are informed by the earlier unambiguous reference to the *Phaedo*.[634] What Philo *means* with the word here is slightly another matter, one that it is the purpose of this section to find out.

3.4.4 *Later Writers*

Our final verdict on the authenticity or otherwise of fragment 7.3 Harris still needs to wait for the results of an additional analysis. This subsection aims to answer the questions if the ideas expressed in the fragment can be found in other writers and if so, what their relation to Philo is. Can we find examples which might amount to references or allusions to the fragment's text? Or are there cases where we could suspect that the author in question

---

[632] I conducted another crude experiment by examining a random sample of ten pages of the PhI. These pages contained a total of 81 words that occur only once in Philo. Since the PhI has 371 pages of concordance, the total number of *hapax* words in Philo will be in the thousands.

[633] Philo uses no cognates of the two last ones, while two other passages (*Mos.* 2.112 and *Spec.* 1.87) each contain the adverb τετραστοιχεί; both are likewise references to Ex 28. The meaning of the verb τοπάζω (5 instances) is unrelated to the gem τόπαζος.

[634] I.e., the concept of practising death. Also the juxtapositioning of sleep and death links the fragment with the dialogue. See below, pp. 203–4.

is the source of the fragment, in full or in part? For this purpose the main notions of the fragment may be noted as follows:

(a) The Phaedonic expression *practice of death*, referred to below as "*the practice.*"
(b) The idea that sleep (including awakening) constitutes an approximation of death and a subsequent revival ("*the simile*").
(c) The reference to those who understand this truth ("*the doxography*").[635]

The examination below is, in the main, based on searches of the TLG database which provides powerful tools for finding occurrences of words, expressions and their combinations. However, the results are dependent on the searcher's ability to look for the right ones and with meaningful parameters. Importantly, such a method can never take the place of actual knowledge of the authors and their works, which in this case is, unfortunately, to a large degree lacking.

As is plausible *a priori* and as, e.g., the *Sentences of Secundus* (early 2nd century CE) show, the first two notions and were ingredients in the intellectual atmosphere of the Greek-speaking world in late antiquity: In *Sentences* 19 and 20 Secundus says, e.g., that sleep is "an image of death (θανάτου εἰκών), ... a principal occupation (ἐπιτήδευμα) of the rich, ... a daily practice (καθημερινὴ μελέτη)."[636] Death for its part is "everlasting sleep, ... the father of sleep." The example shows that there is a risk of hearing echoes of the fragment when all there is are allusions to the *Phaedo*. Therefore, the authors' connection to Philo is an important aspect to be taken into account in the task at hand.

Out of a larger group of authors in whose works I have located passages of interest I have chosen to present two quite different cases in more detail: Clement of Alexandria and (ps.-) John Chrysostom.[637]

---

[635] This third notion, while significant in the fragment itself, cannot be given the same weight as the two others. For it seems evident that someone alluding to or paraphrasing an idea he has read in Philo may well leave out the latter's reference to previous thinkers, while he may or may not similarly refer to Philo.

[636] Plato uses ἐπιτηδεύω too as the verb of *practising* death (64a). See the quotation above, p. 122.

[637] As for the others, the following may be noted: Tertullian (d. c. 220): See his quite anti-Phaedonic *De anima*, the end of Ch. 42 as well as Ch. 43 where *the practice* is alluded to and *the simile* can be found. Jan Hendrik Waszink, *Quinti Septimi Florentis Tertulliani De Anima: Edited with Introduction and Commentary* (Amsterdam: Paris, 1947), on p. 474 actually quotes our fragment as a parallel, but there is no evidence for Tertullian's direct knowledge of Philo; see Waszink, *Tertulliani De Anima*, 14; Runia, *Philo in Early Christian Literature*, 277–81. Origen (d. 254) only has *the simile* a few times; see. e.g., *Selecta in Psalmos*

Clement of Alexandria

Clement of Alexandria (d. c. 215) is the first author to mention Philo by name after Josephus, and he undoubtedly used Philo's works.[638] From the viewpoint of the fragment there are two quite interesting, mutually connected passages in the works of Clement. Let us first look at the fifth book of the *Stromata*:

> Plato, again, in the seventh book of the *Republic* (521c), has called "the day here nocturnal," as I suppose, on account of "the cosmic powers of this present darkness" (Eph 6:12); and the descent of the soul into the body, [he has called] sleep and death, similarly with Heraclitus. And was not this announced, oracularly, of the Saviour, by the Spirit, saying by David, "I lay down and slept;/I woke again, because the Lord will support me." (Ps 3:6) For He not only figuratively calls the resurrection (ἀνάστασιν) of Christ "rising from sleep;" but to the descent of the Lord into the flesh he also applies the figurative term "sleep." The Savior Himself enjoins, "Keep awake" (e.g., Mark 14:38) as much as to say, "Study (μελετᾶτε) how to live, and endeavor to separate the soul from the body (χωρίζειν τὴν ψυχὴν τοῦ σώματος)." (*Strom.* 5.14.105.2–106.1)

(authenticity uncertain) 12.1413.39–43 (ex. Ps 40:9). For Origen and Philo, see Runia, *Philo in Early Christian Literature*, 157–83, Annewies van den Hoek, "Philo and Origen: A Descriptive Catalogue of Their Relationship," SPhA 12 (2000): 44–121 and van den Hoek, "Assessing Philo's Influence in Christian Alexandria: The Case of Origen," in *Shem in the Tents of Japhet: Essays on the Encounter of Judaism and Hellenism*, ed. James L. Kugel (Leiden: Brill, 2002), 223–39. Ps-Athenagoras (third to fourth cent.): See *De resurrectione* 16.4–6 which features both *the simile* and *the doxography* as well as the verb ἀναβιώσκομαι. There are *verba Philonica* in 12.6. See Runia, "Verba Philonica," and *Philo in Early Christian Literature*, 105–9. In Methodius (d. c. 311) there is a noteworthy passage in the *De resurrectione* most easily accessible via Epiphanius, *Panarion* 2.469.14–470.4 (p. 170 in Williams's translation). It features both *the practice* and *the simile*. Methodius in fact argues for resurrection in the same way as Socrates does for reincarnation in the *Phaedo*. He uses the Philonic verb νεκροφορέω thrice in *Res.* (and Philonic influences have been detected in his *Symposium*; see M. Benedetta Zorzi, "The Use of the Terms ἁγνεία, παρθενία, σωφροσύνη, and ἐγκράτεια in the *Symposium* of Methodius of Olympus," in *VC* 63 [2009]: 138–68, pp. 143, 147, 153) but knowledge of the *Phaedo* explains the features in common with the fragment. As for Eusebius (d. 339), his most interesting passage is in *Demonstratio evangelica* 4.16.55 where σκιώδη and ὑπογραμμός appear soon after the Philonic expression "the eyes of understanding." Yet the Philonic inspiration is explainable by *Somn.* 1.199, 206, 215 (cf. *Leg.* 3.102–103). For Eusebius and Philo, see Runia, *Philo in Early Christian Literature*, 212–35. Gregory of Nyssa (d. after 394) has *the simile* and *the doxography* in his *In sanctum pascha* (262.24–263.2), and he also has ὑπογράφω (248.12) and εἰκόνας ἐναργεῖς (256.23), but no firm conclusions can be drawn. On Gregory, see Runia, *Philo in Early Christian Literature*, 243–61.

[638] See Annewies van den Hoek, *Clement of Alexandria and His Use of Philo in the Stromateis: An Early Christian Reshaping of a Jewish Model*, VCSup 3 (Leiden: Brill, 1988) and Runia, *Philo in Early Christian Literature*, 132–56 with further references.

At the end there is a version of *the practice*, expressed in a little different but equally Phaedonic terms: in 67c Socrates refers to the philosopher's orientation away from the bodily things as "separating, so far as possible, the soul from the body (τὸ χωρίζειν ... ἀπὸ τοῦ σώματος τὴν ψυχήν)," this being the definition of physical death in the dialogue (see also 67d). As for *the simile*, here it is incarnation (and not death) that is compared to sleep—but also *to* death, thus likening the two to each other—and the resurrection of Christ to awakening. In her comprehensive study on Clement's use of Philo in the *Stromata* van den Hoek mentions only *Ios.* 126 in this connection, and categorizes the *Strom.* passage quoted as a case of "non-dependence on Philo." She states that "[n]o clear parallel with Philo presents itself."[639] Unfortunately, she has not considered the Philonic fragments. In the *Ios.* passage Philo calls the human life a dream (ὄνειρος).[640]

Clement's reference to Heraclitus above takes us to an earlier passage :

> And as to what, again, they say of sleep, the very same things are to be understood of death. For each exhibits the departure of the soul (ἑκάτερος γὰρ δηλοῖ τὴν ἀπόστασιν τῆς ψυχῆς), the one more, the other less; as we may also get this in Heraclitus. (*Strom.* 4.22.141.1-2)[641]

The simile is again present, but what is most intriguing is the similarity with the fragment's "For it carries images of both clear (ἑκατέρων γὰρ ἐναργεῖς φέρει τὰς ἐικόνας)" and the mind's μετάστασις in the fragment's last sentence. As for its παράστασις (*inter alia*, 'being beside,' 'mental excitement,' 'ardour,' 'exaltation;' LSJ), we may note that it comes close to ἀπόστασις and ἔκστασις if the prepositional prefix is taken in the sense of 'from,' 'out of' etc. Ἔκστασις (e.g., 'standing aside,' 'distraction of mind') is used of Adam's sleep in Gen 2:21 and underlined by Philo in his exegesis thereof in *Leg.* 2.31 and *QG* 1.24.[642] Thus the option of a missing dative noted above would not be the only thinkable way of getting to the gist of the

---

[639] Van den Hoek, *Clement of Alexandria*, 197.
[640] See n. 665 below (p. 205) for a brief quotation. Clement's reference to *Republic* 521c is in the same vein, for there Socrates is explaining his famous parable of the cave and saying that those who can only see the shadows on the wall of the cave (515a) and have not ascended to the noetic reality with the aid of true philosophy are subject to the "day nocturnal," which state is also compared to sleep in 520c-d.
[641] Then follows a quotation from Heraclitus (fr. 26 DK): "Man touches night in himself, when dead and his light quenched; and alive, when he sleeps he touches the dead; and awake, when he shuts his eyes, he touches the sleeper." The translator adds a footnote: "As it stands in the text the passage is unintelligible, and has been variously amended successfully." However, the exact contents are of no great concern to us.
[642] We know that in Philo's view sleeping, and especially dreaming, means the soul's movement (e.g., *Somn.* 1.2, 2.1-2), surely out of the body, and this is what physical death also means. See also *Somn.* 1.41-46 (discussed below, pp. 231-33).

fragment's final sentence, if only we had a little more complete version of it. All in all, "For each exhibits the departure of the soul" in a noteworthy fashion approaches a paraphrase of the fragment's two last sentences.

The doxography is found in both passages of *Strom.* in the sense that Clement appeals to the authority of others; to Plato and Heraclitus in *Strom.* 5, to the unemphatic "them" in *Strom.* 4.[643] Who are the latter? Before the passage quoted, Clement comments on the fact that "they" have called night Euphrone.[644] According to LSJ this appellation goes back to Hesiod, Pindar and others.[645] Thus "they" in the quotation above is probably a reference to traditional Greek views.

With regard to Clement's language more generally, it may be noted that he uses the verb ἀναβιόω thrice (*Strom.* 1.23.154.3, 5.14.103.4; *Protr.* 1.4.4), the noun ὑπογραμμός twice (*Strom.* 5.8.49.1 and *Paed.* 1.9.84.2), and has the plural of ἀληθής as the direct object of φρονέω once (*Strom.* 7.9.53.2).[646] In none of these passages, however, are there any other links with the fragment. We may add that Clement mentions the *Phaedo* seven times by name, and approvingly refers to its ideal of practising death in *Strom.* 3.3.17.5 and 4.3.12.5.

It is interesting that in Maximus our fragment is followed by precisely the passage from *Strom.* 4 which was quoted above. The possibility that Clement is its original source cannot be excluded, but a common theme is a fully plausible explanation. The passages from the *Stromata* would fit well within the class of Clementine texts "in which Platonism and Philonic themes are strikingly brought together," as Runia characterizes one subcategory of what van den Hoek calls Clement's "isolated references" to Philo.[647] It is perhaps not altogether insignificant that of the five passages mentioned in this subcategory four in fact come from *Strom.* 4 and 5. There is an additional match in that *Leg.*, from which the fragment is supposed to come, belongs those works by Philo to which Clement refers

---

[643] There is no pronoun in the text, just the third person plural verb form λέγουσι.
[644] Clement says (*Strom.* 4.22.140.1–2):
But the variety of disposition arises from inordinate affection to material things. And for this reason, as they appear to me, to have called night Euphrone; since then the soul, released (πεπαυμένη) from the perceptions of sense, turns in on itself, and has a truer hold of wisdom (φρονήσεως). Wherefore the mysteries are for the most part celebrated by night, indicating the withdrawal (συστολήν) of the soul from the body, which takes place by night.
[645] After this and before juxtaposing sleep and death Clement cites 1 Thess 5:6–8 where death is absent.
[646] These are, as far as I can tell, the only noteworthy features of the fragment attested in Clement. He does not use the -ιστᾷ forms or the expression ἐξ ὁλοκλήρου.
[647] Runia, *Philo in Early Christian Literature*, 141.

only briefly. I think the *Strom.* passages must collectively be classified as possibly depending on the fragment.

John Chrysostom

I have located two passages of interest in the enormous *Corpus Chrysostomicum* (more than 3.65 million words in the TLG, i.e., about eight times Philo's extant Greek *oeuvre*).[648] The first one comes from *De Lazaro et divite* 59.594.5–7 (ex. Luke 16:19–31), marked as spurious in the TLG. It is part of the author's description of the sad state of Lazarus while he was still alive. The interesting sentence runs, "In his sleep he practised death, death after sleep he sought but nowhere found."[649] We have the combination of *the practice* and *the simile* in a highly concise form: sleep is practising of death—exactly as in the fragment.

The second interesting passage is in a genuine work of John's (d. 407) and has to do with the expression "shadow and outline":

> The Apostle then forbearing to censure these, as either nothing, or at best a shadow and figure of spiritual things (σκιὰν τῶν πνευματικῶν καὶ ὑπογραμμόν), proceeds in a more engaging way to praise the law. (*In epistulam i ad Timotheum* 62.510.42–44)

The context is far removed from sleep and death, but here we have the one and only instance in the whole TLG of the exact combination of "shadow and outline" just as in the fragment. So the next question is, are there any indications of Philo's presence in the surrounding text? Our attention is caught by the expressions less than ten lines earlier: "For when the soul abandons itself to carnal things (πράγμασιν ἑαυτὴν ἐκδῷ σαρκικοῖς), ... the eye of understanding is blinded (πηροῦται τὸ τῆς διανοίας ὄμμα)." The "eye(s) of understanding" is an expression coined by Philo (*Post.* 18; *Plant.* 58, 169) who also seems to be the first author to speak about the eyes of soul becoming blind using the verb πηρόω (*Sacr.* 69, *Det.* 22 *Post.* 8, *Somn.* 1.117, *Spec.* 3.6). But that is not all. The construction ἑαυτόν + a negative

---

[648] In addition, there are fairly commonplace comparisons of sleep to death in John, but they in themselves are not highly relevant: *De Davide et Saule* 54.689.49: "Sleep is nothing else than a temporary death (θάνατος πρόσκαιρος) and daily death (ἐφήμερος τελευτή)" (Cf. 1 Cor 15:31). *In epistulam i ad Corinthios* 61.232.27: "For hence is sleep like unto death (θανάτῳ ἐοικώς), and heaviness of head, and disease, and obliviousness, and an image of dead men's condition (νεκρότητος εἰκών)."

[649] My tr. for θάνατον ἐν τοῖς ὕπνοις ἐμελέτα, θάνατον μετὰ τὸν ὕπνον περιεβλέπετο, καὶ οὐδαμοῦ εὕρισκεν. There is another instance of μελέτη θανάτου in *De studio praesentium* 489.9; the context is praising the ascetic life, which indicates that John was aware of the Socratic meaning of the phrase.

attribute in the dative + πράγμασιν + a form of ἐκδίδωμι is only attested in Philo, *Gig.* 15 before John: certain souls "have abandoned themselves to the unstable things of chance (ἐκδόντες ἀστάτοις καὶ τυχηροῖς πράγμασιν ἑαυτούς) ... which are all related to that dead thing ... the body."[650]

Regarding John's familiarity with Philo's works more generally, Runia states that it is not surprising that "leading Christian authors associated with or influenced by the Antiochene school reveal little acquaintance with Philo."[651] He mentions that there is nevertheless one occurrence of the Philonic verb ἀγαλματοφορέω.[652] This is in fact not the only *verbum Philonicum* found in John. Of those listed by Runia, σεμνοποιέω and συνδιαιωνίζω make a few isolated appearances, as does βελτιόω ('improve') which might perhaps be added to the list despite its general character.[653] We may assume that John had heard of Philo, but the question of whether he is actually utilizing his works is difficult to ascertain, not least because, as Runia has noted, "themes from [Philo's] exegesis and theology have been absorbed into the tradition and authors who use them may not even be aware of their ultimate provenance."[654] John may have been averse to the Alexandrian tradition, but there are, nevertheless occurrences of Philonisms in his works. And it is remarkable that two so exact hits were found: sleep as the practice of death (although no revival) in one treatise, whose exact relation to John we cannot go into, and the expression "shadow and outline" in another one amid fairly clear Philonic echoes. Intriguing as these hits are, however, they do not amount to evidence of knowledge of fragment 7.3 Harris by John or his circles. There is also no reason to regard John as the fragment's author.

---

[650] See p. 132 for a longer quotation. John uses the same construction also in *In Joannem* 59.219.15–16 and *In epistulam ad Ephesios* 62.174.47–48; in these the negative things are τῇ γῇ καὶ τοῖς ταύτης (cf. *QG* 1.51, above, p. 70) and τοῖς πονηροῖς, respectively. Before John, Ephrem the Syrian (d. c. 373) comes close at *In sermonem* 339.2: Πῶς ἐξέδωκας ἑαυτὴν τῇ ματαιότητι καὶ ἐδέσμευσας σαυτὴν τοῖς γηΐνοις πράγμασι.
[651] Runia, *Philo in Early Christian Literature*, 270. In addition, there is, as Runia notes (p. 233), one reference to Philo (and Josephus) in the spurious *In sanctum pascha, sermo 7*, §15, on the question of determining the timing of the Passover feast.
[652] Runia, *Philo in Early Christian Literature*, 109.
[653] These are in John's genuine works. If the spurious ones are included, then we also have a few cases of ζωοπλαστής and μεγαλόπολις. As for βελτιόω, the TLG gives two pre-Philonic instances (although one, a fragment of Chrysippus, actually comes from Galen). Philo has 43, Origen 31, Eusebius 10. The situation of the noun βελτίωσις is quite similar, and it too occurs a few times in John.
[654] David T. Runia, "Philo and the Early Christian Fathers," in *The Cambridge Companion to Philo*, ed. Adam Kamesar (Cambridge: Cambridge University Press, 2009), 210–30, p. 225.

Conclusions

I have not been able to find an author who should be regarded as a more probable source of the fragment than Philo. The fragment's last sentence is a slightly different matter, as both of its key features are found in increasing frequency in the centuries after Philo, or, in fact, after Clement.[655] Clement's statement about sleep and death, "For each exhibits the departure of the soul" is very close to being an interpretative paraphrase of the fragment's last two sentences. Many other passages were found in church fathers that in various ways come close to the fragment, but it is noteworthy that otherwise they do not have much in common with each other. The key notions of the fragment, the practice of death and the analogous relationship between sleep and death, were existent and carried onwards in the Christian tradition—the latter idea notably in connection with the doctrine of resurrection—regardless of whether the fathers were aware of any link to Philo or Plato. On the whole, it is my conclusion that there are no grounds for overruling the traditional ascription of the fragment to Philo.

3.4.5 *Some Tradition History*

The close relationship between sleep and death is an old theme in Greek literature beginning with Homer and Hesiod (e.g., *Il.* 16.672, 682; *Theogonia* 758–759). In mythology, the gods Hypnos and Thanatos are the twins of the goddess Nyx. To take one example from the Classical Period, in Xenophon's *Cyropaedia* Cyrus the Great says in the farewell speech preceding his death (which he has foreseen in a divine vision during sleep):

> "Consider again," he continued, "that there is nothing in the world more nearly akin (ἐγγύτερον) to death than is sleep; and the soul of a human at just such times is revealed in its most divine aspect and at such times, too, it looks forward into the future; for then, it seems, it is most untrammelled (ἐλευθεροῦται)." (*Cyropaedia* 8.7.21)

---

[655] The highest absolute numbers of the -ιστᾷ forms in the period examined are found in John Chrysostom (30), Didymus (29), Ephrem the Syrian (17) and John of Damascus (16), and the only authors that use ἐξ ὁλοκλήρου more than once are Athanasius (5), John Chrysostom (5) and Basil (4). When an index is calculated in which equal weight is given to these two features and which proportions their frequencies to the volumes of the authors' *corpora*, the five authors who clearly stand out are ps.-Macarius (index value 0.25), Ephrem (0.23), Hippolytus (0.22), Didymus (0.20) and John of Damascus (0.16) all the others being < 0.09. These features do thus not occur in authors in whose writings the most relevant contentual parallels can be found.

Philo was aware of the traditional connection between sleep and death in Greek culture. The dead could be said to be "asleep" also in Jewish writings.[656] However, he does not seem to have been inspired by these to any significant degree.[657] In order to understand the fragment, light should be sought from another direction. Plato's *Phaedo* holds several keys.

As already discussed, the phrase "practice of death" is taken from Socrates's teachings in the dialogue, where its subject is the philosopher.[658] The fragment does not elaborate on this ascetic life ideal but instead uses the word μελέτη in roughly the same sense of approximation as σκιά and ὑπογραμμός, so that the choice of expression mainly seems to serve as a pointer to the *Phaedo*. But at the same time it also carries the connotation of the concept, the gist of which may, in Philo's terms, be expressed as dying to the life in the body.[659] On the other hand, one could say that the idea of sleep being rehearsal of physical death means the Platonic phrase is taken in a very narrow and concrete sense. This is not the only place where Philo gives a new meaning to this notion.[660]

A second link with the *Phaedo* has an important bearing on the question as to why Philo uses the word ἀναβίωσις. While the noun does not appear in the dialogue, the verb ἀναβιώσκομαι occurs six times, and in four cases it is used more or less interchangeably with πάλιν γίγνεσθαι to denote the event of reincarnation.[661] Socrates's logic is that since everything is born out of its own opposite, the living must be generated from the dead just as the dead are from the living.[662] This process of regeneration takes place through the reincarnation of souls.

A third connection lies in the fact that in the *Phaedo* Socrates also appeals to the phenomena of sleeping and awakening as a support for the argument just mentioned:

---

[656] E.g., 3 Kgdms 1:21 LXX, Jer 28:39 LXX. See the discussion in Marbury B. Ogle, "The Sleep of Death," in MAAR XI: 81–117, pp. 88–93 (81–88 for Greek and Roman culture).

[657] For example, apart from the fragment, he nowhere speaks of death and sleep in the same sentence. The closest to each other θάνατος and ὕπνος appear in *Migr.* 189–190 (discussed below), where they are separated by 22 words. In a metaphorical expression in *Leg.* 2.27 the mind's death is an amplified form of its sleep. Philo's views of sleep are further discussed below, subsection 3.4.6.

[658] See above, p. 122.

[659] See, e.g., the discussion on *Leg.* 1.107–108 and *Gig.* 14–15 above, p. 64.

[660] See above, p. 124 on *QG* 4.174, *Her.* 292 and *Somn.* 1.151. In the one passage (*Gig.* 14) where Philo uses Plato's terminology strictly in the Socratic sense, there is no connection to sleep. In *Somn.* 1.150 Philo adds it; see below, n. 665.

[661] 71e twice; 72a, d. 72c is more general and 89b (about bringing a *discussion* back to life) metaphorical.

[662] E.g., when something grows, it is first smaller and then bigger: the big "is born" out of the small.

—Well then, said Socrates, is there anything that is the opposite of living (ζῆν), as sleeping (καθεύδειν) is the opposite of being awake (ἐγρηγορέναι)?
—Certainly, said Cebes.
—What?
—Being dead (τεθνάναι), said he.
—Then these two are generated from each other (ἐξ ἀλλήλων τε γίγνεται ταῦτα), and as they are two, so the processes between them are two; is it not so? (*Phaedo* 71c)

Figure 3 illustrates what Socrates is saying. The "processes" (γενέσεις) are printed in italics on the sides.

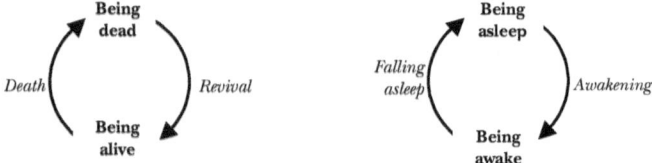

Figure 3. The Comparison between Sleep and Death by Socrates in the *Phaedo*.

Thus we see that Socrates's comparison has an implication that is of great importance in the present context: the whole juxtaposition of sleep and death is in the Phaedonic context *based* on the notion of reincarnation. And so, since what the fragment contains is precisely the juxtaposition of sleep and death in a Phaedonic context, reincarnation is, without question, the *default* meaning of ἀναβίωσις.

A further noteworthy feature of the fragment is that the idea of sleep being the practising of death and the shadow and outline of revival is attributed to previous thinkers. Who is/are being referred to? It is possible that Philo is simply referring to Plato and/or Socrates here.[663] Yet it is interesting to note that in the *Phaedo* Socrates, after ridiculing the "courage" of those who choose to face death because they fear even greater evils and the "self-restraint" of those who refrain from some pleasures only in order to obtain others, comments that virtue should not be purchased in that manner. He then goes on to extol wisdom:

[C]ourage and self-restraint and justice and, in short, true virtue exist only with wisdom (ἀληθὴς ἀρητὴ μετὰ φρονήσεως), whether pleasures and fears and other things of that sort are added or taken away. And virtue which consists in the exchange of such things without wisdom (χωριζόμενα φρονήσεως) is but a painted imitation (σκιαγραφία) of virtue and is really slavish and has nothing healthy or true (ἀληθές) in it; but truth (τὸ ἀληθές) is

---

[663] Cf. Runia, *Philo in Early Christian Literature*, 161, n. 23: "often a plural reference (e.g. some... others) can indicate a single source" in Philo.

in fact a purification from all these things, and self-restraint and justice and courage and wisdom itself (αὐτὴ ἡ φρόνησις) are a kind of purification. (*Phaedo* 69b–c)

Socrates then states that "those men who established the mysteries ... said long ago" that in order to be able to "dwell with the gods" after death (instead of reincarnating, that is) one has to be initiated and purified, and that such souls are presumably "those who have been true philosophers (οἱ πεφιλοσοφηκότες ὀρθῶς)" (69d).[664] The fragment's οἱ τὰ ἀληθῆ πεφρονηκότες comes close to being a very condensed summary of what Socrates is saying here. And there is a further verbal link between Plato's σκιαγραφία and the fragment's σκιὰ καὶ ὑπογραμμός. It is thus quite possible that 69c–d was also in Philo's mind, which makes the fragment's connection to the dialogue even closer.

3.4.6 *Congruity with Philo's Thought*

What is Philo's message in the text of the fragment? We would be in a much better position to answer the question if we had a longer excerpt available and knew the context. As things are, the main point seems to the comparability of sleep and death. However, discussing natural phenomena is not something that Philo would engage in for its own sake, with no theological point to make. The probable reference to reincarnation *is* a theological point, and it is beginning to seem that Philo simply wants to remind his audience of it.

However, the reference to practising death and the (at least rhetorical) equivalence of sleep and that practice suggest also another possible point. Although Philo nowhere else makes an explicit connection between sleep and the Socratic practising of death, their similarity is implied.[665] The following passage from *Migr.* is apposite for demonstrating this. Philo

---

[664] These "mystics" (βάκχοι) are Socrates's ideals and can, no doubt, be identified with those who practise death (64a, 67d–e, 80e, 82c).

[665] In addition, there are other Philonic notions involving sleep that are not equally relevant here. E.g., in *Leg.* 2.25, 30–31; *Her.* 257; *Somn.* 1.80 Philo says that the sleep of the senses is the wakefulness of the mind and *vice versa*. The life of the imperfect or wicked is portrayed as a state of sleep, e.g., in *Leg.* 3.229; *Somn.* 1.121, 165; *Ios.* 140, 142; *QG* 4.62; cf. the opening of the soul's sight as awakening in *Abr.* 70; *Mos.* 1.289; *QG* 4.2; *QE* 2.51, 82. In *Somn.* 1.150 Philo connects the lack of progress in the practiser's life with sleep and death in a reference to Castor and Pollux (*Od.* 11.303). Philo actually seems to want to compare death to sleep here, for he *adds* the latter: "For the life of the practisers is, as one has said, a life 'of alternate days,' sometimes alive *and wakeful* (ζῶν καὶ ἐγρηγορώς), sometimes dead *or asleep* (τεθνεὼς ἢ κοιμώμενος)." A somewhat different viewpoint appears in *Ios.* 125 where the human *life* is called (§126) "that great general universal dream which is dreamt not only by the sleeping but also by the waking."

explains that the soul should, after gaining familiarity with the sense-perceptible and bodily realm, go further:

> Having scrutinized yourselves inquire into your migration from here (τὴν ἐνθένδε μετανάστασιν). It does not proclaim death but immortality.[666] You will be able to observe clear indications (δείγματα σαφῆ) of this [migration] even while held fast in the dens and caves of the body and of the objects of sense: In deep sleep (ἐν τοῖς βαθέσιν ὕπνοις) the mind quits its place (ὑπεξελθών), and, withdrawing (ἀναχωρήσας) from the perceptions and all other bodily faculties, begins to hold converse with itself, fixing its gaze on truth as on a mirror, and, having purged away as defilements all the impressions made upon it by the mental pictures (φαντασιῶν) presented by the senses, it is filled with Divine frenzy and discerns in dreams absolutely true prophecies concerning things to come. (*Migr.* 189–190)

Philo here joins the ancient tradition we saw above in Xenophon connecting sleep with divination.[667] But what is the "migration from here"? Philo uses this phrase of his four times plus twice with the verb μετανίστημι.[668] In *Her.* 98–99 the meaning is similar to *Migr.*, but the tone is even more salvific: the migration is "from the created to the uncreated, from the

---

[666] My tr. for διακινήσαντες αὐτοὺς τὴν ἐνθένδε μετανάστασιν ζητεῖτε, οὐ θάνατον ἀλλ' ἀθανασίαν καταγγέλλουσαν. Although the verb is different, I see here a possible allusion to *Migr.* 7 where God's command to Abraham to leave—as Philo sees it—the body, sense-perception and speech is emphatically said *not* to be the same as the prescription (verb διαγορεύω) of capital punishment. See the quotation above, p. 87.

[667] So also, e.g., *Somn.* 1.2; 2.1–2. Josephus echoes similar ideas:
> Let sleep furnish you with a clearest sign (τεκμήριον . . . ἐναργέστατον) of what I say—sleep, in which the soul, un-distracted by the body, while enjoying in perfect independence the most delightful repose, holds converse with God by right of kinship, ranges the universe and foretells many things that are to come (ἐσομένων).
> (*BJ* 7.349)

The speaker here is Eleazar who advocates collective suicide to his troops, and the primary referent of "what I say" seems to be the view that at death, "freed from the weight that drags it down to earth and clings about it, the soul is restored to its proper sphere" (7.346). The language is quite Platonic; we may also note expressions like "imprisoned in a mortal body (ἐν σώματι θνητῷ δεδεμέναι, 7.344)" and "incarcerated in the body (σώματι συνδεδεμένη, 7.345)." Especially intriguing is the view that while "tainted with all [the body's] miseries, [the soul] is, in sober truth, dead" (7.344). According to my observations, the question of whether Josephus knew and used Philo's *Allegorical Commentary* becomes particularly acute in the afterlife passages of, first and foremost, *BJ* (see below, n. 794 on p. 248 for other examples). My initial answer is affirmative, but this is not the context to discuss the matter further. Sleep being a clear sign and the analogy of death and sleep connect Josephus to our fragment, but the commonalities do not suffice to indicate that Josephus knew it.

[668] Cf. the fragment's use of μεθίστημι and our earlier discussion of Enoch's transference in 3.3.3.

world to its Maker and Father."[669] On one occasion he refers to the Israelites and their Exodus from Egypt (*Mos.* 1.86), once to Adam's having left the Paradise (*Plant.* 34) and twice (*Virt.* 53 and 76) to Moses's death. Of these, the first one is clearly akin to the *Migr.* passage.

Given that in *Migr.* Philo explicitly denies that death is the issue, what is the actual relationship between this migration—of which clear indications may be experienced in sleep—and physical death? Compare *Praem.* 110: the last stage of life is called "the neighbour of death or rather of immortality (θανάτῳ μᾶλλον δ' ἀθανασίᾳ γειτνιῶσα)." The context is the blessing of long life promised *to the righteous*, which means that the proximity between death and immortality is not generally applicable; salvation is probably meant, because reaching immortality fits poorly with anything less. Also in the *Migr.* passage it is hardly the average person whom Philo can think of as experiencing "clear indications" of salvation during sleep, or being "possessed by some philosophic principle" when awake (§191). The point seems to be, not the denial of physical death taking place upon the "migration hence," but playing down its significance on the grounds that something much more important will also occur, something that is not of the nature of a loss but a gain. In this light it seems that the exhortation to inquire into the migration from the state of being held fast in the body points to the permanent post-mortem freedom from everything corporeal that the virtuous can expect. Philo's remark "does not proclaim death but immortality" serves to underline the essential event, not to deny the physical one.[670]

Philo is thus telling us that a foretaste of salvation, which—for the virtuous—will follow physical death, can be had even during the life in the body, i.e., during sleep (§190): ὕπνος is a shadow of μετανάστασις. This he describes as "clear indications" (δείγματα σαφῆ) the meaning of which is the same as that of the ἐναργεῖς ... εἰκόνας of the fragment. Moreover, sleep approaches practising death (in the Socratic sense) through the "with-

---

[669] This is actually Philo's description of "the best of all migrations (ἀποικιῶν)," which is also characterized as "the migration of the soul (μετανισταμένης τῆς ψυχῆς) which passes from astrology to real nature study, from insecure conjecture to firm apprehension." The context is Abram's leaving Chaldea, Gen 15:7. The Chaldeans' reliance on sky-lore is contrasted with the fact that "he who has migrated hence (τὸν δ' ἐνθένδε μεταναστάντα) has given his trust to Him who rides on the heaven and guides the chariot of the whole world, even God"—an obvious allusion to the *Phaedrus*; see esp. 246e–247b.
[670] Cf. *QG* 1.86 quoted and discussed above (p. 174). I think the verb "proclaim" makes *Migr.* 190 different in that here the alternative of taking death in the ethical sense would not make sense.

draw[al] from the perceptions" and "purg[ing] away as defilements all the impressions made ... by the senses."

Although Plato does not explicitly link sleep with the concept practising death in the *Phaedo*, freedom from the senses is an essential ingredient of this practice. After Socrates has put forward the idea that dying, in the sense of alienation from the body and its needs, is what the philosopher will have practised all his life, he starts to elaborate on the reasons for this. One of them is that the ultimate verities (such as absolute justice, beauty and goodness) cannot be approached through the senses (65b–d). The Philosopher, so Socrates,

> approaches each thing, so far as possible, with the reason alone, not introducing sight into his reasoning nor dragging in any of the other senses along with his thinking, [he] employs pure absolute reason in his attempt to search out the pure, absolute essence of things [and] removes himself (ἀπαλλαγείς), so far as possible, from eyes and ears, and, in a word, from his whole body, because he feels that its companionship disturbs the soul and hinders it from attaining truth and wisdom (ἀλήθειάν τε καὶ φρόνησιν). (*Phaedo* 66a)

The ideas presented in *Migr.* and the *Phaedo* come together in an enlightening fashion in *Gig.* To recall, early in the treatise Philo speaks of

> the souls of the genuine philosophers, who from first to last practice dying to the life in the body in order to obtain the portion of incorporeal and immortal life in the presence of the Uncreated and Immortal. (*Gig.* 14)

Later he says of such souls:

> But the people of God are priests and prophets, who have not deigned to obtain rights in the universal commonwealth and to become world citizens but have entirely transcended the sensible (αἰσθητόν) sphere and have migrated (μετανέστησαν) to the intelligible world and dwell there enrolled as citizens of the Commonwealth of Ideas, which are imperishable and incorporeal. (*Gig.* 61)[671]

This is the "migration," one into the world of noetic absolutes, which sleep presents clear indications of in *Migr.* 189, and probably also in the fragment. Thus, in addition to alluding to reincarnation, calling sleep the practice of death resonates with ideas Philo presents elsewhere.

In the analysis of *Cher.* 114 the view of certain scholars of παλιγγενεσία as a salvific second birth was dismissed on grounds that are not valid for

---

[671] Cf. the comment in Winston & Dillon, *Two Treatises*, 270: the people of God (θεοῦ ἄνθρωποι) "plainly... includ[es], in Platonic terms, οἱ φιλοσοφοῦντες ὀρθῶς." As they rightly point out, there are connections to the *Phaedrus* as well.

ἀναβίωσις in the fragment.[672] Hence, this alternative needs to be discussed and compared with the understanding of the "revival" as reincarnation as the final point before drawing the conclusions. The latter option is first summarized.[673]

1. *"Revival" as Reincarnation*

In this alternative the fragment is interpreted as follows:[674]

> *Sleep frees the soul from sense-perception, which is also the goal of practising death.*
> *Falling asleep and physical death have been compared to each other;*
> *sleep is followed by a new awakening and being dead by a new incarnation.*

This interpretation is quite straightforward and does not require assumptions that have no basis in the text itself.[675] We should note that it has several things in common with *Cher.* 114: Death is followed by new birth/life, for which a technical term is used without elaboration. In both texts this happens with a fair degree of self-evidence; no other options are mentioned.[676] Furthermore, both passages have clear links to the *Phaedo*, which must not be ignored; they point to understanding the terms

---

[672] See subsection 3.2.3 on pp. 154–59.

[673] In principle there might be other alternatives as well to consider, because "death" is used in several senses by Philo; see above, n. 215 on p. 64, where three different *states* and three *events* of death were noted in *Leg.* 1.105–108. However, I do not consider it warranted to discuss such alternatives, since I regard Philo's using the Phaedonic formula "practice of death" as an indication that physical death is meant. That is, after all, the very context of Socrates's introducing the whole concept (see above, subsection 2.4.6, pp. 122–24). The philosophers' *practice* of the "release and separation of the soul from the body" (*Phaedo* 67d) involves no suicidal activities: it is a matter of metaphorical practice of literal death.

[674] I omit the two last sentences of the fragment. The first one contains little new substance and the second is too obscure.

[675] It is worth explicitly noting that I understand the fragment's reference to sleep to include awakening, i.e., Philo means the phenomenon of sleep in its entirety, not the *state* of being asleep. Otherwise there would be no point in the whole comparison with death and revival.

[676] This fact alone has nothing to do with the modalities of reincarnation in Philo's thought. In *Cher.* the question is of imperfect souls only. We are in darkness about the immediate context of the fragment, but assuming it is a description of the normal case would make perfect sense and in no way preclude the permanent liberation from the body of those who are pure enough. We may compare this with the myth of Er in the *Republic*: freedom from reincarnation is not mentioned, but this is no grounds for us to posit a contradiction with Plato's other reincarnational texts where it is. Philo's biblical basis in *Leg.* 4 (Gen 3:20–23) deals with the aftermath of the transgression in Paradise, which would tend to favor the assumption that Philo is dealing rather with imperfect than virtuous souls.

210   CHAPTER THREE

παλιγγενεσία and ἀναβίωσις as references to reincarnation.[677] Although the results about these two texts consolidate each other, the meanings of these terms have been established *independently* of each other. For each passage, a reference to transmigration has been concluded to be the likeliest interpretation independent of the other one, but the passages can also be easily read together from this perspective.

2. *"Revival" as Salvific Second Birth*

As an interpretation of the fragment this would mean:

> *Falling asleep and physical death have been compared to each other;*
> *the state of sleep is followed by awakening and the event of death by salvation.*

In this alternative a disparity is introduced in the simile, because a recurrent phenomenon is compared to a one-time event. Moreover, the exact counterpart of being asleep, the *state* of death, is replaced above by the *event*, which further reduces the validity of the simile. For we do not have Philo's view of what he thought the virtuous souls undergo between death and reaching God, and whether it is meaningful to speak of such a state in the first place in the context of his thought. The closest thing that could be thought of is the ascent of the soul to progressively higher spheres, but the fragment contains not even a hint in that direction.[678] Thus the essential comparison must be thought to lie rather between the awakening and the salvific birth, i.e., attaining salvation. Compare Figures 3 (p. 204) and 4:

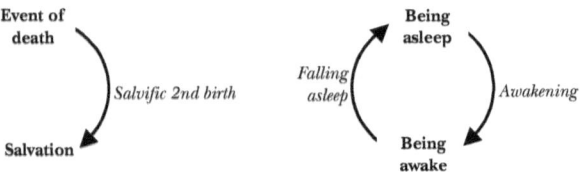

Figure 4. Comparison between Salvific Second Birth and Sleep.

---

[677] For Plutarch too the terms ἀναβίωσις and παλιγγενεσία seem synonymous; see *De Iside et Osiride* 364f (of Osiris; see also 379f), *De E apud Delphos* 389a.

[678] For the ascent, see the discussion of the seventh potential cause of incarnation (above, pp. 53–57). Cf. the flight of souls in *QE* 2.40; in *Cher.* 114 the imperfect souls' lot in the hereafter was being with the incorporeals. Neither notion is alluded to in the fragment.

Admittedly however, the second birth, just like awakening, would represent a *return* to a previous state, given Philo's understanding of the salvation of the pre-existent soul as its return to where it came from.[679] But in that case it would be the corporeal *life* as a whole—and not its end point (death)—that should be compared to sleep.[680] And when we add the fact that the fairly automatic nature (NB. αὖθις) of salvation is not feasible, I find this interpretation of the fragment highly implausible.

3.4.7 *Conclusions*

Nothing found in the above analyses suggests that fragment 7.3 Harris should not be ascribed to Philo. Its last sentence contains unusual linguistic features and is probably both paraphrastic and corrupt, but this cannot be regarded as evidence of a non-Philonic origin of the entire fragment. No author quotes the text before ps.-Maximus Confessor, but echoes of it are quite possibly heard in other patristic sources. In particular, two mutually linked passages in Clement of Alexandria's *Stromata* (books 4 and 5) contain all three chief characteristics of the fragment; there is also some shared vocabulary and syntax.

In the fragment the comparison of sleep, death and revival is clearly connected with Plato's *Phaedo* where the reincarnation-based comparison of death to sleep, the concept of practising death and the use of the verb ἀναβιώσκομαι for rebirth act as the most conspicuous links to the fragment. Philo does not link sleep and death elsewhere in exactly the same way as in the fragment. However, the reference to practising death, not instrumental in the main comparison, implies that Philo wants to remind his audience about this concept. In Philo, as in Plato, it is linked with freedom from the senses, which for its part is connected by Philo with both salvation and also sleep as a giver of a foretaste thereof.

The driving forces of reincarnation are not explicitly dealt with in this brief excerpt, but I think this is a case of "blurred boundaries:"[681] we should take as the Phaedonic background a larger portion of the dialogue than just the exact points Philo explicitly mentions, for example the reasons *why* Socrates advocates practising death. One could say that the main purpose is to make sure that the soul's freedom from the body and

---

[679] See above, p. 31.
[680] The question may be raised, if "death" in the fragment should be understood as a reference to *mortal life*. However, given the distinguishability of mortal life from the death of the soul (see above, p. 47), it is not probable that Philo would liken the former concept to death.
[681] See p. 128.

senses achieved before, and finalised in, physical death is of a permanent sort and that no bodily inclinations remain that would result in the soul's once again ending up in a new incarnation.

3.5 *Conclusions on the Direct Evidence*

In all the main texts discussed in this chapter (*Somn.* 1.137–139, *Cher.* 114, *QE* 2.40 and fr. 7.3 Harris) it was found that Philo is speaking of the idea of reincarnation with approval. The driving forces involved, where these could be identified, were observed to coincide with the potential causes of reincarnation identified in Ch. 2: the mind's tendency to love the body and things corporeal are either mentioned in, or implied by the context of, all the passages. Incomplete monadization seems to be implied in the *Cher.* passage.

With regard to the six-stage model of the mind's fall and rise outlined in Ch. 2, all the main texts examined deal with stages (4) to (6), and so the original cause of incarnation and the original corporealization of the mind are not discussed.[682] However, a noteworthy feature not explicitly encountered in Ch. 2 is the role of the soul's being *accustomed* to the life in the body (*Somn.* 1.139) as one important element—clearly related in thought to the mind's corporealization—in its desire for mortal life. Another important aspect is that in order to be saved, souls must direct their love and desire correctly: steadily towards God (*QE* 2.40). The reincarnating souls desire the mortal life in the body and the objects of sense (*Somn.* 1.139, *Cher.* 117).

Plato's influence is decisive in Philo's reincarnational texts. The latter takes over individual words and concepts of more or less directly Platonic origin (being bound to a mortal body; φιλοσώματος, παλιγγενσία, ἀναβίωσις) and images (the body as a river, prison and grave,[683] the soul's lightness and wings, practising death) as well as a host of more general ideas and expressions used by Plato in his accounts of reincarnation (ἀναπέτομαι, δεσμωτήριον, μέγας ἡγεμών, πολλὴ φλυαρία). However, Philo does not just copy, he also modifies: being born in an animal body is left out, and we have nothing corresponding to Plato's mentions (or long discourses: *Phaedo* 112–114) of the soul's inter-incarnational stay in Hades or Tartarus. Philo demythologizes these places, as was already seen in Ch. 2; in *QE* 2.40 Tartarus represents the human body like in one of its parallels, *QG* 4.234.

---

[682] For the model, see p. 73.
[683] For these there are also antecedents to Plato; see subsection 2.4.4.

Several features were noted to connect the four main passages with each other. In addition, it is worthwhile to highlight the significance of passages that are parallel to these texts. This was already briefly discussed above in the context of the exceptionally clear parallelism between *Somn.* 1.138–139; *Gig.* 6, 12–15 and *Plant.* 14.[684] Given that we are now in a position to state that Philo endorsed reincarnation in the main texts, we must confirm the earlier surmise that these parallels are allusions to the doctrine, because holding another position would require making the wholly arbitrary assumption that Philo's audience did not know the main texts. Equally significant but different kind of parallelism also exists for *QE* 2.40. In addition to the *QG* passage already named, *QE* 2.39 and *Agr.* 89 belong to a group of passages that has important mutual links. In light of our results so far we have all the reason to consider especially the *Agr.* passage as an allusion to reincarnation.

---

[684] See p. 146. If we take the cosmological and angelological discussions into account, the parallelism covers *Somn.* 1.133–141, *Gig.*6–18, and *Plant.* 12–14.

CHAPTER FOUR

SYNTHESIS

4.1 *The Journey of the Soul According to Philo*

In Genesis, the human life on earth has, after a brief period of harmony, a fairly miserable start. Philo never spells out an unequivocal protology, but his grand allegory of the soul with its notion of salvation as the pre-existent mind's *return* to its heavenly state does imply some kind of original fall. In the thought of the Alexandrian the soul enters a vicious state of death which is linked with its striving to attain sense pleasures and its reincarnation. As dead, the soul is buried in the body. As a transgressor, it is imprisoned in it. This state, however, is not irrevocable. The soul can renounce it and regain the incorporeal mode of existence through toil and grace.

But what lies between the fall and salvation? How does the soul advance from its desire for mortal life to virtue and immortality? This section aims at delineating a reincarnational understanding of the soul's journey in Philo's thought based on his anthropological, ethical and soteriological views and on the results of the examination of the direct evidence of his espousing reincarnation. The task involves perusing an extensive network of interrelated terms, concepts, notions and images that Philo employs not only in the directly reincarnational texts examined but also in a large number of other ones primarily in the *Allegorical Commentary* and the *Quaestiones*.

The approach in Chapter 3 can be characterized by stating that each Philonic passage in which *added value*—in the form of a more precise or coherent interpretation—is created by the assumption that reincarnation is spoken of (with approval) counts as part of a cumulative evidence in favor of the view that Philo endorsed the tenet. In this final chapter the viewpoint is different: since we have already reached the conclusion that Philo speaks of reincarnation and that it fits his other views, we are no longer looking for evidence on *what* his position is. Instead, we concentrate more on *how* he uses the idea of transmigration. Yet the results of this chapter as well have a strengthening or weakening effect on the affirmative answer to the central question of this study already reached by this point, depending on the plausibility of a reincarnational reading of the various texts.[685]

The results of Chapters 2 and 3 mean that we have good grounds for expecting that in addition to the clearest mentions of rebirth there are many less explicit ones. In this chapter we turn to some of the vaguer passages and characterize and interpret them in the light of what we have learnt so far. Texts are examined with the assumption that when Philo uses similar vocabulary in similar contexts in different texts, he is speaking of the same things, and that therefore we are entitled to read these texts together. This means assuming that the texts form a whole, and that what is said in one text is, in the absence of evidence to the contrary, implied in the others.

4.1.1 A Synthesis of the Reincarnational Passages

We will begin with an overview of what we have thus far discovered about the Philonic concept of reincarnation. I have drawn up a synthesis of the texts analyzed in Ch. 3 (*Somn.* 1.137–139 (with the parallel at *Gig.* 12–15), *Cher.* 114, *QE* 2.40 and fr. 7.3 Harris). The synthesis presents my understanding of the most important features of Philo's view of reincarnation as it appears in those texts, with some additional features taken from his general anthropological views.[686] A selection of key Greek terms used by Philo is included:

> The air is full of descending and ascending souls. The former are lovers of the body (φιλοσώματος), and they go down to be fast bound (ἐνδέω) in mortal bodies.
>
> The latter are ascending after having exhausted their nature-determined lifespan. Some of them fly up (ἀναπέτομαι) only a short distance and then rush back (ὁρμάω, παλινδρομέω, αὖθις) and are drawn (ὑπσύρω) again to the Tartarus of the body.
>
> These last long for the mortal life (θνητὸς βίος) which they have become used to (συνήθης). If they feel any desire (πόθος) for God, it is too fickle to make them endure the ascent. The irrational parts of their soul still enslave their intellect and curtail its propelling power and make them descend and continue the pursuit of pleasures in bodies. These souls are dead.

---

[685] I want to reiterate here that the goal remains understanding what Philo himself wrote, *not* experimenting on with what degree of credibility reincarnation can be *read into* his texts.

[686] The main texts with their English translations can be found above on pp. 131, 154, 169, and 187, respectively.

> But once a soul pronounces the mortal life (θνητὸς βίος) great folly and its love for God becomes steady, it escapes to incorporeal existence as though from a prison (δεσμωτήριον, εἱρκτή), grave (τύμβος, σῆμα), or river, and is lifted up beyond heaven.[687] Incorporeal it ranges the heights (μετεωροπολέω) with light wings for ever in the presence of God whose leadership and grace enabled it to ascend to the divine city where it started from.
>
> We are reminded of these truths by sleep: until we learn to practise death (μελέτη θανάτου), our falling asleep in death will be followed by our awakening in rebirth (παλιγγενεσία, ἀναβίωσις).

4.1.2 Towards a Reincarnational Understanding of Philo's Individual Eschatology

There is no shortage of Philonic passages that are in marked agreement with the above picture and which complement it in various ways. We have already discussed a large number of them in Chs. 2 and 3. The aim of this section is to look more closely at passages which, for the most part, have thus far only been partially or briefly dealt with, and which relate in important ways to the synthesis presented above. We begin by examining two texts that present a summary of the mind's situation on earth, *Her.* 267–274 and *Spec.* 4.188, the first a broader one, the second, very concise. Key themes are subsequently discussed: love of God vs. the earthly things, the imprisonment of the soul, dying to the life of virtue and drowning in the body.

Being Alien in a Land Not One's Own: Her. 267–274

Her. 267–274 contains a relatively comprehensive account of the journey of the soul. The subject matter is Gen 15:13–14 for which Philo gives his allegorization without secondary biblical lemmas. He first expounds God's words to Abram that his "offspring will be alien (πάροικον) in a land not its own:"

> God does not allow the lover of virtue to dwell (κατοικεῖν) in the body as in one's own land, but only permits him to sojourn (παροικεῖν) there, as in a foreign country.... But the district of the body is kin to every fool; he studies to dwell there, not sojourn. (*Her.* 267)

---

[687] I think the only instance of harmonizing existing *differences* is here; I have chosen to follow *QE* 2.40 and ignored the *ether* of *Somn.* 1.139 as the destination. However, as both passages surely speak of permanent liberation from the body, this difference has no bearing on the validity of my harmony from the viewpoint of the main focus of this study, i.e., whether or not Philo endorsed reincarnation. See below, subsection 4.2.3 on further research.

The occasion gives Philo the opportunity once more to reiterate the difference between dwelling and sojourning in a manner very similar to what was noted at, e.g., *Conf.* 77–78.[688] The incarnate state is to be temporary and not permanent, but could the whole distinction be a matter of right or wrong *attitude*? Surely, that too, but a reincarnational reading adds a second, concrete level of interpretation: this is also a matter of minimizing the number of lives.

Then (§268), alluding to the part of Gen 15:13 which he does not quote—the enslavement, maltreatment and humiliation that take place in this land which is not our "own"—Philo writes, "For the passions of the body are truly bastards, outlanders to the understanding, growths of the flesh in which they have their roots." Here the connection between the body and the passions is not only more explicit than usually, but it is also explained: the passions grow from (verb ἐκφύω) the flesh. Against this connection it is easy to understand why the soul's "prison" is sometimes the body, sometimes the passions.[689] The former is naturally depicted as the soul's place of confinement, but it is also easy to understand the passions as forces that keep it imprisoned.[690]

In *Her.* 269 Philo continues that "the enslavement by the powers of the four passions is for four hundred years," and then (§§ 269–270) describes the ways in which pleasure, desire, grief and fear rule the soul. For example, when desire (ἐπιθυμία) rules, the soul is suffering from a Tantalean punishment, loving that which it does not have;[691] "desire has a power of attraction (ὁλκὸν ... δύναμιν) and forces us to the pursuit (διώκειν) of the desired object (τὸ ποθούμενον)." This kind of insatiability is in full harmony with the idea, most clearly present in *Somn.* 1.139, that the desire for mortal life and sense objects is a key driving force for reincarnation in Philo. It is also easy to see *QE* 2.40 speaking of the reverse situation as far as the non-returning souls are concerned: God is their desired object which they pursue.

For Philo the time limit of four hundred years in Gen 15:13 only stands for the number of the main passions, and he ignores it in his description of the duration of the "heavy slavery of the passions;" instead he says the captivity will last

---

[688] See above, p. 54.
[689] Admittedly, Philo is not fully consistent on this; e.g., in *Leg.* 2.6 the passions are "offspring (ἔκγονα) of sense." But, then again, the difference is quite small, "the senses being the bodily part of the soul" (*Congr.* 21).
[690] Cf. *QG* 3.10 for a very similar interpretation of Gen 15:13–14.
[691] That this last is what ἔρως τῶν ἀπόντων means (*pace* Colson's "yearning for what is not") is shown by *Decal.* 149 and especially *Spec.* 4.80–81.

until God the arbiter and judge makes a separation between the ill-treater and the ill-treated, releases one to full liberty and renders to the other the recompense for its misdeeds. (*Her.* 271)

As in *QE* 2.40, God's action is, in the end, decisive. Philo continues (ex. Gen 15:14):

> It must needs be that the mortal race shall be oppressed by the nation of the passions ... but it is God's will to lighten the evils inherent in us... . God will accomplish the work which is proper to Himself in proclaiming redemption and liberty to the souls that are His suppliants, and not only will He provide release from bonds and a way out from the closely guarded prison, but give us also the viaticum which he here calls "baggage." (*Her.* 272–273)

There is little doubt that the "prison" (εἱρκτή) refers to body, primarily on the basis of the context, but also because this meaning is explicit in §68.[692] Now while grace is a necessary prerequisite of salvation, struggle is also an inevitable part of the life of suppliant souls.[693] This we see in what follows, a condensed summary of the whole journey of the soul from heaven to earth and back again with a recipe for a successful return:

> Whenever the mind, having come down from heaven, is fast bound (ἐνδεθῇ) to the constraints of the body, then, although it is not trapped by any of them like a man–woman or woman–man, it does welcome the pleasant evils. But by remaining in its own nature—a man, verily—it is able to be victor rather than victim in the wrestling-bout, reared as it is in all the lore of the schools. Having received from that lore a longing for contemplation it acquires the sturdy virtues of self-mastery and perseverance. When departing (μετανιστάμενος) and finding the way back to its native (πατρίς) land it takes with it all the fruits of instruction, which are called "baggage." (*Her.* 274) [694]

---

[692] In addition, §109 speaks of a soul "fast bound as in a prison" (ἐν δεσμωτηρίῳ καθειργμένην). Both passages are discussed below, pp. 226, 229, respectively.

[693] That Philo in §§ 271–273 highlights God's role stems from the biblical text, where God's promise to judge the nation enslaving Israel is mentioned.

[694] I have extensively reworked Colson's translation while keeping much of his terminology. The Greek runs, ἐπειδὰν ἄνωθεν ἀπ' οὐρανοῦ καταβὰς ὁ νοῦς ἐνδεθῇ ταῖς σώματος ἀνάγκαις, εἶτα ὑπὸ μηδεμιᾶς δελεασθεὶς οἷα ἀνδρόγυνος ἢ γύνανδρος τὰ ἡδέα ἀσπάσηται κακά, μείνας δὲ ἐπὶ τῆς ἑαυτοῦ φύσεως ἀνὴρ ὄντως τραχηλίζειν μᾶλλον ἢ τραχηλίζεσθαι δύνηται, τοῖς τῆς ἐγκυκλίου μουσικῆς ἐντραφεὶς <παιδεύμασι> ἅπασιν, ἐξ ὧν θεωρίας λαβὼν ἵμερον ἐγκράτειαν καὶ καρτερίαν, ἐρρωμένας ἀρετάς, ἐκτήσατο, μετανιστάμενος καὶ κάθοδον τὴν εἰς τὴν πατρίδα εὑρισκόμενος πάντ' ἐπάγεται τὰ παιδείας, ἅπερ ἀποσκευὴ καλεῖται. The most substantial difference between Colson's rendering and mine is that in his text the mind does *not* welcome the pleasant evils, but I think that would require ἀσπάζεσθαι or ἀσπάσασθαι instead of ἀσπάσηται. For the concessive participle δελεασθείς cf. HWS §2082. As to the οἷα ἀνδρόγυνος ἢ γύνανδρος see Colson's note (PLCL 4.574), and for ἐντραφεὶς <παιδεύμασι> ἅπασιν see PCW and PLCL *ad loc.* (There is some variation and a missing word in the MSS.)

The central teaching in *Her.* 274 seems to be the avoidance of being ensnared by sense objects and everything else that the world has to offer. To the extent that these are not attached to, they can even be "welcomed."[695] The "victims," no doubt, overdo this and become trapped, which brings us back to the "attractive power" of the desired objects (§270). Philo again uses Plato's reincarnational language about being bound to the body.[696] The antidote is precisely that longing for contemplation, i.e., desire for God, whose stability was deemed so crucial in *QE* 2.40, and the words μετανίστημι and πατρίς are used in salvation-related contexts elsewhere.[697]

The Degraded State of the Mind: Spec. 4.188

Book four of the *De specialibus legibus* contains a narrower description of the state of the incarnate mind. Its origin and destination are omitted here, but further insights are gained which we may add to the synthesis presented above. The account can, without hesitation, be extracted from its context, for it is a digression amid a text dealing with entirely different matters—rulers and judges—which can be seamlessly read without the part that we are focusing on (between the dashes):

> But since a vast number of circumstances slip away from or are unnoticed by the human mind—bound (ἐνδεδεμένον) as it is to the troublesome mob of the senses, so competent to mislead and deceive it with false opinions, or rather entombed in a mortal body which may be quite properly called a sepulchre—let no judge be ashamed, when he is ignorant of anything, to confess his ignorance. (*Spec.* 4.188)

The context does have a certain relevance, if we speculate on Philo's train of thought here. The starting point seems to be the imperfection of the human mind in the conditions it finds itself in here on earth: it is bound and entombed in the body.[698] This time, however, it is not the moral side of the confinement but rather the uncertainty of information based on the senses that first comes to Philo's mind, as is quite natural in the context.[699]

---

[695] I find *Leg.* 2.17 speaking of a similar attitude towards the worldly goods: "A created being cannot but make us of pleasure. But the bad person will use it as a perfect good, but the worthy person simply as a necessity, remembering that apart from pleasure nothing in mortal kind comes to existence."
[696] See above, p. 113.
[697] This statement in *Somn.* 1.46 is representative and has several links with the *Her.* passages being discussed: "feeling that you are spending your days in a foreign country as sojourners to be ever seeking for departure (μετανάστασιν) and return to the land of your fathers (εἰς τὴν πατρῷαν γῆν)."
[698] See above, subsection 2.4.1, pp. 113–14.
[699] I have replaced Colson's "seduce" for παραγαγεῖν with "mislead" for this reason.

We have noted the theme of the deceitful nature of the senses and its dual background above.[700] This notion complements our picture of reincarnation in Philo by characterizing the pursuit of sense objects and pleasures as illusory, based on false premises.

Philo calls the senses (or more generally, the irrational part of the soul) a "troublesome mob" (ὄχλος) in several places elsewhere.[701] The soul takes off the "entire encumbrance (ὄγκον) of the body and escap[es] from the troublesome mob (ὄχλον) of the senses" in *Somn.* 1.43, and at *Leg.* 2.77 "our mob-like (λαῶδες καὶ ὄχλον ἔχον) part pines for the dwellings in Egypt, that is, the bodily mass (ὄγκῳ)."[702] In *Deus* 2 we find a solitary case of applying the word directly to the body; Philo speaks of the soul as having "fastened (ἀνημμένη) on it the grievous burden of this fleshly, troublesome mob."

Being entombed in a mortal body as in a grave, highly reminiscent of *Somn.* 1.139, shifts the focus from the practical to deeper issues. A solid link is created to *Leg.* 1.105–108, which is the only other place where Philo, in his extant writings, uses the words ἐντυμβεύω and σῆμα and which, because it speaks of incarnation as a punishment on the already embodied soul, must be considered a likely allusion to reincarnation.[703] Hence we see that the language Philo uses in *Spec.* 4.188 is loaded with allusions and connotations which guide the reader's mind to a quite definite type of texts in both Philo and Plato, texts that either directly speak of or are related to the transmigration of souls.

The Object of the Soul's Love: God or the Earthly Things?

One of the main points that appears in two of the four texts discussed in Ch. 3 is the importance of the love or desire that the mind feels for either God or earthly things, which include the physical body that it inhabits. In *Somn.* 1.138–139 the incarnating souls are body-loving and long for the mortal life, and in *QE* 2.40 the soul's love for God is not stable enough, which naturally relates to the idea that it still finds the mundane sphere more attractive than God. In *Cher.* too, the reincarnating soul's following the senses (§117) is a related phenomenon. Of other texts that have been

---

[700] See n. 283 on p. 88.
[701] See *Leg.* 3.235, *Migr.* 200, *Spec.* 1.298 and *Contempl.* 27. As for the translation of the word, I refer to Colson's note to *Deus* 2: "ὄχλος carries with it the idea both of a mob and the trouble and confusion caused by it."
[702] For these passages see below p. 231, and above, p. 60, respectively. See also Plato's use of ὄχλος for the body in the description of reincarnation in *Tim.* 42c (p. 91 above).
[703] Σῆμα does occur in the poem by Solon quoted at *Opif.* 104. For the *Leg.* passage, see the discussion on incarnation as a punishment (pp. 57–70), where it was concluded that much speaks against taking this as the *original* incarnation.

discussed, we may name just two which have a wider impact on our understanding of Philo's view of reincarnation. *QG* 1.51 features very clearly the mutually excluding nature of the two objects of love: virtue and pleasure.[704] And since the hunt for pleasure and sense objects plays a role also in the other main text on the corporealization of the incarnate mind, *Leg.* 3.251–253, we may note here that corporealization with its corollaries indeed seems to be responsible for the onset of the wheel of reincarnation in Philo and that the six-stage model of the mind's fall and rise fits the evidence available.[705]

There are several other passages in Philo which can be interpreted meaningfully assuming that love of the earthly things makes the soul liable to reincarnate. In Philo's view Er's having "bec[o]me wicked in the sight of the Lord" (*Leg.* 3.71, ex. Gen 38:7) refers to the evil nature of the body not being immediately apparent to everyone, but only "to God and to anyone who is dear to God."[706] The sequel (*ibid.*) sounds, in part, quite familiar:

> For if the mind soars aloft (μετεωροπολῇ) and is being initiated in the mysteries of the Lord, it judges the body to be wicked and hostile; but if it abandons (ἀποστῇ) the investigation (ἐρεύνης) of things divine, it deems [the body] friendly to itself, its kinsman and brother, which is seen in that it takes refuge (καταφεύγει γοῦν) in what is dear to [the body]. (*Leg.* 3.71)[707]

The word for "kinsman" is the same (συγγενές) as the one I translated as "kin" in *Her.* 267; such language aptly describes the corporealized mind's state.[708] Philo does not often call the body the "brother" of the mind or soul. In *Post.* 61 he attributes this notion to body-loving (φιλοσωμάτοις) souls; in *Ebr.* 70–71 and *Fug.* 90–91 (both ex. Ex 32:27) Philo explains

---

[704] See the quotation on p. 70.
[705] For the model, see p. 73.
[706] This is another example of the double dichotomy noted in Philo's anthropology: because the wicked Er's name means '*leathern*,' our exegete has to speak of the evil character of the *body*, although the matter is more complex. *Leg.* 3.69–74 was already briefly discussed above, p. 62; for double dichotomy, see p. 39.
[707] My translation of the two cases of ὅταν in the passage as "if" is based on LSJ: "*whenever*, with a conditional force, so as nearly to = ἐάν, referring to an indef. future." I understand γοῦν here having the force mentioned in HWS §2830: it "commonly confirms a previous general assertion by giving a special instance of its truth," against which Whitaker's "[t]he proof of this is that it takes refuge" is a little strong.
[708] See above, p. 216. *Tim.* 91e (n. 387 on p. 125), where the soul's ξυγγενεία with the earth is coupled with one of the reincarnation-related images borrowed by Philo from Plato, being weighed down, can be seen in the background. *Her.* 267 clearly picks up Philo's earlier discussion about the "suitable" (οἰκεῖος) places of differently orientated souls in §§ 237–239. The "creeping" ones, "because they are kin to what is below (διὰ τὴν πρὸς τὰ κάτω συγγένειαν), shun the region above." §237 is connected to *Tim.* 92a by the exceedingly rare verb ἰλυσπάω ('to wriggle').

Moses's command to the sons of Levi to kill their brothers (together with their neighbours and nearest) to mean getting rid of the body. What is interesting in these last two passages is that in them the mind is described as drowning in the stream of sense objects and passions. Senses and passions were also connected to the danger of drowning in *Agr.* 89, a passage depicting an involuntary return to the body.[709] Furthermore, at *Ebr.* 70, this drowning results in the soul's inability ever to "lift her head heavenwards [and] welcome the divine and noetic natures"—surely the same as "the investigation of things divine" above—, and in *Fug.* 92 the opposite case, ridding the mind of the body, senses and speech results in its being able to "welcome the Sole Existence freely and without distraction."[710]

To come back to *Leg.* 3.71, taking refuge in what is dear to the body corresponds to loving the body, perhaps even to returning to it; cf. *Somn.* 1.44 where "win[ning] in sense-perception a second-best refuge (καταφυγήν)" is presented in parallel with being "forthwith (αὐτίκα) swept down (κατασύρεται) to sense objects," if the soul who has escaped from the body fails in the contemplation of the noetic things.[711] Furthermore, the soaring mind's judgement of the body in the quotation above comes very close to the free souls' "pronouncing [the mortal life] great folly ... [and] rang[ing] the heights for ever" at *Somn.* 1.139.[712]

The ensuing section on the athlete and the philosopher, *Leg.* 3.72, was already discussed above, and its tight connection to *Leg.* 1.105–108 noted.[713] We are now in a position to add that because the athlete represents the mind that takes refuge in the body (*Leg.* 3), it also stands for a body-loving soul in the state of death, entombed in the body (*Leg.* 1). In *Leg.* 3, before coming back to the theme of the ascent at 3.84, Philo presents some reflections on Noah, Melchizedek and Abram, of which we may briefly note the exceptionally bitter tone in relation to the body: e.g., at 3.77 God is spoken of as "hating" pleasure and the body. This is, however, quite in keeping with the biblical text where "God killed [Er]." At 3.74 Philo combines the love for the body and the concept of corpse-bearing employing his verb νεκροφορέω, which he has already used at the outset of his exegesis of Gen 38:7 at *Leg.* 3.69. This further reinforces the connection to 1.108 where the body is called "the baneful corpse."

---

[709] See above, pp. 69, 181–85. For Plato's image of the body as a river and its Philonic applications, see pp. 114–17.
[710] My tr. for τὸ μόνον <ὂν> καθαρῶς καὶ ἀμεθέλκτως ἀσπάσεται.
[711] *Somn.* 1.41–46 is discussed in more detail below, p. 231.
[712] πολλὴν φλυαρίαν αὐτοῦ καταγνοῦσαι ... μετεωροπολοῦσι τὸν αἰῶνα.
[713] See pp. 62–63.

A little later in *Leg.* 3 Philo returns to the same ascent as in 3.71, as revealed by the shared vocabulary. The mind,

> abandoning (ἀποστάς) everything base that leads to mortal things it soars aloft (μετεωροπολῇ) and spends its time in contemplation of the universe and its different parts; when, mounting yet higher, it explores (ἐρευνᾷ) the Deity and His nature, urged by an ineffable love of knowledge; it cannot continue to entertain the doctrines it imbibed originally, but in its desire to improve itself seeks to change its abode for a better one. (*Leg.* 3.84)

The passage is rife with familiar themes: leaving the mortal for the extreme heights where divine visions are experienced, the propelling force of love, changing to a better abode. There is no question that of the reincarnational texts *Somn.* 1.139 and *QE* 2.40 speak of the same flight and the latter of the same love's fickleness. A new detail in the picture is the educational effect on the mind's doctrines coupled with its love of knowledge.

When read from a reincarnational standpoint and taking the other texts that it connects with into account, *Leg.* 3.71 includes a description both of a successful, salvific flight from the body and of an unsuccessful one by a dead soul ending up in another incarnation. Similarly to *QE* 2.40, salvation and taking refuge in the corporeal are presented as alternatives. Since salvation is in any case preceded by the mind's separation from the body, i.e., physical death, the possibility that reincarnation is meant cannot be denied on the grounds that Philo does note expressly declare that he is speaking of afterlife.

Philo's exegesis of Gen 19 in *QG* 4 provides some further relevant examples of texts where the desire for the earthly seems to be presented in a reincarnational context. In 4.46 the angels' exhortation to Lot to escape to the mountain (Gen 19:17) indicates that "the mind begins to take the higher road" whereby it "leav[es] behind earth-bound and low things which those men pursue and admire who are undisciplined." Some Platonic notions then follow: the rise of the light soul to heaven brings to mind the *Phaedrus* (e.g., 249b) and the inspection of the nature, movements etc. of heaven, the *Timaeus* (91e). Plato presents these ideas in explicitly reincarnational contexts.

The angelic message was addressed to the undisciplined mind which should take heed that

> those who strive after low and base and earthly things die[714] in respect of true life—the soul—, wandering about (յածելով [*yacelov*]) in the manner of the dead. But

---

[714] Marcus: "shall die." But մեռանին (*meṙanin*) is present indicative whereas Greek future is commonly rendered as aorist subjunctive; no morphologically distinct future tense exists in classical Armenian (Todd B. Krause, John. A. Greppin and Jonathan Slocum,

> those who desire (գանկացեալ են [c'ankac'eal en]) heavenly things and are borne on high shall be saved alone, exchanging mortal for immortal life. (*QG* 4.46)

We have here a juxtaposition of cherishing corporeal things and leaving the mortal life for higher spheres similar to that in *Somn.* 1.138–139. One is also reminded of the "wandering and going around circle-wise" during the prolonged flight from Egypt at *Migr.* 154.[715] Part of the instructions given by the angels was that the refugees should not look back (Gen 19:17). As it happened, this was too much to ask from Lot's wife who did precisely what was forbidden and turned into a stele of salt as a consequence (v. 26). Philo explains:

> the wife of the mind is symbolically sense-perception, which becomes insolent not only in evil ones but also in those who progress, and it inclines toward sense-perceptible things ... . And for this reason it turns back ... to visible possessions ... and to the properties of pleasant odours and tastes and substances. (*QG* 4.52)[716]

This kind of turning back of sense-perception also in those who are already making progress can well be read together with especially *QE* 2.40, but it also fits well with the idea that the soul's compound constitution may act as a driving force of reincarnation (cf. *Cher.* 114).

The kind of turning to the wrong objects of love as depicted in *QG* 4.52 and *QE* 2.40 may not automatically lead to a long agony in Philo's thought. Swift corrective measures seem possible at least in some cases. In a passage in *Leg.* Philo first tells us that "among the sacrificers of the Passover" those were especially praiseworthy

---

Classical Armenian Online [The University of Texas at Austin, College of Liberal Arts, www.utexas.edu/cola/centers/lrc/eieol/armol-0-X.html], Ch. 24). Mercier: "meurent;" Aucher: "moriuntur."

[715] See Appendix 1. A passage that seems to be connected to both *Migr.* 154 and *QG.* 4.46 is *Praem.* 117:
> the mind which has strayed everywhere in prolonged vagrancy, maltreated by pleasure and lust, the mistresses it honoured so unduly, may well be brought back by the mercy of its Savior from the pathless wild into a road wherein it is resolved to flee without turning—a flight of one banished from evil to salvation, a banishment which may be truly held to be better than a return (καθόδου).

Here again, salvation and return are the alternatives, and reincarnation a plausible interpretation. The connection to *QG* 4.46 lies not only in the mention of wandering but also in the notion of the vain respect that the undisciplined soul pays to things that do not deserve it (see above: "pursue and admire" in *QG*).

[716] Cf. *Cher.* 117 (above, p. 157) where the idea is similar, although in *QG* 4.52 the Arm. for "of ... substances" is հիւթոց [*hiwt'oc'*], for which word NBHL gives ὕλη, στοιχεῖον, βάθος.

who sacrificed earlier (Num 9:3), because when they had crossed over (διαβάντες) from the passions of Egypt, they kept to that crossing (τῇ διαβάσει) and no more rushed (οὐχ ὥρμησαν ἔτι) after them. (*Leg.* 3.94)

These first souls thus do not return. We saw earlier that to Philo the allegorical meaning of Passover is very similar to that of exodus, i.e., the liberation from the body, passions and sense pleasures, and that he extensively utilizes the Platonic notion of the body as a river (which is crossed, verb διαβαίνω) in that context.[717] Thus, once again, permanent liberation from the body and going back (see below) seem to be the alternatives. However, this time the events take, literally, a new turn:

> But to those who sacrificed later (Num 9:11) [Moses] assigns the second place, for after turning (back to the passions) they retraced the wrong steps they had taken (ἀνέδραμον τὴν τροπήν) and, as though they had forgotten their duties, they rushed back (πάλιν ὥρμησαν) to perform them, while the earlier sacrificers held on without turning. (*ibid.*)

These second souls, even though they too had performed the crossing, forgot their "duties (τῶν πρακτέων)" for a while and rushed after the passions of Egypt (desires are thus implied). But now, however, they also rush back.[718] So just like an ascent can turn into a dive, the inverse may also happen. Whether the turning back to the passions means a new incarnation or if the retracing of the wrong steps can somehow take place midair before sinking into a body is not the point Philo is making. It is worth noting that both turns seem contingent ("forgotten") and not inevitable.

There is a parallel to *Leg.* 3.94 in *Leg.* 2 worth noting, for we find at 2.28 the probable meaning of the "duties" (lit. 'what has to be done,' πρακτέον): controlling the passions.[719] A little later Philo explains Adam's trance (Gen

---

[717] See above, subsection 2.4.2, pp. 114–17.
[718] The combination of ὁρμάω and διαβαίνω comes from Gen 31:21: (Jacob, fleeing Laban, "crossed the river and set out for the mountain of Galaad"), which Philo had commented a little earlier saying, e.g., that
> the mind in training ... crosses the river of objects of sense that swamps and drowns (ἐπικλύζοντα καὶ βαπτίζοντα) the soul under the flood (φορᾷ) of the passions, and, when he has crossed it, sets his face (ὁρμᾷ) for the lofty highland, the principle (λόγος) of perfect virtue.... The meaning of [Galaad] is "migration (μετοικία) of witness," for God caused the soul to migrate (μετοικίσαντος) from the passions that are represented by Laban ... and led it on away ... up to the height and greatness of virtue. (*Leg.* 3.18–19)

Here too, the resemblance to the exegesis of Ex 24 in *QE* 2 with its ascent to the mountain, i.e., to God, is not insignificant: Philo says "the divine place" is called Logos" in 2.39; migration under God's leadership is central in 2.40.
[719] Ex. Deut 23:13: Moses "bids the man wear [the 'shovel'] upon his passion, which must be girded up .... And this has to be done (τοῦτο δὲ πρακτέον) whenever the mind, relaxing from the strain of the noetic things, lowers itself to the passions." Numerous

2:21) which he equates with the change that all created things must undergo (only God is immutable):

> But, while some, after being changed, remain so until they are entirely destroyed (ἄχρι παντελοῦς φθορᾶς), others continue so only so far as to experience that to which all flesh is liable, and these forthwith recover (ἀνεσώθησαν). This is why Moses says, "he will not allow the destroyer to enter into your houses to strike" (Ex 12:23): for He does indeed permit the destroyer—"destruction" being the change or turning of the soul—to enter into the soul, ... but God will not let the offspring of "the seeing" Israel be in such wise changed as to receive his death-blow by the change, but will force him to rise (ἀναδραμεῖν) and emerge (ἀνακύψαι) as though from deep water (ὥσπερ ἐκ βυθοῦ) and be restored. (*Leg.* 2.33–34)

It is as if we had here a description of what happens to those who immerse themselves in the corporeal world and the corollaries (desires, pleasures and passions) more than is necessary.[720]

The Imprisonment

We now move onto the next notion, the imprisonment of the soul or mind in several texts of Philo's. We begin with *Her.* 68 where Philo tells us that the intellect which remains "in the prison of the body (ἐν τῇ τοῦ σώματος εἱρκτῇ) of its own free will (καθ' ἑκούσιον γνώμην)" cannot be the heir (of noetic things, §66). A literal, non-reincarnational interpretation—that Philo is speaking about refraining from suicide—would be absurd. Two options remain: the imprisonment must refer to *being subject to* the body and the bodily appetites either in one life or several. The crucial difference between these two is that in the former case the exit from the prison means purely spiritual liberation (independent of physical death) whereas in the latter the question is, *in addition*, of the permanent end of the state of incarnation at next death.

---

verbal links confirm the connection between *Leg.* 3.94 and 2.28–34: in addition to πρακτέος and πάθος, we find ἐπιλανθάνω, τροπή, ἀνατρέχω and the phrase ἄτρεπτος διατελέω in both. In addition, Philo's exegesis of Deut 23:13 and Ex 12:11 in *Leg.* 3 makes the link manifest:
> For God would have us gird up our passions, not wear them flowing and loose. So at the crossing over (διαβάσεως) from them, which is called Passover, He bids that their "loins should be girded up," in other words that their desires should be restrained. (*Leg.* 3.153)

[720] Cf. the idea of the necessary nature of pleasures at *Leg.* 2.17 (n. 695 on p. 219). That the change which is meant in *Leg.* 2.33–34 is directed towards the bodily passions is evident based on 2.28, 31: in the former the mind is said to give up its own objects, embrace the passions and allow itself "to be drawn by bodily necessity;" in the latter Philo equates the mind's trance (ἔκστασις) and change (τροπή) with its sleep: "it falls into a trance when it ceases to be engaged with the noetic objects appropriate to it."

Her. 68 is easy to read in light of *Somn.* 1.138–139. The return by souls that long for mortal life instead of escaping from the body as from a prison can—in spite of the intervening "vacations" between lives—be described *precisely* as remaining voluntarily in the prison of the body. Our interpretation of *Her.* 68 then hinges on whether we assume Philo to mean the same thing or something different when he speaks of the prison of the body and uses the same word in a similar context.[721] In my view, an assumption of consistency should be given precedence if there is no evidence to the contrary. In other words, thinking that Philo does *not* mean transmigration of souls in *Her.* 68 requires the additional supposition that he employs the notion of the imprisonment of the soul in the body in markedly different schemes of individual eschatology.

I think it is rational to try and find a common line of interpretation for all of Philo's references to the soul's involuntary stay in the body, whether the latter be called a prison, grave, foreign land, dwelling, container or garment. He hardly means a different thing with each.[722] Particularly in connection with the metaphor of a foreign land the *entry* thereto is often mentioned in a manner which leaves no room for doubt that the soul's pre-existence and thus its concrete entry into and exit from the body is meant.[723] In that case the exit is *not* a purely spiritual transformation—and this clearly also applies to the soul's "exhumation" (from its grave) and "remission" (from the prison) in *Somn.* 1.139. Likewise, in *Leg.* 2.55 the soul's "disrob[ing] itself of the body" seems to lead to salvation.[724] The various things that symbolize the body may serve to convey somewhat different emphases or aspects. Similarly, in addition to the body, the passions too can be called the grave (*Leg.* 1.106) or prison (*Deus* 111) of the soul without any significant change in meaning; in my view involuntary embodiment is implied in such cases as well.[725]

---

[721] The congruence of the other section in *Her.* where Philo (somewhat indirectly) calls body εἱρκτή (§§ 272–274) with *QE* 2.40 was noted above (pp. 218–19).

[722] The exception is that the *first* incarnation, although perhaps not based on the will of the souls, seems not to be of a penal nature; for the sages it is perhaps the only embodiment. See *Conf.* 77–78 (p. 54).

[723] For the entry into the foreign land–body, see, e.g., *Her.* 274, *Somn.* 1.180–181, *QG* 3.10, 11. In *Ebr.* 99–101 Philo speaks of staying in "the camp of mortality and confusion," i.e., in "the city of the body and mortal life" where the mind is "like a prisoner in the gaol" (ἐν δεσμωτηρίῳ καθειργμένος). §101 is further discussed below, p. 233.

[724] Philo writes, "The soul that loves God, having disrobed itself of the body and the objects dear to it and fled abroad far away from these gains a fixed and assured settlement in the perfect doctrines of virtue."

[725] In *Leg.* this is demonstrated by Philo's stating in 1.108 that the soul has been buried in the body synonymously to the entombment in the passions at 1.106; both are descriptions

Coming back to *Her.* 68, how should the concept of *voluntary prison term* be understood? We may first note that it has a Platonic model, *Phaedo* 82e–83a where Plato in the first instance twice calls the life in the body εἰργμός (= Philo's εἱρκτή; both from εἵργω) and then says the soul is the "chief assistant" in its confinement through its desires.[726] As this is something that only the philosopher understands, the voluntary nature of the imprisonment becomes understandable as the soul's *delusion*: it does not realize its role in its own incarceration, probably not even the incarceration itself.[727] In *Deus* 111 Philo calls the mind a *lover* of the body and the passions (φιλοσώματος καὶ φιλοπαθής[728]), thus suggesting voluntariness, and yet he says it *is cast* (εἰσάγεται) into the prison of the latter. This closely resembles *Somn.* 1.138–139, where too the attainment of the *desired* object leads to being imprisoned. Likewise, the rush to rebirth at *Cher.* 114 cannot be understood as anything but voluntary. In *Deus* Philo also speaks of being trapped by a bait (see below)—an apt image of delusion. On the other hand, pleasures and lusts can also be called "jailers" (*Migr.* 9) in the prison of the body, which refers to their acting to *prevent* the mind's liberation from it (certainly a fitting role for the passions as well). They do this by enticing the mind either to stay in the body, or to enter it, as in the *Deus* passage. There are no indications of this being a protological account. On the contrary, Philo's statements are universal; any soul is in potential danger of being imprisoned: the real prisoners are "those whose character of soul is condemned by nature, as full to the brim of folly" etc. (*Deus* 112). Further, "some do not see the nature of this penalty, but, being *deluded* (ἀπατώμενοι) into counting the harmful as beneficial" enter the prison gladly—and even hope to attain an office there (§113). Philo admonishes his own soul:

> Follow indeed, if thou canst, a life-purpose which is unchained and liberated and free. But, if it be that thou art snared by the hook of passion,

---

of the death of the soul (see above, pp. 57–64, esp. 59). See also Appendix 1 for the convergence of the body and the passions in the *Post.* and *Congr.* passages there discussed.

[726] See a longer quotation above, p. 93.

[727] It is worth noting that this means that the talk of imprisonment represents *an outsider's view*—not necessarily of one who is free from the body but of one who at least understands the reality of the confinement.

[728] Another *verbum Philonicum* with no occurrences before Philo (TLG, Aug. 2014), 23 in him, six in Eusebius, five in Didymus; the rest are individual instances in six different authors.

endure rather to become a prisoner than a prison-keeper. (*Deus* 114–115)[729]

Here one can see that, although the prison is the same, be it of the body or the passions, these in themselves are not fully identical, because the body is the natural container, the passions, containing forces. Thus, *Her.* 68 and *Deus* 111–115 can be interpreted meaningfully if it is assumed they speak of the state the reincarnating soul finds itself in. On the other hand, if one assumes reincarnation is *not* part of the picture, then the validity of using the image of the prison to indicate the body- and passion-loving soul's state is reduced; the exit from it has then to correspond to a mental change, rather than the exit from the body. In addition, the allusion to the *Phaedo* in *Her.* 68 becomes awkward: did Philo refer to Plato's thoroughly reincarnational text but hope—without stating it—that his audience would not think he endorsed the doctrine?

The soul has another delusion conducive to imprisonment: that it is the possessor of everything it perceives through the senses and that it self-sufficiently exerts its own powers. We already encountered this phenomenon above as a leading theme in *Cher*. In his comments on Gen 15:9 in *Her.* Philo writes:

> For which of us does not assert that soul and sense and speech, each and all are his own possession (κτήματ'), thinking falsely (οἰόμενος) that to perceive, to speak, to apprehend, rest with himself alone. (*Her.* 107)

The few who are wise dedicate these three to God (§108), but, says Philo,

> [t]hose, then, who assert their ownership of the three, receive the heritage which their miserable state deserves—a soul malevolent, a chaos of unreasoning passions, bound by a multitude of vices: sometimes mauled by gluttony and lust as in a brothel, sometimes, as it were, shut in a prison (ἐν δεσμωτηρίῳ καθειργμένην) by a multitude of evil deeds, having as its mates malefactors, not of human kind, but habits which an unanimous judgement has declared worthy of arrest. (*Her.* 109)[730]

---

[729] Philo continues, "For through suffering and groaning thou shalt find mercy," whereas aspiring to become a guard in the prison will lead to "its thraldom [being] over thee for the rest of your life" (§115). Colson translates "for ever," but I think the meaning of πάντα τὸν αἰῶνα is here the same as that of ἅπαντα τὸν αἰῶνα at *Mut.* 185 (Colson there renders the phrase in the only sensible way as "the whole length of life"). As to the meaning of being a prison-guard, I take it to mean so an intense indulgence in passions and, by implication, sense-pleasures, as to make them virtually one's "vocation."

[730] I have made exceptionally many small changes to Colson's translation, but they mainly concern the choice of individual words the general idea being unaltered.

The soul's being shut in a prison with bad habits resembles the description of the reincarnating souls of *Somn.* 1.139. This time, however, the body is nowhere to be found—explicitly, that is. But there are indications that the whole "heritage" of those who here stand accused is the bodily life, and that in many incarnations. We may first note that in both texts there is first a desire besetting the soul and then its imprisonment. It therefore seems quite possible that *Her.* 109 is a reference to the two phases of the reincarnation process: being in the discarnate state ("with the incorporeals" in *Cher.* 114) but nevertheless having sensual desires and being drawn to a new embodiment by them, and the actual imprisonment in the incarnate state.[731]

Second, the phenomenon which both being mauled and imprisoned serve to specify in *Her.* 109 is being "bound by a multitude of vices." This expression (πλήθει κακιῶν κατειλημμένην) has one close parallel in Philo:

> For to him who is not as yet firmly bound by vices (ὑπὸ κακίας καταληφθέντι) it is open to repent and return to the virtue, from which he was driven, as to his fatherland. But [he] that is weighed down and enslaved by that fierce and incurable malady ... is thrust forth to the place of the impious. (*Cher.* 2)

Given our previous discussion of the expression "place of the impious," ἀσεβῶν χῶρος, identified with the body in *Congr.* 57, 59, we have reason to suspect a reference to incarnation in the *Her.* passage.[732] That both in *Congr.* 57 and *Agr.* 89 evil deeds (ἀδικήματα), which in *Her.* 109 imprison the soul, are mentioned as playing a role in incarnation (an active one in *Agr.*), points in the same direction.[733] Thus *Her.* 109 can with a significant degree of harmony be read together with passages that refer to reincarnation more openly.

The next example of imprisonment is found in a passage already referred to a few times above. Commenting on God's promise to Jacob in Gen 28:15 to bring him "back to this land" Philo writes,

> For excellent would it have been for the intellect to have remained in its own keeping and not have left its home (ἀποδημῆσαι) for sense-perception; but it does have the "second-best voyage" of returning to itself again. But perhaps in these words he hints at the doctrine of the immortality of the soul: for, as was said a little before, it forsook the heavenly place and came

---

[731] The soul's prostitution in *Her.* 109 and "the familiar and accustomed ways" in *Somn.* 1.139 find common ground in a passage already mentioned, *Spec.* 1.282 (see the quotaton above, p. 138). Only in these two passages (*Somn.* and *Spec.*) are σύντροφος and συνήθης combined in Philo so tightly in expressing something negative.
[732] See above, pp. 65–68.
[733] For the *Agr.* passage, see p. 182. Cf. also *Her.* 186 where God gives freedom from "the cruel and bitter tyranny of passions and evil deeds."

into the body as into a foreign land. But the Father who gave it birth says that he will not permanently disregard it in its imprisonment (καθειργμένην), but will take pity on it and loose its chains, and with certainty escort it free to its mother-city. (*Somn.* 1.180–181)[734]

Philo above indicates that this passage should be read together with what he says earlier in the treatise. The reference is, no doubt, to 1.41–46, where Jacob's coming to Haran is explained:[735] Haran is "a sort of mother-city of the *senses*" (1.41), and the one "who sets forth on a journey (ἀποδημία) from the place of knowledge ... is without fail received by the senses" (1.42). Philo continues:

> For our soul moves by itself: often (πολλάκις μέν) when it has entirely stripped itself of the encumbrance of the body and escaped from the noisy pack of the senses, and often (πολλάκις δέ) when clad in these. What is apprehensible mentally only is the lot of its unclad movement, while to that which takes place with the body fall the objects of sense-perception. If therefore someone is absolutely incapable of exclusively holding converse with the understanding, he finds in sense-perception a second refuge (καταφυγήν), and anyone who becomes balked (ὅστις ἄν σφαλῇ)[736] of the noetic things is forthwith dragged down (κατασύρεται) to those of sense-perception. For the "second-best voyage" is always for those who are not able to enjoy the good voyage to the sovereign mind. (*Somn.* 1.43–44)

Philo then emphasizes the need to minimize the duration of the stay

> in the territory of the senses ... [a stay caused by] the necessities of the body to which he is tied, [for] it is in the city discerned by the mind (ἐν τῇ νοητῇ πόλει) that a long era and life is in store for him. (*Somn.* 1.45–46)

My interpretation of *Somn.* 1.41–46 and 1.180–181 is that both passages contain a description of the mind's incarnation and the eventual return to incorporeal existence. Additionally, 1.43–44 elaborates on the time in-between. But also 1.181 indirectly touches on the interval in at least two

---

[734] Of the earlier references to this passage the only one longer than a mention is on p. 42 where the focus is on the mind's original encounter with the senses.

[735] The mention of *forsaking* the heavenly place (1.181) in fact points to 1.61, where we read, "What Haran is and why the one who *leaves* the Well of the Oath comes to it, has been made evident" (i.e., in 1.41–45). The verb ἀπολείπω occurs in both 1.61 and 1.181, and the identification of the well with heaven is clear. It *has* been made already at 1.24, 39, 40, but in them heaven, although incomprehensible, is rather presented as a region of the physical cosmos than as the metaphysical origin of the mind.

[736] I think Whitaker's/Colson's "a man who has been balked" needs correcting. Not only does it seem improper to speak in terms of man, woman or human, since there is a fair chance we are dealing with the inter-incarnational state, but also the aorist tense becomes misrepresented by the English perfect. The aorist, together with the swift downfall, gives the impression of a fairly rapid pace of events.

ways. It states salvation will come about "with certainty" (ἀσφαλῶς); i.e., there is now no danger of the soul being balked as (often?) before (σφαλῇ at 1.44).[737] And it speaks of the intellect being imprisoned and in chains before being saved, which corresponds to being tied to the necessities of the body in 1.46. [738]

When looking for commonalities between these passage and those discussed in Ch. 3, it is hard not to see a link between the words καθειργμένην and δεσμά of 1.181 and the δεσμωτήριον and εἱρκτῆς of 1.139.[739] There are also notable links to *QE* 2.40: it is hardly to be questioned that "heavenly place" and "mother-city" (1.181) as well as the "land of your fathers" (1.45) and the "noetic city" (1.46) mean the same as the "divine place" and "holy and divine city" of *QE* 2.40, from which some souls do not return.[740] Another link is being dragged down (κατασύρω/ὑποσύρω) in the event of an unsuccessful ascent. At this point (1.44) Philo may even have been thinking of his exegesis of Ex 24:12 in *QE*; at least Ex 24 was in his mind just a little later (1.62) when he has moved onward in his list of points to be clarified to the meaning of the "place" in Gen 28:11. He offers three meanings the middle of which, the divine Logos, stems from Ex 24:10: "And they saw the place, there where the God of Israel stood."[741] This sense is then in 1.68–71, 115–119 applied to Gen 28:11.

My conclusion, based on the above discussion, is that in all the passages mentioned Philo moves in a landscape which he had consistent in his mind. He does use different names and images for things but he does so without contradicting himself. It is on these grounds that *Somn.* 1.41–46, 180–181 can be seen to contain references to and descriptions of reincarnation, even if they are veiled for those who are not knowledgeable of *how* Philo speaks of rebirth. I should like to add that it is hardly a coincidence that the accounts *are* obscure. Their obscurity regarding reincarnation

---

[737] The adverb πολλάκις could also be translated "many times." Cf. *Phaedo* 95d where Socrates restates Cebes's view that from the viewpoint of the fear that the soul will be destroyed at death "it makes no difference ... whether a soul enters into a body once or many times (πολλάκις)." Similarly *Meno* 81c.

[738] The word used in 1.46, σύνδετος, Philo has a tendency to use for the body in contexts that are conducive to the idea of rebirth. See below, pp. 236–38.

[739] Philo surely remembered at 1.181 what he had written in 1.139, since he refers to 1.41–46 as "a little before (μικρῷ πρότερον)."

[740] That πατρίς and μητρόπολις are synonymous, as far as the home and destination of souls are concerned, is clear from *Conf.* 78 where both occur. I would also suggest that a connection existed in Philo's mind between the latter and the verb μετεωροπολέω which is used in corresponding contexts—notably in *Somn.* 1.139.

[741] In *QE* 2.39 those who ascended to the mountain migrated "to a holy and divine place, which is called by another name, Logos."

allows them to be understood meaningfully also in other terms, e.g., as ethical homilies on right conduct. In any case, if the results of the earlier chapters are accepted, i.e., that the direct evidence of Philo's approval of the tenet in certain texts is sufficient and that his other views make his endorsement thereof plausible, then the question of whether the doctrine is seen to be an interpretative key to other texts becomes one of consistency, both of Philo and of his student.

As for Philo, this consistency concerns both views and their expression. Do his views vary? If he uses the same terms time and again in similar contexts, that certainly bespeaks consistency. Let us take another example. In Ex 33:7 Moses "took his tent and pitched it outside the camp, far from the camp," which inspires Philo to write,

> Under this figure he suggests that the Sage is a pilgrim (μέτοικος) who travels (μετανάστης) from peace to war, and from the camp of mortality and confusion to the divine life of peace where strife is not, the life of reasonable and happy souls. (*Ebr.* 100)

The camp symbolizes "the life of the body" (§99); the term is almost the same as in *Gig.* 14 where "the life in the body" in practice refers to the cycle of reincarnation, and thus leaving that camp for "the divine life" amounts to salvation.[742]

Continuing with the theme of going out, Philo moves to Ex 9:29, "As soon as I leave the city, I will spread out my hands to the Lord, and the sounds will stop." The speaker here, says Philo, is "the mind pure and unalloyed," and,

> while it is cooped up in the city of the body and mortal life, it is cabined and cribbed and like a prisoner in the gaol (ἐν δεσμωτηρίῳ καθειργμένος) declares roundly that it cannot even draw a breath of free air. (*Ebr.* 101)

Given the terminological matches there is no reason to think Philo is describing something essentially different than reincarnation in this passage. Once liberated, the mind is then able to employ "its active powers so that the clamours of the passions are at once restrained" (§101). That their

---

[742] *Gig.* μετὰ σωμάτων βίος, *Ebr.* μετὰ σώματος βίος. The difference simply stems from the fact that in *Gig.* souls (in plural) are spoken of, in *Ebr.*, a soul in singular. It may be noted that in *Ebr.* 99 Philo states, "that camp the mind is wont (εἴωθεν) to leave [when] filled with the divine (θεοφορηθείς)," which should be taken to refer to moments of contemplation rather than permanent salvation. It may well mean such temporary exaltation; the idea that a soul at first experiences degrees of the divine only momentarily while still being bound to reincarnation introduces no logical contradiction. In, e.g., *Migr.* 190 a foretaste of the "migration hence" is said by Philo to be achievable during sleep and contemplation (see above, pp. 206–8).

outcries no longer "confuse the ears of the perfect Sage, who has passed elsewhere and resolved no longer to dwell in the same city as [the passions]" (§103) is undoubtedly a reference to the ascent of the mind to God and permanent salvation. Moreover, the implication that the passions were confusing to the sage at an earlier stage is, in my view, tantamount to the aspirant's desire for God not yet being stable enough (*QE* 2.40).

In the search for the more veiled references to reincarnation in Philo those that speak of *returning* to the foreign land/Egypt/prison etc. of the body are of great interest. One such passage is *Mut.* 173 which is part of Philo's commentary on the suspicious delight of the Pharaoh at the arrival of Joseph's brothers (Gen 45:16, §§ 170-174). Pharaoh is identified as "the pleasure-loving mind" who is dissatisfied with only welcoming "the younger sort" to his kingdom; he wants to get the "older thinking" (Jacob implied) as well (Gen 45:18, §§ 172-174). The key point is the interpretation of the Pharaoh's invitation, "come to me, taking along your father and your possessions (τὸν πατέρα καὶ τὰ ὑπάρχοντα ὑμῶν)"—"*to Egypt*," adds Philo and explains:

> come, that is, to this King of terror, who, when our patrimony and truly real goods (τὰ πατρῷα ἡμῶν καὶ τὰ ὄντως ὑπάρχοντα ἀγαθά) had in virtue of their natural liberty left the body behind in their advance, draws them back and throws them with violence into a prison (δεσμωτηρίῳ) of exceeding bitterness. (*Mut.* 173)

That Philo makes the "patrimony and truly real goods" the subject of leaving the body behind is somewhat perplexing. Yet there is no doubt these neuter plurals refer to the progress towards God represented by *Jacob*.[743] It seems, however, that a return may take place even after the mind's advancement out of the body (meaning spiritual progress, not just physical death). What does this mean? Should Philo's comparatively modest characterization of Jacob (who is *not* named) in §172 as "the older thinking (λόγος) in which the frenzy of passions has passed its prime" be understood to mean that there is a danger of a relapse? Not necessarily. It seems that the possibility of a re-imprisonment is a rhetorical device, based solely on Pharaoh's invitation as explained by Philo. It serves to remind the audience that there are forces that try to pull the soul back. In my view the emphatic refusal by "us" to accept the offer at §174 implies that the danger was not imminent.[744]

---

[743] Literally speaking, Jacob cannot return to Egypt as he has not yet been there, but in a universalizing allegory this is not an issue.

[744] The refusal has no basis in the biblical text which Philo cuts short, moving onto the next topic, true joy in Gen 17:17. Nowhere in his extant writings does Philo comment on

That δεσμωτήριον in *Mut.* 173 also refers to the body is fairly obvious based both on the passage's own logic and other factors: In the same way as in *Somn.* 1.139 the destination of the return is implied with certainty by what the non-returners condemn, in this instance the notion of "le[aving] the body behind" before being drawn back "to Egypt" implies the return thereto. It is not immediately obvious what else this could mean than a new incarnation. In my view ἔξω προεληλυθότα τοῦ σώματος does not mean an experience of incorporeity in contemplation, but rather something that is at least intended or thought to be more lasting, possibly permanent. Cf. *Her.* 68 where the combination of ἔξω and προέρχομαι appears several times: The mind "abid[ing] in the prison of the body" is contrasted with "that which, released from its fetters into liberty, has come forth outside the prison walls (ἔξω τειχῶν προεληλυθώς)" (§68); "[h]e who advances 'outside' (ὁ δὲ ἔξω προεληλυθώς) is called not only the seer, but the seer of God, that is Israel" (§78).

We can also note that *Mut.* 173 shares the following features with *Agr.* 88–89: a return to the body, termed Egypt, is envisioned; this return takes place by force, the verb βιάζω in *Mut.*, ἀνὰ κράτος in *Agr.*; and, love of pleasure plays an active role. These are not isolated or chance links, but indications of a pattern that runs through Philo's *Allegorical Commentary*— *on the Soul,* one could add—and, to perhaps a lesser extent, the *Quaestiones*: the soul is stuck in the body, and the prospect of eventual physical death does not represent the end of this state.[745]

Dying to the Life of Virtue and Drowning in the Body: the Case of Cain

In his fundamental description of the death of the soul at the end of book 1 of *Leg.* we found Philo identifying that death with *dying to the life of virtue* (1.107). To recall, Philo starts in 1.105 from the biblical expression "dying the death" (Gen 2:17) which he identifies with the death of the soul and the decay of virtue (*ibid.*), the soul's becoming entombed in and joined to a body (1.106). This is "the penalty-death [which] takes place when the

---

the rest of Gen 45 where the Pharaoh's offers *are* accepted. The next thing Philo knows of Genesis is God's promise at 46:4 to bring Jacob back from Egypt, the "Hades of passions," at *Post.* 29–31. What is noteworthy is that in *Post.* Jacob is neither named nor referred to with any of the usual epithets such as the practiser, one who toils or the supplanter. I think Earp is justified in stating, "Jacob's character of never suffers eclipse with Philo" (PLCL 10.347) and in excluding *Post.* 29–31 from his lists of passages that speak of the patriarch. But in including *Mut.* 171–172 (p. 348) he fails to see that it is a somewhat corresponding case.

[745] See above, subsection 2.3.2 (p. 106–8) for Philo's remarks on death being the end of human ills.

soul dies to the life of virtue (τὸν ἀρετῆς βίον θνῄσκῃ) and is alive only to that of wickedness" (1.107). This is a fine crystallization in ethical terms of the Philonic view of the soul's plight in the wheel of reincarnation. Let us briefly examine the way in which Philo speaks of dying to the life of virtue elsewhere. There is an interesting text in *Det.* which has also another important terminological link to *Leg.* 1.107–108 and 3.72.[746] Philo explains the fratricide by Cain (ex. Gen 4:8, 10):

> For the soul that has extirpated from itself the virtue-loving and God-loving doctrine has died to the life of virtue (τὸν ἀρετῆς τέθνηκε βίον). Abel, therefore, strange as it seems, has both been killed and lives: he is killed out of the mind of the fool, but he is alive with the happy life in God. To this the declaration of Scripture shall be our witness, where Abel is found quite manifestly using his "voice" and "crying out" the wrongs which he has suffered at the hands of a wicked yokefellow (ἃ πέπονθεν ὑπὸ κακοῦ συνδέτου). (*Det.* 48)[747]

It is worthwhile examining the *cause* of dying to the life of virtue: the eradication of the Abel principle by Cain, who is very interestingly characterized here in the same words as *the body* in *Leg.* 1.108, 3.72: Whitaker eliminates the connotation by translating σύνδετος in *Det.* as "brother," but Philo's use of this rare word (five cases in total in the Greek *Corpus Philonicum*) indicates that he employed it exclusively to mean the body; both of the two remaining occurrences speak of τοῦ συνδέτου σώματος ἀνάγκαι (*Somn.* 1.46, 110).[748]

But why is Cain, in effect, equated with the body in *Det.* 48? Philo's interpretation of Gen 4:11 later in *Det.* (§§ 96–103) seems to provide an

---

[746] These were discussed together above, pp. 61–63.
[747] Cain is said to be "ever dying to the way of life directed by virtue" also in *Post.* 45.
[748] There are at least two probable further cases in *QG*. In 2.25 (ex. Gen 7:23) Philo writes:
> But thanks should be given to the Savior and Father for this benefaction also, (namely that [Noah] received a yoke-fellow (ղլծակիցն [*ḣcakic'n*]) and one bound to him (ղկապակիցն [*ḣkapakic'n*])), no longer a ruler over him but under his rule.

Marcus retranslates the words as σύζυγος and συνδέσμιος, respectively; NBHL gives, in addition, ὁμόζυγος and συνδεδεμένος, respectively. Of these, however, the first three do not occur in Philo at all while none of the six cases of συνδέω refers to the body, which is clearly meant here. It is likely that either σύνδετος was one of the two words or that it was the only one, translated by two Armenian words as is usual. Furthermore, the mention of the body no longer ruling the mind serves as a further link to the end of *Leg.* 1, as the reverse case is mentioned in 1.106. In *QG* 2.25 the context is why Noah "remained in the ark—by which is meant the body which is pure of all passions and spiritual diseases—not yet having been enabled to become altogether incorporeal." This may be an allusion to the Noah-mind's still having to reincarnate in spite of its advanced state. The other case is *QG* 3.10 where Philo says "the mind is released from its evil bond (կապակցէ [*kapakc'ē*]), the body."

answer. There the problem demanding a solution is why Cain is "cursed from the earth." Philo writes: "the earthlike in each one of us is discovered to be accountable for our most dire misfortunes" (§98). This element consists of the body and its pleasures as well as the senses and the related passions (§§ 98–99). Philo continues (§100) that "[t]he manner in which the mind becomes 'accursed from the earth'" is indicated by the biblical words that speak of the earth's "open[ing] wide its mouth" (Gen 4:11). This is a reference to the senses (as is the case with many biblical "openings").[749] The ensuing description is worth quoting in its entirety:

> It is a cruel thing that the inlets of the senses should be opened wide for the torrent (φοράν) of the objects of sense to be poured, like a flooding river (ποταμοῦ), into their gaping orifices, with nothing to stay their violent (βίαιον) rush (ὁρμήν). For then the mind, swallowed up (ἐγκαταποθείς) by the huge inpouring, is found to be sunken to the bottom (βύθιος), unable (μηδ' ... δυνάμενος) so much as to rise to the surface (ἀνανήξασθαι) and look out (ὑπερκῦψαι). (*Det.* 100)

We recognize the Platonic motif of the body as the river, i.e., the submerged soul. Philo's most important application of this notion is, for our purposes, the description of incarnation in *Gig.*[750] We have already quoted the relevant passage, but let it be duplicated. Some souls, says Philo,

> descending into the body as though into a stream (ποταμόν) have sometimes been caught in the violent rush of its raging waters (ὑπὸ συρμοῦ δίνης βιαιοτάτης) and swallowed up (κατεπόθησαν), at other times, able (δυνηθεῖσαι) to withstand the rapids (φοράν), they have initially emerged at the surface (ἀνενήξαντο) and then soared back up (πάλιν ἀνέπτησαν) to the place whence they had set out (ὥρμησαν). (*Gig.* 13)

Because the parallelism is so strong, and since the description of incarnation in *Gig.* is one of the two close parallels of *Somn.* 1.138–139, we may hold that, unless there is evidence to show that this is not the case, Philo is speaking of the same things in each text—despite the fact that the imageries in *Det.* and *Somn.* are completely different.[751] Furthermore, the probable reference to reincarnation at *Agr.* 89 fits perfectly: there, the "bottom" of the water to which the mind sinks is explicitly stated to be the body, in the same way as in *Det.* 100 where the mind is "found to be sunken to the

---

[749] The prime example of this is the land of Haran, which means "dug" or "holes" (e.g., *Somn.* 1.41–42, *Migr.* 187–188, *QG* 4.239).
[750] See above, pp. 114–17 for an overview of Philo's versatile use of the image.
[751] Note that also the river metaphor *is* in Philo's mind when he is explaining Jacob's dream of the ladder; see *Somn.* 1.147 (above, p. 97).

bottom" where it is *not* able to do exactly what those who become discarnate in *Gig. are*, i.e., to rise to the surface—and return to God.⁷⁵²

This interpretation makes it more understandable that the somatic appellation σύνδετος is applied to Cain at *Det.* 48: he represents the mind beset by the body and the irrational parts of the soul—in other words, a corporealized one.⁷⁵³ Thus, in relation to Abel, he naturally stands for the quality or state of being so beset.⁷⁵⁴ But how can Abel, "one who refers (all things) to God" (*Sacr.* 2), be said to have been overcome by the body? The answer is in fact present in *Det.* 48; he does not symbolize an individual soul but instead "he is killed *out of* the mind of the *fool.*" That is, the body-oriented life of the fool is characterized by the absence of the Abel principle: "love of self" outweighs and overcomes "love of God."⁷⁵⁵ An Abel soul becomes a Cain.

Cain's connection with the senses, the earth, and the body is made even stronger in the sequel in *Det*. At §§ 101–103 we find notions that bring to mind the compound soul that is the slave of the senses in *Cher.* 117. Philo writes,

> So we see that God cannot but curse the godless and impious Cain, because, opening wide the dens of the compound being (συγκρίματος) he stood open-mouthed desiring greedily all the outward things, praying in his greed to be able both to take them in, and to find room for them for the destruction of Abel, the God-loving doctrine. (*Det.* 103)⁷⁵⁶

---

⁷⁵² See above, pp. 181–85 for a discussion of *Agr.* 88–89, 169, 174. Also *Conf.* 66 (see p. 84) shares this terminology.

⁷⁵³ Cf. Earp's view in PLCL 10.295: "he is occupied with the lower, mortal, earthly level of life."

⁷⁵⁴ In interpreting the same verse as in *Det.* 48 (Gen 4:10) in *QG* 1.70 Philo says that God turns away from the prayers of the evil, "considering that they are dead to true life and bear their body with them like a tomb that they may bury their unhappy soul in it." This is not directly attributed to Cain, but it is presented as the case opposite to Abel, whose voice *is* heard by God.

⁷⁵⁵ So Whitaker in his Analytical Introduction to *Det.* (PLCL 2.198) summarizes the "opposing principles" that Cain and Abel signify to Philo.

⁷⁵⁶ There is the difference that *Cher.* 114 deals with the inter-incarnational state. Despite the senses being part of the *soul* in Philo, he never spells out their role in such a sensual desire in limbo. But cf. *QG* 4.169 (ex. Gen 25:29):

> In the case of the patriarchs, giving up is said to be adding, for when they give up mortal life, they are added to the immortal life. *But the wicked person receives only death, submitting to suffering from incessant hunger for virtue—rather than from that for food and drink.*

The italicized part is my translation of Ὁ δὲ φαῦλος ἔκλειψιν ἀναδέχεται μόνον, λιμὸν ἀρετῆς ὑπομένων ἀδιάστατον μᾶλλον ἢ σίτων καὶ ποτῶν. The wicked soul's "hunger for virtue" must be understood as its *lack* thereof; Philo is playing with the double meaning of the verb ἐκλείπω, occurring in the biblical lemma, as both 'die' and 'be wanting.'

In *Det.* 163 Philo explains what he takes as a contradiction in Gen 4:14, 16, where Cain speaks of God's "driving [him] out from off the earth" and the resultant "be[ing] hidden from [God's] face." For Philo, the former means seeing God: "Were He to expel you from the earthly sphere, He will show you His own image clearly manifested." And yet this cannot be, because (Gen 4:16) "[t]hen Cain went away from the presence of God and lived in the land." Philo solves the problem by explaining v. 14 with v. 16, whereby being driven from the earth ends up meaning going away from God, and hiding from God is tantamount to living on earth: "having turned away from Him you have taken refuge (καταπέφευγας) in earth, i.e., the mortal region." Once again, we meet the notion of taking refuge in the corporeal sphere, a notion that can without contradictions be taken as an allusion to wilful reincarnation.

Philo returns to the theme of Cain's "country" in *Post*: "It is worth while to notice the country also into which [Cain] betakes himself when he has left the presence of God: it is the country called 'Tossing' (σάλος)" (§22).[757] What then follows is yet another apparent description of incarnation:

> In this way the lawgiver indicates that the fool, being a creature of wavering and unsettled impulses (ὁρμαῖς), is subject to tossing and tumult, like the sea lashed (κυμαῖνον) by contrary winds (πρὸς ἐναντίων πνευμάτων) when a storm is raging, and has never even in a dream had experience of quietness and calm. And as at a time when a ship (ναῦς) is tossing at the mercy of the sea, it is capable neither of sailing nor of riding at anchor, but pitched about (διαφερομένη) this way and that it rolls (ἀποκλίνει) in turn to either side (πρὸς ἑκάτερον τοῖχον) and moves uncertainly to and fro (ἀντιρρέπει); even so the worthless man with a mind reeling and storm-driven, powerless (ἀδυνατῶν) to direct his course with any steadiness, is always tossing, ready to make shipwreck of his life. (*Post.* 22)

Not only do the imagery of being in the danger of *sinking* under the water and the *inability* to resist the *impulses* that drive the soul towards the corporeal connect this passage to *Det.* 100, *Gig.* 13 and their parallels discussed above, but, even more importantly, the passage quoted has many close links with the description of re-sinking to the body at *Agr.* 89.[758]

---

[757] I.e., Nod. The same interpretation is given also in *Post.* 32 and *Cher.* 12.
[758] For a quotation, see p. 182. *Agr.* 89 has the following words and expressions for which a counterpart is manifest in *Post.* 22: καθ' ἑκάτερον τοῖχον, νεὼς τρόπον, ἀντιρρεπούσης, κλινομένης and κῦμα. Cf. also "the force of the passions and evil deeds blowing against the unstable soul" in *Agr.* with the "contrary winds" of *Post.* In their commentary on *Agr.* Geljon and Runia (*On Cultivation*) quote *Post.* 22 as a parallel to *Agr.* 89 and list also *Mut.* 107, 186; *Deus* 181; *Ebr.* 22; *Conf.* 23 and *Somn.* 2.13 as parallels containing "[t]he image of the waves of passion (or sense-perception) which roll over the soul or intellect and cause it ultimately to drown." The voyage of Odysseus and its Hellenistic allegorization are

There is another very close parallel to both *Post.* 22 and *Agr.* 89, in *Migr.* In the section §§ 148–155 the fact that "Lot goes with [Abraham]" (Gen 12:4), means in Philo's interpretation difficulties and a huge delay for Israel's getting out of Egypt, i.e., the soul's release from the body.[759] Philo writes,

> "Lot" by interpretation is "inclining away" (ἀπόκλισις). The mind "inclines" (κλίνεται), sometimes turning away from what is good, sometimes from what is bad. Oftentimes both tendencies are observable in one and the same person: for some are irresolute, facers both ways, inclining (ἀποκλίνοντες) to either side (πρὸς ἑκάτερον τοῖχον) like a boat tossed (διαφερόμενον) by contrary winds (ὑπ' ἐναντίων πνευμάτων), or swaying up and down (ἀντιρρέποντες) as though on a pair of scales, incapable (ἀδυνατοῦντες) of becoming firmly settled on one: with such there is nothing praiseworthy even in their taking a turn to the better course; for it is the result not of judgement but of drift (φορᾷ). (*Migr.* 148)

Philo continues that all would have been well had Lot used the opportunity to imitate Abraham and not "retraced his steps (παλινδρομῆσαι) to [ignorance] any more" (§149). As it is, however, Lot's goal is to "create obstacles that pull [Abraham] back (ἀντισπάσματα) and drag him elsewhere and make him slip in this direction or that" (*ibid.*).[760] The resulting "wandering and going around circle-wise" for forty years (§154) now seems an obvious allusion to reincarnation: As long as the Cain–Lot principle is operative in a soul, it will be tossed and overwhelmed and has to remain "in the land" (*Det.* 163, *Post.* 22) instead of swiftly escaping from the body (*Migr.* 151, 154). It is very much worth recalling that being "tossed about and sunken" is something that, in a rare statement, Philo says is the lot of the wicked soul after death in *QG* 2.61.[761]

---

mentioned as models but the notion of the body as a river of the *Timaeus* (43a–d) is not; cf. Runia, *Philo and the* Timaeus, 260–61 where *Agr.* 89 and all the parallels just named are among those listed in connection of the Platonic image.

[759] See also the discussion of *Migr.* 148–155 in Appendix 1.

[760] The words παλινδρομέω (central in both *Somn.* 1.139 and *QE* 2.40) and ἀντίσπασμα (cf. *Mut.* 173, p. 234) occur together also at *Fug.* 22 (also discussed in Appendix 1) in the speech which Philo puts to Jacob's mouth as he is fleeing Laban (and thereby Haran, the land of the senses) and which very naturally reads as a hint at reincarnation:

> [Y]ou, it seems, devised [the merriments etc. of Gen 31:27] as means of diverting (ἀντισπάσματα) me back from flight, to induce me to retrace my steps (παλινδρομήσω) for the sake of the power to cheat and mislead inbred in the senses which I had with difficulty gained strength to tread underfoot.

[761] See p. 83.

We will take one more example of the mind's drowning, this time without Cain. The objects of sense may

> flood (κατέκλυσαν) the ruling mind and press (ἐπίεσαν)[762] it to the lowest abyss (εἰς βυθὸν ἔσχατον), so that it cannot float up to the top (ἀνανήξασθαι) or rise (δυνηθῆναι ἀνασχεῖν) ever so little. (*Mut.* 107)[763]

At *Agr.* 169 the meaning of "the lowest abyss" was, based on *Agr.* 89, above judged to be the body.[764] In *Mut.* 107 the fact that the metaphor of drowning is invoked also leads us to the same conclusion: being pressed into the body most naturally stands for incarnation.[765] The possibility that the descent from a state of mystical contemplation is meant does not at all seem to fit the extreme depth of the destination. In the *Mut.* passage Philo is explaining Num 25, the unholy rites of Baal Peor and the etymology of that name which, according to him, points to the stream of sense-perceptions that pour in from outside.[766] The terminological and thematic connections with the more explicitly reincarnational passages are again so manifest that if we were to reject *Mut.* 107 being a reference to reincarnation an alternative explanation would need to be found for a large number of texts, ultimately including those analyzed in Ch. 3. If such an alternative scheme of individual eschatology were found probable, it would also have a significant impact on the validity of the conclusions reached in Ch. 3.

---

[762] This is Mangey's correction for the ἐπήεσαν of the MSS. which Colson "perhaps" prefers, although he prints Wendland's clearly inferior emendation ἀφεῖσαν. Cf. *Cher.* 2 where the one who is "weighed down (πιεσθέντα) and enslaved" is cast "to the place of the impious"—which in *Congr.* 57, 59 means the body.

[763] There is again marked overlap in vocabulary with *Gig.* 13 which has πρὸς τὴν φορὰν ἀντισχεῖν δυνηθεῖσαι τὸ μὲν πρῶτον ἀνενήξαντο.

[764] See p. 184.

[765] There are three occurrences of the expression "the lowest abyss" in Philo (who is the first to use it), the third being in *Plant.* 144 where, however, the "lowest depth" is that of ignorance and it is wine that is "like a torrent (ὥσπερ χειμάρρους) washing over the soul;" the vocabulary also includes ποταμός and ἐπικλύζω. A similar case is *Ebr.* 22 where the souls are deluged (ἐπικλύζοντες) "by excessive indulgence in food" and "submerge[d] perforce in the depths (βυθόν)." Cf. *Leg.* 3.163: the soul is "overwhelmed by [the gifts of God] as by the rush of a torrent (τῇ φορᾷ χειμάρρου τρόπον ἐπικλυθήσεται)." In my view these passages are indicative of the fact that in addition to a particular sense Philo may use words also in a general, plain sense. Cf. the case of *Fug.* 62 as the exception to Philo's specific use of παλινδρομέω (below, n. 798 in Appendix 1).

[766] In *Timaeus* 43c Plato even derives the word αἴσθησις from this event, i.e., the verb ἀίσσω (so Bury in a note to his translation; Runia, *Philo and the Timaeus*, 261 informs us that this suggestion, which is "likely to be correct," is found in Proclus *In Tim.* 3.332.6 and that Philo had already referred to this etymology in *Her.* 126 and possibly also in *QG* 3.3). Philo's ῥεῦμα in *Mut.* 107 corresponds to Plato's ῥέω.

It would be artificial to take all of Philo's descriptions of the soul's being inundated as isolated. They connect seamlessly with such reincarnational texts as *Gig.* 13–15 and *Agr.* 89 and, somewhat less smoothly, with *Timaeus* 43a–b.[767] The bigger picture which Philo—despite varying his focus—paints, must be seen. Once the soul has ended in the depths of the body, its situation is dire and escaping is not that simple. Philo's way of telling this to his audience forms a network of interrelated images and ideas which is, in my view, *easiest to understand* on the basis of an individual eschatology that includes the idea of reincarnation.

4.1.3 *The Prerequisites of Salvation*

In Ch. 2 a model of the fall and rise of the mind in Philo's thought, consisting of the following six stages, was drafted:

(1) incorporeal existence with God;
(2) incarnation;
(3) corporealization and transgression;
(4) reincarnation until the prerequisites of salvation are met;
(5) liberation from the life in the body; and,
(6) eternal incorporeal existence with God.

Although the model was in the main based on a single passage (*QG* 1.51), it has had a sustained endurance, for the subsequent discussion has failed to elicit reasons why it should be revised. In this subsection the object is to refine it by zooming in on stage four: what kind of phases will a soul go through when it builds up its capacity to fulfil the prerequisites of salvation?

I think we can with reasonable accuracy discern four different cases of the soul's failure to exit the bodily sphere in Philo's thought: (i) ignorance, (ii) unwillingness, (iii) inability and (iv) lack of God's grace. These can be regarded as driving forces of reincarnation and compared with the theoretical ones discussed earlier:[768] On the one hand, Philo cannot be said to hold any prominent doctrine of karma, and a negative attitude towards a body of doctrines or the non-attainment of esoteric knowledge are not the same as ignorance about one's state of imprisonment, which is what I first and foremost mean with (i) in this context. On the other, lack of progress towards perfection can be said to cover cases (i) to (iii). We can

---

[767] In Plato, the image of the body as a river is narrower, more physiological. See above, pp. 114–17.
[768] See the beginning of subsection 2.3.2, p. 90.

describe Philo's soteriology as synergistic: the soul needs to make progress on its own but recognize its dependence on God's grace in order to be saved.[769]

The boundaries between the cases are not clear-cut; e.g., the notion of voluntary imprisonment as discussed above accommodates them all:[770] a soul that *wants* to be reborn (case ii) on earth in order to pursue sense pleasures does *not understand* (i) the fact that when in the body it is a prisoner who *cannot* (iii) just decide to quit the bodily realm when it wants to. Such an ignorant, voluntary prisoner also cannot be the recipient of divine, salvific grace (iv) in Philo's thought. Or if a soul is not able to hold its will steady but gives in to sensual enticements, that is clearly a case of both (ii) and (iii). The numbering (i) to (iv) does, nevertheless, present the rough chronology of these factors in the sense that it is plausibly in this order that these obstacles will need to be removed in the Philonic way of thinking.[771] These four "removals" then correspond to four prerequisites of salvation: *understanding, will, ability and grace.*

When cases (i) to (iii) are related to the recurrent causes of incarnation identified above, we can note that there is no difficulty in fitting them together. The examples in the previous paragraph in fact already go to show this. The corporealized mind which has received the obligation to reincarnate as a punishment for its body-love may very well be, at first, ignorant of its deplorable state. Upon being educated it is probably at first willing and only later able to strive for progressively higher things. Ultimately, it is in Philo's view God who determines if it still has to return on earth.

4.2 Concluding Remarks

4.2.1 Some Reflections on the Results of this Study

This study has found that, beyond reasonable doubt, Philo of Alexandria accepted the tenet of reincarnation.[772] This in itself is not a new result; on

---

[769] On grace, see above, p. 98.
[770] See above, p. 226–29.
[771] I.e., in order to receive grace, the soul has to be interested in salvation and to do its part; for this to happen it needs the willingness, which it cannot have if it is not conscious that it lacks freedom.
[772] Of the definitions of "acceptance" mentioned on p. 4 the following are valid: (1) 'take or receive with consenting mind,' 'receive with favour or approval'; (2) 'receive as adequate or valid,' 'believe;' whereas "tolerate" and "submit to"—and to a lesser extent also

244   CHAPTER FOUR

the contrary, I have merely confirmed what may be called the traditional view on the matter in the modern era.⁷⁷³ What is new is that this confirmation is based on examining Philo's works and views in their entirety with the specific aim of establishing his position on the doctrine. It can now be stated that of the two scholarly quotations presented at the outset of this study the one by Schürer has proved to be very accurate; his words, closely echoing the earlier conclusions of Zeller, "transmigration of souls is in fact the necessary consequence of Philo's premises, though he seldom speaks of it expressly" are a fine crystallization of the matter.⁷⁷⁴

While thus not finding anything radically new *in Philo*, I hope to contribute to something novel *in Philonic research*: in order to hear the Alexandrian's own voice more distinctly we should be reading him with more attention to detail and willingness to draw conclusions than has been the case in scholarship related to Philo's individual eschatology. For I do not think that, e.g., his constant allusions to Plato are just meant to show his erudition; they also have a *content*. His frequent references to Plato's reincarnational passages are like signposts with—in the absence of explicit approval of the tenet—nothing written on them. We should follow them all the way to what they point at, for if we do not, we fail to exploit all the information Philo gives us.

Such an approach is by no means restricted to Philo's use of Plato or any other thinker. It also applies, and with even greater reason, to explaining Philo by Philo. By reading together passages that are similar in both vocabulary and substance and observing closely the way in which our exegete uses key terms, concepts and images we are able to at least approach the thing Philo himself failed to do: building up a description of his views of a given subject. In this study such a method has helped delineate a consistent picture of Philo's view of reincarnation.

4.2.2 *Philo's Reticence about Reincarnation*

I believe David Winston is not far from the truth when he writes,

> Philo's sparse references to reincarnation reveal a reluctance on his part to give undue prominence to a Platonic conception that was essentially alien to Jewish tradition. Hence his failure to map out in any detail the projected

---

"admit" do not seem suitable, for nothing in the evidence examined points to such reluctance as they imply.
⁷⁷³ See above, subsection 1.4.1 on pp. 9–19.
⁷⁷⁴ See above, pp. 3, 14–15.

life histories of the different types of souls and the undoubtedly deliberate vagueness which characterizes his utterances on this matter.[775]

I would like to offer a few observations that in my mind reflect Philo's "deliberate vagueness." In *Deus* 111 Philo first calls the mind "a lover of the body and the passions" but then mentions the passions only when he speaks of the soul's *entrance* to their prison.[776] I find this somewhat similar to *Post.* 156 and *Congr.* 164: the things most closely related to reincarnation (entrance or return) are said of the passions, so that one needs to do some dot-connecting in order to see that the body too, and perhaps in particular, is being meant.[777] Are we witnessing a pattern? One could also add the reincarnational main texts of Ch. 3: even in *Somn.* 1.139, and in *QE* 2.40 for sure, Philo leaves it for us to infer where the returning takes place *to*, and in a different but comparable manner, in *Cher.* 114 and fr. 7.3 Harris he does not openly explain what he means by "regeneration" and "revival." In *Agr.* 89 where the soul sinks to a body, Philo abstains from reiterating that a return is being spoken of.[778] In *Leg.* 1.105–108 he speaks of incarnation as a punishment but fails to explicitly declare that he is talking about an already incarnate soul.[779] In *Leg.* 3.252 he makes a slight change in the biblical text with the result that a reference to reincarnation seems obvious, but he draws no attention to this.[780] In all these cases, not to mention the numerous texts discussed in the present chapter, Philo leaves some detective work for his student.

I think this study has shown that that work is worth doing. After all, it does not take so much digging to unearth a coherent basic scheme of individual eschatology in Philo with reincarnation as an organic part of it. In my view, although Philo is quite silent, he *did want to communicate* to his audience also the view that souls transmigrate. His vagueness is not impenetrable. This enables us to conclude that while he in his surviving works did not want the references to reincarnation to be immediately understood by *anyone* (*Somn.* 1.139 is an exception)[781] he did not want to

---

[775] Winston, *Logos and Mystical Theology*, 42. I would, however, be more cautious about the suggested alienness to Jewish tradition. Such a notion implies that Philo was, if not the first Jew to adopt the tenet, among the first, so that we cannot yet speak of a "Jewish tradition." But the fact is that on the subject of individual eschatology in Hellenistic Judaism before Philo we do not have much to go by.
[776] See above, p. 228.
[777] See Appendix 1.
[778] Above, pp. 181–85.
[779] Above, p. 57.
[780] Above, p. 76. Cf. *Det.* 47 where he explicitly corrects the text of Gen 4:8.
[781] Yet we must acknowledge that we do not know to whom Philo's treatises were originally available. Nothing can be deduced from their finally ending up in Christian hands, for the Jewish rebellion in Alexandria in 116–117 CE led to the annihilation of

hide his position so well that *nobody* can find it. Indeed, the history of Philonic scholarship on this issue bears testimony to precisely this: some scholars have found his references, others have not—or they have considered them isolated or anomalous. The question then becomes, can we better understand Philo's anthropology, ethics, soteriology and individual eschatology with or without reincarnation, and, if without, what is the more probable alternative.[782]

The reasons for Philo's reticence about explicitly speaking of reincarnation would merit a study of its own. Here only some preliminary thoughts can be offered. I think we ought to note that Philo must have thought he had a model for his lack of explicitness, the Bible: Moses does not explicitly speak of reincarnation in the way Plato does, and in this sense Philo had to dig the notion *out of*, or—as some might say—read it *into*, Scripture. He himself felt free to write about reincarnation in ways that are *more* explicit than Moses's. That was, in fact, his job: making accessible to others what he saw as the hidden, allegorical truth.

Yet he did not place reincarnation in plain sight. Winston's view that reincarnation was "essentially alien to Jewish tradition" would be a good explanation.[783] But, as I already pointed out, the concept of "tradition" is problematic here, because we have no knowledge of the history of the idea of reincarnation among Alexandrian Jewry.[784] What we do know, however, is that Philo's allegorical method had its opponents.[785] His reincarnational interpretations of the Pentateuch are a product of that method.[786] And reincarnation was apparently not the only subject on which Philo kept a low profile. Winston also names "the conception of the world as a rational divine being" and his "theory of creation" as such topics.[787] Philo's writings

---

almost the entire Jewish population of the city. Any assumption about the availability of the works in normal conditions loses its validity in such circumstances.

[782] With this I do not mean that anyone who regards Philo's belief in reincarnation as implausible should be able to come up with an alternative scenario before her or his view can be considered. It will be sufficient to demonstrate weaknesses in the methods or conclusions of this study that are serious enough to call the main argument into question.

[783] Winston, *Logos and Mystical Theology*, 42.

[784] Above, n. 775 on p. 245.

[785] See David M. Hay "References to Other Exegetes," in *Both Literal and Allegorical: Studies in Philo of Alexandria's* Questions and Answers on Genesis and Exodus, ed. David M. Hay; BJS 232 (Atlanta: Scholars Press, 1991), 81–97, pp. 86–87 on Philo's attacks on literalists in the *Quaestiones*. He surmises that the reason Philo bothered to report such views was perhaps that "they were extremely important to some members of the Jewish community in Alexandria and Philo felt he had to denounce them."

[786] Indeed, the *Allegorical Commentary* and the *Quaestiones* stand out from the rest of Philo's *oeuvre* in this study. The *Exposition of the Law* has made its lesser contribution.

[787] Winston, *Logos and Mystical Theology*, 31, 47–48. Cf. Mangey's comments above, p. 12.

contain references to the initiated, mysteries, hidden knowledge and oral tradition.[788] These considerations favor the possibility that reincarnation was for Philo an esoteric teaching.[789]

4.2.3 *Further Work*

Although the main question has been answered, much work remains in clarifying the details of the Philonic understanding of reincarnation and Philo's individual eschatology more broadly. Some issues will most probably never be fully solved unless there are discoveries of treatises that are now considered lost. Below are some examples of issues that merit further research.

How detailed an account of reincarnation can eventually be uncovered in Philo's allegory of the soul? For instance, do the patriarchs represent not only different *ways* of reaching God (e.g., *Mut.* 88) but also stages? Or do other biblical figures, e.g., Adam, Cain, Abel, Seth and Noah have a precise, consistent role in Philo's allegories in terms of the prerequisites of salvation and the driving forces for reincarnation?[790] How consistent and detailed palette of reincarnational *vocabulary* did Philo have?[791] How and why do *individual souls* enter the cycle of reincarnation: do they all fall

---

[788] A gross listing of almost 150 passages dealing with themes potentially related to esotericism such as initiation, mysteries, oral tradition, graded teachings, ignorant masses, sensitive matters and the ability to keep silent can be presented as follows: *Leg.* 2.27, 57, 3.3, 27, 71, 100, 219; *Cher.* 16, 32, 42, 48–49, 94; *Sacr.* 60–62, 131; *Det.* 77, 79, 102, 122, 128; *Post.* 118, 131, 173; *Gig.* 54, 57; *Deus* 61; *Agr.* 9, 18, 25; *Plant.* 26, 52, 79, 127; *Ebr.* 88, 146, 189, 198; *Sobr.* 20; *Conf.* 140, 149; *Migr.* 29, 46; *Her.* 76, 295; *Congr.* 19, 27, 105, 121, 180; *Fug.* 19, 85, 97–98, 146, 160, 179; *Mut.* 60, 138, 213; *Somn.* 1.6, 82, 164, 191, 226, 2.3, 78; *Abr.* 122, 147, 200; *Ios.* 59, 90; *Mos.* 1.4, 62, 190, 2.71, 153; *Decal.* 1, 41; *Spec.* 1.25, 200, 2.50, 164, 231, 3.6, 40, 134, 178, 4.47, 60, 107, 148, 150; *Virt.* 10, 147, 178; *Praem.* 24, 62, 121; *Prob.* 2–5, 14, 23, 63, 158; *Contempl.* 25, 28; *Prov.* 2.31; *QG* 3.5, 32, 43, 4.4, 8, 21, 35, 47, 49, 102, 107, 133, 168, 194, 195, 216, 245; *QE* 2.34, 51, 52, 116, unidentified fr. 14 (PAPM) = 20 PLCL.

[789] The differentiation of people according to their level of understanding is in any case inherent in the very idea of allegorical exegesis. The case of reincarnation in the Kabbalah is perhaps a somewhat comparable case: The doctrine initially faced the opposition of mainstream Jewish theology and philosophy, but in its first known literary exposition in the *Sefer ha-Bahir* (12th cent.) it was presented as a self-evident notion, and yet taught as a mystery to initiates only (Gershom Scholem, *Origins of the Kabbalah*; translated by Allan Arkush (Princeton: JPS, 1987), 188, 191–94; *Oxford Concise Dictionary of World Religions*, s.v. *gilgul*). In both Philo and the Kabbalah we thus find the combination of being opposed and yet being apparently unproblematic for the proponent—although for Philo we have no evidence of contemporary opposition to reincarnation specifically. These facts seem to favor an assumption of a *limited* availability of the literary material in both cases.

[790] See n. 526 on p. 164 on the chain Seth–Noah–Abraham–Moses in *Post.*

[791] See pp. 215–16.

separately or is there some notion akin to *original sin* in Philo?⁷⁹² What role and weight can *monadization* ultimately be given in Philo's thought? How does Philo's *soteriology* connect with his *cosmology*: what is the significance and role of the ether or the world of ideas? Do all souls reach the same "altitude" or proximity to God upon being saved? Are some souls incurable like in Plato? If so, what is their fate—can Winston's suggestion of an endless series of reincarnations be upheld for them or do they face, e.g., annihilation?

With certain exceptions, not much attention has been paid in this study to the question of the extent to which Plato's heritage reached Philo directly. What is the role of *Platonist tradition*? How does Philo align himself within Platonism regarding reincarnation?⁷⁹³ What is his own contribution? What about *later Judaism*: What is to be thought of Josephus's remarks about the soul's imprisonment in the body, its being transferred to a new body or being born again?⁷⁹⁴ Some scholars have taken these as references to reincarnation.⁷⁹⁵ Are they correct and what is the relationship between these views and Philo's? What about the "second coming" of reincarnation within Judaism, in the Kabbalah: is it an independent phenomenon or can

---

⁷⁹² Philo's words in *QE* 1.23 might be relevant to this question: "Into every soul at its very birth there enter two powers, the salutary and the destructive." What is this "birth"—the creation of the individual soul or a physical one?

⁷⁹³ E.g., it was noted that Plato's reincarnational image of "changing into animal form" is present in Philo but absent from his allegory of the soul. How was this image used by Platonists? Did Philo anticipate the development in later Platonism that found animal reincarnation unacceptable? See the references in Runia, *Philo and the* Timaeus, 348 and also in Winston, *Logos and Mystical Theology*, 36 who takes Aristotle's criticism of "the Pythagorean notion that 'any soul can find its way into any body'" (*De anima* 407b22) as directed against reincarnation in animal bodies.

⁷⁹⁴ See *BJ* 2.163, 3.373; *AJ* 18.14; *CA* 2.218.

⁷⁹⁵ Ed Parish Sanders, *Judaism: Practice and Belief 63 BCE–66 CE* (London: SCM Press, 1994), 300; Lester L. Grabbe, "Eschatology in Philo and Josephus," in *Death, Life-After-Death, Resurrection and The World-to-Come in the Judaisms of Antiquity*, ed. Alan J. Avery-Peck and Jacob Neusner; vol. 4 of *Judaism in Late Antiquity*, ed. Alan J. Avery-Peck, Jacob Neusner and Bruce Chilton; HO 1.49 (Leiden: Brill, 2000), 163–85, p. 176; John J. Collins, "Eschatology," *The Eerdmans Dictionary of Early Judaism*, 594–97, p. 596; Casey D. Elledge, "Resurrection and Immortality in Hellenistic Judaism: Navigating the Conceptual Boundaries," in *Christian Origins and Hellenistic Judaism: Social and Literary Contexts for the New Testament*, ed. Stanley E. Porter and Andrew W. Pitts (Leiden: Brill, 2013), 101–133, p. 112. Sanders regards reincarnation as Josephus's flirting with his audience. Erkki Koskenniemi, *The Old Testament Miracle-Workers in Early Judaism*; WUNT 2.206 (Tübingen: Mohr Siebeck, 2005), e.g., pp. 269, 278–79, denies such a *tendency* in Josephus with regard to biblical miracles, and states that while he is cautious about *political* issues, he does not tone down *religious* phenomena. In Koskenniemi's view "[a] majority of the Graeco-Roman people had an interest in Eastern, esoteric wisdom;" Josephus "did not write for the sceptics."

the "gnostic" and Neoplatonist influences which Scholem repeatedly mentions have something to do with Philo?[796] Finally, with regard to *Christianity*, does the fact that both Clement of Alexandria and Origen were accused of believing in reincarnation by Photius have any connection to their Jewish predecessor?[797]

---

[796] Scholem, *Origins of the Kabbalah*, e.g., pp. 66–67, 96, 153–54, 176, 210, 228–31, 264–65, 320, 363, 415, 446. With this I am not implying any definite relation between the "Gnostic" views and Philo.

[797] See above, n. 30 on p. 11. It seems that the charges were not *based on* the association of these Platonist church fathers with Philo, as the latter is not accused of espousing the doctrine. It is possible, however, that Philo was dealt with in a less specific manner because he was a Jew. In any case, Photius's characterization of Philo cannot be called flattering.

APPENDICES

Appendix 1. *Philo's Use of* παλινδρομέω

The six occurrences of παλινδρομέω besides *Somn.* 1.139, *QE* 2.40 and *Fug.* 62 are discussed below in order to determine whether Mansfeld can in "Middle Platonist Cento," 144 be said to be right in his assertion that the verb usually "refers to the return to the body" and, if so, in what sense this is true.[798]

1. *Post.* 156:

Post. 155–156 (ex. Ex 15:23, 25) seems quite a clear case of desiring the bodily life:

> When He led us forth out of Egypt, that is out of our bodily passions... [the sense pleasures] ... would pull against us, drawing us on ... and we planned to return (παλινδρομεῖν) to Egypt, the refuge of a dissolute and licentious life.

In §62 Egypt is explicitly identified with the body (at §31, with passions as above). Mansfeld may be said to be correct, but the question arises: *from where* does the returning take place? What was the extent to which and the manner in which "we" had been liberated from the body by the time the plan to return was devised? There are no kind of references to physical death; the passage can be read both with and without the assumption that reincarnation is meant.

2. *Migr.* 149:

In §§ 148–155, taking Abraham as the symbol of the mind and Lot as the symbol of the irrational part of the soul, Philo describes the difficulties which the former faced when it was "abandoning Egypt, all the bodily region," because the latter "went with him" (Gen 12:4). The act of returning is in §149 described, "When [Lot] had set out to follow his steps, it would have been well for him to unlearn ignorance and not to have retraced his steps (παλινδρομῆσαι) to it any more."

Philo continues, "The fact is, however, that he comes with him ... actually to create obstacles which pull him back (ἀντισπάσματα)." Lot's return seems to lead to Abraham's being pulled back, and so (§154) the

---

[798] *Fug.* 62, says Mansfeld, is an exception. There it is good itself (τὸ ἀγαθόν) which *returns* to heaven after visiting the human kind.

journey "from Egypt, the country of the body" to "the inheritance of virtue" takes, not three days but forty years:[799] "for all that time, it wears itself out wandering and going round circle-wise (ἐν κύκλῳ περιάγων) in obedience to the 'manifold' element," i.e., Lot, who wants to "follow after lust's entire genus, including all its species" (ex. Num 11:4, the "rabble" craving Egypt). Thus Lot's return also implies bodily desires. This fits well the idea of reincarnation, as does the delay in abandoning the body because of "going round circlewise."[800]

3. *Congr.* 164:

Like in *Post.* 155–156 above, Philo here too discusses Ex 15:23–25, this time quoting in full (§163) the passage on the plight and murmuring of the Israelites who were unable to find drinkable water after crossing the Red Sea from Egypt, "out of the passions of Egypt," as Philo puts it. Some lose heart because of the uncertainty of the outcome of the struggle in the wilderness and plan to "speed back (παλινδρομεῖν) to Egypt to enjoy passion." Also in *Congr.* Egypt is explicitly linked with the body (see §§ 20–21). That in §§ 83–85 Egypt is again explicitly equated with passion(s), does not annul its identification with the body. Mansfeld's statement is surely accurate again, and reincarnation a possible interpretation. In both expressions, i.e., "out of the passions of Egypt" and "speed back to Egypt" the name of the country can be replaced with "the body" to yield an intelligible meaning, whereas replacing it with "the passions" would be tautological in the first instance. It may also be noted that, just like in *Post.*, Philo refrains from *explicit* identification of Egypt with the body *in the context of the return* thereto. Also, as in both *Post.* and *Migr.*, in *Congr.* there is no mention of physical death or afterlife, so we are not told where the returning takes place from.

---

[799] In both PLCL and PCW the "three days" is assumed to come from Gen 22:3 (the arrival of Abraham and Isaac in three days to the place where the former was supposed to sacrifice the latter), but I think it is obvious that Josh 1:11 is the source. The context is the same as in *Migr.*, reaching the promised land; inheritance is discussed in v. 15. What makes the contexts of *Migr.* and Josh particularly close is the notion of *crossing over* in 1:11, which will have suggested the Passover to Philo, and to which he alludes at §151 (and §25, see above, p. 117). The relevant parts of the Josh verses run,
> ... for yet three days and you are crossing over (διαβαίνετε) this Jordan, when you go in to take possession of the land that the Lord, God of your ancestors, gives you.... the Lord your God gives rest to your kindred, as also to you, and they too inherit the land the Lord your God is giving them. (Josh 1:11, 15)

[800] Cf. *Phaedo* 72b: reincarnation proceeds, according to Socrates, "from opposite to opposite and back again, going round, as it were in a circle (ὡσπερεὶ κύκλῳ περιιόντα)." With the opposites Socrates means the living and the dead; see Figure 3 on p. 204.

4. *Fug.* 22

Fug. 22 deals with the flight of Jacob from Laban (Gen 31:20–21), the constant opponent of the former and the symbol of, in particular, the senses and sense objects.[801] Philo's Jacob rebukes Laban for trying to divert

> me back from flight, to induce me to retrace my steps (παλινδρομήσω) for the sake of the power to cheat and mislead inbred in those senses which I had with difficulty gained strength to tread underfoot.

The destination to which Laban would have wanted to make Jacob return is the world of the senses, which in Philo comes close to signifying the body (e.g., *Somn.* 1.41–46).[802] Mansfeld's claim cannot be rejected, although the link to the body is now more indirect.

5. *Somn.* 2.233:

This passage is about Philo's curious version of Lev 16:17 quoted at 2.231: "'When [the high priest] enters,' it says, 'into the Holy of Holies, he will not be a man until he comes out.'" Philo's interpretation is universalizing and not tied to the high priest:

> If the mind is mastered by the love of the divine ... under the divine impelling force it forgets all else... . But if the inspiration is stayed, and the strong yearning grows weak, it, hastening back (παλινδρομήσας) from the divine things to the human ones becomes a human. (*Somn.* 2.232–233)

The function of the biblical quotation is to exemplify the way in which "the good person" is on the border-line of humanity and incorruption. The deficiency of the yearning as the reason for return is strongly reminiscent of *QE* 2.40.[803] The destination, the human things, is not very precise but will certainly include the bodily things. Mansfeld's view is accepted in a fairly loose sense. Here, more than in the other cases so far, the option of a description of a contemplative flight is obvious (see esp. 2.232). Yet the possibility of this being an allusion to afterlife and reincarnation cannot be excluded.

6. *Abr.* 86:

This is the only time the verb appears in the *Exposition of the Law*, but here too it is located in an allegorical explanation of Abraham's migrations (§§

---

[801] Also of appearances, unreal values, the passions, irrationality and ignorance. See PLCL 10.360–62.

[802] See above, p. 44.

[803] See section 3.3.

68–88): first, from Chaldea (astrological speculations) to Haran (the senses; or, from the great city of the cosmos into the smaller one, the self) and onto the desert (the solitary quest for God). This last migration is for the virtuous few. Philo extols Abraham's endurance: "Who would not have turned around (μετατραπόμενος) and hurried back (ἐπαλινδρόμησεν) homeward, paying little regard to future hopes, but eager to escape his present hardships?" The "land" of departure is again Haran (as in the *Fug.* passage above) and the senses are also explicitly mentioned, and so the direction of the return is again to the corporeal things, as Mansfeld says. The connection to the body is obvious but not made explicit. Afterlife is in no way hinted at, but this cannot be taken to exclude reincarnation.

To conclude: Of the six occurrences of the verb παλινδρομέω examined, in three cases Philo uses it in the context of returning to, or delaying the departure from, Egypt, a leading symbol of the body and passions in his thought. In two cases the return meant is that to Haran, the land of the senses, and once, to the human affairs. Mansfeld's statement of the verb usually referring to the return to the body is acceptable, although "the bodily sphere" would be a more precise expression. However, as far as reincarnation specifically is concerned, in none of the cases can the tenet be said to constitute clearly the most obvious frame of reference for the text. On the other hand, if the starting point of the analysis was that Philo endorsed reincarnation, then all the passages could be read as descriptions thereof. In any case we can say that there is in Philo's thought a notion of *returning to the corporeal realm* and that what seems like a technical term, the verb παλινδρομέω, is repeatedly used in that context.

Appendix 2. *The Text-critical Issues of* Cher. *114*

Below is the part of *Cher.* 114 dealing with the soul in the form printed by Cohn in PCW with his line numbers on the right and the entries of the *apparatus criticus*

πόθεν δὲ ἦλθεν ἡ	8
ψυχή, ποῖ δὲ χωρήσει, πόσον δὲ χρόνον ἡμῖν ὁμοδίαιτος ἔσται; τίς	9
δέ ἐστι τὴν οὐσίαν, ἔχομεν εἰπεῖν; πότε δὲ καὶ ἐκτησάμεθα αὐτήν;	10
πρὸ γενέσεως; ἀλλ' οὐχ ὑπήρχομεν· μετὰ τὸν θάνατον; ἀλλ' οὐκ	11
ἐσόμεθα οἱ μετὰ σωμάτων σύγκριτοι ποιοί, ἀλλ' εἰς παλιγγενεσίαν	12
ὁρμήσομεν οἱ μετὰ ἀσωμάτων σύγκριτοι ποιοί.	13

11, 12 ἀλλ' οὐκ — ποιοί om. AP **12** μετὰ om. M **13** ὁρμήσωμεν H οἱ — ποιοί om. M μετὰ ἀσωμάτων Turn.: μετὰ σώματα ἀσωμάτων AP, μετὰ ἀσώματα ἀσωμάτων GH ἀσύγκριτοι coni. Mang. ποιοί] ποῖοι codd., om. v

In what follows I will discuss three issues: (1) the correction of the two last words into ἀσύγκριτοι (Mangey, Colson, al.) ἄποιοι (Colson, al.), (2) the long omissions in AP and M and (3) the various readings attested for what Turnebus conjectured to be μετὰ ἀσωμάτων.

1. *The Two Last Words*

Colson in PLCL (2.485) states that the "second birth" of Moses in *QE* and the balance of the two clauses justify the emendation of the last two words of *Cher.* 114 to ἀσύγκριτοι ἄποιοι. I think the balance argument can be dismissed, as an antithesis exists in any case between σωμάτων and ἀσωμάτων. The first argument requires a little more detailed examination. Colson continues by stating that, alternatively, "it is possible that Philo is following the Stoic doctrine" in which παλιγγενεσία means the reconstruction of the cosmos after the periodic general conflagration. In this case the passage would be about the survival of souls through this process, and, says Colson, Cohn's reading might stand, "for the soul through this interregnum, though ἀσώματος, would still be σύγκριτος (of fire and air) and ποιός."

The option of Philo's following the said Stoic doctrine can, however, be excluded. He voices his opposition to it mildly in *Spec.* 1.208 and less mildly in *Her.* 228 ("the marvelmongers' fable about the general conflagration"). Furthermore, Philo does not use the term παλιγγενεσία for the post-conflagration reconstruction he mentions in the *Spec.* passage; instead, it is διακόσμησις.[804]

As for the conjecture ἀσύγκριτοι ('not consisting of parts'), if Philo uses it here about the soul, this is the only place where he does so. The word has only seven occurrences in three of which the meaning is 'incomparable,'[805] while in *Deus* 56 and *Mut.* 3 it characterizes the uncompounded nature of God. In *Fug.* 141 and *Somn.* 2.227 the meaning could be either; God is meant. However, Philo does refer to persons in whom the influence of the lower parts of the soul has been eradicated using similar adjectives. For example,

> for he that has an eye to a single aim only [i.e., virtue] is single (ἁπλοῦς) and unmixed (ἀμιγής) and truly smooth and level, but he that sets before him many aims for his life is manifold and mixed and truly rough. (*Migr.* 153)

The words given in Greek above, together with ἀσύγκριτος, are applied to God's nature in the *Deus* passage just mentioned (§56). Thus while these are divine attributes, they do not represent a state which a soul cannot reach. But it is important to note that if the text is to be taken in the form Colson prints it, we are necessarily dealing with a description of highly virtuous souls.[806]

On the other hand, if we take the word as it is attested in the mss., σύγκριτοι, we get a different picture. Against the context of the passage (see subsection 3.2.2) it seems that to retain σύγκριτοι and to understand it as a reference to συνθείς and συνεστώς in *Cher.* 113 is the most natural alternative as it both fits the context and allows us to stay with the MSS. Although the connection between body and soul is severed by death, the body is the only part of the five mentioned in §113 to quit the company; there is no basis in the text for assuming that the irrational parts of the soul are dissolved at death. In §§ 57–60 it is described how the mind, when it still was alone, was but half of the soul and needed to be complemented with the senses, which Philo consistently considers part of the soul, not of the body.[807] Also λόγος, though its meaning may vary considerably, is never considered part of the body by Philo. Here it is part of the irrational soul (as in, e.g., *Leg.* 1.103–104 and *QG* 1.75). Thus more than enough components are left for

---

[804] The treatise *De aeternitate mundi*, standardly included in the Philonic corpus, does have nine occurrences of παλιγγενεσία, all in the Stoic sense. The author of *Aet.* rejects the tenet. For *Aet.*, see above, the end of n. 206 (p. 62).
[805] *Det.* 29, *Gig.* 41, *Ebr.* 43.
[806] I.e., highly monadized ones. See above, pp. 40, 85–90.
[807] The latter is alleged by Burnett, "Philo on Immortality," 450 with no reference to Philo's works.

souls to be still considered σύγκριτοι after death. Colson's correction to ἀσύγκριτοι is unnecessary.

It applies to the conjectural ἄποιος as well that nowhere else does Philo use the word about the soul. It has two main uses in Philo: to describe God (*Leg.* 1.36, 51, 3.36; *Cher.* 67; *Congr.* 61) or the primal matter (or state) of the universe (*Opif.* 22; *Her.* 140; *Fug.* 8–9; *Somn.* 2.45, *Spec.* 1.328, 4.187). When occasionally used otherwise, the word has a negative tone (*Conf.* 85, *Praem.* 130). Thus ἄποιοι is not a word we would expect Philo to use even if παλιγγενεσία in *Cher.* 114 were a case of absorption in God. But if we stick to the MSS. ποιοί the word can without difficulty be interpreted in the context of *Cher.* as a reference to an egotistical sort of *individuality*; note the references to *both* particularity *and* self-centeredness in the cases of Sarai (§5) and Laban (§67). E.g., Laban is characterized as one "whose heart was fixed on particular qualities (ὁ τῶν ποιοτήτων ἠρτμένος)," Jacob as one who "discerns ... the nature which is outside class or category (ὁ τὴν ἄποιον φύσιν ὁρῶν—NB! *not* ἔχων)." Laban's egotism rouses Philo's scorn: "In each case he [in Gen 31:43] adds the 'my,' and his proud talk about himself goes on without ceasing." Cf. also this statement:

> For particulars within a class (τῶν ποιῶν) are of their nature such as to come into being and pass out of it again, but to the potencies which give their form to these particulars (τὰ ἐν μέρει) have received an indestructible existence. (*Cher.* 51)

Thus there is no need to deviate from the extant manuscripts. The word ποιοί refers to the fact that souls belong among τὰ κατὰ μέρος, the individual things that the cosmos consists of (discussed in §§ 109–112).[808]

---

[808] Cf. Runia's comments on *Opif.* 134–135 (*On the Creation*, 325–26): the epithet ἐπὶ μέρους ("individual," §135) "may also be an explication of 'partaking in quality,' [μετέχων ποιότητος, §134] since qualitative features allow individualization to be realised." The connection between having qualities and being individual is present also in the somewhat more specific way in which Philo uses the word ποιός for persons embodying a certain quality. Indeed, Colson translates it with the noun "individual" no less than five times in *Mut.* 121–122.

2. *The Long Omissions in AP and M*

The following diagram shows the readings of the various MSS.

M: ἀλλ' οὐκ ἐσόμεθα οἱ   σωμάτων σύγκριτοι ποιοί,
AP: —
GH: ἀλλ' οὐκ ἐσόμεθα οἱ μετὰ   σωμάτων σύγκριτοι ποιοί,

M: ἀλλ' εἰς παλιγγενεσίαν ὁρμήσομεν. —
AP: ἀλλ' εἰς παλιγγενεσίαν ὁρμήσομεν οἱ μετὰ σώματα ἀσωμάτων σύγκριτοι ποῖοι.
GH   ἀλλ' εἰς παλιγγενεσίαν ὁρμήσομεν οἱ μετὰ ἀσώματα ἀσωμάτων σύγκριτοι (ποῖοι).[809]

In principle it is possible that MS. M (Codex Mediceo-Laurentianus plut.10.20) retains the original reading and that the latter part of the final clause it omits, almost identical as it is with what occurs in the first ἀλλ' clause, represents an accidental duplication. On a closer examination this is, however, highly unlikely. As can be seen from the apparatus of PCW, M is clearly more closely related to A and P, which lack the first ἀλλ' clause, than to G and H which have both clauses. Now if the reading in M is original, there are two alternatives. The first one is that there first occurred an accidental duplication of οἱ μετὰ—ποιοί in an ancestor to both AP and GH, followed by an accidental omission of the first ἀλλ' clause in an ancestor to AP. But this would leave AP more remotely related to M than what GH are. Or, alternatively, G and H belong to a line that became separated from the ancestor of MAP before the duplication of οἱ μετὰ—ποιοί. Here the difficulty is that the ancestor of AP must have developed the same duplication *with* a similar error (discussed under next point) as GH but independently of them. The only sensible assumption is that the omission in AP of the first ἀλλ' clause was produced from the the reading attested in GH through haplography. Thus both the first ἀλλ' clause and the second οἱ μετὰ—ποιοί are original.

3. *The Case of (ἀ)σώματα*

In all the MSS. which have the second οἱ μετά—ποιοί there is an additional word, either σώματα (AP) or ἀσώματα (GH), before the last two/three words. The preposition μετά has many possible meanings with the accusative.[810] However, a substantivized prepositional expression such as οἱ μετὰ

---

[809] The readings in MS. L (Parisinus Graecus 433) are separately mentioned by Cohn only if they differ from H (PCW 1.xvi). Since the last ποιοί (as it surely must be read) is absent in L ("om. v[ulgatus]" in Cohn's apparatus; I have also verified this from a digital copy), it must be missing in H as well.

[810] LSJ gives the following meanings: 1. of motion, *into the middle of, coming into* or *among*; 2. of persons, *in pursuit* or *quest of*; 3. of place, *after, behind*; 4. of time, *after, next to*; 5. in

(ἀ)σώματα is to be understood as a case of ellipsis: a participle needs to be supplied in order to spell out the meaning in full. But as the participle must be able to be supplied from the context, it would in practice have to be one of either εἰμί or γίνομαι.[811] This leaves only one possible sense for οἱ μετὰ (ἀ)σώματα: "we who are among (im)material things." But what would be the meaning of οἱ μετὰ ἀσώματα ἀσωμάτων σύγκριτοι? The accusative necessarily reserves the preposition which would then lead to the highly unlikely combination ἀσωμάτων σύγκριτοι.[812] On these grounds I consider the ἀσώματα variant a corruption, and to read οἱ μετὰ σώματα ἀσωμάτων σύγκριτοι in the sense of "we, compound beings who are among corporeal bodies of (their) incorporeal archetypes" would make no sense in an account of what happens after death. This leads to the conclusion that the original reading was οἱ μετὰ ἀσωμάτων σύγκριτοι ποιοί.[813]

---

order of worth, rank, etc., *next after*; 6. *after, according to*; and, 7. generally, *among, between* (my numbering).

[811] HWS §2147k; cf. §1153c. In the original version of this study ("Reincarnation in Philo," 156–58) I opted for οἱ μετὰ σώματα in the sense of "those *after* (i.e., *in pursuit of*) bodies." I thank Professor David T. Runia for pointing out that, although possible in English, "*being after*" *something* is not proper Greek.

[812] To assume Philo uses σύγκριτος with a bare ablative genitive (ἀσωμάτων) in the meaning "to consist of incorporeals" is unsupported and would give an improbable meaning, for although the parts which the soul consists of are incorporeal, Philo nowhere calls them ἀσώματα. Μετὰ ἀσώματα ἀσωμάτων cannot be taken together, either, to yield any intelligible sense. We could, perhaps, conjecture that the original reading was μετὰ ἀσώματα σωμάτων with the meaning being "we who are among immaterial archetypes of physical bodies." This is close in sense to the reading which I, following Turnebus and Cohn, have adopted (μετὰ ἀσωμάτων), but it would lead to a narrower understanding of the incorporeals than what I deem probable (see subsection 3.2.4).

[813] By an accidental duplication of the letters τα ασωμα this would change into οἱ μετὰ ἀσώματα ἀσωμάτων κτλ., which, for its part could easily change into οἱ μετ' ἀσώματα ἀσωμάτων κτλ. and further into οἱ μετὰ σώματα ἀσωμάτων κτλ.

260 APPENDICES

Appendix 3: *Two Text-critical Issues in* QE 2.40

The following observations and suggestions pertain to sentence *d* of *QE* 2.40, which Marcus translates, "For those who have a quickly satiated passion for reflexion fly upward for only a short distance under divine inspiration and then they immediately return."[814] The first difficulty is the Armenian word correctly translated as "passion," ախտ (*axt*). In Armenian Philo, it primarily renders πάθος, in some cases νόσος.[815] It carries outright negative connotations very hard to fit into our context where something positive must be meant, because its fickleness is seen as negative.[816]

I therefore suggest that the original Greek word here was πόθος, 'longing,' 'yearning,' 'love,' 'desire' (LSJ). We would then be speaking of a "quickly sated desire," in favor of which I think there is a wealth of circumstantial evidence: First, the expression picks up the final words of the previous *solutio*, *QE* 2.39, where those who had reached God "did not fail to see God become clearly visible, but ... fulfilled their great desire (ցանկութիւնն [*c'ankut'iwnn*])[817]." Second, there are parallels to show that Philo uses the combination of "quickly sated" (վաղայագ [*vałayag*]) and "desire" (ցանկութիւն [*c'ankut'iwn*] or a cognate): In *QG* Philo begins the interpretation of Gen 24:28 by saying,

> A virtuous soul is a lover of the good and has a status that is greatly inflexible and unchanging. For when it perceives that someone is not quickly satiated with desire (վաղայագու ցանկացող [*vałayagu c'ankac'oł*]) but is constant and genuine, it rejoices and makes haste. (*QG* 4.116)

---

[814] Terian's rendering in French is the same. See above, p. 169.
[815] According to MI, ախտ (*axt*) renders the former in *QG* 2.54, 59; *QE* 1.19, 2.3; *Contempl.* 2, 6, the latter in *QG* 1.65; *Contempl.* 9, 60. NBHL also gives ἁμαρτία, κακία; ἀρρωστία, ἀσθένεια, μαλακία.
[816] Drummond, *Philo Judaeus*, 2.303 draws attention to what he calls "rational" passions that "strengthen the highest element of our being:" In *Virt.* 144 pity is the "passion (πάθος) that is most indispensable and most closely related to the rational soul." In *Virt.* 75 Moses shows his "genuine feelings (τὰ γνήσια πάθη) of goodwill for the nation" (γνήσιος also means 'legitimate' or 'lawful'). *Spec.* 1.55 speaks of "passion that hates evil and loves God" (tr. Drummond). He further lists four instances of "evil-hating passion" (μισοπόνηρον πάθος) and two of loving one's family (φιλοίκειον πάθος). What Drummond demonstrates is that the word πάθος is not unusable in positive contexts, but his examples also show that in such cases the word needs to be separately defined as something good. It seems that when alone the word unavoidably has a negative tone in Philo. In fact, this is the case also in *Virt.* 144 which Drummond quotes: the gist of what Philo says is surely that compassion is the best of the *lower emotions*; it was classified under grief by the Stoics (Chrysippus, *Fragmenta moralia* 394.17).
[817] NBHL: ἐπιθυμία, ὄρεξις, πόθος, ἔρως. This is not the only possible Armenian word that can be used to translate πόθος. E.g., in *Contempl.* 35, 48, 68 it is փափագումն (*p'ap'agumn*).

A little later, in his exegesis of Gen 24:63 (Isaac's going out "to meditate") Philo has, *inter alia*, this to say:[818]

> the character of the wise man is not quickly sated (վաղայագ [*vałayag*]) but is constant ... [and] he never departs from the company of the *logos*[819] because of his insatiable (անյագ [*anyag*]) and incessant desire (գանկութեանն [*cʻankutʻeann*]) and longing. (*QG* 4.140)[820]

In addition to these examples, the link between ἀψικορία and love or desire is present also in both the *Allegorical Commentary* and the *Exposition of the Law*.[821] The fact that ἀψίκορος occurs in two passages in connection with πάθος is logical (both words are negatively laden) and does not make the latter a feasible option in *QE* 2.40.[822] More generally speaking, the desire or love for God and things divine is very important for Philo; see, e.g. *Post.* 157; *Her.* 70; *Congr.* 105; *Fug.* 164, 195; *Somn.* 2.233, 235; *Abr.* 87; *Spec.* 4.115; *Praem.* 26; *Contempl.* 12–13; *QG* 1.51 4.46.[823] The following is an apposite example in the context of *QE* 2.40:

---

[818] In *QG* 4.139 Isaac is characterized as "desirous (գանկացող [*cʻankacʻoł*]) of wisdom [and] really a lover of God," which is just the kind of desire satisfied in *QE* 2.39 but found fickle in 2.40. The sequel in *QG* 4.140–141 confirms the relevance of these passages for interpreting *QE* 2.40: Isaac's meditation means that "the mind begins to be filled with God and divinely inspired and possessed by God." His looking up refers to the eyes of the mind "which have been educated to look up at higher and ethereal (regions) and others above heaven, and at the nature which is outside the world," the last phrase being a reference to God (and an allusion to the *Phaedrus*; see p. 171).
[819] Marcus: "conversation of speech," but in a footnote he retranslates, "ἀπὸ τῆς ὁμιλίας τῶν λόγων *vel. sim.*"
[820] Karl-Gustav Sandelin, *Wisdom as Nourisher: A Study on an Old Testament Theme, Its Development within Early Judaism and Its Impact on Early Christianity*; Acta Academiae Aboensis A.64:3 (Åbo: Åbo Akademi, 1986), 87 suggests, in connection with *Somn.* 1.50 where insatiable hunger and thirst for the truths of wisdom is mentioned, that Sir. 24:21 is behind this notion in Philo. There wisdom says, "Those who eat me will hunger for more, and those who drink me will thirst for more." The thought is certainly similar, although a common tradition is a more likely explanation than a direct connection; no instances of Philo's using Sirach are recorded by Earp in PLCL 10.
[821] See, e.g., *Det.* 118 and *Spec.* 3.79. In the catalogue of almost 150 negative qualities in *Sacr.* 32 ἀψίκορος comes right after ἐπιμανής ('mad after'), as if provoked by it (cf. *Virt.* 113).
[822] E.g. in *Legat.* 61 we read, "But they say that no pledges of love (ἐν ἔρωτι) are reliable, because love is a passion quicky satiated (διὰ τὸ τοῦ πάθους ἀψίκορον)." In *Virt.* 113 the connection between the words is more remote. Cf. the first surviving instance of the adjective, in Aristotle's *Rhetorica* (1389a): the young are "changeable in their desires (ἐπιθυμίας) and soon tiring (ἀψίκοροι) of them, they desire (ἐπιθυμοῦσι) with extreme ardor, but soon cool."
[823] Many of these are cited in this study; see, e.g., Appendix 1 for *Somn.* 2.233.

The strong yearning (ἱμέρου) to perceive the Existent One gives [the eyes of the soul] wings (πτερωθέντα) to attain not only to the furthest region of the ether, but to overpass the very bounds of the entire universe and speed away toward the Uncreate. (*Plant.* 22)[824]

Thus we change the beginning of sentence *d* of QE 2.40 into "For those in whom the *desire* (for God) is fickle ... " But there are also other issues. That this desire is "for reflection" is problematic given that the Armenian word, խորհրդով (*xorhrdov*), is the instrumental case of խորհուրդ (*xorhurd*).[825] Let us see the whole sentence in Armenian, taking into account the correction of πάθος into πόθος:

Քանզի յորս վալայագ ցանկութիւն է, եղեալ խորհրդով առ սակաւ մի ի վեր՝ թռչունք աստուածազգեստեալք՝ անդէն վալվալակի ընդ կրունկն դարձան.

(*K'anzi yors vałayag c'ankut'iwn ē, ełeal xorhrdov aṙ sakaw mi i ver' t'ṙč'unk' astuacazgestealk'` andēn vałvałaki ənd krunkn darjan*.)

The words following the comma, (եղեալ խորհրդով [*ełeal xorhrdov*]), would literally translate into as something like "having become by [using] the intellect" (~ γεγονὼς λογισμῷ), which is difficult to connect to what precedes it. They should be connected with what follows, առ սակաւ մի ի վեր (*aṙ sakaw mi 'i ver*), "for a short while upward"—but rather than "becoming upward" I propose that that the text speaks of "ascending upward," which can be read if another textual correction of one letter is made: I think that instead of եղեալ (*ełeal*) we should read ելեալ (*eleal*).[826] This change would clarify the meaning of the sentence, and it has the two-fold support of (1) the latter verb (ելանեմ [*elanem*]) appearing both in the biblical lemma being discussed as well as earlier in *QE* 2.40,[827] and of

---

[824] In *Plant.* 23 Philo speaks of "those who crave for wisdom and knowledge with insatiable persistence (ἄπληστοι διατελοῦντες)" being called upwards, and in §§ 24–25 "the mind of the genuine philosopher ... is borne upward insatiably enamoured (ἀκορέστως ἐρασθείς) of all holy happy natures that dwell on high."

[825] NBHL: λογισμός, διαλογισμός, νόημα, διάνοια, διανόημα, ἔννοια, βουλή, συμβούλιον, φρόνημα, ἐνθύμημα. MI: λογισμός, διάνοια, ἐπίνοια, μυστήριον.

[826] The participle ելեալ (*eleal*) is singular while the subject of the sentence is in plural. However, in periphrastic structures "the form of the participle remains unaltered, even in the plural" (Krause, Greppin & Slocum, *Classical Armenian Online*, section 18.2).—There is the weakness that I am assuming that a verb with the meaning 'to become' appears in both the Armenian (because of an error in one letter) and the Greek fr. (because of paraphrasis, see below) without there having been one in the original Greek. But this weakness does not make me change my mind.

[827] In "a holy soul is divinized by ascending (ելանելոյն [*elaneloyn*])." In the lemma, as in the place which I suggest the correction to, the verb is connected with ի վեր (*i ver*), 'up(ward).' It appears in Philo's exegesis of Ex 24 also at *QE* 2.29, 31, 43, 45.

(2) the notion of *ascending with the intellect* being used by Philo elsewhere. In a highly relevant parallel in *Conf.* Philo asks, "What then is the liberty which is really sure and stable?" (§94). It is the service of God, he answers, and continues that those who are engaged therein

> ascend with their intellect (ἀναβαίνειν δὲ τοῖς λογισμοῖς)[828] to the ethereal height, setting before them Moses, the nature beloved of God, to lead them on the way. For then they shall behold the place which in fact is the Logos, where stands God the never changing. (*Conf.* 95–96)

The last sentence, which is followed by a quotation from Ex 24:10, reinforces the relevance of the passage as a parallel to *QE* 2.40; "that which was beneath [God's] feet" in Ex 24:10 is interpreted by Philo as "the sense-perceptible world" (*Conf.* 96). Also the need for guidance in the ascent links *Conf.* 95 to *QE* 2.40, and calling the divine place Logos connects *Conf.* 96 to *QE* 2.39.

At the risk of adding to the number of "ingenious scholars [who] have sometimes identified and corrected mistakes in the [Armenian] translations, even where the Greek originals are not extant," I find these corrections unavoidable.[829] If they are accepted, the whole sentence *d* runs,

---

[828] Colson: "in their thoughts." This may be correct, but in *Conf.* the difference between the two alternatives is not great: this is a mental event, performed *using* the highest part of the soul. Whether or not discarnation is involved will need to be decided case by case. Cf. *Cher.* 31 (ex. Gen 22:6): Abraham wanted to "sever and consume the mortal element away from himself and thus to fly up to God with a naked understanding (ἵνα γυμνῇ διανοίᾳ μετάρσιος πρὸς θεὸν ἀναπτῇ)" (NB. ἀναπέτομαι as in *QE* 2.40). Colson now somewhat ambiguously, "fly upward to God with his understanding stripped of its trammels." See also *Abr.* 88 where the mind "with the intellect sped upwards (ἀναδραμὼν τῷ λογισμῷ) and turned its gaze upon the intelligible nature which is superior to the visible, and upon Him who is maker and ruler (ἡγεμόνα) of both alike." (Note the Platonic echoes in the "gaze" and "ruler.") My point is that the mind is in such ascents not only the subject of the rise but also the instrument thereof in the sense that it has to fulfil certain "technical" specifications such as stability in *QE* 2.40, nakedness in *Cher.* 31; in *Abr.* the ascent is preceded by being freed from the deceptions of the senses. Cf. also *Post.* 137 (ex. Gen 21), where Rebecca, i.e., the soul "enamoured of incorporeal objects has learned by use of the intellect (λογισμῷ) to strip herself completely of the body."

[829] Pontani, "Saying (Almost) the Same Thing," 127. Such criticism is healthy, and as a general rule I am in favor of textual conservatism. In the case of sentence *d* of *QE* 2.40, the Greek original is "not extant" in the sense that it seems paraphrastic (see below). While I fully admit Pontani's point (p. 128) that a translation's "consumption takes place through the target language," my own interest concerns Philo's thought world, which is why it is necessary to try and find the original text. Marcus in the PLCL Supplements suspects a misreading or corruption of the Greek original ranging from a single breathing to five letters on pp. 294 note *f*, 306 n. *a*, 309 n. *k*, 402 n. *b*, 471 n. *k* for *QG*, and pp. 8 n. *d*, 23 n. *h*, 33 n. *a*, 62 n. *l*, 88 n. *a*, 104 n. *e* for *QE*.

For those in whom the desire (for God) is fickle ascend with the intellect for a short while upwards, (being) flying ones carried by God, (and) immediately return.[830]

When this is compared with the surviving Greek text ("In some the intellect becomes fickle, in those who, after having been again carried by wings for a short while, descend right away"), my conclusion is that the latter is somewhat paraphrastic, which is not rare in the Greek fragments.[831] Sentence *f* in *QE* 2.40 in fact shows that the Greek fragment does truncate and interpret the Armenian expressions, stating as it does merely that those who do not return are happy—an attribute not mentioned in the Armenian text. Thus the italics applied to the Greek by Petit in sentences *d* and *f*, as well as the square brackets in *f*, are well placed and to be agreed with.

---

[830] It might be considered that disconnecting խորհրդով (*xorhrdov*) from the word corrected above into "desire" would put the first correction into question; after all, why could Philo not be speaking of those whose craving for God can be characterized as a mere fickle passion? Apart from the support of *QE* 2.39 and *QG* 4.116, 140, I think the most important factor speaking in favor of the correction is that the Greek fragment applies the word ἀψίκορος to something *positive* (λογισμός) like the corrected Armenian. Furthermore, the appearance of "passion" would be quite abrupt and it would not be evident that it should be understood to mean an inadequate kind of love for the divine. I am also not aware of other passages where Philo calls fickle desire for God a "passion."

[831] Within *QE*, Marcus in his notes mentions that a fragment "paraphrases" or "reads more briefly" dozens of times, and one of the latter ones is at the end of *QE* 2.40, which is an obvious case. The MS. in which our fragment of *QE* 2.40 is located (Codex Berolinensis 46), "seems to be paraphrastic" at *QE* 2.28, and also in *QG* 2.12 Marcus notes of it, "Dam. Par. paraphrases."

BIBLIOGRAPHY

Printed Primary Sources

Aeschyli Septem Quae Supersunt Tragoedias. Edited by Denys L. Page. Oxford: Clarendon, 1972.
Aeschylus. *Prometheus vinctus*. In vol. 1 of *Aeschylus, with an English Translation*. Edited and translated by Herbert Weir Smyth. Cambridge, MA: Harvard University Press, 1926.
Andronicus of Rhodes. *On Passions*. In vol. 1 of *Andronici qui fertur libelli Περὶ παθῶν (De affectibus)*. Edited by Xaver Kreuttner. Heidelberg: Winter, 1884.
Apuleius Madaurensis. *Opuscules philosophiques (Du dieu de Socrate, Platon et sa doctrine, Du monde) et fragments*. Translated with a commentary by Jean Beaujeu. Paris: Les Belles Lettres, 1973.
Aristotle. *Ars rhetorica*. Edited by William D. Ross. Oxford: Clarendon, 1959.
———. *De anima*. Edited by William D. Ross. Oxford: Clarendon, 1961
———. *De generatione et corruptione*. In vol. 2 of *The Works of Aristotle*. Translated by R. P. Hardie. Oxford: Clarendon, 1930.
———. *De la génération et de la corruption*. Edited by Charles Mugler. Paris: Les Belles Lettres, 1966
———. *Du ciel*. Edited by P. Moraux. Paris: Les Belles Lettres, 1965
———. *Metaphysica*. Translated by Hugh Tredennick. LCL. Cambridge, MA: Harvard University Press, 1933.
———. *On the Heavens*. Translated by John L. Stocks. Oxford: Clarendon, 1922
———. *Politics*. Translated by H. Rackham. LCL. Cambridge, MA: Harvard University Press, 1932.
———. *Protrepticus*. Edited by Ingemar Düring. Stockholm: Almqvist & Wiksell, 1961.
Athenagoras. *Legatio* and *De Resurrectione*. Edited and translated by William R. Schoedel. Oxford: Clarendon, 1972.
Athenaei Naucratitae deipnosophistarum libri xv. Edited by Georg Kaibel. 3 vols. Leipzig: Teubner, 1887–1890.
Athenaeus. *The Deipnosophists, or, Banquet of the Learned of Athenaeus*. Translated by Charles D. Yonge. London: Bohn, 1854.
Augustine. *City of God* and *Christian Doctrine*. In vol. 2 of *The Nicene and Post-Nicene Fathers*, Series 1. Edited by Philip Schaff. 1886–1889. 14 vols. New York: Christian Literature Publishing, 1887.

Ben Sira. *The Book of Ben Sira in Hebrew: A Text Edition of All Extant Hebrew Manuscripts and a Synopsis of All Parallel Hebrew Ben Sira Texts.* Edited by Pancratius C. Beentjes. Leiden: Brill, 1997.
Chrysippus. *Fragmenta moralia.* In vol. 3 of *Stoicorum veterum fragmenta.* Edited by Hans von Arnim. Leipzig: Teubner, 1903.
Cicero. *De natura deorum.* Translated by H. Rackham. LCL. Cambridge, MA: Harvard University Press, 1933.
———. *Somnium Scipionis: The Dream of Scipio Africanus Minor.* Translated by W. D. M. Pearman. Cambridge: Deighton, Bell & Co., 1883
Clement of Alexandria. *Le protreptique.* Edited and translated by Claude Mondésert. Second edition. Sources chrétiennes 2. Paris: Cerf, 1949.
———. *Le pédagogue,* Edited and translated by Marguerite Harl et al. 3 vols. Sources chrétiennes 70, 108, 158. Paris: Cerf, 1960–1970.
———. *Stromata.* In vols. 2–3 of *Clemens Alexandrinus.* Edited by Ludwig Früchtel, Otto Stählin and Ursula Treu. Third and second edition. Die griechischen christlichen Schriftsteller 52(15), 17. Berlin: Akademie, 1960–1970.
———. *Stromata.* In vol. 2 of *The Ante-Nicene Fathers.* Edited by Alexander Roberts and James Donaldson. 1885–1887. 10 vols. New York: Christian Literature Publishing, 1885.
Demosthenes. *De falsa legatione.* Translated by C. A. Vince and J. H. Vince. LCL. Revised edition. Cambridge, MA: Harvard University Press, 1939.
Diogenes Laertius. *Vitae philosophorum.* Edited by Herbert S. Long. 2 vols. Oxford: Clarendon, 1964.
———. *Lives of eminent philosophers.* Translated by Robert D. Hicks. 2 vols. LCL. Cambridge, MA: Harvard University Press, 1925.
Dionysius of Halicarnassus. *The Roman Antiquities: Books VIII–IX.24.* Translated by Earnest Cary. LCL. Cambridge, MA: Harvard University Press, 1945.
Empedocles. *Fragmenta.* In vol. 1 of *Die Fragmente der Vorsokratiker.* Edited by Hermann Diels and Walther Kranz. 6th editon. Berlin: Weidmann, 1951.
Epiphanius. *Ancoratus* and *Panarion.* Edited by Karl Holl. 3 vols. Die griechischen christlichen Schriftsteller 25, 31, 37. Leipzig: Hinrichs, 1915–1933.
———. *The Panarion of Epiphanius of Salamis: Books II and III, De Fide.* Translated by Frank Williams. Leiden: Brill, 1994.
Ephrem the Syrian. *In sermonem, quem dixit dominus, quod: In hoc mundo pressuram habebitis, et de perfectione hominis.* In vol. 4 of Ὁσίου Ἐφραίμ τοῦ

Σύρου έργα. Edited by K. G. Phrantzoles. Thessalonica: To Perivoli tis Panagias, 1992.

Euripides. *The Suppliants* and *Heracles*. In vol. 1 of *Euripides: The Complete Greek Drama*. Edited by Whitney J. Oates and Eugene O'Neill, Jr. Translated by E. P. Coleridge. New York: Random House, 1938.

———. *Tragicorum Graecorum fragmenta*. Edited by August Nauck. Leipzig: Teubner, 1889.

———. *Alcestis, Heraclidae, Hercules, Supplices*. In *Euripidis fabulae*. Edited by James Diggle. 2 vols. Oxford: Clarendon, 1981–1984.

Eusebius. *Demonstratio evangelica*. Edited by Ivar A Heikel. In vol. 6 of *Eusebius Werke*. Die griechischen christlichen Schriftsteller 23. Leipzig: Hinrichs, 1913.

———. *Praeparatio evangelica*. Edited by Karl Mras. In vol 8. of *Eusebius Werke*. 2 vols. Die griechischen christlichen Schriftsteller 43.1–2. Berlin: Akademie, 1954–1956.

Gregory of Nyssa. *In sanctum Pascha*. Translated by S. G. Hall. In *The Easter Sermons of Gregory of Nyssa. Translation and Commentary: Proceedings of the Fourth International Colloqium on Gregory of Nyssa, Cambridge, England: 11–15 September 1978*. Edited by Andreas Spira and Christoph Klock. Cambridge, MA: Philadelphia Patristic Foundation, 1981.

Georgius Acropolites. *In imaginem beatae virginis* and *Laudatio Petri et Pauli*. In vol. 2 of *Georgii Acropolitae opera*. Edited by August Heisenberg. Leipzig: Teubner, 1903.

Heraclitus. *Fragementa*. In vol. 1 of *Die Fragmente der Vorsokratiker*. Edited by Hermann Diels and Walther Kranz. 6th edition. Berlin: Weidmann 1951.

Herodotus. *Histoires*. Edited by Ph.-E. Legrand. Vol. 2. Paris: Les Belles Lettres, 1930.

Hippolytus. *Refutatio omnium haeresium*. Edited by Miroslav Marcovich. Patristische Texte und Studien 25. Berlin: De Gruyter, 1986.

Homeri Ilias. Edited by Thomas W. Allen. Vols. 2-3. Oxford: Clarendon, 1931.

Homeri Odyssea. Edited by Peter von der Mühll. Basel: Helbing & Lichtenhahn 1962.

Iamblichi Protrepticus ad fidem codicis Florentini. Edited by Hermenegildus Pistelli. Leipzig: Teubner, 1888.

John Chrysostom. *De Lazaro et divite*. In vol. 59 of *Patrologiae graeca*. Edited by Jacques-Paul Migne. Paris, 1862.

———. *In epistulam i ad Timotheum*. In vol. 62 of *Patrologiae graeca*. Edited by Jacques-Paul Migne. Paris, 1862.

———. *Homilies on the First Epistle of St. Paul the Apostle to Timothy*. In vol. 13 of *The Nicene and Post-Nicene Fathers*, Series 1. Edited by Philip Schaff. New York: Christian Literature Publishing, 1889.

Josephus. Translated by Henry St. J. Thackeray et al. 10 vols. LCL. Cambridge: Harvard University Press, 1926–1965.

Lucius Annaeus Cornutus. *Cornuti theologiae Graecae compendium*. Edited by Carl Lang. Leipzig: Teubner 1881.

Menander. *Fragmenta*. In vol. 3 of *Comicorum Atticorum fragmenta*. Edited by Theodor Kock. Leipzig: Teubner 1888.

Methodius of Olympus. *Le banquet*. Edited by Victor-Henry Debidour and Herbert Musurillo. Sources chrétiennes 95. Paris: Cerf, 1963.

Numenius. *Fragments*. Edited by Edouard des Places. Paris: Les Belles Lettres, 1974.

Origen. *Commentaire sur saint Jean*. Edited and translated by Cécile Blanc. Vol. 4. Sources chrétiennes 290. Paris: Cerf, 1982.

———. *Fragmenta in evangelium Joannis (in catenis)*. In vol. 4 of *Origenes Werke*. Edited by E. Preuschen. Die griechischen christlichen Schriftsteller 10. Leipzig: Hinrichs, 1903.

———. *Selecta in Psalmos*. In vol. 12 of Patrologia Graeca. Edited by Jacques-Paul Migne. 162 vols. Paris, 1857-1886.

Philo. Translated by F. H. Colson, G. H. Whitaker and R. Marcus. LCL. Cambridge, MA: Harvard University Press, 1929–1962.

Philonis Alexandrini opera quae supersunt. Edited by Leopold Cohn, Paul Wendland and Siegfried Reiter. 6 vols. Berlin: Reimer, 1896–1915.

Philonis Iudaei in libros Mosis, de mundo opificio, historicos, de legibus; eiusdem libri singulares. Edited by Adrianus Turnebus. Paris: Regiis typis, 1552.

Philonis Judaei opera quae Reperiri potuerunt Omnia. Edited by Thomas Mangey. London: Typis Gulielmi Bowyer, 1742.

Philonis Judaei Paralipomena Armena. Edited and translated into Latin by Joannes Baptista Aucher. 1826. Repr. Hildesheim: Weidmann, 2004.

Philonis Judaei sermones tres hactenus inediti. Edited and translated into Latin by Joannes Baptista Aucher Venice: Typis Coenobii PP. Armenorum in insula S. Lazari, 1822.

Philo. *Fragments of Philo Judaeus*. Edited by J. Rendel Harris. Cambrige, MA: Harvard University Press 1886.

———. *The Works of Philo Judaeus*. Translated by Charles Duke Yonge. London: Bohn, 1854–1890.

———. *Die Werke Philos von Alexandria in deutscher Übersetzung*. Translated by Leopold Cohn, Isaac Heinemann et al. Berlin: de Gruyter, 1909–1964.

———. *Les oeuvres de Philon d'Alexandrie.* Edited by Roger Arnaldez, Jean Pouilloux, Claude Mondésert. Paris: Cerf, 1961–1992.

———. *Philonis Alexandrini* De animalibus*: The Armenian Text with an Introduction, Translation, and Commentary.* Abraham Terian. SPhSup 1. Chico, CA: Scholars Press, 1981.

"Philo of Alexandria, *Quaestiones in Exodum* 2.62–68: Critical Edition." Edited with an introduction, translation and supplementary textual notes by James Royse. Pages 1–68 in SPhA 24 (2012).

Philon d'Alexandrie. *Questions sur la Genèse II, 1–7: Text grec, version arménienne, parallèles latins.* Edited by Joseph Paramelle et al. Cahiers d'Orientalisme, 3. Geneva: Cramer, 1984.

P'iloni Hebrayecʿwoy čaṙkʿ tʿargmanealkʿ i naxneacʿ merocʿ orocʿ hellen bnagirkʿ hasin aṙ mez. [*Sermons by Philo the Jew, the Greek originals of which have reached us.*] [Edited by Garegin Zarbhanalean.] Venice: Mechitarist Press, 1892.

Photius. *Bibliothèque.* Edited by René Henry. 8 vols. Paris: Les Belles Lettres, 1959–1977.

Plato. Translated by Harold North Fowler et al. 12 vols. LCL. Cambridge, MA: Harvard University Press, 1914–1927.

Plato. *Phaedrus.* Edited with English Notes and Dissertations by William H. Thompson. London: Whittaker & Co., 1868.

Platonis opera. Edited by John Burnet. 6 vols. Oxford: Clarendon, 1901–1907.

Plotinus. *Enneades, Books 1–3.* Edited by Paul Henry and Hans-Rudolf Schwyzer. Museum Lessianum. Series philosophica 33. Leiden: Brill, 1951.

Plutarchi moralia. Edited by William R. Paton et al. 7 vols. Leipzig: Teubner, 1925–1971.

Porphyrii philosophi Platonici opuscula selecta. Edited by August Nauck. 2nd edn. Leipzig: Teubner, 1886.

Porphyrus. "Die neuplatonische, fälschlich dem Galen zugeschriebene Schrift Πρὸς Γαῦρον περὶ τοῦ πῶς ἐμψυχοῦνται τὰ ἔμβρυα." Edited by Karl Kalbfleisch. Abhandlungen der königlichen Akademie der Wissenschaften zu Berlin. Berlin: Reimer, 1895.

Posidippi Pellaei quae supersunt omnia. Edited by Colin Austin and Guido Bastianini. Bibliotheca Classica. Milano: LED-Edizioni Universitarie di Lettere Economia Diritto, 2002.

Posidonius. *Die Fragmente.* Edited by Willy Theiler. Vol. 1. Berlin: De Gruyter, 1982.

Pseudo-Caesarius. *Die Erotapokriseis.* Edited by Rudolf Riedinger. Die griechischen christlichen Schriftsteller der ersten Jahrhunderte. Berlin: Akademie, 1989.
Pseudo-Dianysius Halicarnassensis. *Ars rhetorica.* In vol 6 of *Dionysii Halicarnasei quae exstant.* Edited by L. Radermacher and H. Usener. Leipzig: Teubner, 1929
Pseudo-Macarius. *Die 50 geistlichen Homilien des Makarios.* Edited by Hermann Dörries, Erich Klostermann, and Matthias Kroeger. Patristische Texte und Studien 4. Berlin: De Gruyter, 1964.
Pseudo-Maximus Confessor. *Erste kritische Edition einer Redaktion des sacroprofanen Florilegiums* Loci communes. Edited by Sibylle Ihm. Palingenesia LXXIII. Stuttgart: Steiner, 2001.
Pseudo-Plato. *Axiochus.* Translated with notes by Jackson P. Hershbell. Society of Biblical Literature Texts and Translations 21. Graeco–Roman Religion Series 6. Chico, CA: Scholars Press, 1981.
Pythagoras. *Carmen aureum.* In *Theognis.* Edited by Douglas Young (post Ernest Diehl). Second edition. Leipzig: Teubner, 1971
———. *Fragmenta.* In vol. 1 of *Die Fragmente der Vorsokratiker.* Edited by Hermann Diels and Walther Kranz. Sixth edition. Berlin: Weidmann, 1951.
Rossi, Azariah ben Moses de'. *The Light of the Eyes: Azariah de' Rossi: Translated from the Hebrew with an introduction and annotations by Joanna Weinberg.* Yale Judaica Series 31. New Haven: Yale University Press, 2001.
Secundus the silent philosopher: the Greek life of Secundus. Edited and translated by Ben Edwin Perry. Philological monographs 22. Ithaca, N.Y.: American Philological Association, 1964.
Servius, Maurus. *In Vergilii carmina comentarii: Servii Grammatici qui feruntur in Vergilii carmina commentarii.* Edited by Georg Thilo. Leipzig: Teubner, 1881.
Sextus Empiricus. *Pyrrhoniae hypotyposes.* In vol. 1 of *Sexti Empirici opera.* Edited by Hermann Mutschmann. Leipzig: Teubner, 1912.
Sophocles. *Fragmenta.* In vol. 4 of *Tragicorum Graecorum fragmenta.* Edited by Stefan Radt. Göttingen: Vandenhoeck & Ruprecht, 1977.
Tertullian. *De anima.* In vol. 3 of *The Ante-Nicene Fathers.* Edited by Alexander Roberts and James Donaldson. 1885–1887. 10 vols. Repr., Peabody, MA: Hendrickson, 1995.
Theognis. Edited by Douglas Young (post Ernest Diehl), *Theognis,* Second edn. Leipzig: Teubner, 1971.

Xenocrates. *Frammenti.* Edited by Margherita I. Parente. Naples: Bibliopolis, 1982.

Xenophon. *Cyropaedia.* Translated by Walter Miller. LCL. Cambridge, MA: Harvard University Press, 1914.

Manuscripts

John of Damascus. *Parallela sacra.* Parisinus Graecus 923. Bibliothèque National de France.

———. *Eclogae sive Sacra Parallela.* Berolinensis Graecus 46 (*olim* Rupefucaldinus). Staatsbibliothek zu Berlin, shelf-mark Phillips 1450.

Philo of Alexandria. Parisinus Graecus 433. Bibliothèque National de France.

Indices, Dictionaries and Grammars

Awatikʻean G., Siwrmēlean X., Awgerean M. *Nor Baṙgirkʻ Haykazean Lezui. [New Dictionary of the Armenian Language].* Venice: Mechitarist Press 1836–1837.

Borgen, Peder, Kåre Fuglseth and Roald Skarsten. *The Philo Index: A Complete Greek Word Index to the Writings of Philo of Alexandria.* Grand Rapids: Eerdmans, 2000.

Bowker, John, ed. *Oxford Concise Dictionary of World Religions.* Oxford: Oxford University Press, 2000.

Krause, Todd B., John A. C. Greppin and Jonathan Slocum. *Classical Armenian Online.* The University of Texas at Austin, College of Liberal Arts. www.utexas.edu/cola/centers/lrc/eieol/armol-0-X.html.

Lampe G. W. H. *A Patristic Greek Lexicon.* Oxford: Clarendon, 1961.

Lewis, Charlton T. and Charles Short. *A Latin Dictionary: Founded on Andrews' edition of Freund's Latin dictionary: Revised, enlarged, and in great part rewritten.* Oxford: Clarendon, 1879.

Liddell, Henry George and Robert Scott. *A Greek-English Lexicon: Revised and augmented throughout by Sir Henry Stuart Jones with the assistance of Roderick McKenzie.* Oxford: Clarendon, 1940.

New Shorter Oxford English Dictionary CD. Version 1.0.03. Data version: 02.10.96s. Oxford: Oxford University Press; Rotterdam: Electronic Publishing, 1997.

Smyth, Herbert Weir. *A Greek Grammar for Colleges.* New York: American Book, 1920.

Secondary Literature

Alesse, Francesca, ed. *Philo of Alexandria and Post-Aristotelian Philosophy.* SPhA 5. Leiden: Brill, 2008.

Allix, Peter (Pierre). *The Judgement of the Ancient Jewish Church against the Unitarians in the Controversy upon the Holy Trinity and the Divinity of Our Blessed Saviour.* Second edition, corrected by the author. Oxford: Clarendon, 1821.

Ashwin-Siejkowski, Piotr. *Clement of Alexandria on Trial: The Evidence of "Heresy" from Photius' Bibliotheca.* VCSup 101. Leiden: Brill, 2010.

Baer, Richard A. *Philo's Use of the Categories Male and Female.* ALGHJ 3. Leiden: Brill, 1970.

Barclay, John. *Flavius Josephus: Translation and Commentary, Vol. 10: Against Apion.* Leiden: Brill, 2007.

Bentwich, Norman. *Philo-Judaeus of Alexandria.* Philadelphia: JPS, 1910.

Berchman, Robert M. "Arcana Mundi: Magic and Divination in the *De somniis* of Philo of Alexandria." Pages 115–54 in *Mediators of the Divine: Horizons of Prophecy, Divination, Dreams, and Theurgy in Mediterranean Antiquity.* Edited by Robert M. Berchman. SFSHJ 164. Atlanta: Scholars Press, 1998.

Bigg, Charles. *The Christian Platonists of Alexandria: Being the Bampton Lectures of the year 1886.* Oxford: Clarendon, 1913.

Billings, Thomas H. *The Platonism of Philo Judaeus.* Chicago: University of Chicago Press, 1919.

Blum, Claes. "Studies in the Dream-Book of Artemidorus." Diss., University of Uppsala, 1936.

Borgen, Peder. "Heavenly Ascent in Philo." Pages 246–68 in *The Pseudepigrapha and Early Biblical Interpretation.* Edited by James H. Charlesworth and Craig A. Evans. JSPSup 14. Studies in Scripture in Early Judaism and Christianity 2. Sheffield: JSOT Press, 1993.

———. *Philo of Alexandria: An Exegete for His Time.* NovTSup 86. Leiden: Brill, 1997.

Bouffartigue, Jean. "La structure de l'âme chez Philon: terminologie scolastique et métaphores." Pages 59–75 in *Philon d'Alexandrie et la langage de la philosophie. Actes du colloque international organisé par le Centre d'études sur la philosophie hellénistique et romaine de l'Université de Paris XII-Val de Marne.* Edited by Carlos Lévy. Turnhout: Brepols, 1998.

Bréhier, Émile. *Les idées philosophiques et religieuses de Philon d'Alexandrie.* Paris: Alphonse Picard, 1908.

Burnett, Fred W. "Philo on Immortality: A Thematic Study of Philo's Concept of παλιγγενεσία." *CBQ* 46 (1984): 447–70.

Christiansen, Irmgard. *Die Technik der allegorischen Auslegungswissenschaft bei Philon von Alexandrien*. Beiträge zur Geschichte der biblischen Hermeneutik 7. Tübingen: Mohr Siebeck, 1969.

Collins, John. J. "Eschatology." Pages 594–7 in *The Eerdmans Dictionary of Early Judaism*. Edited by John J. Collins and Daniel C. Harlow. Grand Rapids: Eerdmans, 2010.

Conroy, John T. "'The Wages of Sin Is Death:' The Death of the Soul in Greek, Second Temple Jewish, and Early Christian Authors." Ph.D. diss., University of Notre Dame, 2008.

———. "Philo's 'Death of the Soul': Is This Only a Metaphor?" *SPhA* 23 (2011): 23–40.

Conybeare, Fred C. "Cohn's Philo." *The Classical Review* 11.1 (1897): 66–67.

Crispo, Giovanni Battista. *De Ethnicis Philosophis Caute Legendis Disputationum ex Propriis Cuiusque Principiis*. Rome: Aloysij Zannetti, 1594.

Cudworth, Ralph. *The True Intellectual System of the Universe: To Which Are Added the Notes and Dissertations of Dr. J. L. Mosheim*. Translated by John Harrison. London: Thomas Tegg, 1845.

Cumont, Franz. *After Life in Roman Paganism*. New Haven: Yale University Press, 1923.

Dähne, August Ferdinand. *Geschichtliche Darstellung der jüdisch-alexandrinischen Religions-Philosophie*. Halle: Waisenhauses, 1834.

Dey, Joseph. *Παλιγγενεσία: Ein Beitrag zur Erklärung der religionsgeschichtlichen Bedeutung von Tit 3, 5*. NTAbh 27,5. Münster: Aschendorffsche, 1937.

Dillon, John. *The Middle Platonists: A Study of Platonism 80 B.C. to A.D. 220*. Revised edition with new afterword. London: Duckworth, 1996.

———. "The Descent of the Soul in Middle Platonic and Gnostic Theory." Pages 357–64 (section XII) in *The Golden Chain: Studies in the Development of Platonism and Christianity*. Aldershot: Variorum, 1990. Repr. from *The rediscovery of Gnosticism: Proceedings of the International Conference on Gnosticism at Yale, New Haven, Connecticut, March 28-31, 1978*. 2 vols. Edited by Bentley Layton. Studies in the History of Religions 41. Leiden: Brill, 1980.

———. *Alcinous: The Handbook of Platonism*. Oxford: Clarendon, 1993.

———. "Philo of Alexandria and Platonist Psychology." Pages 17–24 in *The Afterlife of the Platonic Soul: Reflections of Platonic Psychology in the Monotheistic Religions*. Edited by Maha Elkaisy-Friemuth and John M. Dillon. Leiden: Brill, 2009.

Dodson, Derek. "Philo's *'De somniis'* in the Context of Ancient Dream Theories and Classifications." *PRSt* 30 (2003): 299–312.

Drummond, James. *Philo Judaeus, or the Jewish-Alexandrian Philosophy.* London: Williams & Norgate, 1888.

Dunderberg, Ismo. "Judas' Anger and the Perfect Human Being." Pages 201–21 in *The Codex Judas Papers. Proceedings of the International Congress on the Tchacos Codex Held at Rice University, Houston, Texas, March 13–16, 2008.* Edited by April D. DeConick. NHMS 71. Leiden: Brill, 2009.

Eisele, Wilfried. *Ein unerschütterliches Reich: Die mittelplatonische Umformung des Parusiegedankens im Hebräerbrief.* BZNW 116. Berlin: de Gruyter, 2003.

Elledge, Casey D. "Resurrection and Immortality in Hellenistic Judaism: Navigating the Conceptual Boundaries." Pages 101–33 in *Christian Origins and Hellenistic Judaism: Social and Literary Contexts for the New Testament.* Edited by Stanley E. Porter and Andrew W. Pitts. Leiden: Brill, 2013.

Elmgren, Henrik. *Philon av Alexandria med särskild hänsyn till hans eskatologiska föreställningar.* [*Philo of Alexandria and his eschatological views.*] Diss., University of Lund. Stockholm: Svenska Kyrkans Diakonistyrelse, 1939.

Fabricius, Johann Albertus. '*Exercitatio de Platonismo Philonis Judaei.*' Diss., Leipzig, 1693.

———. *Bibliotheca Graeca.* 12 vols. Hamburg: Christianum Liebezeit, 1705–1728.

Festugière, Andre-Jean. *La Révélation d'Hermes Trismègiste.* 4 vols. Paris: Lecoffre, 1944–1954.

Fox, Kenneth A. "Paul's Attitude Toward the Body in Romans 6–8: Compared with Philo of Alexandria." Ph.D. diss., University of St. Michael's College, Toronto, 2001.

Fuglseth, Kåre. "The Reception of Aristotelian Features in Philo and the Authorship Problem of *De Aeternitate Mundi.*" Pages 57–67 in *Beyond Reception: Mutual Influences between Antique Religion, Judaism and Early Christianity.* Edited by David Brakke, Anders-Christian Jacobsen and Jörg Ulrich. Early Christianity in the Context of Antiquity 1. Frankfurt am Main: Peter Lang, 2006.

Geljon, Albert C. and David T. Runia, "An Index Locorum to Billings, *The Platonism of Philo Judaeus.*" SPhA 7 (1995): 169–85.

———. *Philo of Alexandria: On Cultivation: Introduction, Translation and Commentary.* PACS 4. Leiden: Brill, 2013.

Gfrörer, August. *Philo und die alexandrinische Theosophie.* 2 vols. Stuttgart: Schweitzerbart, 1831.

Goodenough, Erwin R. *By Light, Light: The Mystic Gospel of Hellenistic Judaism*. New Haven: Yale University Press, 1935.

———. "Philo on Immortality." *HTR* 39.2 (1946): 86–108.

Grabbe, Lester L. "Eschatology in Philo and Josephus." Pages 163–85 in *Death, Life-After-Death, Resurrection and The World-to-Come in the Judaisms of Antiquity*. Edited by Alan J. Avery-Peck and Jacob Neusner. Vol. 4 of *Judaism in Late Antiquity*. HO 1.49. Edited by Alan J. Avery-Peck, Jacob Neusner, and Bruce Chilton. Leiden: Brill, 2000.

Graf, Fritz. "Text and Ritual: The Corpus Eschatologicum of the Orphics." Pages 53–67 in *The "Orphic" Gold Tablets and Greek Religion: Further Along the Path*. Edited by Radcliffe G. Edmonds III. Cambridge: Cambridge University Press, 2010.

Graffigna, Paola. "The Stability of Perfection: The Image of the Scales in Philo of Alexandria." Pages 131–46 in *Italian Studies on Philo of Alexandria*. Edited by Francesca Calabi. Studies in Philo of Alexandria and Mediterranean Antiquity 1. Boston: Brill, 2003.

Gross, Joseph. "Philons von Alexandreia Anschauungen über die Natur des Menschen." Diss., University of Tübingen, 1930.

Grossman, D. C. G. L. *Quaestiones Philoneae*. Leipzig: Friedricus Fleischer, 1829.

Hay, David M. "References to Other Exegetes." Pages 81–97 in *Both Literal and Allegorical: Studies in Philo of Alexandria's Questions and Answers on Genesis and Exodus*. Edited by David M. Hay. BJS 232. Atlanta: Scholars Press, 1991.

Heinemann, Isaak. *Philons griechische und judische Bildung: Kulturvergleichende Untersuchungen zu Philons Darstellung der judischen Gesetze*. Breslau: M. & H. Marcus, 1932.

Helleman, Wendy E. "Philo of Alexandria on Deification and Assimilation to God." *SPhA* 2 (1990): 51–71.

Herriot, Édouard. *Philon le Juif: Essai sur l'ecole juive d'Alexandrie*. Paris: Librairie Hachette, 1898.

Herzog, Karl. *Spekulativ-psychologische Entwicklung der Grundlagen und Grundlinien des philonischen Systems*. Nuremberg: Rottner & Keller, 1911.

Hilgert, Earle. "*The Quaestiones:* Texts and Translations." Pages 1–15 in *Both Literal and Allegorical. Studies in Philo of Alexandria's Questions and Answers on Genesis and Exodus*. Edited by David M. Hay. BJS 232. Atlanta: Scholars Press, 1991.

Hoek, Annewies van den. *Clement of Alexandria and His Use of Philo in the Stromateis: An Early Christian Reshaping of a Jewish Model*. VCSup 3. Leiden: Brill, 1988.

———. "Philo and Origen: A Descriptive Catalogue of Their Relationship." *SPhA* 12 (2000): 44–121.
———. "Assessing Philo's Influence in Christian Alexandria: The Case of Origen." Pages 223–39 in *Shem in the Tents of Japhet: Essays on the Encounter of Judaism and Hellenism*. Edited by James L. Kugel. Leiden: Brill, 2002.
Holladay, Carl R. *Theios Aner in Hellenistic-Judaism: A Critique of the Use of This Category in New Testament Christology*. SBLDS 40. Missoula: Scholars Press, 1977.
Huffman, Carl A. *Philolaus of Croton: Pythagorean and Presocratic*. Cambridge: Cambridge University Press, 1993.
Kamesar, Adam. "Biblical Interpretation in Philo." Pages 65–91 in *The Cambridge Companion to Philo*. Edited by Adam Kamesar. Cambridge: Cambridge University Press, 2009.
Katz, Peter. *Philo's Bible: The Aberrant Text of Bible Quotations in Some Philonic Writings and its Place in the Textual History of the Greek Bible*. Cambridge: Cambridge University Press, 1950.
Keller, Carl-A. "La réincarnation: vue d'ensemble des problèmes." Pages 1–35 in *La réincarnation: Théories, raisonnements et appréciations*. Edited by Carl-A. Keller. Bern: Lang, 1986.
Kennedy, Harry. A. A. *Philo's Contribution to Religion*. London: Hodder & Stoughton, 1919.
Kessels, A. H. M. "Ancient Systems of Dream-Classification." *Mnemosyne*, 4/ 22.3 (1969): 389–424.
Knuuttila, Simo. "Notes on the *Timaeus*." Pages 363–81 in Plato, *Teokset* 5. Helsinki: Otava, 1982.
Koester, Helmut. *History, Culture, and Religion of the Hellenistic Age*. Vol. 1 of *Introduction to the New Testament*. Second edition. New York: de Gruyter, 1995.
Koskenniemi, Erkki. *The Old Testament Miracle-Workers in Early Judaism*. WUNT 2.206. Tübingen: Mohr Siebeck, 2005.
Kraye, Jill. "Ficino in the Firing Line: A Renaissance Neoplatonist and His Critics." Pages 37797 in *Marsilio Ficino: His Theology, His Philosophy, His Legacy*. Edited by Michael J. B. Allen, Valery Rees, and Martin Davies. Leiden: Brill, 2002.
Le Clerc, Jean. *Joanni Clerici epistolae criticae et ecclesticae*. Amsterdam: Typographiae huguetanorum, 1700.
Leopold, J. "Philo's Vocabulary and Word Choice." Pages 137–40 in David Winston and John Dillon, *Two Treatises of Philo of Alexandria: A*

Commentary on De Gigantibus and Quod Deus Sit Immutabilis. BJS 25. Chico, CA.: Scholars Press, 1983.

Lévy, Carlos. "Philo's Ethics." Pages 146–71 in *The Cambridge Companion to Philo.* Edited by Adam Kamesar. Cambridge: Cambridge University Press, 2009.

Mackie, Scott D. "The Passion of Eve and the Ecstasy of Hannah: Sense Perception, Passion, Mysticism, and Misogyny in Philo of Alexandria, *De ebrietate* 143–52." *JBL* 133.1 (2014): 141–63.

Mansfeld, Jaap. "Heraclitus, Empedocles, and Others in a Middle Platonist Cento in Philo of Alexandria." *VC* 39 (1985): 131–56.

Marcus, Ralph. "The Armenian Translation of Philo's *Quaestiones in Genesim et Exodum.*" *JBL* 49.1 (1930): 61–64.

———. "An Armenian-Greek Index to Philo's *Quaestiones* and *De Vita Contemplativa.*" *JAOS* 53.3 (1933): 251–82.

———. "A 16th Century Hebrew Critique of Philo (Azariah dei Rossi's *Meor Eynayim,* Pt. I, cc. 3–6)." *HUCA* 21 (1948): 29–71.

Méasson, Anita. *Du char ailé de Zeus à l'Arche d'Alliance: Images et mythes platoniciens chez Philon d'Alexandrie.* Paris: Études Augustiniennes, 1986.

Meyer, Annegret. *Kommt und seht: Mystagogie im Johannesevangelium ausgehend von Joh 1,35–51.* Würzburg: Echter, 2005.

Muradyan, Gohar. "The Armenian Version of Philo Alexandrinus." Pages 51–85 in *Studies on the Ancient Armenian Version of Philo's Works.* Edited by Sara Mancini Lombardi and Paola Pontani. SPhA 6. Leiden: Brill, 2011.

Nikiprowetzky, Valentin. "L'Exégèse de Philon d'Alexandrie dans le *De Gigantibus* et le *Quod Deus.*" Pages 5–75 in David Winston and John Dillon, *Two Treatises of Philo of Alexandria: A Commentary on De Gigantibus and Quod Deus Sit Immutabilis.* BJS 25. Chico, CA: Scholars Press, 1983.

Ogle, Marbury B. "The Sleep of Death." MAAR XI (1933): 81–117.

Olivieri, Maurizio. "Philo's *De providentia*: A Work Between Two Traditions." Pages 87–124 in *Studies on the Ancient Armenian Version of Philo's Works.* Edited by Sara Mancini Lombardi and Paola Pontani. SPhA 6. Leiden: Brill, 2011.

Pascher, Joseph. Η ΒΑΣΙΛΙΚΗ ΟΔΟΣ: *Der Königsweg zu Wiedergeburt und Vergottung bei Philon von Alexandria.* Studien zur Geschichte und Kultur des Altertums, Bd. 17, Heft 3 and 4. Paderborn: Ferdinand Schöningh, 1931.

Paz, Yakir. Review of Albert C. Geljon and David T. Runia, *Philo of Alexandria: On Cultivation: Introduction, Translation and Commentary. Bryn Mawr*

Classical Review 2013.10.61, bmcr.brynmawr.edu/2013/2013-10-61.html.
Pearce, Sarah. *The Land of the Body: Studies in Philo's Representation of Egypt.* WUNT 1.208. Tübingen: Mohr Siebeck, 2007.
Pétau, Denis. *Opus de Theologicis Dogmatibus, in Hac Novissima Editione Auctius.* 5 vols. Venice: Andreae Poleti, 1745.
Petit, Françoise. *L'ancienne version latine des* Questions sur la Genèse *de Philon d'Alexandrie.* 2 vols. TUGAL 113–114. Berlin: Akademie, 1973.
Pontani, Paola. "Saying (Almost) the Same Thing." Pages 125–46 in *Studies on the Ancient Armenian Version of Philo's Works.* Edited by Sara Mancini Lombardi and Paola Pontani. SPhA 6. Leiden: Brill, 2011.
Priestley, Joseph. "Of the Platonism of Philo." *The Theological Repository* 4 (1784): 408–20.
Radice, Roberto & Runia, David T. *Philo of Alexandria: An Annotated Bibliography 1937–1986.* VCSup 8. Leiden: Brill, 1988.
Raphael, Paull Simcha. *Jewish Views of the Afterlife.* Second edition. Lanham, MD: Rowman & Littlefield, 2009.
Reddoch, Michael J. "Dream Narratives and Their Philosophical Orientation in Philo of Alexandria." Ph.D. diss., University of Cincinnati, 2010.
Reydams-Schils, Gretchen. "Philo of Alexandria on Stoic and Platonist Psycho-Physiology: The Socratic Higher Ground." Pages 169–95 in *Philo of Alexandria and Post-Aristotelian Philosophy.* Edited by Francesca Alesse. SPhA 5. Leiden: Brill, 2008. Repr. with minor corrections from *Ancient Philosophy*, vol. 22.1 (2002): 124–47.
Ritter, Heinrich. *The History of Ancient Philosophy.* Translated from the German by Alexander J. W. Morrison. 4 vols. London: Bohn, 1838–1846.
Royse, James R. *The Spurious Texts of Philo of Alexandria: A Study of Textual Transmission and Corruption with Indexes to the Major Collections of Greek Fragments.* Leiden: Brill, 1991.
———. "Reverse Indexes to Philonic Texts in the Printed Florilegia and Collections of Fragments." *SPhA* 5 [1993]: 156–79.
———. "The Works of Philo." Pages 32–64 in *The Cambridge Companion to Philo.* Edited by Adam Kamesar. Cambridge: Cambridge University Press, 2009.
———. "Philo of Alexandria, *Quaestiones in Exodum* 2.62–68: Critical Edition." *SPhA* 24 (2012): 1–68.
Runia, David T. "Philo's *De aeternitate mundi*: The Problem of Its Interpretation." *VC* 35 (1981): 105–51.

———. "Philo of Alexandria and the Timaeus of Plato." Ph.D. diss., Free University of Amsterdam, 1983.

———. "The Structure of Philo's Allegorical Treatises: A Review of Two Recent Studies and Some Additional Comments." *VC* 38 (1984): 209–256.

———. *Philo of Alexandria and the Timaeus of Plato*. Philosophia Antiqua 44. Leiden: Brill, 1986.

———. "Further Observations on the Structure of Philo's Allegorical Treatises." *VC* 41 (1987): 105–138.

———. Review of Anita Méasson, *Du char ailé de Zeus à l'Arche d'Alliance: Images et mythes platoniciens chez Philon d'Alexandrie*, *VC* 42 (1988): 290–5.

———. "Secondary Texts in Philo's *Quaestiones*." Pages 47–79 in *Both Literal and Allegorical: Studies in Philo of Alexandria's Questions and Answers on Genesis and Exodus*. Edited by David M. Hay. BJS 232. Atlanta: Scholars Press, 1991.

———. "Verba Philonica, ΑΓΑΛΜΑΤΟΦΟΡΕΙΝ, and the Authenticity of the *De Resurrectione* Attributed to Athenagoras." *VC* 46.4 (1992): 313–27.

———. *Philo in Early Christian Literature: A Survey*. CRINT III.3. Minneapolis: Fortress, 1993.

———. "Why Does Clement of Alexandria Call Philo 'the Pythagorean'?" *VC* 49 (1995): 1–22.

———. "The Text of the Platonic Citations in Philo of Alexandria." Pages 261–91 in *Studies in Plato and the Platonic Tradition: Essays Presented to John Whittaker*. Edited by Mark Joyal. Aldershot: Ashgate, 1997.

———. *Philo of Alexandria: An Annotated Bibliography for 1987–1996 with Addenda for 1937–1986*. VCSup 57. Leiden: Brill, 2000.

———. *On the Creation of the Cosmos According to Moses: Introduction, Translation, and Commentary*. PACS 1. Atlanta: Society of Biblical Literature, 2001.

———. "Theodicy in Philo of Alexandria." Pages 576–604 in *Theodicy in the World of the Bible*. Edited by Antti Laato and Johannes De Moor. Leiden: Brill, 2003.

———. "Philo and the Early Christian Fathers." Pages 210–30 in *The Cambridge Companion to Philo*. Edited by Adam Kamesar. Cambridge: Cambridge University Press, 2009.

———. *Philo of Alexandria: an Annotated Bibliography 1997–2006 with addenda for 1987–1996*. VCSup 109. Leiden: Brill, 2012.

Ryle, Herbert Edward. *Philo and Holy Scripture, or the Quotations of Philo from the Books of the Old Testament*. London: Macmilan, 1895.

Sandelin, Karl-Gustav. "Die Auseinandersetzung mit der Weisheit in 1. Korinther 15." ThD diss., Åbo Akademi University, 1976.

──. *Wisdom as Nourisher: A Study on an Old Testament Theme, Its Development within Early Judaism and Its Impact on Early Christianity.* Acta Academiae Aboensis A.64:3. Åbo: Åbo Akademi, 1986.

Sanders, Ed Parish. *Judaism: Practice and Belief 63 BCE–66 CE.* London: SCM Press, 1994.

Sandmel, Samuel. *Philo of Alexandria: An Introduction.* New York: Oxford University Press, 1979.

Schäfer, Peter. *The Origins of Jewish Mysticism.* Tübingen: Mohr Siebeck, 2009.

Schibli, Hermann S. "Xenocrates' Daemons and the Irrational Soul." *CQ* New Series 43.1 (1993): 143–67.

Scholem, Gershom. *Origins of the Kabbalah.* Translated by Allan Arkush. Princeton: JPS, 1987.

Schürer, Emil. *A History of the Jewish People in the Time of Jesus Christ.* Translated by Sophia Taylor and Peter Christie. 2 divs., 5 vols. New York: Scribner's, 1885–1891.

Schürer, Emil and Charles Bigg. "Philo." Pages 409–13 in vol. 21 of *The Encyclopaedia Britannica. A Dictionary of Arts, Sciences, Literature and General Information.* Eleventh edition. Cambridge: Cambridge University Press, 1911.

Seland, Torrey. *Reading Philo: A Handbook to Philo of Alexandria.* Grand Rapids: Eerdmans, 2014.

Sellin, Gerhard. *Der Streit um die Auferstehung der Toten: Eine religionsgeschichtliche und exegetische Untersuchung von 1 Korinther 15.* Göttingen: Vandenhoeck & Ruprecht, 1986.

Siegert, Folker. *Philon von Alexandrien: Über die Gottesbezeichnung „wohltätig verzehrendes Feuer" (De Deo): Rückübersetzung des Fragments aus dem Armenischen, deutsche Übersetzung und Kommentar.* WUNT 46. Tübingen: Mohr Siebeck, 1988.

──. "Philo and the New Testament." Pages 175–209 *The Cambridge Companion to Philo.* Edited by Adam Kamesar. Cambridge: Cambridge University Press, 2009.

Sirinian, Anna. "'Armenian Philo': A Survey of the Literature." Pages 7–44 in *Studies on the Ancient Armenian Version of Philo's Works.* Edited by Sara Mancini Lombardi and Paola Pontani. SPhA 6. Leiden: Brill, 2011.

Skarsten, Roald. "Forfatterproblemet ved De Aeternitate Mundi i Corpus Philonicum." Ph.D. diss., University of Bergen, 1987.

Smallwood, Mary E. *Philonis Alexandrini Legatio ad Gaium: Introduction, translation and commentary.* Leiden: Brill, 1961.

Sterling, Gregory. "Which Version of the Greek Bible Did Philo Read?" Pages 89–128 in *Pentateuch Traditions in the Late Second Temple Period: Proceedings of the International Workshop in Tokyo, August 28–31, 2007.* Edited by Akio Moriva and Gohei Hata. JSJSup 158. Leiden: Brill, 2012.

Stettner, Walter. *Die Seelenwanderung bei Griechen und Römern.* Tübingen beiträge zur Altertumswissenschaft 22. Stuttgart: Kohlhammer, 1934.

Tarrant, Harold. "Myth as a Tool of Persuasion in Plato" Pages 19–31 (essay VII) in *From the Old Academy to Later Neo-Platonism: Studies in the History of Platonic Thought.* Variorum collected studies series. Farnham: Ashgate, 2011. Repr. from *Antichthon* 24 (1990): 19–31.

Terian, Abraham. "Syntactical Peculiarities in the Translations of the Hellenizing School." *St. Nersess Theological Review* 13 (2008): 15–24. Repr. from *First International Conference on Armenian Linguistics: Proceedings: The University of Penssylvania, Philadelphia, July 11–14, 1979.* Edited by John A. C. Greppin. Delmar: Caravan, 1980.

Termini, Cristina. "Philo's Thought within the Context of Middle Judaism." Pages 95–123 in *The Cambridge Companion to Philo.* Edited by Adam Kamesar Cambridge: Cambridge University Press, 2009.

Thatcher, Tom. "Philo on Pilate: Rhetoric or Reality?" in *ResQ* 37.4 (1995): 215-218.

Tobin, Thomas H. *The Creation of Man: Philo and the History of Interpretation.* Washington, DC: Catholic Biblical Association of America, 1983.

Torallas Tovar, Sofia. "Philo of Alexandria on Sleep." Pages 41–52 in *Sleep.* Edited by Th. Wiedemann and Ken Dowden. Nottingham Classical Literature Studies 8. Bari: Levante, 2003.

Vollenweider, Samuel. "Reinkarnation—ein abendländisches Erbstück." Pages 327–46 in *Horizonte neutestamentlicher Christologie: Studien zu Paulus und zur frühchristlichen Theologie.* WUNT 144. Tübingen: Mohr Siebeck, 2002. Repr. from *Der Evangelische Erzieher* 47.2 (1995): 141–58.

Waszink, Jan Hendrik. *Quinti Septimi Florentis Tertulliani De Anima: Edited with Introduction and Commentary.* Amsterdam: Paris, 1947.

Wilberding, James. *Porphyry:* To Gaurus On How Embryos Are Ensouled *and* On What is in our Power. London: Bristol Classical Press, 2011.

Wilson, Walter. *On Virtues: Introduction, Translation and Commentary.* PACS 3. Leiden: Brill, 2010.

Winston, David. *Philo of Alexandria:* The Contemplative Life, The Giants, *and Selections: Translation and introduction.* London: SPCK, 1981.

———. *Logos and Mystical Theology in Philo of Alexandria*. Cincinnati: Hebrew Union College Press, 1985.

Winston, David and John Dillon. *Two Treatises of Philo of Alexandria: A Commentary on* De Gigantibus *and* Quod Deus Sit Immutabilis. BJS 25. Chico, CA: Scholars Press, 1983.

Wolff, Moritz. *Die philonische Philosophie in ihrem Hauptmomenten dargestellt*. Gothenburg: Bonnier, 1858.

Wolfson, Harry Austryn. *Philo: Foundations of Religious Philosophy in Judaism, Christianity, and Islam*. 2 vols. Cambridge, MA: Harvard University Press, 1948.

Wright, Archie T. "Some Observations of Philo's *De gigantibus* and Evil Spirits in Second Temple Judaism." *JSJ* 36.4 (2005): 471–88.

Yli-Karjanmaa, Sami. "The *Timaeus*, Philo Judaeus and Reincarnation." Pages 217–43 in *Människan i universum: Platons Timaios och dess tolkningshistoria: Texter från Platonsällskapets symposium i Åbo 2007*. [*The Human Being in the Universe: Plato's Timaeus and Its History of Interpretation: Papers from the Symposium of the Nordic Plato Society in Turku, Finland, 2007.*] Edited by Gunnar af Hällström. Åbo: Åbo Akademis förlag, 2009.

———. "Reincarnation in Philo of Alexandria." Th.D. diss., Åbo Akademi University, 2013.

———. "'Call Him Earth:' On Philo's Allegorization of Adam in the *Legum allegoriae*." In *Where Are You, Adam? Papers from the Conference in Turku, Finland, in August 2014*. Edited by Antti Laato and Lotta Valve. Studies in the Reception History of the Bible 7. Åbo: Åbo Akademi University; Winona Lake: Eisenbrauns, forthcoming.

———. "Philo of Alexandria." In *A Companion to the Reception of Plato in Antiquity*. Edited by Harold Tarrant, François Renaud, Dirk Baltzly and Danielle A. Layne Moore. Leiden: Brill, forthcoming.

Zeller, Dieter. "The Life and Death of the Soul in Philo of Alexandria: The Use and Origin of a Metaphor." *SPhA* 7 (1995): 19–55.

Zeller, Eduard. *Die nacharistotelische Philosophie*. Vol. 3.2 of *Die Philosophie der Griechen in ihrer geschichtlichen Entwicklung*. Sixth edition. Hildesheim: Olms, 1963

Zorzi, M. Benedetta. "The Use of the Terms ἁγνεία, παρθενία, σωφροσύνη, and ἐγκράτεια in the *Symposium* of Methodius of Olympus." *VC* 63 (2009): 138–68.

INDICES

Index locorum

1. *Septuagint and Pseudepigrapha*

Genesis
1–3	4
1:27	34, 50
2:6	163
2:7	5, 35–36, 42, 50, 58, 70, 74
2:8	75
2:17	23, 57, 79, 235
2:17b	38
2:18	86
2:21	198, 226
3:1b–8a	58
3:7	58
3:8	87
3:13–14	38
3:19	51, 70, 73, 76, 78
3:20–23	189, 209
3:21	42, 78
3:22	47, 189
3:23	67
3:24	67, 150
4:1–2	150
4:8	10, 236
4:10	238
4:11	236
4:14	16, 239
4:15	82, 121
4:16	117
4:25	163–64
5:24	174–175
7:23	236
9:1–2	22
9:6	82, 104
11:2	54
12:1	87
12:4	240, 251
15:7	207
15:9	229
15:13–14	216, 219
15:15	32
15:16	106
17:1	109
18:33	53
19:17	223–24
19:26	224
21	263
22:3	252
22:6	263
23:4	50, 54–55
24:28	260
24:63	261
25:8	108
25:15	139
25:29	238
26:2–3	55
26:34	180
27:39	68
27:43	37
28:10–11	129
28:11	232
28:12	130, 132
28:12–15	129
28:15	42, 230
31	129
31:20–21	253
31:21	225
31:27	240
31:43	257
37	129
37:17	40
38:7	62, 221–22
40	129
41	129
45	235
45:16	234
45:18	234
46:4	235
47:9	55
48	109
48:15–16	109

Exodus
2:22	55
3:6	98
9:29	233
12:2–23	167
12:11	117, 226
12:23	226
15:2–18	182–83
15:17	65–66

15:17–18	65	3 Kingdoms	
15:23	25, 251	1:21	203
15:23–25	252	Esther	
20:25	167	E:3 (8:12c)	48
21:12	104		
21:26	56	2 Maccabees	
22:21–28:34	167	2:28	190
22:6	138	7:9	191
24	173, 225, 262		
24:2	40	4 Maccabees	
24:10	232, 263	1:1	89
24:11	180	2:21	89
24:12	17, 168, 232	3:2	89
24:13	155, 173	3:5	89
24:15	155	17:18	193
24:16	155		
24:18	155	Psalms	
24:9	155	3:6	197
25:20	190	118:176	151
25:40	190		
28:17	195	Proverbs	
31:2–3	34, 190	13:9	151
31:3	34, 50	22:8	90
32:27	88, 221		
33:7	233	Ecclestiastes	
33:13	178	12:7	142
34:28	175	Job	
35:31	34	4:8	90
Leviticus		27:3	34
8:29	89	33:4	34
10:2	51	Wisdom of Solomon	
11:44	151	17:1	151
16:17	253	17:13	170
21:1	151		
25:23	103, 152	Sirach	
Numers		24:21	261
9:11	225	40:11	142
11:4	252	Isaiah	
15:30	82	21:4	151
21:5–6	60		
25	241	Jeremiah	
Deuteronomy		28:39	203
10:9	97	Ezekiel	
17:16	69	4:14	151
23:13	225–26	44:25	151
29:20	65	1 Enoch	
30:15	19, 189	Entire work	148
32:8	65		
Joshua			
1:11, 15	252		

2. New Testament

Mark
- 14:38 — 197

Luke
- 16:9 — 165
- 16:19–31 — 200

1 Cor
- 8:8 — 193
- 15:31 — 200

Gal
- 6:7 — 90

Eph
- 6:12 — 197

1 Thess
- 5:6–8 — 199

Hebr
- 8:5 — 190
- 10:1 — 190

1 Peter
- 2:21 — 190

3. Philonic Works

Abr. (De Abrahamo)
- 7 — 179
- 8 — 121
- 17–26 — 175
- 33 — 121
- 47 — 154, 175, 179
- 55 — 119
- 57–58 — 54, 56
- 64 — 107
- 68–88 — 54, 254
- 70 — 205
- 79 — 98
- 86 — 140
- 86–88 — 253–54
- 87 — 261
- 88 — 88, 263
- 100 — 96
- 103 — 66
- 121 — 110
- 122 — 247
- 135 — 48
- 135–136 — 112
- 147 — 105, 247
- 156–164 — 56
- 164 — 56
- 200 — 247
- 223 — 97
- 230 — 107
- 255–259 — 107
- 256 — 95
- 258 — 32, 39, 73, 107–8, 156
- 270 — 192

Aet. (De aeternitate mundi)
- Entire work — 62, 256
- 29 — 117
- 111 — 61

Agr. (De agricultura)
- 9 — 247
- 18 — 247
- 25 — 63, 247
- 31 — 122
- 42 — 37
- 46 — 37, 122
- 48 — 48
- 64–65 — 31
- 80 — 183
- 83 — 37, 122
- 88 — 115, 182
- 88–89 — 69, 115, 235
- 89 — 37, 69, 84–85, 115, 181–82, 184–85, 213, 222, 230, 237, 239–40, 241–42, 245
- 98 — 100, 119
- 100 — 119
- 101 — 181
- 158–160 — 184
- 159 — 37
- 163–164 — 119
- 164 — 136
- 169 — 61, 160, 183–85, 241
- 169–173 — 184
- 169–178 — 183
- 171 — 119
- 174–175 — 184–85

Anim. (De animalibus)
- 85 — 21

Cher. (De cherubim)
- Entire work — 150
- 1 — 67
- 1–2 — 67
- 1–39 — 150
- 2 — 67–68, 81, 154, 230, 241
- 5 — 257
- 9 — 157, 191
- 10 — 100
- 12 — 239
- 16 — 247

23–24	157		210, 212, 215, 224,
26	59		228, 238, 245, 255
28–29	161	114–117	153
31	31, 89, 263	115	39, 101, 151, 153,
32	247		160–62
40	158	115–117	162
40–130	150	116	37, 151, 157, 184
42	151, 247	116–117	102, 161
43–47	163	116–118	158
48	151	117	151, 157, 212, 220,
48–49	247		224, 238
49	151, 159	117–118	157
49–50	96	118–19	151
51	119, 151, 257	120	31, 103, 106
51–52	151	121	103
52	100, 150	124	151
54	191		
57	157	*Conf. (De confusione linguarum)*	
57–58	41	21	36–37
57–60	256	23	239
58	42	24	122
58–60	43	30	115–16
60	159	36	136
65	151	60–82	54
66	157	66	31, 84, 238
67	257	70	116
68	150, 157	75–83	55
69	157	77	56
69–71	157, 158	77–78	31–32, 44, 54–55,
70	122		73, 217, 227
71	151, 157	77–79	81
75	157	77–82	33, 54
79 ff.	162	78	80, 173, 232
83	151, 161	78–79	56
89	194	80	55
93	151	82	55
94	247	85	257
95	97	92	114
98–107	97, 99	94–96	263
101	151	97	110
105	194	106	114
106–107	151	122	82, 119
108	152	126	37
109	152	137	110
109–112	161, 257	140	247
109–113	161	149	247
110	151	169	109
110–112	152	169–182	109
113	33, 36, 102, 152,	174	159–60
	156–57, 256	174	176–77, 145, 160
113–118	152, 154, 161	176–177	10
113–119	102–3, 153, 162	177	114
114	7, 16, 33, 85, 101–2,	190	190
	129, 150–67, 208,		

Congr. (De congressu eruditionis gratia)

19	247
20–21	252
21	56, 217
26	36
27	105, 247
56–57	66
56–59	66, 81
57	66, 68–69
57	59, 230
60	66
61	257
79	96
81	95
83–85	252
84	37
97	37
105	247, 261
106	116
110	37
121	247
132	96
163–164	252
164	140, 245
180	247

Contempl. (De vita contemplativa)

2	260
6	260
9	260
10–12	54
12–13	261
20	105
25	247
27	220
28	247
57–64	112
60	260

Decal. (De decalogo)

1	247
31	117
41	247
58	96
80	23, 120–21
87	77
101	192
106	105
106–107	105
110	120–21
111	104, 121
113	121
114	121
149	217
176	192

Deo (De Deo)

7	105

Det. (Quot deterius potiori insidiari soleat)

16	126
22	200
27	40
29	256
32	123
34	123–24
35	194
37	164
48	236, 238
48–49	124
49	119, 123
61	152
65	37
70	100, 119, 124
74–75	119
77	79, 247
86	34, 50
96–103	236
98–100	237
100	182, 237, 239
101–103	238
102	247
118	261
122	247
128	77, 247
138	155
163	31, 154, 240
167–169	100
168	36
178	19, 68, 82, 100

Deus (Quod Deus sit immutabilis)

2	111, 220
3	77
4	192
14–15	126
22	96, 123
45	21
46	36
47	21
56	31, 256
61	247
75	107
76	98
107	98
109–111	136
110	110
111	38, 120, 227–28, 245
111–115	228–29
117–119	105

134	77	85	152, 247
135	111	90–91	221
136–139	174	90–92	88–89
150	31, 141	91	116
173	77	92	222
181	239	97	96
		97–98	247
Ebr. (De ebrietate)		110	31
8	37	113	100, 119
22	239, 241	130–131	66
28	97	141	98, 256
43	256	146	247
49	96	160	247
69	89	164	261
69–72	99	179	247
70	36, 89, 222	194–195	96
70–71	221	195	261
88	247	213	37
98	77		
99	159	*Gig. (De gigantibus)*	
99–101	227	6	134
99–101	103, 233–34	6–11	144
100–103	96	6, 12–14	145
101	31, 47, 120	6–15	1, 13
104	126	6, 12–15	115, 132, 213
111	122	6–18	13–14, 132, 213
124	31	7	27
143–52	56	7–11	27
145	98, 160	8	134, 160
146	247	12–15	39, 215
164	138	13	31–32, 115, 237,
189	247		239, 241
198	105, 247	13–14	96, 99, 113, 123
		13–15	85, 242
Fragments Harris		14	5, 64, 99, 116, 123,
6.1	189		150, 160, 203, 208,
7.1	189		233
7.3	7, 124, 129, 155,	14–15	203
	168, 186–213, 215,	15	13, 64, 100, 201
	245	16	146, 149
8.1	189	27	50
		30–31	39
Fug. (De fuga et inventione)		31	21, 100, 111, 125
8–9	257	41	256
19	247	53	31
22	140, 240, 253	54	152, 247
46–47	54	56	136
55	81	57	247
55–56	119	61	111, 208
59	51		
60	82	*Her. (Quis rerum divinarum heres sit)*	
61	68	45	66, 170
62	47	46	160
69	36	52	28, 36
78	119	52–53	119

57	34	*Ios. (De Iosepho)*	
58	98	59	105, 247
58–61	50	90	247
60	98	125–130	104
64	97, 99	126	198
68	31, 120, 218, 226–	129	107
	29, 235	140	142, 205
69	88, 139	151	66
70	261	264	114
71	38, 88		
74	88	*Leg. (Legum allegoriae)*	
76	105, 247	Original Book 2	79
78	235	Original Book 4	79, 189, 209
78–79	125	1.10	194
84	37	1.15	155
85	31, 88, 120	1.26	152, 159
98–99	206	1.29	77, 152
107–109	229–30	1.31	77
109	218, 230	1.31–32	36, 74
126	241	1.31–38	5
140	257	1.31–42	35–36, 58
183	86	1.31–62	51
185	97	1.32	58
186	98, 230	1.34	36, 50
228	255	1.34–35	75
231	35	1.36	257
234	138	1.42	77
237–239	221	1.43	75
239	97, 99	1.45	75
239–240	31	1.45–46	75
240	45, 48, 73, 81	1.49–52	162
243	39	1.51	257
255	116	1.76	119
257	41, 205	1.77	96
267	221	1.79	75
267–274	216–219	1.81	195
272–274	227	1.82	77
273	98, 120	1.88	77
274	31, 114, 227	1.91	110
276	108	1.92–93	75
282	117, 136	1.95	110
282–283	33, 108	1.103–104	256
283	107	1.105	23, 58, 65
290	119	1.105, 107	68
292	124, 203	1.105–106	38
293–299	106	1.105–108	39, 48, 58–59, 62–64, 78–79, 100, 119, 209, 220, 222, 235–36, 245
294	106		
295	247		
315	31		
		1.106	28, 39, 57, 59, 136, 141, 227, 236
Hypoth. (Hypothetica)			
Entire work	55	1.106–107	24, 60
11.13	55	1.107	48, 57–59, 64–65, 124
		1.107–108	81, 203

1.108	14, 16, 31, 58–59, 62, 64, 141, 222, 227	3.33	162
		3.36	257
		3.36–39	74
2.1	86	3.39–48	87
2.2–3	86	3.41	139
2.6	42, 217	3.42	31, 61, 98, 120
2.9	122	3.44	87
2.17	219, 226	3.45	194
2.22	31, 114	3.47	100
2.24	41, 43	3.52	74, 119
2.25	205	3.55	58
2.25–30	41	3.56	162
2.27	203, 247	3.59–68	38
2.28	225	3.61	38
2.28–34	226	3.69	39, 63, 81, 222
2.30–31	205	3.69–74	62
2.31	198	3.71	221–23, 247
2.33–34	226	3.71–72	62, 63
2.39	77	3.72	222, 236
2.40	77	3.74	31, 63, 81, 222
2.44	77	3.77	222
2.46	194	3.78	162
2.49–50	41	3.80	75
2.53	96	3.84	222–23
2.55	31, 227	3.94	77, 225–26
2.57	247	3.95–96	34
2.63	136	3.97–100	54
2.64	96	3.100	247
2.68–70	162	3.103	193
2.70	77	3.106	75
2.73	79	3.111	42
2.77	39, 81, 100, 220	3.113	119
2.77–78	60, 119	3.127–140	89
2.78	68, 77	3.128–140	89
2.80	61, 81	3.131	96
2.82	61	3.137	95, 99
2.82–83	119	3.140	37
2.83	61, 160	3.141	85
2.86	77	3.147–148	75
2.87	119	3.150	75
2.91	37	3.151	114
2.100	77	3.152	126
2.102	37	3.153–159	99
2.103	116	3.161	35, 58
2.104	98	3.163	241
3.1	65–66, 68	3.165	116
3.1–2	65, 173	3.168	75
3.1–48	87	3.172	116
3.2	65, 75	3.189	37
3.3	247	3.191	39
3.7	65–66	3.193	96, 100
3.14	77, 116	3.195	77, 162
3.18	116	3.198	162
3.18–19	225	3.201 ff.	162
3.27	247	3.207	158

3.219	247	153	256
3.222	75, 77	154	224
3.224	38	171	61
3.229	205	184	143
3.235	220	184–195	54
3.240	170	187	43
3.244	37	187–188	237
3.249	138	189	108, 208
3.251	74–76	189–190	206
3.251–253	20, 59, 73, 221	190	207, 233
3.252	51, 74–75, 77, 245	190–191	88
3.252–253	78, 81	192	88
3.253	78	195	54
		197	31
Legat. (Legatio ad Gaium)		200	88, 89, 220
5	171	209	38
49	170	212	122
61	261	214	37
103	170	216–220	54
325	165	223	37
		225	23
Migr. (De migratione Abrahami)			
2	87, 99, 139	*Mos. (De vita Mosis)*	
7	87, 206	1.4	247
7–12	190	1.43	121
9	31, 120, 228	1.62	247
12	139	1.86	207
13	54	1.96	66
14	31	1.190	37, 247
16	31	1.204	23
18	36	1.289	205
20	117	2.13	48
21	31	2.60	165
25	98, 117	2.65	165
28	31	2.69	180
29	247	2.71	247
46	247	2.99	110
62	37	2.100	104
63	57	2.112	195
67	95, 97	2.153	247
74–75	164	2.209–210	155
76	191	2.263	17
88	54	2.267	104
90	159	2.288	37, 40, 47, 108, 175
93	31	2.291	174
124	98		
128	177	*Mut. (De mutatione nominum)*	
131	177	3	256
133	106–7	10	110
148	77, 182	18	109
148–155	240, 251	24	110
149	140	26	110
150	178	27	109–10
151	117	28	110
152–155	100	29	110

30–32	109	151–152	71
33	39, 175	152	100
33–38	175	154	34, 37
36	39, 114	158	100, 126
37	158		
38	31, 175	*Plant. (De plantatione)*	
60	247	11–14	132
72	143	12–14	144, 213
81–82	99	14	1, 33, 45, 49, 81, 115, 118, 132, 134, 136, 145–46, 159, 160, 213
88	247		
95–96	119		
96	100		
107	239, 241	18–27	34
124	23, 96	22	143, 262
138	247	23–25	262
170–174	234	24–25	96, 99
171–172	235	26	247
172	37	34	207
172–174	234	37	119
173	39, 234–35, 240	44–46	119
174	39	46	65, 68, 81
184	86, 105	49	107
185	68, 229	52	247
186	239	58	200
208–209	96	64	97, 99
213	170, 192, 247	79	247
218	98	86	110
219	138	94	37
222	98	97	77
239–240	97	122	119
		127	247
Opif. (De opificio mundi)		144	192, 241
7	192	147	28, 39, 119, 136
8–9	105	169	200
16	159		
21–22	105	*Post. (De posteritate Caini)*	
22	257	5	117, 136
54	56	8	200
67	190–91	13	178
69	35, 172	18	200
69–71	54, 56	22	107, 182, 239–40
70	143, 171	29–31	235
72	110	31	251
77	96	32	239
77–78	56	39	119
78	17	43	98, 193
84	145	45	119, 124, 236
100	59, 155	61	221
104	220	62	251
113	23	73	23, 100
134–135	257	73–74	119
135	34, 37, 50, 73, 105, 107–8	97	37
		101	96, 99
137	31	117	190
151	52, 77	118	247

124	163–64	1.4	37, 116
124–125	164	1.7	178, 179
125	164	1.15	96
125–127	163	1.19	39, 260
127	163	1.23	248
131	247	2.3	260
132	77	2.9	139
137	31, 263	2.13	159
154	98	2.14	139
155–156	251	2.28	264
156	140, 245	2.29	40, 173, 262
157	261	2.31	262
170	172–73, 163	2.34	105, 247
170–174	164	2.39	181, 185–86, 232, 260–61, 264
173	152, 247		
173–174	164	2.39–40	181, 225
		2.40	7, 17, 61, 129, 140, 167–86, 210, 212–13, 215–16, 218–20, 223–24, 227, 232, 234, 240, 245, 251, 260–64

Praem. (De praemiis et poenis)

10–66	164		
15–21	175		
24	105, 247		
26	54, 89, 261		
40	86, 192	2.43	173, 262
41–43	54	2.45	83, 97, 262
62	85, 247	2.46	154–56, 173
69	82, 107	2.51	95, 99, 205, 247
70–73	82	2.52	247
81	96	2.82	205
110	136, 207	2.96	37
117	31, 224	2.116	247
120–121	31	Fr. 3 PAPM	123
121	247	Fr. 14 PAPM	247
130	257	Fr. 15 PAPM	47, 119
159	119		

QG (Quaestiones in Genesim)

Prob. (Quod omnis probus liber sit)

		1.4	35, 42, 70
2–5	247	1.6	54
3–4	96	1.8	42
13	112	1.10	37
14	247	1.16	108, 155–56
19	151	1.24	198
23	105, 247	1.33	119
63	247	1.45	119
75–76	119	1.50	35, 37
104	141	1.51	19–20, 37, 47, 51, 70, 72–73, 76–79, 81, 119, 201, 221, 242, 261
159–160	106		

Prov. (De providentia)

Passage numbering 39		1.53	31, 42, 53, 78
2.17	39	1.55	47, 81, 105
2.31	105, 247	1.56	119
2.35–36	82	1.65	260
		1.70	31, 81, 119, 141, 238

QE (Quaestiones in Exodum)

Entire work	167	1.70–71	16

1.75	28, 119, 256	4.102	247
1.76	121	4.107	247
1.85	178–179	4.111	21, 100
1.86	174, 178, 207	4.116	260, 264
2.9	119	4.133	121, 247
2.12	98, 264	4.139	261
2.13	104	4.140	261, 264
2.22	119	4.140–141	261
2.23	119	4.152	100, 108, 119
2.25	236	4.153	31
2.27	31	4.159	37
2.34	56, 170	4.165	37
2.54	260	4.166	34
2.57	100, 119	4.168	247
2.59	35, 260	4.169	155, 238
2.61	40, 51, 83–84, 183, 240	4.171	69
		4.173	124
2.69	31, 99	4.174	203
3.3	171, 241	4.178	31, 173
3.5	247	4.185	139
3.10	31, 73, 217, 236	4.188	132, 136, 145
3.10	11, 227	4.194	247
3.11	31, 33, 108, 155, 173	4.195	97, 99–100, 139, 247
3.12	106	4.216	247
3.18	37	4.228	139
3.32	247	4.234	31, 69, 81, 83–84, 180–83, 185–86, 212–13
3.39	170		
3.43	247		
3.45	31, 73	4.235	119
3.52	100	4.238	119
4.1	31, 42	4.239	237
4.2	205	4.240	119
4.4	247	4.242	85
4.8	105, 159, 247	4.245	247
4.21	54, 247	OL addition 10	180
4.29	53, 81, 132, 135		
4.30	37	*Sacr. (De sacrificiis Abelis et Caini)*	
4.35	37, 97, 247	2	238
4.45	178–179, 184	3	77
4.46	37, 96, 99–100, 119, 223–24, 261	5	159
		7	37
4.47	98, 247	21	194
4.49	247	32	261
4.51	100	33	152
4.52	224	49	38
4.59	139	60	152
4.62	205	60–62	247
4.74	31, 45, 48–51, 53–55, 57, 81	62	152
		63	107, 116
4.75	31, 96	69	200
4.77	63	72	39
4.78	31	74	194
4.46	224	123	107
4.94	31	131	247

INDICES

137	37	1.138	16, 26, 45, 47, 49, 81, 113–14, 118, 134–38, 148
Sobr. (De sobrietate)			
20	105, 247	1.138–139	1, 10, 17, 20, 81, 100, 171, 176, 213, 220, 224, 227–28, 237
56–58	96		
62	97, 99		
Somn. (De somniis)			
1.2	129, 198, 206	1.138–141	115, 145
1.6	247	1.138–143	160
1.24	231	1.138–146	10
1.26	31, 108, 170	1.139	14, 17, 19–20, 26, 31, 33, 47, 99, 120, 138–43, 147–49, 168, 175, 212, 216–17, 220–23, 227, 230, 232, 235, 240, 245, 251
1.30	59		
1.31	110, 159		
1.34	35		
1.36	175		
1.39	40, 231		
1.41–42	237		
1.41–46	43, 222, 231–32, 253	1.140–141	10, 132
		1.141	134
1.43	31, 220	1.145	143
1.43–44	160	1.146–149	130, 132
1.44	61, 222	1.147	31, 100, 146, 191, 237
1.46	31, 173, 219, 236		
1.50	261	1.147–148	97, 99
1.52–60	54	1.150	205
1.54	143	1.150–151	119
1.55–56	54	1.150–152	130
1.59	56	1.151	66, 124, 170, 203
1.59–60	81	1.152	77, 98
1.60	56	1.153–156	130
1.61	231	1.164	247
1.62	232	1.165	205
1.68–71	232	1.176–178	50
1.71	138	1.180–181	43, 227, 231–32
1.80	205	1.181	31–32, 173, 232
1.82	247	1.191	247
1.84	37	1.206	190
1.110	236	1.213	37
1.110–111	95	1.226	247
1.111	138	1.255	108
1.115–119	232	1.256	108
1.117	200	2.1–2	198, 206
1.119	77	2.3	247
1.121	205	2.13	239
1.122	77	2.45	257
1.133–141	213	2.54	122
1.133–145	132	2.70	119
1.134–141	144, 147	2.78	152, 247
1.134–143	13, 16	2.109	31, 116
1.134–145	130	2.112	136
1.135	160	2.198	96, 100
1.136	134	2.227	256
1.137	118, 133–34, 144	2.231–233	253
1.137–139	7, 46, 129–50, 212, 215	2.233	140, 261
		2.233, 235	261

2.234	37	3.178	247
2.234–235	119	3.184–192	56
2.235	124	3.185	56
2.237	31, 37, 63	3.191	56, 81
2.259	23	4.34	82
2.267	122	4.47	247
		4.60	247

Spec. (De specialibus legibus)

1.25	247	4.80–81	217
1.36–38	54	4.107	247
1.37–40	171	4.114	100, 126
1.44	54	4.115	261
1.55	260	4.141	85
1.66	159	4.148	247
1.87	195	4.150	247
1.100	126	4.167	107
1.200	247	4.187	257
1.207	143, 171	4.188	31, 59, 114, 141, 216, 219–20
1.208	255		
1.214–215	37		

Virt. (De virtutibus)

1.259–260	97	10	105, 247
1.269	37, 39, 96	53	207
1.281–282	138	74	114
1.282	230	75	260
1.298	220	76	207
1.328	257	87	120–21
1.339	56	113	95, 261
1.345	119	144	260
2.2	104	147	247
2.44–45	54	171–174	82
2.44–46	171	178	247
2.50	112, 247	189	37
2.52	54	205	23, 92
2.95	107		
2.145	116		
2.147	96, 116		
2.164	247	## 4. Plato	
2.224	105		

Cratylus

2.225	104	396a	105
2.229	104	398b–c	133
2.231	105, 247	399d	105
2.243	104	400b–c	60
2.248	104	400c	59, 119
3.1	171		
3.1–2	54		

Crito

3.6	200, 247	48b	91
3.37–42	112		
3.40	247		

Gorgias

3.79	261	493a	59–60
3.84	104	523b	120
3.90	104	523b–524a	18
3.99	28, 120–21	525c	120
3.119	106, 192		
3.134	247		

INDICES 297

Laws
Entire work 2
   869b 104
   870d–e 94, 104, 140
   904c 140

Meno
   81b 2, 93, 151
   81c 232
   81e 25
   86b 25

Phaedo
Entire work 2, 21, 39, 55, 85, 97, 124, 126, 167, 199, 203, 211
   62d 151
   64a 96, 122, 124, 205
   64c 122
   64e–65a 122
   65c–d 122
   66a 122, 208
   66c 140
   66e–67a 122
   67a 98, 141
   67b–c 151
   67c 198
   67c–d 122
   67d 39, 107, 198, 209
   67d–e 113, 122, 205
   67e 96
   68b–c 135
   69b–c 205
   69c 142
   69d 205
   70c 151
   71b 191
   71c 204
   71c–d 151, 191
   71e 203
   72a 151
   72a, d 203
   72b 252
   72c 203
   77d 191
   79b 151
   79c 151
   79c–d 151
   79d 151
   80a 39, 151
   80a–d 161
   80b 40
   80e 113, 205
   80e–81a 96, 123
   80e–83e 91–92

   81a 151, 187
   81a–b 113
   81a–b, e 113
   81b 92, 100, 151
   81b–c 40
   81b–e 136
   81c 18, 40, 84, 123–24
   81c–d 133, 142
   81c, e 92
   81e 113–14, 139–40
   82a 139
   82b 151
   82b–c 93
   82c 205
   82e 93, 119–20
   82e–83a 228–29
   83a 88
   88a 191
   88b 107
   89b 203
   91e–92a 113
   92b–c 151
   94b, d–e 151
   95d 232
   103c 191
   107c 91
   107c–d 93
   107e 118
   108c 118, 137
   109b 142
   109b–110a 142
   112–114 69
   113a 118, 137, 151
   113d 18
   113d–114c 91
   114b 93, 120
   114c 93, 96, 99

Phaedrus
Entire work 2, 16, 20, 24, 28, 39–40, 55, 97, 171, 186, 261
   244a–257b 111
   246a 69, 142
   246c 69, 142–43
   246c–d 142
   246d–249d 111
   246e 133, 172
   246e–247b 207
   247a 69
   247a–b 133
   247c 171
   247e 171
   248a 171, 180
   248a–b 172

248a–c	69	30b	21
248b–c	142, 171	34c	39
248c	52, 93, 124, 191	41a	142
248c–e	172	41b	49
248e	93, 142	41d	34, 114, 118, 133, 144
248e ff.	136		
248e–249a	113, 118, 123	41d–42d	126
249a	18, 69, 94, 113, 172	41e	133
249a–b	125	41e–42a	52
249b	93, 119, 142, 223	41e–42c	91
249c	93	41e–42d	18, 34
249d	69, 142	42a	79
250c	119, 141	42a–b	91–92
251b	142, 180	42a–c	21, 27
256b	142	42b	79, 96, 142
256d	142	42b ff.	140
260c–d	90	42b–c	91
274e–275c	25	42c	23–24, 120–21, 140, 220
Republic		42c–d	91
Entire work	2, 24, 40, 125	42d	25, 114, 133
498d	191	42e	117
515a	198	42e–43a	118
517b	120	42e–43b	114
519b	191	43	115
520c–d	173, 198	43a	69, 97, 113
521c	197–198	43a–b	242
611c–d	115	43a–d	114, 240
611e	115	43b	85
612e	94	43c	241
614b–621b	94	44b	113–14
614c	18, 94	44d	113
615a	90	47a–c	56
617b–c	126	51e	21
617d	118, 136–37	69c–e	36
618e	91	69e	113
620a	139	81e	142
621a	106	89b	118, 137
621c	94, 117	90a	125, 133
		90b–92c	91
Statesman		90d	125
272e	2	90e–92b	92
		91a–c	24
Symposium		91a–92c	120
211e	140	91d–92c	21–22
		91e	21, 100, 125, 223
Theaetetus		91e–92a	125, 221
176a–b	86, 171	92a	125
		92b	100
Timaeus		92b–c	92
Entire work	2, 20–24, 27, 39–40, 50, 55, 69, 92–94, 97, 111, 119, 130, 136	92c	21, 23, 99

5. Other Ancient Authors

Aeschylus
Prometheus vinctus
936 — 52

Alcinous
Didaskalikos
15.1 — 144
16.1 — 118
16.1–2 — 144
16.2 — 118
25.1 — 57
25.2 — 57
25.6 — 45, 144

Apuleius
De Deo Socratis
137–140 — 144
De dogmate Platonis
204–205 — 144

Aristotle
De anima
407b22 — 248
413b25–28 — 21
415b — 105
429a22–26 — 21
430a22–23 — 21
De caelo
300a11–17 — 138
De generatione et corruptione
336b9–13 — 137
337a24 — 138
Metaphysica
988b31 — 191
Protrepticus
106–107 — 63
110 — 141
Rhetorica
1389a — 261
1406b10 — 90

Athenaeus
Deipnosophistae
4.157c — 59

Augustine
City of God
7.6 — 134

Chrysippus
Fragmenta moralia
394.17 — 260

Cicero
De natura deorum
1.27 — 35
Somnium Scipionis
4 (= *De re publica* 6.12) — 137

Clement of Alexandria
Paedagogus
1.9.84.2 — 199
Protrepticus
1.4.4 — 199
9.88.2 — 157
Stromateis
1.23.154.3 — 199
1.72.4 — 147
2.100.3 — 147
3.3.17.5 — 199
4.3.12.5 — 199
4.22.141.1–2 — 198–99
4.122.140.1–2 — 199
5.14.103.4 — 199
5.14.105.2–106.1 — 197, 199
5.8.49.1 — 199
7.9.53.2 — 199

Demosthenes
De falsa legatione
19.262 — 77

Diogenes Laertius
Vitae philosophorum
7.143 — 35

Dionysius of Halicarnassus
Ant. Rom.
8.1.2 — 67

Ephrem the Syrian
In sermonem
339.2 — 201

Euripides
Alcestis
1003 — 133
Heraclidae
218 — 170
Supplices
531–534 — 142

GEORGIUS ACROPOLITES
In imaginem beatae virginis
4	193
13	193
17	193

Laudatio Petri et Pauli
9.27–29	193
23.11	193

GREGORY OF NYSSA
In sanctum pascha
262.24–263.2	197

HERACLITUS
Fragments DK
26	198
36	61
62	61

HESIOD
Theogonia
119	170
758–759	202

HOMER
Iliad
16.672	202
16.682	202

Odyssey
4.392	54
10.513	69
12.118	82

IAMBLICHUS
Protrepticus
47.21–48.9	59, 63

JOHN CHRYSOSTOM
De Davide et Saule
54.689.49
De studio praesentium
489.9	200

In epistulam ad Ephesios
62.174.47–48	201

In epistulam i ad Corinthios
61.232.27	200

In epistulam i ad Timotheum
62.510.42–44	200
62.510.43	190

In Joannem
59.219.15–16	201

JOSEPHUS
Antiquitates Judaicae
18.14	248
18.297	165

Contra Apionem
2.218	248

De bello Judaico
2.163	248
3.373	248
7.344–349	206

MENANDER
Fragments Kock
724	48

NUMENIUS
Fragments Des Places
32,34–35	134

ORIGEN
Fragmenta in evangelium Joannis (in catenis)
57.12–13	188

Commentary on St. John
19.21	189

PHOTIUS
Bibliotheca
cod. 8	11, 26
cod. 105	11
cod. 109	11, 26

PLOTINUS
Enneads
1.7.3	57

PLUTARCH
De esu carnium ii
2.998c	150

De exilio
607c	137

De E apud Delphos
389a	210

De Iside et Osiride
364f	210

Quaestiones convivales
722d	166

PORPHYRY
Ad Gaurum
48.26–28	46
49.1	46

De abstinentia
1.31.13–15	42
2.46.4–5	42
8.14	52
8.30	134
8.32	134

POSIDIPPUS
Epigrams
74	192

PROCLUS
In Tim.
3.332.6	241

PSEUDO-ANDRONICUS OF RHODES
On passions
4.1.32	135

PSEUDO-CAESARIUS
Quaestiones et responsiones
214.72–3	193

PSEUDO-DIONYSIUS OF HALICARNASSUS
Ars rhetorica
8.12.37	141

PSEUDO-JOHN CHRYSOSTOM
De Lazaro et divite
59.594.5–7	200

In sanctum pascha
7.15	201

PSEUDO-MACARIUS
Homiliae spirituales
47.114	190

PSEUDO-MAXIMUS CONFESSOR
Loci communes
sermo xxix	186

PSEUDO-ORIGEN
Selecta in Psalmos
12.1413.39–43	197

PSEUDO-PHILOLAUS
Fragments DK
14	59

PSEUDO-PLATO
Axiochus
365d–e	154
365e	161
371c	66
371e	66, 154

PYTHAGORICA
Fragments DK
8	150

Golden Verses
70–71	142

SERVIUS
Commentary on the Aeneid
3.68	150

SECUNDUS
Sententiae
19–20	196

SEXTUS EMPIRICUS
Pyrrhoniae hypotyposes
3.230	63

SOPHOCLES
Fragments Radt
755	151

STOBAEUS
Anthologium
1.49.39.44–53	45

XENOCRATES
Fragments Parente
236–237	133

XENOPHON
Cyropaedia
8.7.21	202

Topical Index

Aaron	89	Athanasius	202
Abel	163–64, 236, 238, 247	Athenaeus	59–60
		Augustine	134
Abihu	51	Baal Peor	241
Abraham	32, 50, 53–56, 66, 87, 106–108, 125, 164–65, 177, 206, 240, 247, 251–54, 263	Balaam	84
		Basil	192, 202
		Bezaleel	190
		body	
Abram	109, 207, 216, 222. *See also* Abraham	container of the soul	31, 227
Acheron	68	dwelling of the soul	31, 227
Acropolites, Georgius	193	foreign land, place of sojourn	31–32, 43–44, 50, 54–55, 58, 80, 106, 217, 227, 231
Adam	5, 20, 35, 41–42, 47–48, 51–52, 58, 65, 67, 70–71, 74, 78–79, 163, 198, 207, 225, 247	garment of the soul	31, 227, 231, 263
		love of, the soul's	46–47, 62, 113, 135–36, 147–49, 166, 212, 215, 220–22, 228, 243
Adrasteia	52		
Aeschylus	52		
Aesop	188		
Alcinous	45–46, 48–50, 52, 57, 118, 144		
Alexander Polyhistor	134	prison of the soul	1, 14, 31, 44, 60–61, 92–93, 113, 119, 136, 141, 148, 150, 214, 216–17, 226, 227–28
Allegorical Commentary	9, 31, 37, 66, 82, 112, 119, 122, 129, 150, 152, 162–63, 206, 214, 235, 246, 261		
		tomb of the soul	1, 14, 28, 31, 58, 60, 119, 141, 148, 150, 212, 214, 216, 219, 222, 227
angels	10, 14, 53, 97, 130, 132, 134–36, 144–46, 159–60, 213, 223–224		
Antiochene theology	201	breath of life	33–36, 51, 75
		Cain	82, 100, 121, 150, 158, 163–64, 184, 235–36, 238–39, 240–41, 247
Antonius Monachus	186		
Apuleius	144, 200		
Aristotle	21, 42, 59–60, 62–63, 79, 90, 105, 136–38, 141, 188, 191–92, 248, 261	Calvenus Taurus	45, 49–50, 52
		Castor	205
		Cebes	92, 139, 204, 232
		Chaldea	54, 143, 207, 254
arithmology	1, 45, 49, 81, 131, 137–38, 155, 217	Christ	193, 197–98
		Christian tradition and Philo	3, 11, 249
Armenian Philo	35, 40, 42, 47, 54, 68–69, 72, 83–84, 97, 129, 139, 155–56, 167–70, 172, 174, 176–78, 180–81, 223–24, 236, 260–64	Chrysippus	201
		Cicero	35, 137
		city, metaphorical. *See also* fatherland, heavenly	
		air as	133
Artemidorus	130	body as	227, 233
astrology	143, 207, 254	of the senses	231

			240, 251–52, 254
of the soul	87	Elijah	173–74, 176, 185
self as	254	Eliphaz	65–66
the divine	32–33, 65, 140, 169, 173, 176, 179, 181, 185, 216, 231–32	Empedocles	16, 52, 136–37
		Enoch	138, 173–76, 179, 185, 193, 206
the world as	103, 254	Ephrem the Syrian	201–2
Clearchus the Peripatetic	60	Epimenides	191
Clement of Alexandria	11, 15, 26, 59, 147, 192, 197–99, 202, 249	Er (Genesis)	62, 221–22
		Er (*Republic*)	28, 94, 125, 209
		Esau	65, 69, 180
Codex Berolinensis	46, 168, 186–87, 264	esotericism	90, 104, 134, 147, 151–52, 154, 167, 199, 205, 221, 242, 247–48
conflagration of the world (Stoic tenet)	255–56	Essenes	10
		ether	1, 48, 73, 107–8, 131, 134, 142–43, 147–49, 169, 216, 248, 262
contemplation, mystical in Philo	53–54, 56, 87–88, 172, 178, 180, 183, 218–19, 222–23, 233, 235, 253	Euphrone	199
		Euripides	133, 142, 170, 191
		Eusebius	201, 228
		Euxitheus the Pythagorean	60
corporealization of the mind	48, 51, 70–81, 84, 127, 150, 166, 212, 221, 238, 242	Eve	5, 38, 42, 58, 65, 163
		exodus	31, 116–17, 207, 225
		Exposition of the Law	5, 9, 246, 253, 261
Crates	191	fatherland, heavenly	55, 219, 232
creatio ex nihilo	105	Gaius Caligula	165
Cyril of Alexandria	42, 192	Galen	140, 201
Cyrus the Great	202	genres, Philonic.	See *Allegorical Commentary, Exposition of the Law, Quaestiones*
daemons	13–14, 41, 66, 132–34, 136–37, 144, 146, 149		
Danaids	66	gilgul	247
death		Glaucus	115
of soul	See soul, death of	"Gnostic" views	249
practising	81, 96, 122–24, 187, 196, 199, 200, 203, 211–12, 216	grace, God's	90, 98, 128, 214, 216, 218, 242–43
deception, by/of sense-perception	88, 139, 219, 220, 263	Gregory of Nazianzen	192–93
		Gregory of Nyssa	42, 192
Demiurge	114, 133	Hades.	See underworld
demonadization	41–43	*hapax legomena*	140, 191, 194–95
Demosthenes	76	Haran	38, 43, 54, 231, 237, 240, 254
Didymus Caecus	141, 202, 228		
Diodorus Siculus	140	Hebrew language	76, 82, 116, 142
Dionysius of Halicarnassus	67	meaning of "Hebrew" as 'migrant'	117
double dichotomy	39–40, 44, 62, 161, 221	Hesiod	170, 199, 202
Egypt as the symbol of the body	31, 69, 116–17, 132, 182, 220, 225, 235,	Heraclitus	16, 61, 63–64, 108, 197–99

Herod Agrippa	165	Miriam	183
heroes	132, 134, 146	monadization	41, 43, 85–90, 116, 127, 166, 173, 175, 212, 215, 248, 256
Hippocrates	140		
Hippolytus	202		
Homer	202	mortal life	1, 47–48, 51, 80, 99–100, 123, 133, 136, 138–39, 147–49, 175, 184, 212, 214–17, 220, 222, 224, 227, 233, 238
homoerotic behavior	112. See also pederasty		
HWS	76, 218, 221, 259		
Hypnos	202		
Iamblichus	42, 45, 59	Moses	10, 12, 17, 24, 32, 34, 38, 40–41, 54–55, 65, 89, 108–9, 112, 117, 132, 136, 155, 164, 168, 170–71, 173–74, 177–78, 180, 182–83, 190, 207, 222, 225–26, 233, 246–47, 255, 260, 263
imitation of God	14		
immortality	5, 18–19, 28, 34, 36–37, 46–47, 70–71, 92–93, 96–100, 105, 108, 114, 123, 133, 142, 156, 175, 181, 206–8, 214, 224		
Indian religions	90, 156		
Irenaeus	42	mysticism in Philo. See contemplation	
Isaac	55, 69, 252, 261	myth	18, 19, 24–25, 65–66, 68, 111, 120, 125, 171, 180
Israel	218, 226, 232, 235, 240		
Israelites	116, 207, 252	Nadab	51
Jacob	17, 55, 129, 160, 225, 230–31, 234–35, 237, 240, 253, 257	NBHL	42, 54, 83–84, 105, 139, 174, 178, 180, 224, 236, 260, 262
John Chrysostom	190, 200, 201–2	NETS	2, 82
John of Damascus	167, 186, 202	nirvana	156
Joseph	40, 117, 234	Noah	38, 136, 164–65, 222, 236, 247
Josephus	165, 197, 201, 206, 248		
Joshua	173	number symbolism. See arithmology	
Julian, emperor	192	Numenius	134
Kabbalah	1, 247–48	Nyx	202
karma	90, 242	OL	68–69, 180
Laban	225, 240, 253, 257	Origen	11–12, 15, 26, 52, 188–89, 192, 196–97, 201, 249
Lachesis	118		
land of the impious	65–67, 69–70, 154, 230, 241. See also underworld	original sin	73, 248
		Orphics	59–60, 119
		Paradise	20, 41, 51–52, 65, 67, 75, 207, 209
Lazarus (Luke 16)	200		
Lethe	94, 117	Parisinus Graceus 923	186–87
Levi	88, 97, 222	Passover	31, 99, 116–17, 201, 224–26, 252
Lot	117, 138, 177, 223–24, 240, 251–52		
		Paul, apostle	200
LSJ	34, 63, 165, 170, 198–99, 221, 258, 260	pederasty	94, 112–13, 172
		periods of time	1, 16, 18, 45, 49, 113, 117–18, 125, 132, 136–38, 144
Melchizedek	222		
Methodius	192, 197	Pharaoh	183, 234–35
MI	42, 83, 139, 176, 178, 260, 262	Pherecydes	191
		PhI	39, 163, 170, 193, 195
Milky Way	134		

INDICES

Philolaus	59, 133	Pseudo-John	
Photius	11, 26, 249	Chrysostom	200–203
Pindar	199	Pseudo-Macarius	190, 202
place of the impious.	*See* land of the impious	Pseudo-Maximus Confessor	186–187, 199, 211
		Pseudo-Origen	197
Plato	xi–xii, 2–3, 7, 10–12, 14, 16–25, 27–30, 33–34, 36, 39–40, 42, 45–46, 57, 59, 69, 84, 88–100, 104–6, 111–15, 118–28, 130–131, 133–35, 137, 139–40, 142–43, 146–47, 149–51, 167, 171, 181, 186, 188–89, 191–92, 197, 199, 202–5, 209, 211–12, 219–20, 222–23, 225, 228–29, 237, 240–42, 244, 246, 248	Pseudo-Philolaus	59–60, 63
		Pseudo-Plato	66
		Pseudo-Philo	42
		purgatory	61
		Pyriphlegethon	68
		Pythagoras	52, 134, 150
		Pythagoreanism	15, 24, 55, 59–60, 133–34, 138, 142, 147, 150, 155, 248
		QGUM	35, 42, 47, 72
		Quaestiones (Philo's *QGE*)	13, 35, 37, 119, 167–68, 178, 180, 214, 235, 246
		reading together of parallels	x, 7–8, 50, 66, 85, 146, 180–86, 210, 213, 215–16, 224, 227, 230–31, 237, 244
Platonism	2, 15–16, 20, 22, 33, 39, 45, 57, 61, 66, 72, 90, 111, 118–19, 128, 133–34, 136, 144, 146, 199, 248–49		
Plotinus	55, 57	Rebecca	38, 263
Plutarch	41, 133, 137, 140, 150, 166, 191–92, 210	rebellion by the Jews in Alexandria in 116–117 CE	245
Pollux	205	reincarnation	
Porphyry	42, 46	"rejection" by Philo	15, 17–18, 20, 22, 147
Posidippus	192		
Posidonius of Apamea	130	as an eternal punishment in Philo	19, 79, 248
pre-existence of soul.	*See* soul, pre-existence of	belief in, by Essenes, according to de' Rossi	10
prepositions			
instrumental use of ἐκ in *Legat.* 325	165	driving forces of	6, 44, 46, 51, 53, 57, 78, 85, 89, 90–101, 115, 127, 135, 149, 162, 166, 186, 211–12, 217, 224, 242, 247
soteriology centered on ἐκ in *Leg.* 3.39–48	87		
protology	4, 35–36, 42, 44, 50, 57–58, 66–67, 71, 74–75, 78–79, 214, 228	essential characteristics of belief systems espousing	6, 90
Proclus	241	in animal bodies	21–25, 27–28, 92, 119–22, 125, 137, 212, 248
Pseudo-Andronicus of Rhodes	135		
Pseudo-Caesarius	193		
Pseudo-Dionysius of Halicarnassus	141	in the Kabbalah	1, 247

resurrection	6, 18, 156, 188, 191, 197–98, 202	structural features, of texts	67–68, 102, 131, 152–54, 166, 176
rhetorics	102, 158	Tantalus	66, 217
salvation, prerequisites of	4, 57, 73, 90–101, 127, 150, 218, 242–43, 247	Tartarus. textual corrections	See underworld 103, 153–54, 157, 159, 170, 193, 255–64
Sarah	32, 107–08, 156		
Sarai	257. See also Sarah	Thanatos	202
Scylla	82	Themistius	192
Sefer ha-Bahir	247	Theodoret of Cyrrhus	192
Septuagint, text of	34, 48, 76–77, 82, 116, 145, 188	Tiberius Caesar	165
Servius	150	Timna	66
Seth	163–64, 247	Tityus	66
Sextus Empiricus	63	TLG	8, 39, 45–46, 49, 63, 140, 166, 170, 178, 188, 190–93, 195–96, 200–1, 228
Simmias	92, 123–24		
Socrates	2, 25, 39, 52, 60, 69, 86, 92, 94, 111, 115, 123–24, 135, 139, 141–42, 197–98, 200, 203–5, 209, 232, 252		
		tunics of skin.	See Gen 3:21 in Index locorum
Solon	220	underworld	24
Sophocles	151	Hades	65–66, 70, 94, 120, 125, 134, 170, 180, 185, 212, 235
soul			
banishment of	65		
death of	23–24, 27–28, 37, 39, 47–48, 57–64, 71–72, 80–81, 100, 119, 124, 214–15, 206, 228, 235	Tartarus	66, 68–70, 120, 137, 169, 170, 172–73, 176–77, 180–81, 183, 185, 212, 215
		universal allegory	4–5, 35, 42, 58, 66, 71, 74–75, 78–79, 228, 234, 253
drowning of	66, 100, 114, 132, 181–82, 216, 222, 225, 237	Varro	134
		Velleius	35
mortal portion of	36	verba Philonica	62–63, 192–94, 197, 201, 228
pre-existence of	1, 4, 12–13, 20, 31–36, 72, 101–6, 115, 144, 146, 211, 214, 227. See also demonadisation	watcher tradition (1 Enoch)	148
		wings of the soul	1, 24, 69, 94, 124, 142–43, 147, 149, 170, 172, 180–81, 212, 216, 262, 264
six-stage model of fall and rise of	73–74, 78–80, 127, 212, 221, 242–43	Xenocrates	41, 133
		Xenophon	112, 202, 206
Sisyphus	66	Zeus	19, 105, 147, 171
Stobaeus	45		
Stoicism	14, 21, 35–36, 39, 152, 157, 165, 255–56, 260		

Index of Modern Authors

Alesse, Francesca	26		125, 133–34, 143, 147, 160, 208
Allix, Peter (Pierre)	12		
Annala, Pauli	x	Dodson, D. S.	130
Ashwin-Siejkowski, Piotr	26	Drummond, James	13, 33–34, 170, 260
Aucher, Joannes Baptista	35, 40, 42, 47, 52, 72, 83, 139, 168, 224	Dunderberg, Ismo	89
		Earp, J. W.	59, 100, 235, 238, 261
		Eisele, Wilfried	26–27, 130, 132, 143
Baer, Richard	33, 143		
Barclay, John	55	Elledge, Casey D.	248
Bentwich, Norman	15–16, 20, 150	Elmgren, Henrik	17, 143, 158
Berchman, Robert M.	130	Fabricius, Johann Albert	11–12, 143
Bigg, Charles	15		
Billings, Thomas H.	13, 20, 36, 114, 121, 133, 143	Festugière, André-Jean	172
Blum, Claes	130	Fowler, Harold North	142
Borgen, Peder	143, 174	Fuglseth, Kåre	62
Bouffartigue, Jean	42	Geljon, Albert C.	1, 13, 20, 27, 63–64, 122, 182–84, 239
Bréhier, Émile	16		
Burnet, J.	142		
Burnett, Fred W	3, 18, 151–52, 156, 158, 163, 165, 167, 256	Gförer, August	13
		Goodenough, Erwin R.	17, 40, 66, 108, 156, 158, 170
Bury, R. G.	241		
Christiansen, Irmgard	15, 130, 143	Gorez, Jean	159
Cohn, Leopold	103, 130, 152, 154, 156–58, 255, 258–59	Grabbe, Lester	248
		Graf, Fritz	59–60
		Graffigna, Paola	26
Collins, John. J.	248	Greppin, John A. C.	262
Colson, F. H.	16, 49, 56, 101–3, 109–10, 112, 116–17, 136–38, 143, 149, 152–54, 156–59, 161–62, 165, 217–20, 229, 231, 241, 255–57, 263	Gross, Joseph	13
		Grossman, D.	13
		Harris, J. Rendel	167, 186–87, 189
		Hay, David M.	246
		Heinemann, Isaac	16, 116
		Helleman, Wendy	170–71
		Henry, R.	11
Conroy, John T. Jr.	27–29, 37, 63, 170	Herriot, Édouard	14
Conybeare, Fred. C.	130	Herzog, Karl	13
Coomaraswamy, Ananda K.	156	Hilgert, Earle	168
		Hoek, Annewies van den	197–99
Crispo, Giovanni Battista	11–12	Holladay, Carl A.	15, 171
Cudworth, Ralph	13	Huffman, Carl A.	59, 63, 133
Cumont, Franz	13	Ihm, Sibylle	186
Dähne, August Ferdinand	13	Ionsius, Iohannes	12
		Kahn, Jean-Georges	55
Dey, Joseph	151, 156–58, 166	Kamesar, Adam	26, 201
Dibelius, Martin	156	Katz, Peter	76
Dillon, John	20, 45–46, 49, 67, 111, 117–18, 123,	Keller, Carl-A.	6, 13, 90
		Kennedy, Harry A. A.	13
		Kessels, A. H. M.	130

Knuuttila, Simo	24	Ritter, Heinrich	13
Kock, Theodor	48	Rossi, Azariah de'	9, 10, 143
Koester, Helmut	21	Royse, James	9, 62, 168, 186, 189
Koskenniemi, Erkki	x, 248		
Krause, Todd B.	262	Runia, David T.	x–xi, 1, 3, 5–6, 9, 11–13, 18–25, 27, 31, 33–34, 38, 52, 56, 59, 62–64, 79, 92, 96, 108, 111, 114–15, 117, 121–22, 125, 133, 144, 146–47, 155, 164, 170–72, 183–84, 189–90, 192, 196–97, 199, 201, 204, 239–41, 248, 257
Kraye, Jill	11		
Laato, Antti	x		
Lampe, G. W. H.	188		
Le Clerc, Jean	13		
Leopold, J.	111		
Lévy, Carlos	26		
Lucchesi, E.	168		
Mackie, Scott D.	56		
Mangey, Thomas	12, 157, 159, 186–87, 241, 246, 255		
Mansfeld, Jaap	16, 61, 63–64, 140, 143, 251–54	Ryle, Herbert Edward	76
Marcus, Ralph	10, 35, 42, 47, 53, 68, 69, 83–84, 97, 108, 139, 155, 168–70, 174, 178, 180–81, 223, 236, 260–61, 263–64	Sandelin, Karl-Gustav	x, 36, 261
		Sanders, E. P.	248
		Sandmel, Samuel	62
		Savinel, Pierre	16, 47, 148
		Schäfer, Peter	64
		Schibli, Hermann S.	133
Martikainen, Jouko	x	Scholem, Gershom	247, 249
Méasson, Anita	19, 50, 63, 114–15, 121, 123, 125–26, 134, 137, 140, 142, 146–48, 171–72	Schürer, Emil	3, 14, 15, 244
		Seland, Torrey	26
		Sellin, Gerhard	36
		Siegert, Folker	5, 6
		Sirinian, Anna	168
Mercier, Charles	35, 42, 47, 53, 69, 83, 139, 224	Skarsten, Roald	62
		Slocum, Jonathan	262
Meyer, Annegret	26, 130, 143	Smyth, Herbert Weir	52
Mosheim, J. L. von	13	Stettner, Walter	15
Muradyan, Gohar	170	Tarrant, Harold	25
Nikiprowetzky, Valentin	67	Terian, Abraham	x, 42, 168–69, 176, 260
Ogle, Marbury B.	203	Termini, Cristina	6, 26, 81, 156, 166, 170
Olivieri, Maurizio	40		
Otto, Jennifer	147	Thatcher, Tom	165
Paramelle, J.	168	Tobin, Thomas H.	xii, 21
Pascher, Joseph	13, 36, 156, 171	Torallas Tovar, Sofia	130
Pearce, Sarah	26, 31, 63, 121	Turnebus, Adrianus	158, 255, 259
Pétau, Denis	10–11, 16, 143	Vollenweider, Samuel	1, 143
Petavius. See Pétau		Waszink, J. H.	196
Petit, Françoise	68–69, 76, 169–70, 177, 180, 189, 264	Weinberg, Joanna	9
		Wendland, Paul	88, 126, 189, 241
		Whitaker, G. H.	49, 57, 59, 73, 75–76, 124, 131, 221, 231, 236, 238
Pontani, Paola	35, 168, 263		
Priestley, Joseph	13		
Radice, Roberto	18	Wilberding, James	46–47
Raphael, Paull Simcha	26	Winston, David	xii, 1, 19–20, 44–45, 48–51, 72, 79, 123, 125, 143, 147, 208, 244–46, 248
Reddoch, Michael J.	16, 26, 130, 137, 143		
Reydams-Schils, Gretchen	39		

Wolff, Moritz	13	Yonge, Charles Duke	49, 72, 158, 165, 188
Wolfson, Harry Austryn	6, 9, 18, 156	Zeller, Dieter	13, 57, 63–64
Wright, Archie T.	148–49	Zeller, Eduard	3, 14, 244
Yli-Karjanmaa, Sami	20, 35, 51, 74, 92	Zorzi, M. Benedetta	197

www.ingramcontent.com/pod-product-compliance
Lightning Source LLC
Chambersburg PA
CBHW021819300426
44114CB00009BA/239